COMPLETE ANGLICAN
HYMNS OLD & NEW

Acknowledgements

The publishers wish to express their gratitude to the copyright holders who have granted permission to include their material in this book.

Every effort has been made to trace the copyright holders of all the songs in this collection and we hope that no copyright has been infringed. Apology is made and pardon sought if the contrary be the case, and a correction will be made in any reprint of this book.

Important Copyright Information

We would like to remind users of this hymnal that the reproduction of any song texts or music without the permission of the copyright holder is illegal. Details of all copyright holders are clearly indicated under each song.

Many of the song *texts* may be covered either by a Christian Copyright Licensing (CCL) licence or a Calamus licence. If you possess a CCL or Calamus licence, it is essential that you check your instruction manual to ensure that the song you wish to use is covered.

If you are *not* a member of CCL or Calamus, or the song you wish to reproduce is not covered by your licence, you must contact the copyright holder direct for their permission.

Christian Copyright Licensing (Europe) Ltd., have also now introduced a *Music Reproduction Licence*. Again, if you hold such a licence it is essential that you check your instruction manual to ensure that the song you wish to reproduce is covered. The reproduction of any music not covered by your licence is both illegal and immoral.

If you are interested in joining CCL or Calamus they can be contacted at the following addresses:

Christian Copyright Licensing (Europe) Ltd. P.O. Box 1339, Eastbourne, East Sussex. BN 21 1AD.
Tel: 01323 417711, Fax: 01323 417722

Calamus, 30 North Terrace, Mildenhall, Suffolk, IP28 7AB.
Tel: 01638 716579, Fax: 01638 510390.

First published in Great Britain in 2000 by
KEVIN MAYHEW LIMITED
Buxhall, Stowmarket
Suffolk IP14 3BW

Compilation © Kevin Mayhew Ltd 2000

The following editions are available.

Words edition	Catalogue No.1413131	ISMN No. M 57004 700 0
	ISBN-10: 1 84003 566 8	ISBN-13: 978 184003 566 7
Organ/choir	Catalogue No. 1413134	ISMN No. M 57004 699 7
	ISBN-10: 1 84003 565 X	ISBN-13: 978 184003 565 0

Printed and bound by CPI Group (UK) Ltd, Croydon, CR0 4YY

FOREWORD

Hymns Old & New was first published in 1986, to be followed a decade later by *Hymns Old & New, New Anglican Edition*. *New Anglican* has amply justified its claim to be 'the most exhaustive and all-embracing collection of hymns available' and has proved to be one of the country's most popular and widely used hymn books, reprinting on numerous occasions.

The continuing rich outpouring of new Christian hymns and worship songs since their publication is a sign of the vitality of the Church. This flow of contemporary material springs naturally from the earlier tradition in which it is firmly rooted, addressing contemporary issues in the unequivocal context of the underlying truth of our faith.

It became evident to us that this was an appropriate time to enlarge *New Anglican* to embrace the best of the new material, whilst taking the opportunity to include further treasures from an earlier age. *Complete Anglican Hymns Old & New* is the result.

There is much here to accommodate all preferences, with something suitable for every occasion and season; but, of course, it would be surprising (and disappointing), in an eclectic collection of this kind, if everything in it had an immediate and universal appeal. Most importantly, within the covers of this book, many new and exciting discoveries await the user.

Complete Hymns Old & New is at once traditional and radical. The radical aspects will be self-evident in what follows and in the texts of some of the new hymns we have included. It is traditional partly because a large number of the texts have stood the test of time; and it is 'traditional' in another sense, for the process of critical scrutiny and rewriting of established texts has itself a long and honourable history. Throughout the time hymns have been in use they have been reviewed, adapted and rewritten; many of the hymns now regarded as classics are in reality very different from the original texts.

This is the tradition in which we, as an editorial panel, felt ourselves to be placed, and we sought to discharge our responsibilities as faithfully as we were able. We were a diverse group of people both denominationally and doctrinally: a diversity which was vital to the breadth and richness of the hymnody we were considering. Yet there were some basic principles upon which we were absolutely of common mind.

We wanted the overall tone of the book to be positive: to bear witness to the abundant grace and unconditional love of God; to enable the Church to sing of the *Good News* of salvation; to celebrate humanity as God's creation, fallen though we are, and affirm the essential goodness of the world which he has made and to which he has shown himself to be committed even unto death. Of course, we recognise the reality of sin and evil, and we would not for a moment deny that the world can be a dark and fearful place, but as Christians we believe we are called to point to the light that is never overcome; the darkness of the *background* to that is then self-evident.

We were also concerned that the book should use positive and appropriate images, and decided that militarism and triumphalism were, therefore, not appropriate. We recognise that military imagery is used in the Bible, but history, including current events, shows only too clearly the misuse to which those images are open. All too often in the Christian and other religions, texts advocating *spiritual* warfare are used to justify the self-serving ambitions behind *temporal* conflicts. Christian 'triumph' is the triumph of love which 'is not envious or boastful or arrogant' (1 Corinthians 13:4): the triumph of the cross.

Another fundamental principle was the use of inclusive language in referring to the human race. Rare exceptions were only made for very clear reasons and after much deliberation. Non-copyright texts were amended by members of the editorial panel while those by living authors were referred back. We are grateful to the authors concerned for their willingness to co-operate.

Some traditional hymns have been difficult for congregations to sing effectively because of variations in metre from verse to verse. Most of those, except for those few which are so well-known that it would be counterproductive, have now been adapted so that the words fit easily and consistently to the tune. A classic example, of course, is *God is working his purpose out:* a deservedly well-loved hymn which is now much easier to sing well and therefore more enjoyable for all concerned.

We were also aware that a number of hymns which have served well down the ages are now being seriously questioned. Some hymns are clearly manipulative, often written by adults for children and trying to impose values which were in reality more social and cultural than religious. In other cases we felt that God was being pushed out of this world at times when we should be looking to find him within it. In cases such as this, we attempted to redress the emphasis by rewriting, rather than by deleting well-loved hymns from the book. Whether that has been worthily done will be for the churches to decide as they use the texts.

In applying our criteria, we inevitably encountered a problem: there are a number of hymns which, however doubtful the text, are rightly loved for their music; and music is an essential part of our glorifying God in worship. We then had to establish another final criterion: ultimately, what we say to and about God and each other matters, and no dubious text would be included solely because of its tune. The solution we found was, in certain cases, to commission new texts to be sung to those tunes, hence such new hymns as *Stand up, stand up for Jesus, God is our strength from days of old* and *Onward, Christian pilgrims.*

While thus occupied with the classic texts we were also aware of the enormous number of new hymns and worship songs of recent years. Jesus said that being involved in the kingdom of heaven means treasuring things both old and new, and so we turned our attention to the new. Here we found an almost bewildering diversity. As well as the offerings of communities such as Taizé and Iona, we took into account a wide range of new hymns and songs, from texts using traditional metres to the freely expressive styles with which the Church has been blessed through the renewal movement. Through these modern texts we restate the ancient traditions of the faith, explore new insights, proclaim hope, protest, express solidarity with the poor, call ourselves and others to penitence and faith; and in all that we celebrate the eternal Mystery who surrounds, embraces and permeates creation. In other words, we do what hymns have always done.

As the number of hymns has increased to over nine hundred, we felt it would be useful to divide the book into various sections. This has been done purely as an aid to the user of the book as we certainly do not wish to 'compartmentalise' any hymns or songs. We have added a Children's Section, a Chant Section and a section containing Music for the Eucharist. These headings have also been used in the Index of Uses and the Index for the Common Lectionary.

The singing of hymns and psalms in worship pre-dates Christianity. It is something that Jesus himself would have been familiar with in the temple, and he certainly sang at the Last Supper – 'After psalms had been sung they left for the Mount of Olives', writes Matthew. What a wonderful tradition we share!

We hope that in this diverse and approachable collection of hymns we have sown some seeds; that is all we can do. It is in the worship of the churches that those seeds must be brought to glorious flower.

GEOFFREY MOORE – Compiler

SUSAN SAYERS – Liturgical Adviser

MICHAEL FORSTER – Theological Editor

KEVIN MAYHEW – Publisher

CONTENTS

COMPLETE ANGLICAN
HYMNS OLD & NEW

1 Dave Bilbrough
© 1977 *Kingsway's Thankyou Music*

Abba, Father, let me be
yours and yours alone.
May my will for ever be
more and more your own.
Never let my heart grow cold,
never let me go.
Abba, Father, let me be
yours and yours alone.

2 Henry Francis Lyte (1793-1847)

1. Abide with me,
fast falls the eventide;
the darkness deepens;
Lord, with me abide:
when other helpers fail,
and comforts flee,
help of the helpless,
O abide with me.

2. Swift to its close
ebbs out life's little day;
earth's joys grow dim,
its glories pass away;
change and decay
in all around I see;
O thou who changest not,
abide with me.

3. I need thy presence
ev'ry passing hour;
what but thy grace can foil
the tempter's pow'r?
Who like thyself my guide
and stay can be?
Through cloud and sunshine,
Lord, abide with me.

4. I fear no foe
with thee at hand to bless;
ills have no weight,
and tears no bitterness.
Where is death's sting?
Where, grave, thy victory?
I triumph still,
if thou abide with me.

5. Hold thou thy cross
before my closing eyes;
shine through the gloom,
and point me to the skies;
heav'n's morning breaks,
and earth's vain shadows flee;
in life, in death, O Lord,
abide with me.

3 Percy Dearmer (1867-1936)
© *Oxford University Press*

1. A brighter dawn is breaking,
and earth with praise is waking;
for thou, O King most highest,
the pow'r of death defiest.

2. And thou hast come victorious,
with risen body glorious,
who now for ever livest,
and life abundant givest.

3. O free the world from blindness,
and fill the earth with kindness,
give sinners resurrection,
bring striving to perfection.

4. In sickness give us healing,
in doubt thy clear revealing,
that praise to thee be given
in earth as in thy heaven.

4 St. Germanus (c. 634-c. 734) trans.
John Mason Neale (1818-1866) alt.

1. A great and mighty wonder,
a full and holy cure!
The Virgin bears the infant
with virgin-honour pure:

Repeat the hymn again!
'To God on high be glory,
and peace on earth shall reign.'

2. The Word becomes incarnate,
and yet remains on high;
and cherubim sing anthems
to shepherds from the sky:

Continued overleaf

3. While thus they sing your monarch,
   those bright angelic bands,
   rejoice, ye vales and mountains,
   ye oceans, clap your hands:

   Repeat the hymn again!
   'To God on high be glory,
   and peace on earth shall reign.'

4. Since all he comes to ransom
   by all be he adored,
   the infant born in Bethl'em,
   the Saviour and the Lord:

5 Robert Bridges (1844-1930) from J. Heerman (1585-1647)
   alt. based on an 11th century Latin meditation

1. Ah, holy Jesu,
   how hast thou offended,
   that so to judge thee
   mortals have pretended?
   By foes derided,
   by thine own rejected,
   O most afflicted.

2. Who was the guilty?
   Who brought this upon thee?
   Alas, O Lord,
   my treason hath undone thee.
   'Twas I, Lord Jesu,
   I it was denied thee:
   I crucified thee.

3. Lo, the good shepherd
   for the sheep is offered;
   the slave hath sinnèd,
   and the Son hath suffered;
   for our atonement
   Christ himself is pleading,
   still interceding.

4. For me, kind Jesu,
   was thy incarnation,
   thy mortal sorrow,
   and thy life's oblation;
   thy death of anguish
   and thy bitter passion,
   for my salvation.

5. Therefore, kind Jesu,
   since I cannot pay thee,
   I do adore thee,
   and will ever pray thee,
   think on thy pity
   and thy love unswerving,
   not my deserving.

6 William Henry Draper (1855-1933) alt.
   © J. Curwen & Sons Ltd.

1. All creatures of our God and King,
   lift up your voice and with us sing
   alleluia, alleluia!
   Thou burning sun with golden beam,
   thou silver moon with softer gleam:

   O praise him, O praise him,
   alleluia, alleluia, alleluia!

2. Thou rushing wind that art so strong,
   ye clouds that sail in heav'n along,
   O praise him, alleluia!
   Thou rising morn, in praise rejoice,
   ye lights of evening, find a voice:

3. Thou flowing water, pure and clear,
   make music for thy Lord to hear,
   alleluia, alleluia!
   Thou fire so masterful and bright,
   that givest us both warmth and light:

4. Dear mother earth, who day by day
   unfoldest blessings on our way,
   O praise him, alleluia!
   The flow'rs and fruits that in thee grow,
   let them his glory also show.

5. All you with mercy in your heart,
   forgiving others, take your part,
   O sing ye, alleluia!
   Ye who long pain and sorrow bear,
   praise God and on him cast your care:

6. And thou, most kind and gentle death,
   waiting to hush our latest breath,
   O praise him, alleluia!
   Thou leadest home the child of God,
   and Christ our Lord the way hath trod:

7. Let all things their Creator bless,
and worship him in humbleness,
O praise him, alleluia!
Praise, praise the Father, praise the Son,
and praise the Spirit, Three in One.

7 vs: 1-4 unknown, vs: 5-7 Damian Lundy (b. 1944-1997)
© Additional words 1996, 1999 Kevin Mayhew Ltd.

1. Alleluia . . .

2. Jesus is Lord . . .

3. And I love him . . .

4. Christ is risen . . .

*Additional verses may be composed to suit
the occasion. For example:*

5. Send your Spirit . . .

6. Abba, Father . . .

7. Come, Lord Jesus . . .

8 Donald Fishel (b. 1950)
© 1973 Word of God Music Administered by CopyCare

*Alleluia, alleluia,
give thanks to the risen Lord,
alleluia, alleluia, give praise to his name.*

1. Jesus is Lord of all the earth.
He is the King of creation.

2. Spread the good news o'er all the earth.
Jesus has died and is risen.

3. We have been crucified with Christ.
Now we shall live for ever.

4. God has proclaimed the just reward:
'Life for us all, alleluia!'

5. Come, let us praise the living God,
joyfully sing to our Saviour.

9 Christopher Wordsworth (1807-1885)

1. Alleluia, alleluia,
hearts to heav'n and voices raise;
sing to God a hymn of gladness,
sing to God a hymn of praise:
he who on the cross a victim
for the world's salvation bled,
Jesus Christ, the King of Glory,
now is risen from the dead.

2. Christ is risen, Christ the first-fruits
of the holy harvest field,
which will all its full abundance
at his second coming yield;
then the golden ears of harvest
will their heads before him wave,
ripened by his glorious sunshine,
from the furrows of the grave.

3. Christ is risen, we are risen;
shed upon us heav'nly grace,
rain, and dew, and gleams of glory
from the brightness of thy face;
that we, with our hearts in heaven,
here on earth may fruitful be,
and by angel-hands be gathered,
and be ever, Lord, with thee.

4. Alleluia, alleluia,
glory be to God on high;
alleluia to the Saviour,
who has gained the victory;
alleluia to the Spirit,
fount of love and sanctity;
alleluia, alleluia,
to the Triune Majesty.

10 Hubert J. Richards (b. 1921), based on Psalm 100
© 1996 Kevin Mayhew Ltd.

Alleluia, alleluia. *Alleluia, alleluia.*
Alleluia, *alleluia.*

1. All the earth, sing out to the Lord.
Serve the Lord with joy in your heart;
come into his presence with song.

Continued overleaf

Alleluia, alleluia. *Alleluia, alleluia.*
Alleluia, *alleluia.*

2. Come and bring your gifts to the Lord.
   Come before him, singing his praise;
   he is Lord, and he is our God.

3. God is good, his love never ends;
   he is always true to his word,
   he is faithful, age upon age.

11 Hubert J. Richards (b. 1921), based on Psalms 103 and 105
© 1995 Kevin Mayhew Ltd.

Alleluia, alleluia, alleluia.

1. Praise God, who forgives all our sins
   and heals us of ev'rything evil;
   he rescues our life from the grave
   and clothes us in mercy and love.

2. Our God is all kindness and love,
   so patient and rich in compassion;
   not treating us as we deserve:
   not paying us back for our sins.

3. As heaven is high over earth,
   so strong is his love for his people.
   As far as the east from the west,
   so far he removes all our sins.

4. As fathers take pity on sons,
   we know God will show us compassion;
   for he knows of what we are made:
   no more than the dust of the earth.

12 William Chatterton Dix (1837-1898) alt. the editors
© This version 1999 Kevin Mayhew Ltd.

1. Alleluia, sing to Jesus,
   his the sceptre, his the throne;
   alleluia, his the triumph,
   his the victory alone:
   hark, the songs of peaceful Sion
   thunder like a mighty flood:
   Jesus, out of ev'ry nation,
   hath redeemed us by his blood.

2. Alleluia, not as orphans
   are we left in sorrow now;
   alleluia, he is near us,
   faith believes, nor questions how;
   though the cloud from sight received him
   when the forty days were o'er,
   shall our hearts forget his promise,
   'I am with you evermore'?

3. Alleluia, bread of angels,
   here on earth our food, our stay;
   alleluia, here the sinful
   come to you from day to day.
   Intercessor, friend of sinners,
   earth's redeemer, plead for me,
   where the songs of all the sinless
   sweep across the crystal sea.

4. Alleluia, King eternal,
   he the Lord of lords we own;
   alleluia, born of Mary,
   earth his footstool, heav'n his throne;
   he within the veil has entered
   robed in flesh, our great High Priest;
   he on earth both priest and victim
   in the Eucharistic Feast.

13 William John Sparrow-Simpson (1859-1952) alt.
© Novello & Co. Ltd.

1. All for Jesus! All for Jesus!
   This our song shall ever be;
   for we have no hope nor Saviour
   if we have not hope in thee.

2. All for Jesus! thou wilt give us
   strength to serve thee hour by hour;
   none can move us from thy presence
   while we trust thy love and pow'r.

3. All for Jesus! at thine altar
   thou dost give us sweet content;
   there, dear Saviour, we receive thee
   in thy holy sacrament.

4. All for Jesus! thou hast loved us,
all for Jesus! thou hast died,
all for Jesus! thou art with us,
all for Jesus, glorified!

5. All for Jesus! All for Jesus!
This the Church's song shall be,
till at last the flock is gathered
one in love, and one in thee.

14 St Theodulph of Orleans (d. 821)
trans. John Mason Neale

All glory, laud and honour,
to thee, Redeemer King,
to whom the lips of children
made sweet hosannas ring.

1. Thou art the King of Israel,
thou David's royal Son,
who in the Lord's name comest,
the King and blessed one.

2. The company of angels
are praising thee on high,
and mortals, joined with all things
created, make reply.

3. The people of the Hebrews
with palms before thee went:
our praise and prayer and anthems
before thee we present.

4. To thee before thy passion
they sang their hymns of praise:
to thee now high exalted
our melody we raise.

5. Thou didst accept their praises,
accept the prayers we bring,
who in all good delightest,
thou good and gracious king.

15 Aodh Mac Cathmhaoil (1571-1626) trans. George Otto
Simms (1910-1991) © *Oxford University Press.*
Used by permission from 'Irish Church Praise'

1. All hail and welcome, holy child,
you poor babe in the manger.
So happy and rich it is you are
tonight inside your castle.

2. God bless you, Jesus, once again!
Your life in its young body,
your face more lovely than the sun –
a thousand welcomes, baby!

3. Tonight we greet you in the flesh;
my heart adores my young king.
You came to us in human form –
I bring you a kiss and a greeting.

16 Edward Perronet (1726-1792)
adapted by Michael Forster (b. 1946)
© *This version 1999 Kevin Mayhew Ltd.*

1. All hail the pow'r of Jesus' name,
let angels prostrate fall;
bring forth the royal diadem

and crown him, crown him, crown him,
crown him Lord of all.

2. Crown him, all martyrs of your God,
who from his altar call;
praise him whose way of pain you trod,
and crown him . . .

3. O prophets faithful to his word,
in matters great and small,
who made his voice of justice heard,
now crown him . . .

4. All sinners, now redeemed by grace,
who heard your Saviour's call,
now robed in light before his face,
O crown him . . .

5. Let every tribe and every race
who heard the freedom call,
in liberation, see Christ's face,
and crown him . . .

6. Let every people, every tongue
to him their heart enthral:
lift high the universal song
and crown him . . .

17 Tricia Richards
© 1987 Kingsway's Thankyou Music

1. All heav'n declares
   the glory of the risen Lord.
   Who can compare
   with the beauty of the Lord?
   For ever he will be
   the Lamb upon the throne.
   I gladly bow the knee
   and worship him alone.

2. I will proclaim
   the glory of the risen Lord.
   Who once was slain
   to reconcile us all to God.
   For ever you will be
   the Lamb upon the throne.
   I gladly bow the knee
   and worship you alone.

18 Graham Kendrick (b. 1950), based on Philippians 3:8-12
© 1993 Make Way Music

1. All I once held dear, built my life upon,
   all this world reveres, and wars to own,
   all I once thought gain I have
       counted loss;
   spent and worthless now, compared
       to this.

   Knowing you, Jesus, knowing you,
   there is no greater thing.
   You're my all, you're the best,
   you're my joy, my righteousness,
   and I love you, Lord.

2. Now my heart's desire is to know
       you more,
   to be found in you and known as yours.
   To possess by faith what I could not earn,
   all-surpassing gift of righteousness.

3. Oh, to know the pow'r of your risen life,
   and to know you in your sufferings.
   To become like you in your death,
       my Lord,
   so with you to live and never die.

19 Robert Bridges (1844-1930), based on 'Meine Hoffnung
stehet feste' by Joachim Neander (1650-1680)
© Oxford University Press

1. All my hope on God is founded;
   he doth still my trust renew.
   Me through change and chance
       he guideth,
   only good and only true.
   God unknown, he alone
   calls my heart to be his own.

2. Human pride and earthly glory,
   sword and crown betray his trust;
   what with care and toil he buildeth,
   tow'r and temple, fall to dust.
   But God's pow'r, hour by hour,
   is my temple and my tow'r.

3. God's great goodness aye endureth,
   deep his wisdom, passing thought:
   splendour, light and life attend him,
   beauty springeth out of naught.
   Evermore, from his store,
   new-born worlds rise and adore.

4. Still from earth to God eternal
   sacrifice of praise be done,
   high above all praises praising
   for the gift of Christ his Son.
   Christ doth call one and all:
   ye who follow shall not fall.

20 Roy Turner
© 1984 Kingsway's Thankyou Music

1. All over the world the Spirit is moving,
   all over the world,
   as the prophets said it would be.
   All over the world there's a mighty
       revelation
   of the glory of the Lord,
   as the waters cover the sea.

2. All over this land the Spirit is
       moving . . .

3. All over the Church the Spirit is
   moving . . .

4. All over us all the Spirit is
   moving . . .

5. Deep down in my heart the Spirit
   is moving . . .

21 William Kethe (d. 1594)

1. All people that on earth do dwell,
   sing to the Lord with cheerful voice;
   him serve with fear, his praise forth tell,
   come ye before him and rejoice.

2. The Lord, ye know, is God indeed,
   without our aid he did us make;
   we are his folk, he doth us feed
   and for his sheep he doth us take.

3. O enter then his gates with praise,
   approach with joy his courts unto;
   praise, laud and bless his name always,
   for it is seemly so to do.

4. For why? the Lord our God is good:
   his mercy is for ever sure;
   his truth at all times firmly stood,
   and shall from age to age endure.

5. To Father, Son and Holy Ghost,
   the God whom heav'n and earth adore,
   from us and from the angel-host
   be praise and glory evermore.

22 Francis Bland Tucker (1895-1984) based on Philippians 2:5-11 © 1982 Church Pension Fund

1. All praise to thee,
   for thou, O King divine,
   didst yield the glory
   that of right was thine,
   that in our darkened hearts
   thy grace might shine:
   Alleluia.

2. Thou cam'st to us
   in lowliness of thought;
   by thee the outcast
   and the poor were sought,
   and by thy death
   was God's salvation wrought:
   Alleluia.

3. Let this mind be in us
   which was in thee,
   who wast a servant
   that we might be free,
   humbling thyself
   to death on Calvary:
   Alleluia.

4. Wherefore, by God's
   eternal purpose,
   thou art high exalted
   o'er all creatures now,
   and giv'n the name to which
   all knees shall bow:
   Alleluia.

5. Let ev'ry tongue confess
   with one accord
   in heav'n and earth
   that Jesus Christ is Lord;
   and God the Father
   be by all adored:
   Alleluia.

23 Sebastian Temple (1928-1997) © 1967 OCP Publications

1. All that I am, all that I do,
   all that I'll ever have, I offer now to you.
   Take and sanctify these gifts
   for your honour, Lord.
   Knowing that I love and serve you
   is enough reward.
   All that I am, all that I do,
   all that I'll ever have I offer now to you.

Continued overleaf

2. All that I dream, all that I pray,
   all that I'll ever make I give to you today.
   Take and sanctify these gifts
   for your honour, Lord.
   Knowing that I love and serve you
   is enough reward.
   All that I am, all that I do,
   all that I'll ever have I offer now to you.

24 Susan Sayers (b. 1946), based on Psalm 98
   © 1995 Kevin Mayhew Ltd.

All the ends of the earth have seen
the salvation of our God.

1. Let us sing a new song to the Lord
   for the wonderful things he has done;
   by his holy and powerful arm,
   his salvation is brought to us all.

2. His salvation is known on the earth,
   all the nations can see he is just;
   he will never neglect to be true
   to the people he knows as his own.

3. Ev'ry part of creation has seen
   the salvation our God has bestowed.
   Let the earth shout aloud to our God,
   and the universe ring with delight.

4. O sing songs to our God with the harp,
   and with music sing praise to the Lord;
   let the horn and the trumpet give voice,
   we acknowledge the Lord who is King.

25 Cecil Frances Alexander (1818-1895)

All things bright and beautiful,
all creatures great and small,
all things wise and wonderful,
the Lord God made them all.

1. Each little flow'r that opens,
   each little bird that sings,
   he made their glowing colours,
   he made their tiny wings.

2. The purple-headed mountain,
   the river running by,
   the sunset and the morning
   that brightens up the sky.

3. The cold wind in the winter,
   the pleasant summer sun,
   the ripe fruits in the garden,
   he made them every one.

4. The tall trees in the greenwood,
   the meadows for our play,
   the rushes by the water,
   to gather ev'ry day.

5. He gave us eyes to see them,
   and lips that we might tell
   how great is God Almighty,
   who has made all things well.

26 18th century-Latin
   trans. Edward Caswall (1814-1878) alt. the editors
   © 1999 This version Kevin Mayhew Ltd.

1. All you who seek a comfort sure
   in trouble and distress,
   whatever sorrow vex the mind,
   or guilt the soul oppress.

2. Jesus, who gave himself for you
   upon the cross to die,
   opens to you his sacred heart;
   O, to that heart draw nigh.

3. You hear how kindly he invites;
   you hear his words so blest:
   'All you that labour, come to me,
   and I will give you rest.'

4. What meeker than the Saviour's heart?
   As on the cross he lay,
   it did his murderers forgive,
   and for their pardon pray.

5. Jesus, the joy of saints on high,
   the hope of sinners here,
   attracted by those loving words
   to you I lift my prayer.

6. Wash then my wounds in that dear blood
   which forth from you does flow;
   by grace a better hope inspire,
   and risen life bestow.

27 Christopher Ellis (b. 1949)
© 1999 Kevin Mayhew Ltd

1. Almighty God, we come to make
      confession,
   for we have sinned in thought and
      word and deed.
   We now repent in honesty and sorrow;
   forgive us, Lord, and meet us in
      our need.

2. Forgiving God, I come to make
      confession
   of all the harm and hurt that
      I have done;
   of bitter words and many selfish
      actions,
   forgive me, Lord, and make me
      like your Son.

3. Forgiving God, I come to make
      confession
   of all that I have failed to do this day;
   of help withheld, concern and
      love restricted,
   forgive me, Lord, and lead me in
      your way.

4. Redeeming God, we come to seek
      forgiveness,
   for Jesus Christ has died to set us free.
   Forgive the past and fill us with
      your Spirit
   that we may live to serve you joyfully.

28 Somerset Corry Lowry (1855-1932)
© Oxford University Press

1. A man there lived in Galilee
   like none who lived before,
   for he alone from first to last
   our flesh unsullied wore;
   a perfect life of perfect deeds
   once to the world was shown,
   that people all might mark his steps
   and in them plant their own.

2. A man there died on Calvary
   above all others brave;
   the human race he saved and blessed,
   himself he scorned to save.
   No thought can gauge the weight
      of woe
   on him, the sinless, laid;
   we only know that with his blood
   our ransom price was paid.

3. A man there reigns in glory now,
   divine, yet human still;
   that human which is all divine
   death sought in vain to kill.
   All pow'r is his; supreme he rules
   the realms of time and space;
   yet still our human cares and needs
   find in his heart a place.

29 vs 1-4 John Newton (1725-1807) alt.
v 5 John Rees (1828-1900)

1. Amazing grace! How sweet the sound
   that saved a wretch like me.
   I once was lost, but now I'm found;
   was blind, but now I see.

2. 'Twas grace that taught my heart to fear,
   and grace my fears relieved.
   How precious did that grace appear
   the hour I first believed.

3. Through many dangers, toils and snares
   I have already come.
   'Tis grace that brought me safe thus far,
   and grace will lead me home.

4. The Lord has promised good to me,
   his word my hope secures;
   he will my shield and portion be
   as long as life endures.

5. When we've been there a thousand years,
   bright shining as the sun,
   we've no less days to sing God's praise
   than when we first begun.

30
John L. Bell (b. 1949) and Graham Maule (b. 1958)
© 1989 WGRG Iona Community

1. Among us and before us,
   Lord, you stand
   with arms outstretched
   and bread and wine at hand.
   Confronting those
   unworthy of a crumb,
   you ask that to your table
   we should come.

2. Who dare say No,
   when such is your resolve
   our worst to witness,
   suffer and absolve,
   our best to raise in lives
   by God forgiv'n,
   our souls to fill on earth
   with food from heav'n?

3. Who dare say No,
   when such is your intent
   to love the selves
   we famish and resent,
   to cradle our
   uncertainties and fear,
   to kindle hope as
   you in faith draw near?

4. Who dare say No,
   when such is your request
   that each around your table
   should be guest,
   that here the ancient word
   should live as new
   'Take, eat and drink –
   all this is meant for you.'?

5. No more we hesitate
   and wonder why;
   no more we stand indiff'rent,
   scared or shy.
   Your invitation leads us
   to say 'Yes',
   to meet you where you nourish,
   heal and bless.

31
Dave Bilbrough
© 1983 Kingsway's Thankyou Music

1. An army of ordinary people,
   a kingdom where love is the key,
   a city, a light to the nations,
   heirs to the promise are we.
   A people whose life is in Jesus,
   a nation together we stand.
   Only through grace are we worthy,
   inheritors of the land.

   A new day is dawning,
   a new age to come,
   when the children of promise
   shall flow together as one:
   a truth long neglected,
   but the time has now come,
   when the children of promise
   shall flow together as one.

2. A people without recognition,
   but with him a destiny sealed,
   called to a heavenly vision:
   his purpose shall be fulfilled.
   Come, let us stand strong together,
   abandon ourselves to the King.
   His love shall be ours for ever,
   this vict'ry song shall we sing.

32
Charles Wesley (1707-1788)

1. And can it be that I should gain
   an int'rest in the Saviour's blood?
   Died he for me, who caused his pain?
   For me, who him to death pursued?
   Amazing love! How can it be
   that thou, my God, shouldst die
     for me?

   Amazing love! How can it be
   that thou, my God, shouldst die
     for me?

2. 'Tis myst'ry all! th'Immortal dies:
   who can explore his strange design?
   In vain the first-born seraph tries
   to sound the depths of love divine!
   'Tis mercy all! Let earth adore,
   let angel minds inquire no more.

3. He left his Father's throne above
   so free, so infinite his grace;
   emptied himself of all but love,
   and bled for Adam's helpless race;
   'tis mercy all, immense and free;
   for, O my God, it found out me.

4. Long my imprisoned spirit lay
   fast bound in sin and nature's night;
   thine eye diffused a quick'ning ray,
   I woke, the dungeon flamed with light;
   my chains fell off, my heart was free;
   I rose, went forth, and followed thee.

5. No condemnation now I dread;
   Jesus, and all in him, is mine!
   Alive in him, my living Head,
   and clothed in righteousness divine,
   bold I approach the eternal throne,
   and claim the crown, through Christ
      my own.

33 William Blake (1757-1827)

1. And did those feet in ancient time
   walk upon England's mountains green?
   And was the holy Lamb of God
   on England's pleasant pastures seen?
   And did the countenance divine
   shine forth upon our clouded hills?
   And was Jerusalem builded here
   among those dark satanic mills?

2. Bring me my bow of burning gold!
   Bring me my arrows of desire!
   Bring me my spear! O clouds unfold!
   Bring me my chariot of fire!
   I will not cease from mental fight,
   nor shall my sword sleep in my hand,
   till we have built Jerusalem
   in England's green and pleasant land.

34 William Bright (1824-1901)

1. And now, O Father, mindful of the love
   that bought us, once for all, on Calv'ry's
      tree,
   and having with us him that pleads above,
   we here present, we here spread forth to
      thee
   that only off'ring perfect in thine eyes,
   the one true, pure, immortal sacrifice.

2. Look, Father, look on his anointed face,
   and only look on us as found in him;
   look not on our misusings of thy grace,
   our prayer so languid, and our faith so
      dim:
   for lo, between our sins and their reward
   we set the Passion of thy Son our Lord.

3. And then for those, our dearest and our
      best,
   by this prevailing presence we appeal:
   O fold them closer to thy mercy's breast,
   O do thine utmost for their souls' true
      weal;
   from tainting mischief keep them pure
      and clear,
   and crown thy gifts with strength to
      persevere.

4. And so we come: O draw us to thy feet,
   most patient Saviour, who canst love us
      still;
   and by this food, so aweful and so sweet,
   deliver us from ev'ry touch of ill:
   in thine own service make us glad and
      free,
   and grant us never more to part with
      thee.

35

v 1 unknown, based on John 13:34-35
vs 2-4 Aniceto Nazareth, based on John 15 and 1 Cor. 13
© 1984, 1999 Kevin Mayhew Ltd.

A new commandment I give unto you:
that you love one another as I have loved you,
that you love one another as I have loved you.

1. By this shall all know
   that you are my disciples
   if you have love one for another. *(Repeat)*

2. You are my friends
   if you do what I command you.
   Without my help you can do nothing.
   (Repeat)

3. I am the true vine,
   my Father is the gard'ner.
   Abide in me: I will be with you. *(Repeat)*

4. True love is patient,
   not arrogant nor boastful;
   love bears all things, love is eternal.
   (Repeat)

36 James Montgomery (1771-1854)

1. Angels from the realms of glory,
   wing your flight o'er all the earth;
   ye who sang creation's story
   now proclaim Messiah's birth:

   Come and worship
   Christ, the new-born King:
   come and worship,
   worship Christ, the new-born King.

2. Shepherds, in the field abiding,
   watching o'er your flocks by night,
   God with us is now residing,
   yonder shines the infant Light:

3. Sages, leave your contemplations;
   brighter visions beam afar:
   seek the great Desire of Nations;
   ye have seen his natal star:

4. Saints before the altar bending,
   watching long in hope and fear,
   suddenly the Lord, descending,
   in his temple shall appear:

5. Though an infant now we view him,
   he shall fill his Father's throne,
   gather all the nations to him;
   ev'ry knee shall then bow down:

37 Francis Pott (1832-1909) alt.

1. Angel-voices ever singing
   round thy throne of light,
   angel-harps for ever ringing,
   rest not day nor night;
   thousands only live to bless thee,
   and confess thee Lord of might.

2. Thou who art beyond the farthest
   mortal eye can see,
   can it be that thou regardest
   our poor hymnody?
   Yes, we know that thou art near us
   and wilt hear us constantly.

3. Yea, we know that thou rejoicest
   o'er each work of thine;
   thou didst ears and hands and voices
   for thy praise design;
   craftsman's art and music's measure
   for thy pleasure all combine.

4. In thy house, great God, we offer
   of thine own to thee;
   and for thine acceptance proffer
   all unworthily,
   hearts and minds and hands and voices
   in our choicest psalmody.

5. Honour, glory, might and merit,
   thine shall ever be,
   Father, Son and Holy Spirit,
   blessèd Trinity.
   Of the best that thou hast given
   earth and heaven render thee.

38
Fred Pratt Green (b. 1903)
© 1974 Stainer & Bell Ltd.

1. An upper room did our Lord prepare
   for those he loved until the end:
   and his disciples still gather there,
   to celebrate their risen friend.

2. A lasting gift Jesus gave his own:
   to share his bread, his loving cup.
   Whatever burdens may bow us down,
   he by his cross shall lift us up.

3. And after supper he washed their feet
   for service, too, is sacrament.
   In him our joy shall be made
     complete –
   sent out to serve, as he was sent.

4. No end there is! We depart in peace,
   he loves beyond our uttermost:
   in ev'ry room in our Father's house
   he will be there, as Lord and host.

39
Timothy Dudley-Smith (b. 1926)
© Timothy Dudley-Smith

1. A purple robe, a crown of thorn,
   a reed in his right hand;
   before the soldiers' spite and scorn
   I see my Saviour stand.

2. He bears between the Roman guard
   the weight of all our woe;
   a stumbling figure bowed and scarred
   I see my Saviour go.

3. Fast to the cross's spreading span,
   high in the sunlit air,
   all the unnumbered sins of man
   I see my Saviour bear.

4. He hangs, by whom the world was made,
   beneath the darkened sky;
   the ever-lasting ransom paid,
   I see my Saviour die.

5. He shares on high his Father's throne
   who once in mercy came;
   for all his love to sinners shown
   I sing my Saviour's name.

40
Michael Forster (b. 1946), based on Isaiah 60:1-6
© 1993 Kevin Mayhew Ltd.

1. Arise to greet the Lord of light,
   you people of his choice.
   In uncreated glory bright,
   he bursts upon our inward sight,
   and bids the heart rejoice,
   and bids the heart rejoice!

2. Towards his light shall kings be drawn
   this majesty to see;
   and in the brightness of the dawn
   shall see the world in hope reborn,
   in justice full and free,
   in justice full and free.

3. The holy light in Judah's skies
   calls sages from afar.
   The hope of kings they recognise
   which, in the virgin mother's eyes,
   outshines the guiding star,
   outshines the guiding star.

4. This majesty for long concealed
   from longing human sight,
   in Jesus Christ is now revealed,
   and God's eternal promise sealed
   in love's unending light,
   in love's unending light.

41
John Mason Neale (1818-1866)

1. Around the throne of God a band
   of glorious angels ever stand;
   bright things they see, sweet harps
     they hold,
   and on their heads are crowns of gold.

Continued overleaf

2. Some wait around him, ready still
   to sing his praise and do his will;
   and some, when he commands
      them, go
   to guard his servants here below.

3. Lord, give thy angels ev'ry day
   command to guide us on our way,
   and bid them ev'ry evening keep
   their watch around us while we sleep.

4. So shall no wicked thing draw near,
   to do us harm or cause us fear;
   and we shall dwell, when life is past,
   with angels round thy throne at last.

42 Peter West, Mary Lou Locke and Mary Kirkbride
© 1979 Peter West/Integrity's Hosanna! Music/Kingsway's
Thankyou Music

Ascribe greatness to our God, the Rock,
his work is perfect and all his ways are
   just.
A God of faithfulness
and without injustice,
good and upright is he.

43 Charles Coffin (1676-1749)
trans. John Chandler (1806-1876)

1. As now the sun's declining rays
   at eventide descend,
   e'en so our years are sinking down
   to their appointed end.

2. Lord, on the cross thine arms were
      stretched
   to draw the nations nigh;
   O grant us then that cross to love,
   and in those arms to die.

3. To God the Father, God the Son,
   and God the Holy Ghost,
   all glory be from saints on earth
   and from the angel host.

44 Psalm 42 in 'New Version' (Tate and Brady, 1696)

1. As pants the hart for cooling streams
   when heated in the chase,
   so longs my soul, O God, for thee,
   and thy refreshing grace.

2. For thee, my God, the living God,
   my thirsty soul doth pine:
   O when shall I behold thy face,
   thou majesty divine?

3. Why restless, why cast down, my soul?
   hope still, and thou shalt sing
   the praise of him who is thy God,
   thy health's eternal spring.

4. To Father, Son and Holy Ghost,
   the God whom we adore,
   be glory, as it was, is now,
   and shall be evermore.

45 Martin Nystrom, based on Psalm 42:1-2
© 1983 Restoration Music Ltd.
Administered by Sovereign Music UK

1. As the deer pants for the water,
   so my soul longs after you.
   You alone are my heart's desire
   and I long to worship you.

   You alone are my strength, my shield,
   to you alone may my spirit yield.
   You alone are my heart's desire
   and I long to worship you.

2. I want you more than gold or silver,
   only you can satisfy.
   You alone are the real joy-giver
   and the apple of my eye.

3. You're my friend and you are my brother,
   even though you are a king.
   I love you more than any other,
   so much more than anything.

46 Jancis Harvey
© Jancis Harvey. Used by Permission

1. A still small voice in the heart of the city,
   a still small voice on the mountain,
   through the storms that are raging
   or the quiet of the evening,
   it can only be heard if you listen.

2. The voice of God in a place that is
       troubled,
   the voice of God in the dawning,
   through the noise of the shouting,
   through the stillness of the sleeping,
   it can only be heard if you listen.

3. Give time to hear, give us love that
       will listen,
   give wisdom for understanding,
   there's a voice of stillness
   that to each of us is speaking,
   it can only be heard if you listen.

47 John Daniels
*© 1979 Word's Spirit of Praise Music
Administered by CopyCare*

As we are gathered, Jesus is here;
one with each other, Jesus is here;
joined by the Spirit, washed in the blood,
part of the body, the church of God.
As we are gathered, Jesus is here;
one with each other, Jesus is here.

48 Fred Kaan (b. 1929)
© 1968 Stainer & Bell Ltd

1. As we break the bread
   and taste the life of wine,
   we bring to mind our Lord,
   Man of all time.

2. Grain is sown to die;
   it rises from the dead,
   becomes through human toil
   our daily bread.

3. Pass from hand to hand
   the living love of Christ!
   Machines and people raise
   bread for this feast.

4. Jesus binds in one
   our daily life and work;
   he is of humankind
   symbol and mark.

5. Having shared the bread
   that died to rise again,
   we rise to serve the world
   scattered as grain.

49 William Chatterton Dix (1837-1898)

1. As with gladness men of old
   did the guiding star behold,
   as with joy they hailed its light,
   leading onward, beaming bright;
   so, most gracious Lord, may we
   evermore be led to thee.

2. As with joyful steps they sped,
   to that lowly manger-bed,
   there to bend the knee before
   him whom heav'n and earth adore,
   so may we with willing feet
   ever seek thy mercy-seat.

3. As their precious gifts they laid,
   at thy manger roughly made,
   so may we with holy joy,
   pure, and free from sin's alloy,
   all our costliest treasures bring,
   Christ, to thee our heav'nly King.

4. Holy Jesu, ev'ry day
   keep us in the narrow way;
   and, when earthly things are past,
   bring our ransomed souls at last
   where they need no star to guide,
   where no clouds thy glory hide.

Continued overleaf

5. In the heav'nly country bright
   need they no created light,
   thou its light, its joy, its crown,
   thou its sun which goes not down;
   there for ever may we sing
   alleluias to our King.

50

Henry Twells (1823-1900) alt.

1. At even, ere the sun was set,
   the sick, O Lord, around thee lay;
   O in what divers pains they met!
   O with what joy they went away!

2. Once more 'tis eventide, and we
   oppressed with various ills draw near;
   what if thy form we cannot see?
   We know and feel that thou art here.

3. O Saviour Christ, our woes dispel;
   for some are sick, and some are sad,
   and some have never loved thee well,
   and some have lost the love they had.

4. And some have found the world is vain,
   yet from the world they break not free;
   and some have friends who give them
      pain,
   yet have not sought a friend in thee.

5. And none, O Lord, has perfect rest,
   for none is wholly free from sin;
   and they who fain would serve thee best
   are conscious most of wrong within.

6. O Christ, thou hast been human too,
   thou hast been troubled, tempted, tried;
   thy kind but searching glance can view
   the very wounds that shame would hide.

7. Thy touch has still its ancient pow'r;
   no word from thee can fruitless fall:
   hear, in this solemn evening hour,
   and in thy mercy heal us all.

51

Jacapone da Todi (d. 1306)
trans. Edward Caswall (1814-1878)

1. At the cross her station keeping,
   stood the mournful mother weeping,
   close to Jesus to the last.

2. Through her heart, his sorrow sharing,
   all his bitter anguish bearing,
   now at length the sword has passed.

3. O, how sad and sore distressed
   was that mother highly blest,
   of the sole-begotten One.

4. Christ above in torment hangs;
   she beneath beholds the pangs
   of her dying glorious Son.

5. Is there one who would not weep,
   whelmed in miseries so deep,
   Christ's dear mother to behold?

6. Can the human heart refrain
   from partaking in her pain,
   in that mother's pain untold?

7. Bruised, derided, cursed, defiled,
   she beheld her tender child,
   all with bloody scourges rent.

8. For the sins of his own nation,
   saw him hang in desolation,
   till his spirit forth he sent.

9. O thou mother! Fount of love!
   Touch my spirit from above,
   make my heart with thine accord.

10. Make me feel as thou hast felt;
    make my soul to glow and melt
    with the love of Christ my Lord.

11. Holy Mother, pierce me through,
    in my heart each wound renew
    of my Saviour crucified.

12. Let me share with thee his pain
    who for all my sins was slain,
    who for me in torments died.

13. Let me mingle tears with thee,
    mourning him who mourned for me,
    all the days that I may live.

14. By the cross with thee to stay,
    there with thee to weep and pray,
    this I ask of thee to give.

52 David Fox (b. 1956)
© David Fox

1. At the dawning of creation
   when the world began to be,
   God called forth the world's foundations
   from the deep chaotic sea.

2. When the Lord delivered Israel
   out of Egypt's bitter yoke,
   then the parting of the waters
   of the living water spoke.

3. Water from the rock of Moses,
   water from the temple's side,
   water from the heart of Jesus,
   flow in this baptismal tide.

4. Thus united in this water
   each to all, and each to Christ;
   to his life of love he calls us
   by his total sacrifice.

53 'Ad regias Agni dapes'
trans. Robert Campbell (1814-1868)

1. At the Lamb's high feast we sing
   praise to our victorious King,
   who hath washed us in the tide
   flowing from his piercèd side;
   praise we him, whose love divine
   gives his sacred blood for wine,
   gives his body for the feast,
   Christ the victim, Christ the priest.

2. Where the paschal blood is poured,
   death's dark angel sheathes his sword;
   faithful hosts triumphant go
   through the wave that drowns the foe.
   Praise we Christ, whose blood was shed,
   paschal victim, paschal bread;
   with sincerity and love
   eat we manna from above.

3. Mighty victim from above,
   conqu'ring by the pow'r of love;
   thou hast triumphed in the fight,
   thou hast brought us life and light.
   Now no more can death appal,
   now no more the grave enthral:
   thou hast opened paradise,
   and in thee thy saints shall rise.

4. Easter triumph, Easter joy,
   nothing now can this destroy;
   from sin's pow'r do thou set free
   souls new-born, O Lord, in thee.
   Hymns of glory and of praise,
   risen Lord, to thee we raise;
   holy Father, praise to thee,
   with the Spirit, ever be.

54 Caroline Maria Noel (1817-1877)

1. At the name of Jesus
   ev'ry knee shall bow,
   ev'ry tongue confess him
   King of glory now;
   'tis the Father's pleasure
   we should call him Lord,
   who, from the beginning,
   was the mighty Word.

2. At his voice creation
   sprang at once to sight,
   all the angels' faces,
   all the hosts of light,
   thrones and dominations,
   stars upon their way,
   all the heav'nly orders
   in their great array.

Continued overleaf

3. Humbled for a season;
   to receive a name
   from the lips of sinners
   unto whom he came,
   faithfully he bore it,
   spotless to the last,
   brought it back victorious
   when from death he passed.

4. Bore it up triumphant
   with its human light,
   through all ranks of creatures
   to the central height,
   to the throne of Godhead,
   to the Father's breast,
   filled it with the glory
   of that perfect rest.

5. In your hearts enthrone him;
   there let him subdue
   all that is not holy,
   all that is not true;
   crown him as your captain
   in temptation's hour;
   let his will enfold you
   in its light and pow'r.

6. Truly, this Lord Jesus
   shall return again,
   with his Father's glory,
   with his angel train;
   for all wreaths of empire
   meet upon his brow,
   and our hearts confess him
   King of glory now.

55 Graham Kendrick (b. 1950)
   © 1988 Make Way Music

At this time of giving,
gladly now we bring
gifts of goodness and mercy
from a heav'nly King.

1. Earth could not contain the treasures
   heaven holds for you,
   perfect joy and lasting pleasures,
   love so strong and true.

2. May his tender love surround you
   at this Christmastime;
   may you see his smiling face
   that in the darkness shines.

3. But the many gifts he gives
   are all poured out from one;
   come, receive the greatest gift,
   the gift of God's own Son.

Last two choruses and verses:

Lai, lai, lai . . . etc

56 Charles Wesley (1707-1788)

1. Author of life divine,
   who hast a table spread,
   furnished with mystic wine
   and everlasting bread,
   preserve the life thyself hast giv'n,
   and feed and train us up for heav'n.

2. Our needy souls sustain
   with fresh supplies of love,
   till all thy life we gain,
   and all thy fulness prove,
   and, strengthened by thy perfect grace,
   behold without a veil thy face.

57 John Raphael Peacey (1896-1971)
   based on Ephesians 5:6-20
   © Revd Mary J. Hancock

1. Awake, awake: fling off the night!
   for God has sent his glorious light;
   and we who live in Christ's new day
   must works of darkness put away.

2. Awake and rise, in Christ renewed,
   and with the Spirit's pow'r endued.
   The light of life in us must glow,
   and fruits of truth and goodness show.

3. Let in the light; all sin expose
   to Christ, whose life no darkness knows.
   Before his cross for guidance kneel;
   his light will judge and, judging, heal.

4. Awake, and rise up from the dead,
   and Christ his light on you will shed.
   Its pow'r will wrong desires destroy,
   and your whole nature fill with joy.

5. Then sing for joy, and use each day;
   give thanks for everything alway.
   Lift up your hearts; with one accord
   praise God through Jesus Christ our Lord.

58 Thomas Ken (1637-1711) alt.

1. Awake, my soul, and with the sun
   thy daily stage of duty run;
   shake off dull sloth, and joyful rise
   to pay thy morning sacrifice.

2. Redeem thy mis-spent time that's past,
   and live this day as if thy last;
   improve thy talent with due care;
   for the great day thyself prepare.

3. Let all thy converse be sincere,
   thy conscience as the noon-day clear;
   think how all-seeing God thy ways
   and all thy secret thoughts surveys.

4. Wake, and lift up thyself, my heart,
   and with the angels bear thy part,
   who all night long unwearied sing
   high praise to the eternal King.

PART TWO

5. Glory to thee, who safe hast kept
   and hast refreshed me whilst I slept;
   grant, Lord, when I from death shall
     wake,
   I may of endless light partake.

6. Lord, I my vows to thee renew;
   disperse my sins as morning dew;
   guard my first springs of thought
     and will,
   and with thyself my spirit fill.

7. Direct, control, suggest, this day,
   all I design or do or say;
   that all my pow'rs, with all their might,
   in thy sole glory may unite.

This Doxology is sung after either part

8. Praise God, from whom all blessings
     flow,
   praise him, all creatures here below,
   praise him above, angelic host,
   praise Father, Son and Holy Ghost.

59 Isaac Watts (1674-1748), based on Isaiah 40: 28-31

1. Awake, our souls; away, our fears;
   let ev'ry trembling thought be gone;
   awake and run the heav'nly race,
   and put cheerful courage on.

2. True, 'tis a strait and thorny road,
   and mortal spirits tire and faint;
   but they forget the mighty God
   that feeds the strength of ev'ry saint.

3. The mighty God, whose matchless pow'r
   is ever new and ever young,
   and firm endures, while endless years
   their everlasting circles run.

4. From thee, the overflowing spring,
   our souls shall drink a fresh supply,
   while such as trust their native strength
   shall melt away, and drop, and die.

5. Swift as an eagle cuts the air,
   we'll mount aloft to thine abode;
   on wings of love our souls shall fly,
   nor tire amidst the heav'nly road.

60
Graham Kendrick (b. 1950)
© 1993 Make Way Music

1. Beauty for brokenness,
   hope for despair,
   Lord, in the suffering,
   this is our prayer.
   Bread for the children,
   justice, joy, peace,
   sunrise to sunset
   your kingdom increase.

2. Shelter for fragile lives,
   cures for their ills,
   work for the craftsmen,
   trade for their skills.
   Land for the dispossessed,
   rights for the weak,
   voices to plead the cause
   of those who can't speak.

   God of the poor,
   friend of the weak,
   give us compassion, we pray,
   melt our cold hearts,
   let tears fall like rain.
   Come, change our love
   from a spark to a flame.

3. Refuge from cruel wars,
   havens from fear,
   cities for sanctu'ry,
   freedoms to share.
   Peace to the killing fields,
   scorched earth to green,
   Christ for the bitterness,
   his cross for the pain.

4. Rest for the ravaged earth,
   oceans and streams,
   plundered and poisoned,
   our future, our dreams.
   Lord, end our madness,
   carelessness, greed;
   make us content with
   the things that we need.

5. Lighten our darkness,
   breathe on this flame,
   until your justice
   burns brightly again;
   until the nations
   learn of your ways,
   seek your salvation
   and bring you their praise.

61
'Te lucis ante terminum' (pre 8th century)
trans. John Mason Neale (1818-1866)

1. Before the ending of the day,
   Creator of the world, we pray,
   that with thy wonted favour thou
   wouldst be our guard and keeper now.

2. From all ill dreams defend our eyes,
   from nightly fears and fantasies;
   tread under foot our ghostly foe,
   that no pollution we may know.

3. O Father, that we ask be done,
   through Jesus Christ thine only Son,
   who, with the Holy Ghost and thee,
   doth live and reign eternally. Amen.

62
Thomas Pestel (1585-1659) alt.

1. Behold, the great Creator makes
   himself a house of clay,
   a robe of virgin flesh he takes
   which he will wear for ay.

2. Hark, hark! the wise eternal Word
   like a weak infant cries;
   in form of servant is the Lord,
   and God in cradle lies.

3. This wonder struck the world amazed,
   it shook the starry frame;
   squadrons of angels stood and gazed,
   then down in troops they came.

4. Glad shepherds run to view this sight;
   a choir of angels sings,
   and eastern sages with delight
   adore this King of kings.

5. Join then, all hearts that are not stone,
   and all our voices prove;
   to celebrate this Holy One,
   the God of peace and love.

63
Michael Forster (b. 1946), based on Isaiah 11:1-10
© 1993 Kevin Mayhew Ltd.

1. Behold, the Saviour of the nations
   shall spring from David's royal line,
   to rule with mercy all the peoples,
   and judge with righteousness divine!

2. He shall delight in truth and wisdom,
   with justice for the meek and poor,
   and reconcile his whole creation,
   where beasts of prey shall hunt no more.

3. Here may his word, with hope abounding,
   unite us all in peace and love,
   to live as one with all creation,
   redeemed by mercy from above.

4. Prepare the way with awe and wonder;
   salvation comes on judgement's wing,
   for God will purify his people,
   and 'Glory!' all the earth shall sing.

64
Horatius Bonar (1808-1889), based on 1 John 4:7

1. Beloved, let us love: for love is of God;
   in God alone love has its true abode.

2. Beloved, let us love: for those who love,
   they only, are his children from above.

3. Beloved, let us love: for love is rest,
   and those who do not love cannot
   be blessed.

4. Beloved, let us love: for love is light,
   and those who do not love still live
   in night.

5. Beloved, let us love: for only thus
   shall we see God, the Lord who first
   loved us.

65
Elizabeth C. Clephane (1830-1869) alt.

1. Beneath the cross of Jesus
   I fain would take my stand,
   the shadow of a mighty rock
   within a weary land;
   a home within a wilderness,
   a rest upon the way,
   from burning heat at noontide and
   the burden of the day.

2. O safe and happy shelter!
   O refuge tried and sweet!
   O trysting place where heaven's love
   and heaven's justice meet!
   As to the holy patriarch
   that wondrous dream was giv'n,
   so seems my Saviour's cross to me
   a ladder up to heav'n.

3. There lies, beneath its shadow,
   but on the farther side,
   the darkness of an awful grave
   that gapes both deep and wide;
   and there between us stands the cross,
   two arms outstretched to save;
   a watchman set to guard the way
   from that eternal grave.

4. Upon that cross of Jesus
   mine eye at times can see
   the very dying form of One
   who suffered there for me;
   and from my stricken heart, with tears,
   two wonders I confess –
   the wonders of redeeming love,
   and my unworthiness.

5. I take, O cross, thy shadow
   for my abiding place!
   I ask no other sunshine than
   the sunshine of his face;
   content to let the world go by,
   to reckon gain as loss –
   my sinful self, my only shame,
   my glory all – the cross.

66 Unknown, based on Psalm 46

1. Be still and know that I am God. *(x3)*

2. I am the Lord that healeth thee. *(x3)*

3. In thee, O Lord, I put my trust. *(x3)*

67 David J. Evans
© 1986 Kingsway's Thankyou Music

1. Be still, for the presence of the Lord,
   the Holy One, is here.
   Come, bow before him now,
   with reverence and fear.
   In him no sin is found,
   we stand on holy ground.
   Be still, for the presence of the Lord,
   the Holy One, is here.

2. Be still, for the glory of the Lord
   is shining all around;
   he burns with holy fire,
   with splendour he is crowned.
   How awesome is the sight,
   our radiant King of light!
   Be still, for the glory of the Lord
   is shining all around.

3. Be still, for the power of the Lord
   is moving in this place;
   he comes to cleanse and heal,
   to minister his grace.
   No work too hard for him,
   in faith receive from him.
   Be still, for the power of the Lord
   is moving in this place.

68 Katherina von Schlegel (b. 1697)
trans. Jane L. Borthwick, alt.

1. Be still, my soul: the Lord is at your side;
   bear patiently the cross of grief and pain;
   leave to your God to order and provide;
   in ev'ry change he faithful will remain.
   Be still, my soul: your best, your
      heav'nly friend,
   through thorny ways, leads to a joyful end.

2. Be still, my soul: your God will undertake
   to guide the future as he has the past.
   Your hope, your confidence let nothing
      shake,
   all now mysterious shall be clear at last.
   Be still, my soul: the tempests still obey
   his voice, who ruled them once on Galilee.

3. Be still, my soul: the hour is hastening on
   when we shall be for ever with the Lord,
   when disappointment, grief and fear
      are gone,
   sorrow forgotten, love's pure joy restored.
   Be still, my soul: when change and tears
      are past,
   all safe and blessèd we shall meet at last.

69 Isaac Williams (1802-1865)

1. Be thou my guardian and my guide,
   and hear me when I call;
   let not my slipp'ry footsteps slide,
   and hold me lest I fall.

2. The world, the flesh, and Satan dwell
   around the path I tread;
   O save me from the snares of hell,
   thou quick'ner of the dead.

3. And if I tempted am to sin,
   and outward things are strong,
   do thou, O Lord, keep watch within,
   and save my soul from wrong.

4. Still let me ever watch and pray,
   and feel that I am frail;
   that if the tempter cross my way,
   yet he may not prevail.

70 Irish 8th century, trans. Mary Byrne (1880-1931)
and Eleanor Hull (1860-1935)
© Copyright control

1. Be thou my vision, O Lord of my heart,
   naught be all else to me save that thou art;
   thou my best thought in the day and
      the night,
   waking or sleeping, thy presence my light.

2. Be thou my wisdom, be thou my
      true word,
   I ever with thee and thou with me, Lord;
   thou my great Father, and I thy true heir;
   thou in me dwelling, and I in thy care.

3. Be thou my breastplate, my sword for
      the fight,
   be thou my armour, and be thou
      my might,
   thou my soul's shelter, and thou my
      high tow'r,
   raise thou me heav'nward, O Pow'r of
      my pow'r.

4. Riches I need not, nor all the
      world's praise,
   thou mine inheritance through all my days;
   thou, and thou only, the first in my heart,
   high King of heaven, my treasure thou art!

5. High King of heaven, when battle is done,
   grant heaven's joy to me, O bright
      heav'n's sun;
   Christ of my own heart, whatever befall,
   still be my vision, O Ruler of all.

71 Timothy Dudley-Smith (b. 1926), based on Daniel 2
      © Timothy Dudley-Smith

1. Beyond all mortal praise
   God's name be ever blest,
   unsearchable his ways,
   his glory manifest;
   from his high throne,
   in pow'r and might,
   by wisdom's light,
   he rules alone.

2. Our times are in his hand
   to whom all flesh is grass,
   while as their Maker planned
   the changing seasons pass.
   He orders all:
   before his eyes
   earth's empires rise,
   her kingdoms fall.

3. He gives to humankind,
   dividing as he will,
   all pow'rs of heart and mind,
   of spirit, strength and skill:
   nor dark nor night
   but must lay bare
   its secrets, where
   he dwells in light.

4. To God the only Lord,
   our fathers' God, be praise;
   his holy name adored
   through everlasting days.
   His mercies trace
   in answered prayer,
   in love and care,
   and gifts of grace.

72 Bob Gillman
      © 1977 Kingsway's Thankyou Music

Bind us together, Lord,
bind us together with cords
that cannot be broken.
Bind us together, Lord,
bind us together, Lord,
bind us together in love.

1. There is only one God,
   there is only one King.
   There is only one Body,
   that is why we sing:

2. Fit for the glory of God,
   purchased by his precious Blood,
   born with the right to be free:
   Jesus the vict'ry has won.

3. We are the fam'ly of God,
   we are his promise divine,
   we are his chosen desire,
   we are the glorious new wine.

73
Dieter Trautwein (b. 1928), tr. Fred Kaan (b. 1929)
© 1985 Stainer & Bell Ltd

1 Bless, and keep us, God, in your
   love united,
from your family never separated.
You make all things new as we
   follow after;
whether tears or laughter, we belong to you.

2. Blessing shrivels up when your children
   hoard it;
move us then to share, for we can afford it.
Blessing only grows in the act of sharing,
in a life of caring; love that heals and grows.

3. Fill your world with peace, such as
   you intended.
Teach us to prize the earth, love,
   replenish, tend it.
God, uplift, fulfil all who sow in sadness:
let them reap with gladness, by your
   kingdom thrilled.

4. You renew our life, changing tears
   to laughter;
we belong to you, so we follow after.
Bless and keep us, God, in your love
   united,
never separated from your living Word.

74
Frances Jane van Alstyne (Fanny J. Crosby) (1820-1915)

1. Blessed assurance, Jesus is mine:
   O what a foretaste of glory divine!
   Heir of salvation, purchase of God;
   born of his Spirit, washed in his blood.

   This is my story, this is my song,
   praising my Saviour all the day long.
   (Repeat)

2. Perfect submission, perfect delight,
   visions of rapture burst on my sight;
   angels descending, bring from above
   echoes of mercy, whispers of love.

3. Perfect submission, all is at rest,
   I in my Saviour am happy and blest;
   watching and waiting, looking above,
   filled with his goodness, lost in his love.

75
Hubert J. Richards (b. 1921), based on Psalm 96
© 1996 Kevin Mayhew Ltd.

Blessed be God for ever, amen. (x3)

1. Come, sing a new song to the Lord,
   come, sing to the Lord, all the earth,
   and ring out your praises to God.

2. Come, tell of all his wondrous deeds,
   come, thank him for all he has done,
   and offer your gifts to the Lord.

3. Let all creation shout for joy;
   come worship the Lord in his house,
   the Lord who made heaven and earth.

76
Mike Anderson (b. 1956)
© 1999 Kevin Mayhew Ltd.

Bless the Lord, my soul!
Bless the Lord, my soul!
Let all that is within me praise his name!
(Repeat)

1. Praise the Lord on cymbals,
   praise the Lord on drums,
   praise the Lord
   for all that he has done.

2. Praise the Lord on trumpet,
   praise the Lord in song,
   praise him all
   who stand before his throne.

3. Praise him for his mercy,
   praise him for his pow'r,
   praise him for
   his love which conquers all.

77

vs 1 and 3 John Keeble (1792-1866)
vs 2 and 4 William John Hall's 'Psalms and Hymns' (1836), alt.

1. Blest are the pure in heart,
   for they shall see our God;
   the secret of the Lord is theirs,
   their soul is Christ's abode.

2. The Lord who left the heav'ns
   our life and peace to bring,
   to dwell in lowliness with us,
   our pattern and our King.

3. Still to the lowly soul
   he doth himself impart,
   and for his dwelling and his throne
   chooseth the pure in heart.

4. Lord, we thy presence seek;
   may ours this blessing be:
   give us a pure and lowly heart,
   a temple meet for thee.

78

Hubert J. Richards (b. 1921)
© 1996 Kevin Mayhew Ltd.

1. Blest are you, Lord of creation,
   you provide the bread we offer,
   fruit of your earth and work of our hands.

   Blest be the Lord for ever, Amen. (Repeat)

2. Blest are you, Lord of creation,
   you provide the wine we offer,
   fruit of your earth and work of our hands.

3. Blest are you, Lord of creation,
   look with favour on our off'rings,
   pour out your Spirit over these gifts.

79

'Lucis Creator Optime' trans. unknown

1. Blest Creator of the light,
   making day with radiance bright,
   thou didst o'er the forming earth
   give the golden light its birth.

2. Thou didst mark the night from day
   with the dawn's first piercing ray;
   darkness now is drawing nigh;
   listen to our humble cry.

3. May we ne'er by guilt depressed
   lose the way to endless rest;
   nor with idle thoughts and vain
   bind our souls to earth again.

4. Rather may we heav'nward rise
   where eternal treasure lies;
   purified by grace within,
   hating ev'ry deed of sin.

5. Holy Father, hear our cry
   through thy Son our Lord most high,
   whom our thankful hearts adore
   with the Spirit evermore.

80

Geoffrey Ainger (b. 1925)
© 1964 Stainer & Bell Ltd.

1. Born in the night, Mary's child,
   a long way from your home;
   coming in need, Mary's child,
   born in a borrowed room.

2. Clear shining light, Mary's child,
   your face lights up our way;
   light of the world, Mary's child,
   dawn on our darkened day.

3. Truth of our life, Mary's child,
   you tell us God is good;
   prove it is true, Mary's child,
   go to your cross of wood.

4. Hope of the world, Mary's child,
   you're coming soon to reign;
   King of the earth, Mary's child,
   walk in our streets again.

81

John L. Bell (b. 1949) and Graham Maule (b. 1958)
© 1989 WGRG, Iona Community
(Wild Goose Publications 1989)

1. Bread is blessed and broken,
   wine is blessed and poured:
   take this and remember
   Christ the Lord.

2. Share the food of heaven
   earth cannot afford.
   Here is grace in essence –
   Christ the Lord.

Continued overleaf

3. Know yourself forgiven,
   find yourself restored,
   meet a friend for ever –
   Christ the Lord.

4. God has kept his promise
   sealed by sign and word:
   here, for those who want him –
   Christ the Lord.

82 Josiah Conder (1789-1855)

1. Bread of heav'n, on thee we feed,
   for thy flesh is meat indeed;
   ever may our souls be fed
   with this true and living bread;
   day by day with strength supplied
   through the life of him who died.

2. Vine of heav'n, thy blood supplies
   this blest cup of sacrifice;
   Lord, thy wounds our healing give,
   to thy cross we look and live:
   Jesus, may we ever be
   grafted, rooted, built in thee.

83 Reginald Heber (1783-1826)

1. Bread of the world in mercy broken,
   wine of the soul in mercy shed,
   by whom the words of life were spoken,
   and in whose death our sins are dead.

2. Look on the heart by sorrows broken,
   look on the tears by sinners shed;
   and be thy feast to us the token
   that by thy grace our souls are fed.

84 Edwin Hatch (1835-1889), alt. the Editors
© 1999 Kevin Mayhew Ltd.

1. Breathe on me, Breath of God,
   fill me with life anew,
   that as you love, so may I love,
   and do what you would do.

2. Breathe on me, Breath of God,
   until my heart is pure:
   until my will is one with yours
   to do and to endure.

3. Breathe on me, Breath of God,
   fulfil my heart's desire,
   until this earthly part of me
   glows with your heav'nly fire.

4. Breathe on me, Breath of God,
   so shall I never die,
   but live with you the perfect life
   of your eternity.

85 Reginald Heber (1783-1826)

1. Brightest and best
   of the sons of the morning,
   dawn on our darkness
   and lend us thine aid;
   star of the east,
   the horizon adorning,
   guide where our infant
   Redeemer is laid.

2. Cold on his cradle
   the dew-drops are shining;
   low lies his head
   with the beasts of the stall;
   angels adore him
   in slumber reclining,
   Maker and Monarch
   and Saviour of all.

3. Say, shall we yield him,
   in costly devotion,
   odours of Edom,
   and off'rings divine,
   gems of the mountain,
   and pearls of the ocean,
   myrrh from the forest,
   or gold from the mine?

4. Vainly we offer
   each humble oblation,
   vainly with gifts
   would his favour secure:
   richer by far
   is the heart's adoration,
   dearer to God
   are the prayers of the poor.

86 Richard Mant (1776-1848)

1. Bright the vision that delighted
   once the sight of Judah's seer;
   sweet the countless tongues united
   to entrance the prophet's ear.

2. Round the Lord in glory seated
   cherubim and seraphim
   filled his temple, and repeated
   each to each the alternate hymn:

3. 'Lord, thy glory fills the heaven;
   earth is with its fulness stored;
   unto thee be glory given,
   holy, holy, holy, Lord.'

4. Heav'n is still with glory ringing,
   earth takes up the angels' cry,
   'Holy, holy, holy,' singing,
   'Lord of hosts, the Lord most high.'

5. With his seraph train before him,
   with his holy Church below,
   thus unite we to adore him,
   bid we thus our anthem flow:

6. 'Lord, thy glory fills the heaven;
   earth is with its fulness stored;
   unto thee be glory given,
   holy, holy, holy, Lord.'

87 Janet Lunt

Broken for me, broken for you,
the body of Jesus, broken for you.

1. He offered his body, he poured out
   his soul;
   Jesus was broken, that we might
   be whole.

2. Come to my table and with me dine;
   eat of my bread and drink of my wine.

3. This is my body given for you;
   eat it remembering I died for you.

4. This is my blood I shed for you,
   for your forgiveness, making you new.

88 Richard Gillard

1. Brother, sister, let me serve you,
   let me be as Christ to you;
   pray that I may have the grace to
   let you be my servant, too.

2. We are pilgrims on a journey,
   fellow trav'llers on the road;
   we are here to help each other
   walk the mile and bear the load.

3. I will hold the Christlight for you
   in the night-time of your fear;
   I will hold my hand out to you,
   speak the peace you long to hear.

4. I will weep when you are weeping;
   when you laugh, I'll laugh with you.
   I will share your joy and sorrow
   till we've seen this journey through.

5. When we sing to God in heaven,
   we shall find such harmony,
   born of all we've known together
   of Christ's love and agony.

6. Brother, sister, let me serve you,
   let me be as Christ to you;
   pray that I may have the grace to
   let you be my servant, too.

89

Steven Fry
© 1994 Deep Fryed Music/Word Music/Maranatha! Music/
Administered by CopyCare

By his grace we are redeemed,
by his blood we are made clean,
and we now can know him face to face.
By his pow'r we have been raised,
hidden now in Christ by faith,
we will praise the glory of his grace.

90

Noel and Tricia Richards
© 1989 Kingsway's Thankyou Music

By your side I would stay;
in your arms I would lay.
Jesus, lover of my soul,
nothing from you I withhold.

Lord, I love you, and adore you;
what more can I say?
You cause my love to grow stronger
with every passing day.
(Repeat)

91

J B De Santeuil (1630-1697)
trans. Henry William Baker (1821-1877)

1. Captains of the saintly band,
lights who lighten ev'ry land,
princes who with Jesus dwell,
judges of his Israel.

2. On the nations sunk in night
ye have shed the Gospel light;
sin and error flee away;
truth reveals the promised day.

3. Not by warrior's spear and sword,
not by art of human word,
preaching but the Cross of shame,
rebel hearts for Christ ye tame.

4. Earth, that long in sin and pain
groaned in Satan's deadly chain,
now to serve its God is free
in the law of liberty.

5. Distant lands with one acclaim
tell the honour of your name,
who, wherever man has trod,
teach the mysteries of God.

6. Glory to the Three in One
while eternal ages run,
who from deepest shades of night
called us to his glorious light.

92

Eddie Espinosa, based on Isaiah 64:8
© 1982 Mercy/Vineyard Publishing
Administered by CopyCare

Change my heart, O God,
make it ever true;
change my heart, O God,
may I be like you.
You are the potter, I am the clay;
mould me and make me:
this is what I pray.

93

Mary MacDonald (1817-1890)
trans. Lachlan MacBean (1853-1931)
© Copyright control

1. Child in the manger, infant of Mary;
outcast and stranger, Lord of all;
child who inherits all our transgressions,
all our demerits on him fall.

2. Once the most holy child of salvation
gently and lowly lived below;
now as our glorious mighty Redeemer,
see him victorious o'er each foe.

3. Prophets foretold him, infant of wonder;
angels behold him on his throne;
worthy our Saviour of all their praises;
happy for ever are his own.

94

John Byrom (1692-1763) alt.

1. Christians, awake! salute the happy
morn,
whereon the Saviour of the world was
born;
rise to adore the mystery of love,
which hosts of angels chanted from
above:
with them the joyful tidings first begun
of God incarnate and the Virgin's Son.

2. Then to the watchful shepherds it was
    told,
  who heard th' angelic herald's voice,
    'Behold,
  I bring good tidings of a Saviour's birth
  to you and all the nations on the earth:
  this day hath God fulfilled his promised
    word,
  this day is born a Saviour, Christ the
    Lord.'

3. He spake; and straightway the celestial
    choir
  in hymns of joy, unknown before,
    conspire;
  the praises of redeeming love they sang,
  and heav'n's whole orb with alleluias
    rang:
  God's highest glory was their anthem
    still,
  peace on the earth, in ev'ry heart good
    will.

4. To Bethl'em straight th'enlightened
    shepherds ran,
  to see, unfolding, God's eternal plan,
  and found, with Joseph and the blessèd
    maid,
  her Son, the Saviour, in a manger laid:
  then to their flocks, still praising God,
    return,
  and their glad hearts with holy rapture
    burn.

5. O may we keep and ponder in our mind
  God's wondrous love in saving lost
    mankind;
  trace we the babe, who hath retrieved our
    loss,
  from his poor manger to his bitter cross;
  tread in his steps assisted by his grace,
  till our first heav'nly state again takes
    place.

6. Then may we hope, th'angelic hosts
    among,
  to sing, redeemed, a glad triumphal song:
  he that was born upon this joyful day
  around us all his glory shall display;
  saved by his love, incessant we shall sing
  eternal praise to heav'n's almighty King.

95
John E. Bowers (b. 1923)
© *John E. Bowers*

Christians, lift up your hearts,
and make this a day of rejoicing;
God is our strength and song;
glory and praise to his name!

1. Praise for the Spirit of God,
  who came to the waiting disciples,
  there in the wind and the fire
  God gave new life to his own:

2. God's mighty pow'r was revealed
  when those who once were so fearful
  now could be seen by the world
  witnessing bravely for Christ.

3. Praise that his love overflowed
  in the hearts of all who received him,
  joining together in peace
  those once divided by sin:

4. Strengthened by God's mighty pow'r
  the disciples went out to all nations,
  preaching the gospel of Christ,
  laughing at danger and death:

5. Come, Holy Spirit, to us,
  who live by your presence within us,
  come to direct our course,
  give us your life and your pow'r.

6. Spirit of God, send us out
  to live to your praise and your glory;
  yours is the pow'r and the might,
  ours be the courage and faith:

96

Brian Wren (b. 1936)
© 1969, 1995 Stainer & Bell Ltd

1. Christ is alive! Let Christians sing.
   The cross stands empty to the sky.
   Let streets and homes with praises ring.
   Love, drowned in death, shall never die.

2. Christ is alive! No longer bound
   to distant years in Palestine,
   but saving, healing, here and now,
   and touching ev'ry place and time.

3. In ev'ry insult, rift and war,
   where colour, scorn or wealth divide,
   Christ suffers still, yet loves the more,
   and lives, where even hope has died.

4. Women and men, in age and youth,
   can feel the Spirit, hear the call,
   and find the way, the life, the truth,
   revealed in Jesus, freed for all.

5. Christ is alive, and comes to bring
   good news to this and ev'ry age,
   till earth and sky and ocean ring
   with joy, with justice, love and praise.

97

'Urbs beata Jerusalem', (c.7th century)
trans. John Mason Neale, (1818-1866) alt.

1. Christ is made the sure foundation,
   Christ the head and cornerstone,
   chosen of the Lord, and precious,
   binding all the Church in one,
   holy Zion's help for ever,
   and her confidence alone.

2. To this temple, where we call you,
   come, O Lord of hosts, today;
   you have promised loving kindness,
   hear your servants as we pray,
   bless your people now before you,
   turn our darkness into day.

3. Hear the cry of all your people,
   what they ask and hope to gain;
   what they gain from you, for ever
   with your chosen to retain,
   and hereafter in your glory
   evermore with you to reign.

4. Praise and honour to the Father,
   praise and honour to the Son,
   praise and honour to the Spirit,
   ever Three and ever One,
   One in might and One in glory,
   while unending ages run.

98

Latin (before 9th century)
trans. John Chandler (1806-1876)

1. Christ is our cornerstone,
   on him alone we build;
   with his true saints alone
   the courts of heav'n are filled:
   on his great love our hopes we place
   of present grace and joys above.

2. O then with hymns of praise
   these hallowed courts shall ring;
   our voices we will raise
   the Three in One to sing;
   and thus proclaim in joyful song,
   both loud and long, that glorious name.

3. Here, gracious God, do thou
   for evermore draw nigh;
   accept each faithful vow,
   and mark each suppliant sigh;
   in copious show'r on all who pray
   each holy day thy blessings pour.

4. Here may we gain from heav'n
   the grace which we implore;
   and may that grace, once giv'n,
   be with us evermore,
   until that day when all the blest
   to endless rest are called away.

99

Fred Pratt Green (b. 1903)
© 1969 Stainer & Bell Ltd

1. Christ is the world's Light, he and
      none other;
   born in our darkness, he became
      our Brother;
   if we have seen him, we have seen
      the Father:
   Glory to God on high.

2. Christ is the world's Peace, he and
     none other;
   no-one can serve him and despise
     another;
   who else unites us, one in God the Father?
   Glory to God on high.

3. Christ is the world's Life, he and
     none other;
   sold once for silver, murdered here,
     our Brother -
   he who redeems us, reigns with
     God the Father:
   Glory to God on high.

4. Give God the glory, God and
     none other;
   give God the glory, Spirit, Son
     and Father;
   give God the glory, God in Man
     my Brother:
   Glory to God on high.

100 George Wallace Briggs (1875-1959)
        © Oxford University Press

1. Christ is the world's true light,
   its captain of salvation,
   the daystar clear and bright
   of ev'ry race and nation;
   new life, new hope awakes,
   where'er we own his sway:
   freedom her bondage breaks,
   and night is turned to day.

2. In Christ all races meet,
   their ancient feuds forgetting,
   the whole round world complete,
   from sunrise to its setting:
   when Christ is throned as Lord,
   all shall forsake their fear,
   to ploughshare beat the sword,
   to pruning-hook the spear.

3. One Lord, in one great name
   unite us all who own thee;
   cast out our pride and shame
   that hinder to enthrone thee;
   the world has waited long,
   has travailed long in pain;
   to heal its ancient wrong,
   come, Prince of Peace, and reign!

101 John L. Bell (b. 1949) and Graham Maule (b. 1958)
        © 1989 WGRG, Iona Community

1. Christ's is the world in which we move,
   Christ's are the folk we're summoned
     to love,
   Christ's is the voice which calls us to care,
   and Christ is the one who meets us here.

   To the lost Christ shows his face;
   to the unloved he gives his embrace;
   to those who cry in pain or disgrace,
   Christ makes with his friends a
     touching place.

2. Feel for the people we most avoid,
   strange or bereaved or never employed;
   feel for the women, and feel for the men
   who fear that their living is all in vain.

3. Feel for the parents who've lost their child,
   feel for the women whom men
     have defiled,
   feel for the baby for whom there's
     no breast,
   and feel for the weary who find no rest.

4. Feel for the lives by life confused,
   riddled with doubt, in loving abused;
   feel for the lonely heart, conscious of sin,
   which longs to be pure but fears to begin.

102

Latin, ascribed to Rabanus Maurus (776-856)
trans. Athelstan Riley (1858-1945)
© Hymns Ancient & Modern

1. Christ, the fair glory
   of the holy angels,
   thou who hast made us,
   thou who o'er us rulest,
   grant of thy mercy,
   unto us thy servants
   steps up to heaven.

2. Send thy archangel,
   Michael, to our succour;
   peacemaker blessèd,
   may he banish from us
   striving and hatred,
   so that for the peaceful
   all things may prosper.

3. Send thy archangel,
   Gabriel, the mighty;
   herald of heaven,
   may he from us mortals
   spurn the old serpent,
   watching o'er the temples
   where thou art worshipped.

4. Send thy archangel,
   Raphael, the restorer
   of the misguided ways
   of those who wander,
   who at thy bidding
   strengthens soul and body
   with thine anointing.

5. May the blest Mother
   of our God and Saviour,
   may the assembly
   of the saints in glory,
   may the celestial
   companies of angels
   ever assist us.

6. Father Almighty,
   Son and Holy Spirit,
   God ever blessèd,
   be thou our preserver;
   thine is the glory
   which the angels worship,
   veiling their faces.

103

Michael Weisse (c. 1480-1534)
trans. Catherine Winkworth (1827-1878) alt.

1. Christ the Lord is ris'n again,
   Christ hath broken ev'ry chain.
   Hark, angelic voices cry,
   singing evermore on high,
   Alleluia.

2. He who gave for us his life,
   who for us endured the strife,
   is our paschal Lamb today;
   we too sing for joy, and say:
   Alleluia.

3. He who bore all pain and loss
   comfortless upon the cross,
   lives in glory now on high,
   pleads for us, and hears our cry:
   Alleluia.

4. He whose path no records tell,
   who descended into hell,
   who the strongest arm hath bound,
   now in highest heav'n is crowned.
   Alleluia.

5. He who slumbered in the grave
   is exalted now to save;
   now through Christendom it rings
   that the Lamb is King of kings.
   Alleluia.

6. Now he bids us tell abroad
   how the lost may be restored,
   how the penitent forgiv'n,
   how we too may enter heav'n.
   Alleluia.

7. Thou, our paschal Lamb indeed,
   Christ, thy ransomed people feed;
   take our sins and guilt away;
   let us sing by night and day:
   Alleluia.

104

Michael Saward (b. 1932)
© *Michael Saward/Jubilate Hymns*

1. Christ triumphant, ever reigning,
   Saviour, Master, King.
   Lord of heav'n, our lives sustaining,
   hear us as we sing:

   Yours the glory and the crown,
   the high renown, th'eternal name.

2. Word incarnate, truth revealing,
   Son of Man on earth!
   Pow'r and majesty concealing
   by your humble birth:

3. Suff'ring servant, scorned, ill-treated,
   victim crucified!
   Death is through the cross defeated,
   sinners justified:

4. Priestly King, enthroned for ever
   high in heav'n above!
   Sin and death and hell shall never
   stifle hymns of love:

5. So, our hearts and voices raising
   through the ages long,
   ceaselessly upon you gazing,
   this shall be our song:

105

Charles Wesley (1707-1788)

1. Christ, whose glory fills the skies,
   Christ, the true, the only light,
   Sun of Righteousness arise,
   triumph o'er the shades of night;
   Dayspring from on high, be near;
   Daystar, in my heart appear.

2. Dark and cheerless is the morn
   unaccompanied by thee;
   joyless is the day's return,
   till thy mercy's beams I see,
   till they inward light impart,
   glad my eyes, and warm my heart.

3. Visit then this soul of mine,
   pierce the gloom of sin and grief;
   fill me, radiancy divine,
   scatter all my unbelief;
   more and more thyself display,
   shining to the perfect day.

106

Samuel Johnson (1822-1882) alt.

1. City of God, how broad and far
   outspread thy walls sublime!
   Thy free and loyal people are
   of ev'ry age and clime.

2. One holy Church, one mighty throng,
   one steadfast, high intent;
   one working band, one harvest-song,
   one King omnipotent.

3. How purely hath thy speech come
   down
   from earth's primeval youth!
   How grandly hath thine empire grown
   of freedom, love and truth!

4. How gleam thy watch-fires through
   the night
   with never-fainting ray!
   How rise thy tow'rs, serene and bright,
   to meet the dawning day!

5. In vain the surge's angry shock,
   in vain the drifting sands;
   unharmed upon th'eternal Rock
   th'eternal city stands.

107

John L. Bell (b. 1949) and Graham Maule (b. 1958)
© 1987 WGRG, Iona Community

Cloth for the cradle,
cradle for the child,
the child for our ev'ry joy and sorrow;
find him a shawl that's woven by us all
to welcome the Lord
of each tomorrow.

1. Darkness and light
   and all that's known by sight,
   silence and echo fading,
   weave into one a welcome for the Son,
   set earth its own maker serenading.

2. Claimant and queen,
   wage earners in between,
   trader and travelling preacher,
   weave into one a welcome for the Son,
   whose word brings new life to ev'ry
   creature.

3. Hungry and poor,
   the sick and the unsure,
   wealthy, whose needs are stranger,
   weave into one a welcome for the Son,
   leave excess and want beneath the
   manger.

4. Wrinkled or fair,
   carefree or full of care,
   searchers of all the ages,
   weave into one a welcome for the Son,
   the Saviour of shepherds and of sages.

108

Sue McClellan (b. 1951), John Paculabo (b. 1946)
Keith Ryecroft (b. 1949)
© 1974 Kingsway's Thankyou Music

1. Colours of day dawn into the mind,
   the sun has come up, the night is behind.
   Go down in the city, into the street,
   and let's give the message
   to the people we meet.

So light up the fire and let the flame burn,
open the door, let Jesus return,
take seeds of his Spirit, let the fruit grow,
tell the people of Jesus, let his love show.

2. Go through the park, on into the town;
   the sun still shines on; it never goes down.
   The light of the world is risen again;
   the people of darkness
   are needing our friend.

3. Open your eyes, look into the sky,
   the darkness has come, the sun came to die.
   The evening draws on, the sun disappears,
   but Jesus is living,
   and his Spirit is near.

109

Graham Kendrick (b. 1950)
© 1989 Make Way Music

1. Come and see, come and see,
   come and see the King of love;
   see the purple robe
   and crown of thorns he wears.
   Soldiers mock, rulers sneer
   as he lifts the cruel cross;
   lone and friendless now,
   he climbs towards the hill.

We worship at your feet,
where wrath and mercy meet,
and a guilty world
is washed by love's pure stream.
For us he was made sin —
oh, help me take it in.
Deep wounds of love
cry out 'Father, forgive.'
I worship, I worship
the Lamb who was slain.

2. Come and weep, come and mourn
   for your sin that pierced him there;
   so much deeper
   than the wounds of thorn and nail.
   All our pride, all our greed,
   all our fallenness and shame;
   and the Lord has laid
   the punishment on him.

3. Man of heaven, born to earth
   to restore us to your heaven.
   Here we bow in awe
   beneath your searching eyes.
   From your tears comes our joy,
   from your death our life shall spring;
   by your resurrection power
   we shall rise.

110
Christopher Idle (b. 1938), based on Revelation 4,5
© Christopher Idle/Jubilate Hymns

1. Come and see the shining hope
   that Christ's apostle saw;
   on the earth, confusion,
   but in heav'n an open door,
   where the living creatures
   praise the lamb for evermore:
   Love has the victory for ever!

   Amen, he comes! to bring his own reward!
   Amen, praise God! for justice now restored;
   kingdoms of the world become the
   *   kingdoms of the Lord:*
   Love has the victory for ever!

2. All the gifts you send us, Lord,
   are faithful, good, and true;
   holiness and righteousness
   are shown in all you do:
   who can see your greatest gift
   and fail to worship you?
   Love has the victory for ever!

3. Power and salvation
   all belong to God on high!
   So the mighty multitudes of heaven
   make their cry,
   singing Alleluia!
   where the echoes never die:
   Love has the victory for ever!

111
Brian Wren (b. 1936)
© 1986 Stainer & Bell Ltd

1. Come, build the church - not heaps of
       stone
   in safe, immobile, measured walls,
   but friends of Jesus, Spirit-blown,
   and fit to travel where he calls.

2. Come, occupy with glad dissent
   where death and evil fence the ground,
   and pitch a Resurrection-Tent
   where peace is lived, and love is found.

3. Exposed upon the open ground
   to screams of war in East and West,
   our ears will catch a deeper sound:
   the weeping of the world's oppressed.

4. In wearied face, or frightened child,
   in all they know, and need to say,
   the living Christ shall stand revealed.
   Come, let us follow and obey!

112
Unknown, alt.

Come, come, come to the manger,
children, come to the children's King;
sing, sing, chorus of angels,
star of morning o'er Bethlehem sing.

1. He lies 'mid the beasts of the stall,
   who is Maker and Lord of us all;
   the wintry wind blows cold and dreary,
   see, he weeps, the world is weary;
   Lord, have pity and mercy on me!

Continued overleaf

2. He leaves all his glory behind,
   to be Saviour of all humankind,
   with grateful beasts his cradle chooses,
   thankless world his love refuses;
   Lord, have pity and mercy on me!

   Come, come, come to the manger,
   children, come to the children's King;
   sing, sing, chorus of angels,
   star of morning o'er Bethlehem sing.

3. To the manger of Bethlehem come,
   to the Saviour Emmanuel's home;
   the heav'nly hosts above are singing,
   set the Christmas bells a-ringing;
   Lord, have pity and mercy on me!

113 Isaac Watts (1674-1748)

1. Come dearest Lord, descend and dwell
   by faith and love in ev'ry breast;
   then shall we know and taste and feel
   the joys that cannot be expressed.

2. Come, fill our hearts with inward strength,
   make our enlargèd souls possess
   and learn the height and breadth and length
   of thine unmeasurable grace.

3. Now to the God whose pow'r can do
   more than our thoughts or wishes know,
   be everlasting honours done
   by all the Church, through Christ his Son.

114 'Discendi, amor santo' by Bianco da Siena (d. 1434)
trans. Richard F. Littledale, (1833-1890) alt.

1. Come down, O Love divine,
   seek thou this soul of mine,
   and visit it with thine own ardour glowing;
   O Comforter, draw near,
   within my heart appear,
   and kindle it, thy holy flame bestowing.

2. O let it freely burn,
   till earthly passions turn
   to dust and ashes in its heat consuming;
   and let thy glorious light
   shine ever on my sight,
   and clothe me round, the while my
      path illuming.

3. Let holy charity
   mine outward vesture be,
   and lowliness become mine inner clothing;
   true lowliness of heart,
   which takes the humbler part,
   and o'er its own shortcomings weeps
      with loathing.

4. And so the yearning strong,
   with which the soul will long,
   shall far outpass the pow'r of human
      telling;
   nor can we guess its grace,
   till we become the place
   wherein the Holy Spirit makes
      his dwelling.

115 Michael Forster (b. 1946)
© 2000 Kevin Mayhew Ltd

1. Come, faithful pilgrims all,
   give God the glory.
   Let all who hear his call
   tell out his story:
   how he set Israel free
   from Egypt's slavery,
   and called them out to be
   a pilgrim people.

2. Out on the desert way,
   in all its starkness,
   faith led them through the day,
   and lit their darkness.
   No written guarantee,
   no easy certainty,
   just God's great call to be
   a pilgrim people.

3. Let all the world rejoice
in exsultation
let every silent voice
sing of salvation.
Loose all the chains that bind,
set free both heart and mind,
and make all humankind
a pilgrim people.

116 Simon Browne (1680-1732) and others

1. Come, gracious Spirit, heav'nly Dove,
with light and comfort from above;
be thou our guardian, thou our guide,
o'er ev'ry thought and step preside.

2. The light of truth to us display,
and make us know and choose thy way;
plant faith and love in ev'ry heart,
that we from God may ne'er depart.

3. Lead us to Christ, the living Way,
nor let us from our shepherd stray;
lead us to holiness, the road
that brings us to our home in God.

4. Lead us to heav'n, that we may share
fullness of joy for ever there;
lead us to God, the heart's true rest,
to dwell with him, for ever blest.

117 Charles Wesley (1707-1788)

1. Come, Holy Ghost, our hearts inspire,
let us thine influence prove;
source of the old prophetic fire,
fountain of life and love.

2. Come, Holy Ghost – for, moved by thee,
thy prophets wrote and spoke –
unlock the truth, thyself the key,
unseal the sacred book.

3. Expand thy wings, celestial Dove,
brood o'er our nature's night;
on our disordered spirits move,
and let there now be light.

4. God, through himself, we then shall
know,
if thou within us shine;
and sound, with all thy saints below,
the depths of love divine.

118

vs. 1-3, 5: John Cosin (1594-1672)
after Rabanus Maurus (c. 776-856) alt.
v. 4: Michael Forster (b. 1946)
© v.4: 1993 Kevin Mayhew Ltd.

1. Come, Holy Ghost, our souls inspire,
and lighten with celestial fire;
thou the anointing Spirit art,
who dost thy sev'nfold gifts impart.

2. Thy blessèd unction from above
is comfort, life, and fire of love;
enable with perpetual light
the dullness of our blinded sight.

3. Anoint and cheer our soilèd face
with the abundance of thy grace:
keep far our foes, give peace at home;
where thou art guide no ill can come.

4. Show us the Father and the Son,
in thee and with thee, ever one.
Then through the ages all along,
this shall be our unending song.

5. 'Praise to thy eternal merit,
Father, Son and Holy Spirit.'
Amen.

119

Michael Forster (b. 1946)
based on 1 Corinthians 12: 4-11
© 1992 Kevin Mayhew Ltd.

1. Come, Holy Spirit, come!
Inflame our souls with love,
transforming ev'ry heart and home
with wisdom from above.
O let us not despise
the humble path Christ trod,
but choose, to shame the worldly-wise,
the foolishness of God.

Continued overleaf

2. All-knowing Spirit, prove
   the poverty of pride,
   by knowledge of the Father's love
   in Jesus crucified.
   And grant us faith to know
   the glory of that sign,
   and in our very lives to show
   the marks of love divine.

3. Come with the gift to heal
   the wounds of guilt and fear,
   and to oppression's face reveal
   the kingdom drawing near.
   Where chaos longs to reign,
   descend, O holy Dove,
   and free us all to work again
   the miracle of love.

4. Spirit of truth, arise;
   inspire the prophet's voice:
   expose to scorn the tyrant's lies,
   and bid the poor rejoice.
   O Spirit, clear our sight,
   all prejudice remove,
   and help us to discern the right,
   and covet only love.

5. Give us the tongues to speak,
   in ev'ry time and place,
   to rich and poor, to strong and weak,
   the word of love and grace.
   Enable us to hear
   the words that others bring,
   interpreting with open ear
   the special song they sing.

6. Come, Holy Spirit, dance
   within our hearts today,
   our earthbound spirits to entrance,
   our mortal fears allay.
   And teach us to desire,
   all other things above,
   that self-consuming holy fire,
   the perfect gift of love!

120 Isaac Watts (1674-1748) alt.

1. Come, let us join our cheerful songs
   with angels round the throne;
   ten thousand thousand are their tongues,
   but all their joys are one.

2. 'Worthy the Lamb that died,' they cry,
   'to be exalted thus.'
   'Worthy the Lamb,' our lips reply,
   'for he was slain for us.'

3. Jesus is worthy to receive
   honour and pow'r divine;
   and blessings, more than we can give,
   be, Lord, for ever thine.

4. Let all creation join in one
   to bless the sacred name
   of him that sits upon the throne,
   and to adore the Lamb.

121 Robert Walmsley (1831-1905)

1. Come, let us sing of a wonderful love,
   tender and true;
   out of the heart of the Father above,
   streaming to me and to you:
   wonderful love
   dwells in the heart of the Father above.

2. Jesus, the Saviour, this gospel to tell,
   joyfully came;
   came with the helpless and hopeless to
      dwell,
   sharing their sorrow and shame;
   seeking the lost,
   saving, redeeming at measureless cost.

3. Jesus is seeking the wanderers yet;
   why do they roam?
   Love only waits to forgive and forget;
   home! weary wanderer, home!
   Wonderful love
   dwells in the heart of the Father above.

4. Come to my heart, O thou wonderful
       love,
   come and abide,
   lifting my life till it rises above
   envy and falsehood and pride;
   seeking to be
   lowly and humble, a learner of thee.

122

Howard Charles Adie Gaunt (1902-1983)
© Oxford University Press

1. Come, Lord, to our souls come down,
   through the gospel speaking;
   let your words, your cross and crown,
   lighten all our seeking.

2. Drive out darkness from the heart,
   banish pride and blindness;
   plant in ev'ry inward part
   truthfulness and kindness.

3. Eyes be open, spirits stirred,
   minds new truth receiving;
   lead us, Lord, by your own Word;
   strengthen our believing.

123

George Herbert (1593-1633)

1. Come, my Way, my Truth, my Life:
   such a way as gives us breath;
   such a truth as ends all strife;
   such a life as killeth death.

2. Come, my Light, my Feast, my Strength:
   such a light as shows a feast;
   such a feast as mends in length;
   such a strength as makes his guest.

3. Come, my Joy, my Love, my Heart:
   such a joy as none can move;
   such a love as none can part;
   such a heart as joys in love.

124

Frances M Kelly
© 1999 Kevin Mayhew Ltd

Come, O Lord, inspire us
with the pow'r of your love,
that your Word may take flesh,
that your kingdom may come.
Come, O Lord, inspire us
with the pow'r of your love,
that your Name may be sung
and your will may be done.

1. When the poor are lifted up,
   and when the weak are strong,
   we have the right to sing 'Alleluia!
   When the mighty are laid low,
   the dispossessed made rich,
   we have the right to sing 'Alleluia!'

2. When the hungry want no more
   and when the sick are healed,
   we have the right to sing 'Alleluia!'
   When the darkness holds no fear
   and each new dawn brings hope,
   we have the right to sing 'Alleluia!'

3. When the pow'r of hate lies crushed
   and there's no ground for war,
   we have the right to sing 'Alleluia!'
   When the lion and the lamb
   lie peaceful, all is calm,
   we have the right to sing 'Alleluia!'

125

Patricia Morgan and Dave Bankhead
© 1984 Kingsway's Thankyou Music

Come on and celebrate
his gift of love, we will celebrate
the Son of God who loved us
and gave us life.
We'll shout your praise, O King,
you give us joy nothing else can bring;
we'll give to you our offering
in celebration praise.

Come on and celebrate, celebrate,
celebrate and sing,
celebrate and sing to the King. *(Repeat)*

126
George Wallace Briggs (1875-1959)
© *Oxford University Press*

1. Come, risen Lord,
   and deign to be our guest;
   nay, let us be thy guests;
   the feast is thine;
   thyself at thine own board
   make manifest,
   in thine own sacrament
   of bread and wine.

2. We meet, as in
   that upper room they met;
   thou at thy table,
   blessing, yet dost stand:
   'This is my body'
   – so thou givest yet;
   faith still receives the cup
   as from thy hand.

3. One body we,
   one body who partake,
   one Church united
   in communion blest;
   one name we bear,
   one bread of life we break,
   with all thy saints on earth
   and saints at rest.

4. One with each other,
   Lord, for one in thee,
   who art one Saviour
   and one living Head;
   then open thou our eyes,
   that we may see:
   be known to us
   in breaking of the bread.

127
Stephen Langton (d. 1228)
trans Edward Caswall (1814-1878) alt.

1. Come, thou Holy Spirit, come,
   and from thy celestial home
   shed a ray of light divine;
   come, thou Father of the poor,
   come, thou source of all our store,
   come, within our bosoms shine.

2. Thou of comforters the best,
   thou the soul's most welcome guest,
   sweet refreshment here below;
   in our labour rest most sweet,
   grateful coolness in the heat,
   solace in the midst of woe.

3. O most blessèd Light divine,
   shine within these hearts of thine,
   and our inmost being fill;
   where thou art not, we have naught,
   nothing good in deed or thought,
   nothing free from taint of ill.

4. Heal our wounds; our strength renew;
   on our dryness pour thy dew;
   wash the stains of guilt away;
   bend the stubborn heart and will;
   melt the frozen, warm the chill;
   guide the steps that go astray.

5. On the faithful, who adore
   and confess thee, evermore
   in thy sev'nfold gifts descend:
   give them virtue's sure reward,
   give them thy salvation, Lord,
   give them joys that never end.

128
Charles Wesley (1707-1788)

1. Come, thou long expected Jesus,
   born to set thy people free;
   from our fears and sins release us;
   let us find our rest in thee.

2. Israel's strength and consolation,
   hope of all the earth thou art;
   dear desire of ev'ry nation,
   joy of ev'ry longing heart.

3. Born thy people to deliver;
   born a child and yet a king;
   born to reign in us for ever;
   now thy gracious kingdom bring.

4. By thine own eternal Spirit,
   rule in all our hearts alone:
   by thine all-sufficient merit,
   raise us to thy glorious throne.

129 Gerard Markland (b. 1953)
© 1998 Kevin Mayhew Ltd.

1. Come to me, come, my people;
   learn from me, be humble of heart.

2. I your Lord, I your master;
   learn from me, be humble of heart.

3. Follow me to my Father;
   learn from me, be humble of heart.

4. In my death, in my rising;
   learn from me, be humble of heart.

5. Be transformed by my Spirit;
   learn from me, be humble of heart.

6. Glory be to my Father;
   learn from me, be humble of heart.

130 Martin E. Leckebusch (b. 1962)
© 1999 Kevin Mayhew Ltd

1. Come, wounded Healer, your
      suff'rings reveal –
   the scars you accepted, our anguish to
      heal.
   Your wounds bring such comfort in
      body and soul
   to all who bear torment and yearn to
      be whole.

2. Come, hated Lover, and gather us near,
   your welcome, your teaching, your
      challenge to hear:
   where scorn and abuse cause rejection
      and pain,
   your loving acceptance makes hope live
      again!

3. Come, broken Victor, condemned to a
      cross –
   how great are the treasures we gain
      from your loss!
   Your willing agreement to share in our
      strife
   transforms our despair into fullness of
      life.

131 Job Hupton (1762-1849)
and John Mason Neale (1818-1866) alt.

1. Come, ye faithful, raise the anthem,
   cleave the skies with shouts of praise;
   sing to him who found the ransom,
   Ancient of eternal days,
   God of God, the Word incarnate,
   whom the heav'n of heav'n obeys.

2. Ere he raised the lofty mountains,
   formed the seas or built the sky,
   love eternal, free and boundless,
   moved the Lord of Life to die,
   fore-ordained the Prince of princes
   for the throne of Calvary.

3. There, for us and our redemption,
   see him all his life-blood pour!
   There he wins our full salvation,
   dies that we may die no more;
   then arising, lives for ever,
   reigning where he was before.

4. High on yon celestial mountains
   stands his sapphire throne, all bright,
   midst unending alleluias
   bursting from the saints in light;
   Sion's people tell his praises,
   victor after hard-won fight.

5. Bring your harps, and bring your
      incense,
   sweep the string and pour the lay;
   let the earth proclaim his wonders,
   King of that celestial day;
   he the Lamb once slain is worthy,
   who was dead and lives for ay.

6. Laud and honour to the Father,
   laud and honour to the Son,
   laud and honour to the Spirit,
   ever Three and ever One,
   consubstantial, co-eternal,
   while unending ages run.

132 St. John of Damascus (d. c. 754)
trans. John Mason Neale (1816-1866) alt.

1. Come, ye faithful, raise the strain
   of triumphant gladness:
   God hath brought his Israel
   into joy from sadness;
   loosed from Pharaoh's bitter yoke
   Jacob's sons and daughters;
   led them with unmoistened foot
   through the Red Sea waters.

2. 'Tis the spring of souls today;
   Christ hath burst his prison,
   and from three days' sleep in death
   as a sun hath risen:
   all the winter of our sins,
   long and dark, is flying
   from his light, to whom we give
   laud and praise undying.

3. Now the queen of seasons, bright
   with the day of splendour,
   with the royal feast of feasts,
   comes its joy to render;
   comes to glad Jerusalem,
   who with true affection
   welcomes in unwearied strains
   Jesu's resurrection.

4. Alleluia now we cry
   to our King immortal,
   who triumphant burst the bars
   of the tomb's dark portal;
   Alleluia, with the Son,
   God the Father praising;
   Alleluia yet again
   to the Spirit raising.

133 Henry Alford (1810-1871) alt.

1. Come, ye thankful people, come,
   raise the song of harvest-home!
   All is safely gathered in,
   ere the winter storms begin;
   God, our maker, doth provide
   for our wants to be supplied;
   come to God's own temple, come;
   raise the song of harvest-home!

2. We ourselves are God's own field,
   fruit unto his praise to yield;
   wheat and tares together sown,
   unto joy or sorrow grown;
   first the blade and then the ear,
   then the full corn shall appear:
   grant, O harvest Lord, that we
   wholesome grain and pure may be.

3. For the Lord our God shall come,
   and shall take his harvest home,
   from his field shall purge away
   all that doth offend, that day;
   give his angels charge at last
   in the fire the tares to cast,
   but the fruitful ears to store
   in his garner evermore.

4. Then, thou Church triumphant, come,
   raise the song of harvest-home;
   all be safely gathered in,
   free from sorrow, free from sin,
   there for ever purified
   in God's garner to abide:
   come, ten thousand angels, come,
   raise the glorious harvest-home!

134 Jan Berry (b. 1953)
© 1999 Kevin Mayhew Ltd

1. Creating God, we bring our song
      of praise
   for life and work that celebrate
      your ways:
   the skill of hands, our living with
      the earth,
   the joy that comes from knowing
      our own worth.

2. Forgiving God, we bring our cries
      of pain
   for all that shames us in our search
      for gain:
   the hidden wounds, the angry scars
      of strife,
   the emptiness that saps and
      weakens life.

3. Redeeming God, we bring our trust
   in you,
   our fragile hope that all may be
   made new:
   our dreams of truth, of wealth that all
   may share,
   of work and service rooted deep in prayer.

4. Renewing God, we offer what shall be
   a world that lives and works in harmony:
   when peace and justice, once so
   long denied,
   restore to all their dignity and pride.

135
7th century
Trans John Mason Neale (1818-1866) alt.

1. Creator of the starry height,
   thy people's everlasting light,
   Jesu, redeemer of us all,
   hear thou thy servants when they call.

2. Thou, grieving at the helpless cry
   of all creation doomed to die,
   didst come to save our fallen race
   by healing gifts of heav'nly grace.

3. When earth was near its evening hour,
   thou didst, in love's redeeming pow'r,
   like bridegroom from his chamber, come
   forth from a Virgin-mother's womb.

4. At thy great name, exalted now,
   all knees in lowly homage bow;
   all things in heav'n and earth adore,
   and own thee King for evermore.

5. To thee, O Holy One, we pray,
   our judge in that tremendous day,
   ward off, while yet we dwell below,
   the weapons of our crafty foe.

6. To God the Father, God the Son
   and God the Spirit, Three in One,
   praise, honour, might and glory be
   from age to age eternally.
   (Amen.)

136
William Sparrow-Simpson (1859-1952)
© Novello & Co Ltd.

1. Cross of Jesus, cross of sorrow,
   where the blood of Christ was shed,
   perfect man on thee was tortured,
   perfect God on thee has bled.

2. Here the King of all the ages,
   throned in light ere worlds could be,
   robèd in mortal flesh is dying,
   crucified by sin for me.

3. O mysterious condescending!
   O abandonment sublime!
   Very God himself is bearing
   all the sufferings of time!

4. Evermore for human failure
   by his Passion we can plead;
   God has borne all mortal anguish,
   surely he will know our need.

5. This - all human thought surpassing -
   this is earth's most awful hour,
   God has taken mortal weakness!
   God has laid aside his pow'r!

6. Once the Lord of brilliant seraphs,
   winged with love to do his will,
   now the scorn of all his creatures,
   and the aim of ev'ry ill.

7. Up in heav'n, sublimest glory
   circled round him from the first;
   but the earth finds none to serve him,
   none to quench his raging thirst.

8. Who shall fathom that descending,
   from the rainbow-circled throne,
   down to earth's most base profaning
   dying desolate alone.

9. From the 'Holy, Holy, Holy,
   we adore thee, O most high,'
   down to earth's blaspheming voices
   and the shout of 'Crucify'.

10. Cross of Jesus, cross of sorrow,
    where the blood of Christ was shed,
    perfect man on thee was tortured,
    perfect God on thee has bled.

137
Matthew Bridges (1800-1894)

1. Crown him with many crowns,
the Lamb upon his throne;
hark, how the heav'nly anthem drowns
all music but its own:
awake, my soul, and sing
of him who died for thee,
and hail him as thy matchless King
through all eternity.

2. Crown him the Virgin's Son,
the God incarnate born,
whose arm those crimson trophies won
which now his brow adorn;
fruit of the mystic Rose,
as of that Rose the Stem,
the Root, whence mercy ever flows,
the Babe of Bethlehem.

3. Crown him the Lord of love;
behold his hands and side,
rich wounds, yet visible above,
in beauty glorified:
no angel in the sky
can fully bear that sight,
but downward bends each burning eye
at mysteries so bright.

4. Crown him the Lord of peace,
whose pow'r a sceptre sways
from pole to pole, that wars may cease,
absorbed in prayer and praise:
his reign shall know no end,
and round his piercèd feet
fair flow'rs of paradise extend
their fragrance ever sweet.

5. Crown him the Lord of years,
the Potentate of time,
Creator of the rolling spheres,
ineffably sublime.
All hail, Redeemer, hail!
for thou hast died for me;
thy praise shall never, never fail
throughout eternity.

138
Michael Forster (b. 1946)
© 1992 Kevin Mayhew Ltd.

1. Cry 'Freedom!' in the name of God,
and let the cry resound;
proclaim for all that freedom
which in Jesus Christ is found,
for none of us is truly free
while anyone is bound.

Cry 'Freedom!' cry 'Freedom!'
in God's name!
Cry 'Freedom!' cry 'Freedom!'
in God's name!

2. Cry 'Freedom!' for the victims
of the earthquake and the rain:
where wealthy folk find shelter
and the poor must bear the pain;
where weapons claim resources
while the famine strikes again.

3. Cry 'Freedom!' for dictators
in their fortresses confined,
who hide behind their bodyguards
and fear the open mind,
and bid them find true freedom
in the good of humankind.

4. Cry 'Freedom!' in the church when
honest doubts are met with fear;
when vacuum-packed theology
makes questions disappear;
when journeys end before they start
and mystery is clear!

5. Cry 'Freedom!' when we find ourselves
imprisoned in our greed,
to live in free relationship
and meet each other's need.
From self released for others' good
we should be free indeed!

139 John L. Bell (b. 1949) and Graham Maule (b.1958)
© 1987 WGRG, Iona Community

Dance and sing, all the earth,
gracious is the hand that tends you:
love and care ev'rywhere,
God on purpose sends you.

1. Shooting star and sunset shape
   the drama of creation;
   lightning flash and moonbeam share
   a common derivation.

2. Deserts stretch and torrents roar
   in contrast and confusion;
   treetops shake and mountains soar
   and nothing is illusion.

3. All that flies and swims and crawls
   displays an animation;
   none can emulate or change
   for each has its own station.

4. Brother man and sister woman,
   born of dust and passion,
   praise the one who calls you friends
   and makes you in his fashion.

5. Kiss of life and touch of death
   suggest our imperfection:
   crib and womb and cross and tomb
   cry out for resurrection.

140 Mike Anderson (b. 1956)
© 1999 Kevin Mayhew Ltd.

Dance in your Spirit,
we dance in your Spirit,
we dance in your Spirit of joy! (Repeat)

1. Jesus, you showed us the way to live,
   and your Spirit sets us free,
   free now to sing, free to dance and shout,
   'Glory, glory' to your name.

2. Jesus, you opened your arms for us,
   but we nailed them to a cross;
   but you are risen and now we live,
   free from, free from ev'ry fear.

3. Your Spirit brings peace and gentleness,
   kindness, self-control and love,
   patience and goodness and faith and joy,
   Spirit, Spirit fill us now.

141 Michael Forster (b. 1946)
© 1993 Kevin Mayhew Ltd.

1. Day of wrath and day of wonder,
   whence hope has fled!
   See the body torn asunder,
   blood freely shed.
   Stripped of majesty we saw him,
   human sight recoiled before him,
   yet it was our sorrows tore him;
   for us he bled.

2. Day of hope and day of glory,
   though unperceived!
   See redemption's dreadful story,
   long, long conceived.
   Evil pow'rs, in downfall lying,
   knowing death itself is dying,
   hear the voice triumphant crying,
   'All is achieved!'

3. Day of majesty and splendour,
   here ends the race!
   Christ, our Priest, our soul's defender,
   us will embrace.
   He who walked this earth before us,
   tried and tempted, yet victorious,
   calls us to the kingdom glorious,
   O perfect grace!

142 Brian Wren (b. 1936)
from John 12:32-33 and Romans 15-7
© 1973, 1996 Stainer & Bell Ltd.

1. Dear Christ, uplifted from the earth,
   your arms stretched out above
   through ev'ry culture, ev'ry birth,
   to draw an answ'ring love.

2. Still east and west your love extends
   and always, near and far,
   you call and claim us as your friends
   and loves us as we are.

Continued overleaf

3. Where age and gender, class and race,
   divides us to our shame,
   you see a person and a face,
   a neighbour with a name.

4. May we, accepted as we are,
   yet called in grace to grow,
   reach out to others, near and far,
   your healing love to show.

143 George Ratcliffe Woodward (1848-1934)
after T. Clausnitzer (1619-1684)
© *Copyright control*

1. Dearest Jesu, we are here,
   at thy call, thy presence owning;
   pleading now in holy fear
   that great sacrifice atoning:
   Word incarnate, much in wonder
   on this myst'ry deep we ponder.

2. Jesu, strong to save – the same
   yesterday, today, for ever –
   make us fear and love thy name,
   serving thee with best endeavour:
   in this life, O ne'er forsake us,
   but to bliss hereafter take us.

144 John Greenleaf Whittier (1807-1892)

1. Dear Lord and Father of mankind,
   forgive our foolish ways!
   Re-clothe us in our rightful mind,
   in purer lives thy service find,
   in deeper rev'rence praise,
   in deeper rev'rence praise.

2. In simple trust like theirs who heard,
   beside the Syrian sea,
   the gracious calling of the Lord,
   let us, like them, without a word,
   rise up and follow thee,
   rise up and follow thee.

3. O Sabbath rest by Galilee!
   O calm of hills above,
   where Jesus knelt to share with thee
   the silence of eternity,
   interpreted by love!
   Interpreted by love!

4. Drop thy still dews of quietness,
   till all our strivings cease;
   take from our souls the strain and stress,
   and let our ordered lives confess
   the beauty of thy peace,
   the beauty of thy peace.

5. Breathe through the heats of our desire
   thy coolness and thy balm;
   let sense be dumb, let flesh retire;
   speak through the earthquake,
       wind and fire,
   O still small voice of calm!
   O still small voice of calm!

145 Howard Charles Adie Gaunt (1902-1983)
© *Oxford University Press*

He took

1. Dear Lord, to you again our gifts
       we bring,
   this bread our toil, this wine our ecstasy,
   poor and imperfect though they both
       must be;
   yet you will take a heart-free offering.
   Yours is the bounty, ours the
       unfettered will
   to make or mar, to fashion good or ill.

He blessed

2. Yes, you will take and bless, and
       grace impart
   to make again what once your
       goodness gave,
   what we half crave, and half refuse
       to have,
   a sturdier will, a more repentant heart.
   You have on earth no hands, no hearts
       but ours;
   bless them as yours, ourselves, our will,
       our pow'rs.

3. Break bread, O Lord, break down our
   wayward wills,
   break down our prized possessions, break
   them down;
   let them be freely given as your own
   to all who need our gifts, to heal their ills.
   Break this, the bread we bring, that all
   may share
   in your one living body, everywhere.

He gave

4. Our lips receive your wine, our hands
   your bread;
   you give us back the selves we
   offered you,
   won by the cross, by Calvary made new,
   a heart enriched, a life raised from the
   dead.
   Grant us to take and guard your
   treasure well,
   that we in you, and you in us may dwell.

3. Sun, who all my life dost brighten,
   Light, who dost my soul enlighten,
   Joy, which through my spirit floweth,
   Fount, which life and health
   bestoweth,
   at thy feet I cry, my Maker,
   let me be a fit partaker
   of this blessèd food from heaven,
   for our good, thy glory, given.

4. Jesus, Bread of Life, I pray thee,
   let me gladly here obey thee;
   never to my hurt invited,
   be thy love with love requited:
   from this banquet let me measure,
   Lord, how vast and deep its treasure;
   through the gifts thou here dost
   give me,
   as thy guest in heav'n receive me.

146 Johann Franck (1618-1677)
trans. Catherine Winkworth (1827-1878)

1. Deck thyself, my soul, with gladness,
   leave the gloomy haunts of sadness;
   come into the daylight's splendour,
   there with joy thy praises render
   unto him whose grace unbounded
   hath this wondrous banquet founded:
   high o'er all the heav'ns he reigneth,
   yet to dwell with thee he deigneth.

2. Now I sink before thee lowly,
   filled with joy most deep and holy,
   as with trembling awe and wonder
   on thy mighty works I ponder:
   how, by mystery surrounded,
   depth no mortal ever sounded,
   none may dare to pierce unbidden
   secrets that with thee are hidden.

147 Mike Anderson (b. 1956)
© 1999 Kevin Mayhew Ltd.

1. Deep within my heart I know Jesus
   loves me,
   deep within my heart I know he loves me.
   Guilt and shame are conquered in his name,
   and I'm alive now.
   Deep within my heart I know he loves me.

2. Deep within my heart I know I'm forgiven,
   deep within my heart I know that I'm free.
   Free from sin, a new life to begin,
   and I'm alive now.
   Deep within my heart I know that I'm free.

3. Deep within my heart Jesus' love is healing,
   deep within my heart he is healing me.
   Tears like rain are flooding out the pain,
   and I'm alive now.
   Deep within my heart he is healing me.

148
George Ratcliffe Woodward (1848-1934)
© SPCK

1. Ding dong, merrily on high!
In heav'n the bells are ringing;
ding dong, verily the sky
is riv'n with angels singing.

Gloria, hosanna in excelsis!
Gloria, hosanna in excelsis!

2. E'en so here below, below,
let steeple bells be swungen,
and io, io, io,
by priest and people sungen.

3. Pray you, dutifully prime
your matin chime, ye ringers;
may you beautifully rhyme
your evetime song, ye singers.

149
J. B. de Santeuil (1630-1697)
trans. Isaac Williams (1802-1865) alt.

1. Disposer supreme,
and Judge of the earth,
thou choosest for thine
the meek and the poor;
to frail earthen vessels,
and things of no worth,
entrusting thy riches
which ay shall endure.

2. Those vessels are frail,
though full of thy light,
and many, once made,
are broken and gone;
thence brightly appeareth
thy truth in its might,
as through the clouds riven
the lightnings have shone.

3. Like clouds are they borne
to do thy great will,
and swift as the winds
about the world go:
the Word with his wisdom
their spirits doth fill;
they thunder, they lighten,
the waters o'erflow.

4. Their sound goeth forth,
'Christ Jesus the Lord!'
then Satan doth fear,
his citadels fall;
as when the dread trumpets
went forth at thy word,
and one long blast shattered
the Canaanites' wall.

5. O loud be their cry,
and stirring their sound,
to rouse us, O Lord,
from slumber of sin:
the lights thou hast kindled
in darkness around,
O may they awaken
our spirits within.

6. All honour and praise,
dominion and might,
to God, Three in One,
eternally be,
who round us hath shed
his own marvellous light,
and called us from darkness
his glory to see.

150
Gerard Markland (b. 1953), based on Isaiah 43:1-4
© 1978 Kevin Mayhew Ltd.

Do not be afraid, for I have redeemed you.
I have called you by your name;
you are mine.

1. When you walk through the waters,
I'll be with you.
You will never sink beneath the waves.

2. When the fire is burning
all around you,
you will never be consumed by the flames.

3. When the fear of loneliness
is looming,
then remember I am at your side.

4. When you dwell in the exile
   of the stranger,
   remember you are precious in my eyes.

5. You are mine, O my child,
   I am your Father,
   and I love you with a perfect love.

151 Phineas Fletcher (1582-1650)

1. Drop, drop, slow tears,
   and bathe those beauteous feet,
   which brought from heav'n
   the news and Prince of peace.

2. Cease not, wet eyes,
   his mercies to entreat;
   to cry for vengeance
   sin doth never cease.

3. In your deep floods
   drown all my faults and fears;
   nor let his eye
   see sin, but through my tears.

152 Aurelius Clemens Prudentius (348-c. 413) trans. Edward Caswall (1814-1878) alt.

1. Earth has many a noble city;
   Bethl'em, thou dost all excel:
   out of thee the Lord from heaven
   came to rule his Israel.

2. Fairer than the sun at morning
   was the star that told his birth,
   to the world its God announcing,
   seen in fleshly form on earth.

3. Eastern sages at his cradle
   make oblations rich and rare;
   see them give in deep devotion
   gold and frankincense and myrrh.

4. Sacred gifts of mystic meaning:
   incense doth their God disclose,
   gold the King of kings proclaimeth,
   myrrh his sepulchre foreshows.

5. Jesu, whom the Gentiles worshipped
   at thy glad Epiphany,
   unto thee with God the Father
   and the Spirit glory be.

153 William Whiting (1825-1878), alt.

1. Eternal Father, strong to save,
   whose arm doth bind the restless wave,
   who bidd'st the mighty ocean deep
   its own appointed limits keep:
   O hear us when we cry to thee
   for those in peril on the sea.

2. O Saviour, whose almighty word
   the winds and waves submissive heard,
   who walkedst on the foaming deep,
   and calm, amid its rage, didst sleep:
   O hear us when we cry to thee
   for those in peril on the sea.

3. O sacred Spirit, who didst brood
   upon the waters dark and rude,
   and bid their angry tumult cease,
   and give, for wild confusion, peace:
   O hear us when we cry to thee
   for those in peril on the sea.

4. O Trinity of love and pow'r,
   our brethren shield in danger's hour.
   From rock and tempest, fire and foe,
   protect them whereso'er they go,
   and ever let there rise to thee
   glad hymns of praise from land and sea.

154 John White Chadwick (1840-1904) alt.

1. Eternal Ruler of the ceaseless round
   of circling planets singing on their way;
   guide of the nations from the night
      profound
   into the glory of the perfect day;
   rule in our hearts, that we may ever be
   guided and strengthened and upheld
      by thee.

Continued overleaf

2. We are of thee, the children of thy love,
by virtue of thy well-belovèd Son;
descend, O Holy Spirit, like a dove,
into our hearts, that we may be as one:
as one with thee, to whom we ever tend;
as one with him, our Brother and our
    Friend.

3. We would be one in hatred of all wrong,
one in our love of all things
    sweet and fair,
one with the joy that breaketh into song,
one with the grief that trembles into
    prayer,
one in the pow'r that makes thy
    children free
to follow truth, and thus to follow thee.

4. O clothe us with thy heav'nly armour,
    Lord,
thy trusty shield, thy sword of love
    divine;
our inspiration be thy constant word;
we ask no victories that are not thine:
give or withhold, let pain or pleasure be;
enough to know that we are
    serving thee.

155 John Hampden Gurney (1802-1862)

1. Fair waved the golden corn
in Canaan's pleasant land,
when full of joy, some shining morn,
went forth the reaper-band.

2. To God so good and great
their cheerful thanks they pour;
then carry to his temple-gate
the choicest of their store.

3. Like Israel, Lord, we give
our earliest fruits to thee,
and pray that, long as we shall live,
we may thy children be.

4. Thine is our youthful prime,
and life and all its pow'rs;
be with us in our morning time,
and bless our evening hours.

5. In wisdom let us grow,
as years and strength are giv'n,
that we may serve thy Church below,
and join thy saints in heav'n.

156 Thomas Benson Pollock (1836-1896)

1. Faithful Shepherd, feed me
in the pastures green;
faithful Shepherd, lead me
where thy steps are seen.

2. Hold me fast, and guide me
in the narrow way;
so, with thee beside me,
I shall never stray.

3. Daily bring me nearer
to the heav'nly shore;
may my faith grow clearer,
may I love thee more.

4. Hallow ev'ry pleasure,
ev'ry gift and pain;
be thyself my treasure,
though none else I gain.

5. Day by day prepare me
as thou seest best,
then let angels bear me
to thy promised rest.

157 Timothy Dudley-Smith (b.1926)
based on Luke 2:29-32
© Timothy Dudley-Smith

1. Faithful vigil ended,
watching, waiting cease;
Master, grant thy servant
his discharge in peace.

2. All the Spirit promised,
all the Father willed,
now these eyes behold it
perfectly fulfilled.

3. This thy great deliv'rance
   sets thy people free;
   Christ, their light, uplifted
   all the nations see.

4. Christ, thy people's glory!
   watching, doubting, cease;
   grant to us thy servants
   our discharge in peace.

158

Gerard Markland (b. 1953), based on Psalm 139
© 1998 Kevin Mayhew Ltd.

Father God, gentle Father God,
my Lord of consolation,
I lift up my heart to you.

1. O Lord, you search me,
   you know me, my ev'ry move.
   My thoughts you read from afar,
   all my ways lie there before you.

2. My heart, my innermost being
   was made by you.
   My body, secretly formed in the womb
   was always with you.

3. What place, what heavens could
   hide me away from you.
   Were I to fly to the ends of the sea,
   your hand would guide me.

4. Your works, your knowledge, your love
   are beyond my mind.
   My Lord, I thank you for these
   and the wonder of my being.

5. O Lord, come search me, come find
   what is in my heart,
   that I may never stray far
   from your path of life eternal.

159

Ian Smale
© 1984 Kingsway's Thankyou Music

Father God,
I wonder how I managed to exist
without the knowledge of your parenthood
and your loving care.
But now I am your child,
I am adopted in your family
and I can never be alone,
'cause, Father God, you're there beside me.
I will sing your praises,
I will sing your praises,
I will sing your praises,
for evermore.

160

Graham Kendrick (b. 1950)
© 1981 Kingsway's Thankyou Music

1. Father God, we worship you,
   make us part of all you do.
   As you move among us now,
   we worship you.

2. Jesus King, we worship you,
   help us listen now to you.
   As you move among us now,
   we worship you.

3. Spirit pure, we worship you,
   with your fire our zeal renew.
   As you move among us now,
   we worship you.

161

Maria Willis (1824-1908)

1. Father, hear the prayer we offer:
   not for ease that prayer shall be,
   but for strength that we may ever
   live our lives courageously.

2. Not for ever in green pastures
   do we ask our way to be;
   but the steep and rugged pathway
   may we tread rejoicingly.

Continued overleaf

3. Not for ever by still waters
   would we idly rest and stay;
   but would smite the living fountains
   from the rocks along our way.

4. Be our strength in hours of weakness,
   in our wand'rings be our guide;
   through endeavour, failure, danger,
   Father, be thou at our side.

162 Jenny Hewer (b. 1945)
    © 1975 Kingsway's Thankyou Music

1. Father, I place into your hands
   the things I cannot do.
   Father, I place into your hands
   the things that I've been through.
   Father, I place into your hands
   the way that I should go,
   for I know I always can trust you.

2. Father, I place into your hands
   my friends and family.
   Father, I place into your hands
   the things that trouble me.
   Father I place into your hands
   the person I would be,
   for I know I always can trust you.

3. Father, we love to see your face,
   we love to hear your voice,
   Father, we love to sing your praise
   and in your name rejoice.
   Father, we love to walk with you
   and in your presence rest,
   for we know we always can trust you.

4. Father, I want to be with you
   and do the things you do.
   Father, I want to speak the words
   that you are speaking too.
   Father, I want to love the ones
   that you will draw to you,
   for I know that I am one with you.

163 Stewart Cross (1928-1989)
    © Mrs M. Cross. Used by permission

1. Father, Lord of all creation,
   ground of Being, Life and Love;
   height and depth beyond description
   only life in you can prove:
   you are mortal life's dependence:
   thought, speech, sight are ours by grace;
   yours is ev'ry hour's existence,
   sov'reign Lord of time and space.

2. Jesus Christ, the Man for Others,
   we, your people, make our prayer:
   help us love – as sisters, brothers –
   all whose burdens we can share.
   Where your name binds us together
   you, Lord Christ, will surely be;
   where no selfishness can sever
   there your love the world may see.

3. Holy Spirit, rushing, burning
   wind and flame of Pentecost,
   fire our hearts afresh with yearning
   to regain what we have lost.
   May your love unite our action,
   nevermore to speak alone:
   God, in us abolish faction,
   God, through us your love make known.

164 Latin (c. 10th century)
    trans. Alfred E. Alston (1862-1927)

1. Father most holy,
   merciful and loving,
   Jesu, Redeemer,
   ever to be worshipped,
   life-giving Spirit,
   Comforter most gracious,
   God everlasting.

2. Three in a wondrous
   Unity unbroken,
   One perfect Godhead,
   love that never faileth,
   light of the angels,
   succour of the needy,
   hope of all living.

3. All thy creation
   serveth its Creator,
   thee ev'ry creature
   praiseth without ceasing;
   we too would sing thee
   psalms of true devotion:
   hear, we beseech thee.

4. Lord God Almighty,
   unto thee be glory,
   One in Three Persons,
   over all exalted.
   Thine, as is meet, be honour,
   praise and blessing
   now and for ever.

165 Edward Cooper (1770-1833)

1. Father of heav'n, whose love profound
   a ransom for our souls hath found,
   before thy throne we sinners bend,
   to us thy pard'ning love extend.

2. Almighty Son, incarnate Word,
   our Prophet, Priest, Redeemer, Lord,
   before thy throne we sinners bend,
   to us thy saving grace extend.

3. Eternal Spirit, by whose breath
   the soul is raised from sin and death,
   before thy throne we sinners bend,
   to us thy quick'ning pow'r extend.

4. Thrice Holy! Father, Spirit, Son;
   mysterious Godhead, Three in One,
   before thy throne we sinners bend,
   grace, pardon, life, to us extend.

166 Terrye Coelho (b. 1952)
© 1972 Maranatha! Music. Administered by CopyCare

1. Father, we adore you,
   lay our lives before you.
   How we love you!

2. Jesus, we adore you . . .

3. Spirit, we adore you . . .

167 Donna Adkins (b. 1940)
© 1976 Maranatha! Music. Administered by CopyCare

1. Father, we love you,
   we worship and adore you,
   glorify your name in all the earth.
   Glorify your name, glorify your name,
   glorify your name in all the earth.

2. Jesus, we love you . . .

3. Spirit, we love you . . .

168 Fred Kaan (b. 1929)
© 1968 Stainer & Bell Ltd.

1. Father, who in Jesus found us,
   God, whose love is all around us,
   who to freedom new unbound us,
   keep our hearts with joy aflame.

2. For the sacramental breaking,
   for the honour of partaking,
   for your life our lives remaking,
   young and old, we praise your name.

3. From the service of this table
   lead us to a life more stable,
   for our witness make us able;
   blessings on our work we claim.

4. Through our calling closely knitted,
   daily to your praise committed,
   for a life of service fitted,
   let us now your love proclaim.

169 John Samuel Bewley Monsell (1811-1875), alt.

1. Fight the good fight with all thy might;
   Christ is thy strength, and Christ thy right;
   lay hold on life, and it shall be
   thy joy and crown eternally.

2. Run the straight race through God's
         good grace,
   lift up thine eyes and seek his face;
   life with its way before us lies;
   Christ is the path, and Christ the prize.

Continued overleaf

3. Cast care aside, lean on thy guide;
his boundless mercy will provide;
trust, and thy trusting soul shall prove
Christ is its life, and Christ its love.

4. Faint not nor fear, his arms are near;
he changeth not, and thou art dear;
only believe, and thou shalt see
that Christ is all in all to thee.

170 John Raphael Peacey (1896-1971)
© The Revd. Mary J. Hancock. Used by permission

1. Filled with the Spirit's pow'r,
with one accord
the infant Church
confessed its risen Lord.
O Holy Spirit,
in the Church today
no less your pow'r
of fellowship display.

2. Now with the mind of Christ
set us on fire,
that unity
may be our great desire.
Give joy and peace;
give faith to hear your call,
and readiness
in each to work for all.

3. Widen our love, good Spirit,
to embrace
in your strong care
the people of each race.
Like wind and fire
with life among us move,
till we are known as Christ's,
and Christians prove.

171 Horatius Bonar (1808-1889) alt.

1. Fill thou my life, O Lord my God,
in ev'ry part with praise,
that my whole being may proclaim
thy being and thy ways.

2. Not for the lip of praise alone,
nor e'en the praising heart,
I ask, but for a life made up
of praise in ev'ry part.

3. Praise in the common things of life,
its goings out and in;
praise in each duty and each deed,
however small and mean.

4. Fill ev'ry part of me with praise:
let all my being speak
of thee and of thy love, O Lord,
poor though I be and weak.

5. So shalt thou, Lord, receive from me
the praise and glory due;
and so shall I begin on earth
the song for ever new.

6. So shall each fear, each fret, each care,
be turnèd into song;
and ev'ry winding of the way
the echo shall prolong.

7. So shall no part of day or night
unblest or common be;
but all my life, in ev'ry step,
be fellowship with thee.

172 Timothy Dudley-Smith (b. 1926)
© Timothy Dudley-Smith

1. Fill your hearts with joy and gladness,
sing and praise your God and mine!
Great the Lord in love and wisdom,
might and majesty divine!
He who framed the starry heavens
knows and names them as they shine.
Fill your hearts with joy and gladness,
sing and praise your God and mine!

2. Praise the Lord, his people, praise him!
Wounded souls his comfort know.
Those who fear him find his mercies,
peace for pain and joy for woe;
humble hearts are high exalted,
human pride and pow'r laid low.
Praise the Lord, his people, praise him!
Wounded souls his comfort know.

3. Praise the Lord for times and seasons,
   cloud and sunshine, wind and rain;
   spring to melt the snows of winter
   till the waters flow again;
   grass upon the mountain pastures,
   golden valleys thick with grain.
   Praise the Lord for times and seasons,
   cloud and sunshine, wind and rain.

4. Fill your hearts with joy and gladness,
   peace and plenty crown your days!
   Love his laws, declare his judgements,
   walk in all his words and ways;
   he the Lord and we his children,
   praise the Lord, all people, praise!
   Fill your hearts with joy and gladness,
   peace and plenty crown your days!

173 Unknown
trans. John Mason Neale (1818-1866) alt.

1. Finished the strife of battle now,
   gloriously crowned the victor's brow;
   sing with gladness, banish sadness:
   Alleluia, alleluia!

2. After the death that him befell,
   Jesus Christ has harrowed hell;
   songs of praising we are raising:
   Alleluia, alleluia!

3. On the third morning he arose,
   shining with vict'ry o'er his foes;
   earth is singing, heav'n is ringing:
   Alleluia, alleluia!

4. Lord, by your wounds on you we call,
   you, by your death, have freed us all;
   may our living be thanksgiving:
   Alleluia, alleluia!

174 John Henry Newman (1801-1890) alt.

1. Firmly I believe and truly
   God is Three and God is One;
   and I next acknowledge duly
   manhood taken by the Son.

2. And I trust and hope most fully
   in the Saviour crucified;
   and each thought and deed unruly
   do to death as he has died.

3. Simply to his grace and wholly
   light and life and strength belong,
   and I love supremely, solely,
   him the holy, him the strong.

4. And I hold in veneration,
   for the love of him alone,
   holy Church as his creation,
   and her teachings as his own.

5. Adoration ay be given,
   with and thro' th'angelic host,
   to the God of earth and heaven,
   Father, Son and Holy Ghost.

   *When the tune 'Alton' is used the following
   last line is added:*
   Amen. Father, Son and Holy Ghost.

175 Graham Kendrick (b. 1950)
© *1998 Ascent Music*

1. First light is upon our faces,
   first light of the morning sun,
   first sight of a new creation,
   first hour of the age to come.

2. New life from the earth is waking,
   first shoots of the second birth,
   first bloom of an endless springtime,
   first bud of the tree of life.

3. First rays of the sun of justice,
   first note of the freedom song,
   first breath of the coming Spirit,
   first shout from the conquered tomb.

4. First light is the Father's glory,
   first light is the risen one,
   first born over all creation,
   we greet the unconquered Son.

Continued overleaf

5. First sound of a sacred rhythm,
first beat of a diff'rent drum,
first step of a dance with heaven,
first joy of the world to come.

6. Last sigh of an age that's passing,
last chill of a winter's breath,
last night of the king of terrors,
last days of the sting of death.

7. First light is the Father's glory,
first light is the risen Son,
the first and the last of all things,
Jesus the Light has come!

176 Michael Cockett (b. 1938)
© 1978 Kevin Mayhew Ltd.

Follow me, follow me,
leave your home and family,
leave your fishing nets and boats
upon the shore.
Leave the seed that you have sown,
leave the crops that you've grown,
leave the people you have known
and follow me.

1. The foxes have their holes
and the swallows have their nests,
but the Son of Man
has no place to lie down.
I do not offer comfort,
I do not offer wealth,
but in me will all happiness be found.

2. If you would follow me,
you must leave old ways behind.
You must take my cross and
follow on my path.
You may be far from loved ones,
you may be far from home,
but my Father will welcome you at last.

3. Although I go away
you will never be alone,
for the Spirit will be
there to comfort you.
Though all of you may scatter,
each follow his own path,
still the Spirit of love will lead you home.

177 William Walsham How (1823-1897)

1. For all the saints
who from their labours rest,
who thee by faith
before the world confessed,
thy name, O Jesus,
be for ever blest.

Alleluia, alleluia!

2. Thou wast their rock,
their fortress and their might;
thou, Lord, their captain
in the well-fought fight;
thou in the darkness drear
their one true light.

3. O may thy soldiers,
faithful, true and bold,
fight as the saints
who nobly fought of old,
and win, with them,
the victor's crown of gold.

4. O blest communion!
fellowship divine!
we feebly struggle,
they in glory shine;
yet all are one in thee,
for all are thine.

5. And when the strife is fierce,
the warfare long,
steals on the ear
the distant triumph song,
and hearts are brave again,
and arms are strong.

6. The golden evening
   brightens in the west;
   soon, soon to faithful
   warriors cometh rest;
   sweet is the calm of
   paradise the blest.

7. But lo! There breaks
   a yet more glorious day;
   the saints triumphant
   rise in bright array:
   the King of glory
   passes on his way.

8. From earth's wide bounds,
   from ocean's farthest coast,
   through gates of pearl
   streams in the countless host,
   singing to Father,
   Son and Holy Ghost.

178 William Walsham How (1823-1897)
Adapted by Michael Forster (b. 1946)
© 2000 Kevin Mayhew Ltd

1. For all the saints, who from their
   labours rest,
   who thee by faith before the world
   confessed,
   thy name, O Jesus, be forever blest:
   Alleluia!

2. Thou wast their rock, their refuge and
   their might,
   thou, Lord, the vision ever in their sight;
   thou in the darkness drear their
   one true light.
   Alleluia!

3. O may thy servants, faithful, true
   and bold,
   strive for thy kingdom as the saints
   of old,
   and win with them a glorious crown
   of gold:
   Alleluia!

4. O blest communion, fellowship divine!
   We feebly struggle, they in glory shine,
   yet all are one in thee, for all are thine:
   Alleluia!

5. And when the road is steep, the
   journey long,
   steals on the ear the distant
   welcome song,
   and hope is bright again, and faith
   is strong:
   Alleluia!

6. The golden evening brightens in
   the west,
   soon, soon to faithful pilgrims
   cometh rest:
   sweet is the calm of Paradise the blest:
   Alleluia!

7. But lo! There breaks a yet more
   glorious day,
   the saints triumphant rise in bright array:
   the King of glory passes on his way:
   Alleluia!

8. From earth's wide bounds, from ocean's
   farthest coast,
   through gates of pearl streams in the
   countless host,
   singing to Father, Son and Holy Ghost.
   Alleluia!

179 Richard Mant (1776-1848)

1. For all thy saints, O Lord,
   who strove in thee to live,
   who followed thee, obeyed, adored,
   our grateful hymn receive.

2. For all thy saints, O Lord,
   who strove in thee to die,
   and found in thee a full reward,
   accept our thankful cry.

Continued overleaf

3. Thine earthly members fit
   to join thy saints above,
   in one communion ever knit,
   one fellowship of love.

4. Jesu, thy name we bless,
   and humbly pray that we
   may follow them in holiness,
   who lived and died for thee.

5. All might, all praise, be thine,
   Father, co-equal Son,
   and Spirit, bond of love divine,
   while endless ages run.

180 Rosamond E. Herklots (1905-1987) alt.
© Oxford University Press

1. 'Forgive our sins as we forgive',
   you taught us, Lord, to pray;
   but you alone can grant us grace
   to live the words we say.

2. How can your pardon reach and bless
   the unforgiving heart
   that broods on wrongs, and will not let
   old bitterness depart?

3. In blazing light your Cross reveals
   the truth we dimly knew:
   what trivial debts are owed to us,
   how great our debt to you!

4. Lord, cleanse the depths within
      our souls,
   and bid resentment cease.
   Then, bound to all in bonds of love,
   our lives will spread your peace.

181 Dave Richards
© 1977 Kingsway's Thankyou Music

For I'm building a people of power
and I'm making a people of praise,
that will move through this land by my
Spirit,
and will glorify my precious name.

Build your church, Lord,
make us strong, Lord,
join our hearts, Lord,
through your Son.
Make us one, Lord, in your body,
in the kingdom of your Son.

182 John Raphael Peacey (1896-1971)
© The Revd. Mary J. Hancock. Used by permission

1. For Mary, mother of our Lord,
   God's holy name be praised,
   who first the Son of God adored,
   as on her child she gazed.

2. The angel Gabriel brought the word
   she should Christ's mother be;
   Our Lady, handmaid of the Lord,
   made answer willingly.

3. The heav'nly call she thus obeyed,
   and so God's will was done;
   the second Eve love's answer made
   which our redemption won.

4. She gave her body for God's shrine,
   her heart to piercing pain,
   and knew the cost of love divine
   when Jesus Christ was slain.

5. Dear Mary, from your lowliness
   and home in Galilee,
   there comes a joy and holiness
   to ev'ry family.

6. Hail, Mary, you are full of grace,
   above all women blest;
   and blest your Son, whom your embrace
   in birth and death confessed.

183 Fred Kaan (b. 1929)
© 1975, 1988 Stainer & Bell Ltd

1. For ourselves no longer living,
   let us live for Christ alone;
   of ourselves more strongly giving,
   go as far as he has gone:
   one with God who chose to be
   one with us to set us free.

2. If we are to live for others,
   share as equals human worth,
   join the round of sisters, brothers,
   that encircles all the earth:
   all the fullness earth affords,
   is the people's, is the Lord's.

3. Fighting fear and exploitation
   is our daily common call;
   finding selfhood, building nations,
   sharing what we have with all.
   As the birds that soar in flight,
   let us rise towards the light.

4. Let us rise and join the forces
   that combine to do God's will,
   wisely using earth's resources,
   human energy and skill.
   Let us now, by love released,
   celebrate the future's feast!

184 Folliot Sandford Pierpoint (1835-1917)

1. For the beauty of the earth,
   for the beauty of the skies,
   for the love which from our birth
   over and around us lies:

   Lord of all, to thee we raise
   this our sacrifice of praise.

2. For the beauty of each hour
   of the day and of the night,
   hill and vale and tree and flow'r,
   sun and moon and stars of light:

3. For the joy of human love,
   brother, sister, parent, child,
   friends on earth, and friends above,
   pleasures pure and undefiled:

4. For each perfect gift of thine,
   to our race so freely giv'n,
   graces human and divine,
   flow'rs of earth and buds of heav'n:

5. For thy Church which evermore
   lifteth holy hands above,
   off'ring up on ev'ry shore
   her pure sacrifice of love:

185 Fred Pratt Green (b. 1903)
© *1970 Stainer & Bell Ltd*

1. For the fruits of his creation,
   thanks be to God;
   for his gifts to ev'ry nation,
   thanks be to God;
   for the ploughing, sowing, reaping,
   silent growth while we are sleeping,
   future needs in earth's safe keeping,
   thanks be to God.

2. In the just reward of labour,
   God's will is done;
   in the help we give our neighbour,
   God's will is done;
   in our world-wide task of caring
   for the hungry and despairing,
   in the harvests we are sharing,
   God's will is done.

3. For the harvests of his Spirit,
   thanks be to God;
   for the good we all inherit,
   thanks be to God;
   for the wonders that astound us,
   for the truths that still confound us,
   most of all, that love has found us,
   thanks be to God.

186 Fred Kaan (b. 1929)
© *1968 Stainer & Bell Ltd.*

1. For the healing of the nations,
   Lord, we pray with one accord;
   for a just and equal sharing
   of the things that earth affords.
   To a life of love in action
   help us rise and pledge our word.

Continued overleaf

2. Lead us, Father, into freedom,
   from despair your world release;
   that, redeemed from war and hatred,
   all may come and go in peace.
   Show us how through care and goodness
   fear will die and hope increase.

3. All that kills abundant living,
   let it from the earth be banned;
   pride of status, race or schooling
   dogmas that obscure your plan.
   In our common quest for justice
   may we hallow life's brief span.

4. You, creator-God, have written
   your great name on humankind;
   for our growing in your likeness
   bring the life of Christ to mind;
   that by our response and service
   earth its destiny may find.

187 James Quinn (b. 1919)
© 1969 Geoffrey Chapman

1. Forth in the peace of Christ we go;
   Christ to the world with joy we bring;
   Christ in our minds, Christ on our lips,
   Christ in our hearts, the world's
     true King.

2. King of our hearts, Christ makes us kings;
   kingship with him his servants gain;
   with Christ, the Servant-Lord of all,
   Christ's world we serve to share
     Christ's reign.

3. Priests of the world, Christ sends us forth
   this world of time to consecrate,
   our world of sin by grace to heal,
   Christ's world in Christ to re-create.

4. Prophets of Christ, we hear his Word:
   he claims our minds to search his ways;
   he claims our lips to speak his truth;
   he claims our hearts to sing his praise.

5. We are his Church, he makes us one:
   here is one hearth for all to find;
   here is one flock, one Shepherd-King;
   here is one faith, one heart, one mind.

188 Charles Wesley (1707-1788) alt.

1. Forth in thy name, O Lord, I go,
   my daily labour to pursue;
   thee, only thee, resolved to know,
   in all I think or speak or do.

2. The task thy wisdom hath assigned
   O let me cheerfully fulfil;
   in all my works thy presence find,
   and prove thy good and perfect will.

3. Thee may I set at my right hand,
   whose eyes my inmost substance see,
   and labour on at thy command,
   and offer all my works to thee.

4. Give me to bear thy easy yoke,
   and ev'ry moment watch and pray,
   and still to things eternal look,
   and hasten to thy glorious day.

5. For thee delightfully employ
   whate'er thy bounteous grace hath giv'n,
   and run my course with even joy,
   and closely walk with thee to heav'n.

189 Henry Downton (1818-1885)

1. For thy mercy and thy grace,
   faithful through another year,
   hear our song of thankfulness;
   Jesus, our Redeemer, hear.

2. In our weakness and distress,
   Rock of Strength, be thou our stay;
   in the pathless wilderness
   be our true and living Way.

3. Keep us faithful, keep us pure,
   keep us evermore thine own.
   Help, O help us to endure,
   fit us for thy promised crown.

4. So within thy palace gate
   we shall praise on golden strings
   thee, the only potentate,
   Lord of lords and King of kings.

190 George Hunt Smyttan (1822-1870)
adapted by Michael Forster (b. 1946)
© 1999 Kevin Mayhew Ltd.

1. Forty days and forty nights
   you were fasting in the wild;
   forty days and forty nights,
   tempted still, yet unbeguiled.

2. Sunbeams scorching all the day,
   chilly dew-drops nightly shed,
   prowling beasts about your way,
   stones your pillow, earth your bed.

3. Let us your endurance share,
   and from earthly greed abstain,
   with you vigilant in prayer,
   with you strong to suffer pain.

4. Then if evil on us press,
   flesh or spirit to assail,
   Victor in the wilderness,
   help us not to swerve or fail.

5. So shall peace divine be ours;
   holy gladness, pure and true:
   come to us, angelic powers,
   such as ministered to you.

6. Keep, O keep us, Saviour dear,
   ever constant by your side,
   that with you we may appear
   at th'eternal Eastertide.

191 Jean Holloway (b. 1939)
© 1995 Kevin Mayhew Ltd.

1. Forty days and forty nights
   in Judah's desert Jesus stayed;
   all alone he fought temptation,
   all alone he fasted, prayed.
   When the heat of passion rules me,
   when I feel alone, betrayed,
   Lord, you meet me in the desert,
   strong in faith and unafraid.

2. In the garden, his disciples
   slept the darkest hours away,
   but our Lord did not condemn them
   when they would not watch or pray.
   Make me constant in your service,
   keeping watch both night and day.
   Give me grace that I may never
   such a love as yours betray.

3. When the rooster crowed at daybreak,
   Peter's fear and panic grew.
   He denied three times the charge
   that Jesus was a man he knew.
   When my love for you is challenged,
   when the faithful ones are few,
   give me courage and conviction
   to proclaim my Lord anew.

4. Soldiers came, the Galilean
   was arrested, bound and tried,
   and upon a wooden cross
   the Son of God was crucified.
   In the darkest hour of torture,
   Jesus raised his head and cried,
   'Why hast thou forsaken me?',
   and faithful to the end, he died.

5. With a sword they pierced his side –
   himself, they jeered, he could not save;
   Joseph then prepared the body
   with sweet spices for the grave.
   This the precious, broken body
   which for me my Saviour gave;
   such a love as his I long for,
   such a faith as his I crave.

192
Isaac Watts (1674-1748), based on Psalm 117

1. From all that dwell below the skies
let the Creator's praise arise:
let the Redeemer's name be sung
through ev'ry land by ev'ry tongue.

2. Eternal are thy mercies, Lord;
eternal truth attends thy word:
thy praise shall sound from shore to shore,
till suns shall rise and set no more.

193
Translated from the Latin of Caelius Sedulius by John Ellerton (1826-1893)

1. From east to west, from shore to shore,
let ev'ry heart awake and sing
the holy Child whom Mary bore,
the Christ, the everlasting King.

2. Behold, the world's creator wears
the form and fashion of a slave,
our very flesh our Maker shares,
his fallen creature, man, to save.

3. For this how wondrously he wrought!
A maiden, in her lowly place,
became, in ways beyond all thought,
the chosen vessel of his grace.

4. She bowed her to the angel's word
declaring what the Father willed,
and suddenly the promised Lord
that pure and hallowed temple filled.

5. He shrank not from the oxen's stall,
he lay within the manger-bed,
and he whose bounty feedeth all,
at Mary's breast himself was fed.

6. And while the angels in the sky
sang praise above the silent field,
to shepherds poor, the Lord most high,
the one great shepherd was revealed.

7. All glory for that blessed morn
to God the Father ever be,
all praise to thee, O virgin-born,
and praise, blest Spirit, unto thee.

194
Liturgy of St. James trans. Charles William Humphreys (1840-1921)

1. From glory to glory advancing,
we praise thee, O Lord;
thy name with the Father and Spirit
be ever adored.
From strength unto strength we go
forward
on Sion's highway,
to appear before God
in the city of infinite day.

2. Thanksgiving and glory and worship
and blessing and love,
one heart and one song have the saints
upon earth and above.
Evermore, O Lord, to thy servants
thy presence be nigh;
ever fit us by service on earth
for thy service on high.

195
Graham Kendrick (b. 1950)
© 1983 Kingsway's Thankyou Music

1. From heav'n you came, helpless babe,
entered our world, your glory veiled;
not to be served but to serve,
and give your life that we might live.

This is our God, the Servant King,
he calls us now to follow him,
to bring our lives as a daily offering
of worship to the Servant King.

2. There in the garden of tears,
my heavy load he chose to bear;
his heart with sorrow was torn.
'Yet not my will but yours,' he said.

3. Come see his hands and his feet,
the scars that speak of sacrifice,
hands that flung stars into space,
to cruel nails surrendered.

4. So let us learn how to serve,
and in our lives enthrone him;
each other's needs to prefer,
for it is Christ we're serving.

196

Michael Forster (b. 1946), based on the Didaché
© *1992 Kevin Mayhew Ltd.*

1. From many grains, once scattered far
      and wide,
   each one alone, to grow as best it may,
   now safely gathered in and unified,
   one single loaf we offer here today.
   So may your Church, in ev'ry time
      and place,
   be in this meal united by your grace.

2. From many grapes, once living on the vine,
   now crushed and broken under
      human feet,
   we offer here this single cup of wine:
   the sign of love, unbroken and complete.
   So may we stand among the crucified,
   and live the risen life of him who died.

3. From many places gathered, we are here,
   each with a gift that we alone can bring.
   O Spirit of the living God, draw near,
   make whole by grace our broken offering.
   O crush the pride that bids us stand alone;
   let flow the love that makes our spirits one.

197

Graham Kendrick (b. 1950)
© *1988 Make Way Music*

1. From the sun's rising unto the sun's setting,
   Jesus our Lord, shall be great in the earth;
   and all earth's kingdoms shall be
      his dominion,
   all of creation shall sing of his worth.

   Let ev'ry heart, ev'ry voice,
   ev'ry tongue join with spirits ablaze;
   one in his love, we will circle the world
   with the song of his praise.
   O let all his people rejoice,
   and let all the earth hear his voice.

2. To ev'ry tongue, tribe and nation he
      sends us,
   to make disciples, to teach and baptise.
   For all authority to him is given;
   now, as his witnesses, we shall arise.

3. Come, let us join with the Church from
      all nations,
   cross ev'ry border, throw wide ev'ry door;
   workers with him as he gathers his harvest,
   till earth's far corners our Saviour adore.

198

Michael Forster (b. 1946)
© *1992 Kevin Mayhew Ltd.*

1. From the very depths of darkness
   springs a bright and living light;
   out of falsehood and deceit
   a greater truth is brought to sight;
   in the halls of death, defiant,
   life is dancing with delight!
   The Lord is risen indeed!

   Christ is risen! Hallelujah! (x3)
   The Lord is risen indeed!

2. Jesus meets us at the dawning
   of the resurrection day;
   speaks our name with love, and gently
   says that here we may not stay:
   'Do not cling to me, but go to all
   the fearful ones and say,
   "The Lord is risen indeed!" '

3. So proclaim it in the high-rise,
   in the hostel let it ring;
   make it known in Cardboard City,
   let the homeless rise and sing:
   'He is Lord of life abundant,
   and he changes everything;
   the Lord is risen indeed!'

4. In the heartlands of oppression,
   sound the cry of liberty;
   where the poor are crucified,
   behold the Lord of Calvary;
   from the fear of death and dying,
   Christ has set his people free;
   the Lord is risen indeed!

Continued overleaf

Christ is risen! Hallelujah! (x3)
The Lord is risen indeed!

5. To the tyrant, tell the gospel
   of a love that can't be known
   in a guarded palace-tomb,
   condemned to live and die alone:
   'Take the risk of love and freedom;
   Christ has rolled away the stone!
   The Lord is risen indeed!'

6. When our spirits are entombed
   in mortal prejudice and pride;
   when the gates of hell itself
   are firmly bolted from inside;
   at the bidding of his Spirit,
   we may fling them open wide;
   The Lord is risen indeed!.

199 Jean Holloway (b. 1939)
© 1994, 1999 Kevin Mayhew Ltd.

Gather around, for the table is spread,
welcome the food and rest!
Wide is our circle, with Christ at the head,
he is the honoured guest.
Learn of his love, grow in his grace,
pray for the peace he gives;
here at this meal, here in this place,
know that his Spirit lives!
Once he was known
in the breaking of bread,
shared with a chosen few;
multitudes gathered
and by him were fed,
so will he feed us too.

200 Christine McCann (b. 1951)
© 1978 Kevin Mayhew Ltd.

1. Gifts of bread and wine, gifts we've offered,
   fruits of labour, fruits of love, taken,
   offered, sanctified, blessed and broken;
   words of one who died;

   'Take my body, take my saving blood.'
   Gifts of bread and wine: Christ our Lord.

2. Christ our Saviour, living presence here,
   as he promised while on earth:
   'I am with you for all time,
   I am with you in this bread and wine.'

3. To the Father, with the Spirit,
   one in union with the Son,
   for God's people, joined in prayer,
   faith is strengthened by the food we share.

201 Traditional

1. Give me joy in my heart, keep me praising,
   give me joy in my heart, I pray.
   Give me joy in my heart, keep my praising,
   keep me praising till the end of day.

   Sing hosanna! Sing hosanna!
   Sing hosanna to the King of kings!
   Sing hosanna! Sing hosanna!
   Sing hosanna to the King!

2. Give me peace in my heart,
   keep me resting . . .

3. Give me love in my heart,
   keep me serving . . .

4. Give me oil in my lamp,
   keep me burning . . .

202 Henry Smith.
© 1978 Integrity's Hosanna! Music
Administered by Kingsway's Thankyou Music

Give thanks with a grateful heart,
give thanks to the Holy One,
give thanks because he's given
Jesus Christ, his Son.
And now let the weak say, 'I am strong',
let the poor say, 'I am rich',
because of what the Lord has done for us.
And now let the weak say, 'I am strong',
let the poor say, 'I am rich',
because of what the Lord has done for us

203
Isaac Watts (1674-1748), based on Psalm 136 alt.

1. Give to our God immortal praise;
   mercy and truth are all his ways:
   wonders of grace to God belong,
   repeat his mercies in your song.

2. Give to the Lord of lords renown,
   the King of kings with glory crown:
   his mercies ever shall endure
   when earthly pow'rs are known no more.

3. He sent his Son with pow'r to save
   from guilt and darkness and the grave:
   wonders of grace to God belong,
   repeat his mercies in your song.

4. Through earthly life he guides our feet,
   and leads us to his heav'nly seat:
   his mercies ever shall endure
   when earthly pow'rs are known no more.

204
Isaac Watts (1674-1748) alt.

1. Give us the wings of faith to rise
   within the veil, and see
   the saints above, how great their joys,
   how bright their glories be.

2. Once they were mourning here below,
   their couch was wet with tears;
   they wrestled hard, as we do now,
   with sins and doubts and fears.

3. We ask them whence their vict'ry came:
   they, with united breath,
   ascribe the conquest to the Lamb,
   their triumph to his death.

4. They marked the footsteps that he trod,
   his zeal inspired their breast,
   and, foll'wing their incarnate God,
   they reached the promised rest.

5. Our glorious Leader claims our praise
   for his own pattern giv'n;
   while the great cloud of witnesses
   show the same path to heav'n.

205
John Newton (1725-1807)
based on Isaiah 33:20-21, alt.

1. Glorious things of thee are spoken,
   Zion, city of our God;
   he whose word cannot be broken
   formed thee for his own abode.
   On the Rock of Ages founded,
   what can shake thy sure repose?
   With salvation's walls surrounded,
   thou may'st smile at all thy foes.

2. See, the streams of living waters,
   springing from eternal love,
   well supply thy sons and daughters,
   and all fear of want remove.
   Who can faint while such a river
   ever flows their thirst to assuage?
   Grace which, like the Lord, the giver,
   never fails from age to age.

3. Round each habitation hov'ring,
   see the cloud and fire appear
   for a glory and a cov'ring,
   showing that the Lord is near.
   Thus they march, the pillar leading,
   light by night and shade by day;
   daily on the manna feeding
   which he gives them when they pray.

4. Saviour, if of Zion's city
   I through grace a member am,
   let the world deride or pity,
   I will glory in thy name.
   Fading is the worldling's pleasure,
   boasted pomp and empty show;
   solid joys and lasting treasure
   none but Zion's children know.

206
'Viva, viva, Gestù', 18th century, trans. Edward Caswall (1814-1878), alt.

1. Glory be to Jesus
   who, in bitter pains,
   poured for me the lifeblood
   from his sacred veins.

2. Grace and life eternal
   in that blood I find:
   blest be his compassion,
   infinitely kind.

3. Blest, through endless ages,
   be the precious stream
   which, from endless torment,
   did the world redeem.

4. There the fainting spirit
   drinks of life her fill;
   there, as in a fountain,
   laves herself at will.

5. Abel's blood for vengeance
   pleaded to the skies,
   but the blood of Jesus
   for our pardon cries.

6. Oft as it is sprinkled
   on our guilty hearts
   Satan in confusion
   terror-struck departs.

7. Oft as earth exulting
   wafts its praise on high
   angel hosts rejoicing,
   make their glad reply.

8. Lift, then, all your voices,
   swell the mighty flood;
   louder still and louder,
   praise the precious blood.

207
Charles Wesley (1707-1788) alt.

1. Glory, love, and praise, and honour
   for our food, now bestowed,
   render we the Donor.
   Bounteous God, we now confess thee;
   God, who thus blessest us,
   meet it is to bless thee.

2. Thankful for our ev'ry blessing,
   let us sing Christ the Spring,
   never, never ceasing.
   Source of all our gifts and graces
   Christ we own; Christ alone
   calls for all our praises.

3. He dispels our sin and sadness,
   life imparts, cheers our hearts,
   fills with food and gladness.
   Who himself for all hath given,
   us he feeds, us he leads
   to a feast in heaven.

208
Thomas Ken (1637-1710)

1. Glory to thee, my God, this night
   for all the blessings of the light;
   keep me, O keep me, King of kings,
   beneath thine own almighty wings.

2. Forgive me, Lord, for thy dear Son,
   the ill that I this day have done,
   that with the world, myself and thee,
   I, ere I sleep, at peace may be.

3. Teach me to live, that I may dread
   the grave as little as my bed;
   teach me to die, that so I may
   rise glorious at the aweful day.

4. O may my soul on thee repose,
   and with sweet sleep mine eyelids close;
   sleep that may me more vig'rous make
   to serve my God when I awake.

5. Praise God, from whom all blessings flow;
   praise him, all creatures here below;
   praise him above, ye heav'nly host;
   praise Father, Son and Holy Ghost.

209

Howard Charles Adie Gaunt (1902-1983)
© Oxford University Press

1. Glory to thee, O God,
   for all thy saints in light,
   who nobly strove and conquered
   in the well fought fight.
   Their praises sing,
   who life outpoured
   by fire and sword for Christ their King.

2. Thanks be to thee, O Lord,
   for saints thy Spirit stirred
   in humble paths to live thy life and
   speak thy word.
   Unnumbered they,
   whose candles shine
   to lead our footsteps after thine.

3. Lord God of truth and love,
   'thy kingdom come', we pray;
   give us thy grace to know thy truth and
   walk thy way:
   that here on earth
   thy will be done,
   till saints in earth and heav'n are one.

210

Fred Kaan (b. 1929)
© 1997 Stainer & Bell Ltd

1. God! As with silent hearts we bring
   to mind
   how hate and war diminish humankind,
   we pause - and seek in worship
   to increase
   our knowledge of the things that make
   for peace.

2. Hallow our will as humbly we recall
   the lives of those who gave and give
   their all.
   We thank you, Lord, for women,
   children, men
   who seek to serve in love, today as then.

3. Give us deep faith to comfort those
   who mourn,
   high hope to share with all the
   newly born,
   strong love in our pursuit of
   human worth:
   'lest we forget' the future of this earth.

4. So, Prince of Peace, disarm our trust
   in pow'r,
   teach us to coax the plant of peace
   to flow'r.
   May we, impassioned by your
   living Word,
   remember forward to a world restored.

211

Book of Hours (1514)

God be in my head,
and in my understanding;
God be in mine eyes,
and in my looking;
God be in my mouth,
and in my speaking;
God be in my heart,
and in my thinking;
God be at mine end,
and at my departing.

212

Carol Owens
© 1972 Bud John Songs/EMI Christian Music
Publishing. Administered by CopyCare

1. God forgave my sin in Jesus' name.
   I've been born again in Jesus' name.
   And in Jesus' name I come to you
   to share his love as he told me to.

   He said: 'Freely, freely you have received;
   freely, freely give.
   Go in my name, and because you believe,
   others will know that I live.'

2. All pow'r is giv'n in Jesus' name,
   in earth and heav'n in Jesus' name.
   And in Jesus' name I come to you
   to share his pow'r as he told me to.

Continued overleaf

3. God gives us life in Jesus' name,
   he lives in us in Jesus' name.
   And in Jesus' name I come to you
   to share his peace as he told me to.

213
John L. Bell (b. 1949) and Graham Maule (b. 1958)
© 1989 WGRG, Iona Community

1. God, in the planning and purpose of life,
   hallowed the union of husband and wife:
   this we embody where love is displayed,
   rings are presented and promises made.

2. Jesus was found, at a similar feast,
   taking the roles of both waiter and priest,
   turning the worldly towards the divine,
   tears into laughter and water to wine.

3. Therefore we pray that his Spirit preside
   over the wedding of bridegroom
         and bride,
   fulfilling all that they've hoped will
         come true,
   lighting with love all they dream of and do.

4. Praise then the Maker, the Spirit, the Son,
   source of the love through which two are
         made one.
   God's is the glory, the goodness and grace
   seen in this marriage and known in
         this place.

214
Graham Kendrick (b. 1950)
© 1985 Kingsway's Thankyou Music

God is good, we sing and shout it,
God is good, we celebrate.
God is good, no more we doubt it,
God is good, we know it's true.

And when I think of his love for me,
my heart fills with praise
and I feel like dancing.
For in his heart there is room for me
and I run with arms opened wide.

215
Marie Lydia Pereira (b. 1920)
© 1999 Kevin Mayhew Ltd

1. God is love, God is love,
   God is love for us.
   He lives by love, he works by love,
   and his sun comes shining through.

2. God is life, God is life,
   God is life for us.
   His life keeps us from sin and strife,
   and his sun comes shining through.

3. God is food, God is food,
   God is food for us.
   He is our food, our saving good,
   and his sun comes shining through.

4. God is light, God is light,
   God is light for us.
   His light shines out through the
         darkest night,
   and his sun comes shining through.

5. God is peace, God is peace.
   God is peace for us.
   And through his peace all quarrels cease,
   and his sun comes shining through.

6. God is joy, God is joy,
   God is joy for us.
   The purest joy, the deepest joy,
   and his sun comes shining through.

7. God is strength, God is strength,
   God is strength for us.
   The greatest strength, unfailing strength,
   and his sun comes shining through.

8. God is truth, God is truth,
   God is truth for us.
   The surest truth, unchanging truth,
   and his sun comes shining through.

216

Percy Dearmer (1867-1936) alt.
© Oxford University Press

1. God is love: his the care,
   tending each, ev'rywhere.
   God is love, all is there!
   Jesus came to show him,
   that we all might know him!

   Sing aloud, loud, loud!
   Sing aloud, loud, loud!
   God is good! God is truth!
   God is beauty! Praise him!

2. None can see God above;
   we can share life and love;
   thus may we Godward move,
   seek him in creation,
   holding ev'ry nation.

3. Jesus lived on the earth,
   hope and life brought to birth
   and affirmed human worth,
   for he came to save us
   by the truth he gave us.

4. To our Lord praise we sing,
   light and life, friend and King,
   coming down, love to bring,
   pattern for our duty,
   showing God in beauty.

217

Timothy Rees (1874-1939) alt.
© Geoffrey Chapman, an imprint of Cassell plc.
Used by permission

1. God is love: let heav'n adore him;
   God is love: let earth rejoice;
   let creation sing before him,
   and exalt him with one voice.
   He who laid the earth's foundation,
   he who spread the heav'ns above,
   he who breathes through all creation,
   he is love, eternal Love.

2. God is love: and he enfoldeth
   all the world in one embrace;
   with unfailing grasp he holdeth
   ev'ry child of ev'ry race.
   And when human hearts are breaking
   under sorrow's iron rod,
   then they find that self-same aching
   deep within the heart of God.

3. God is love: and though with blindness
   sin afflicts the human soul,
   God's eternal loving-kindness
   guides and heals and makes us whole.
   Sin and death and hell shall never
   o'er us final triumph gain;
   God is love, so love for ever
   o'er the universe must reign.

218

Timothy Dudley-Smith, based on Psalm 62
© Timothy Dudley-Smith

1. God is my great desire,
   his face I seek the first;
   to him my heart and soul aspire,
   for him I thirst.
   As one in desert lands,
   whose very flesh is flame,
   in burning love I lift my hands
   and bless his name.

2. God is my true delight,
   my richest feast his praise,
   through silent watches of the night,
   through all my days.
   To him my spirit clings,
   on him my soul is cast;
   beneath the shadow of his wings
   he holds me fast.

3. God is my strong defence
   in ev'ry evil hour;
   in him I face with confidence
   the tempter's pow'r.
   I trust his mercy sure,
   with truth and triumph crowned:
   my hope and joy for evermore
   in him are found.

219

Richard Bewes, based on Psalm 46
© Richard Bewes Jubilate Hymns

1. God is our strength and refuge,
   our present help in trouble;
   and we therefore will not fear,
   though the earth should change!
   Though mountains shake and tremble,
   though swirling floods are raging,
   God the Lord of hosts is with us
      evermore!

2. There is a flowing river,
   within God's holy city;
   God is in the midst of her – she shall not
      be moved!
   God's help is swiftly given,
   thrones vanish at his presence
   God the Lord of hosts is with us
      evermore!

3. Come, see the works of our maker,
   learn of his deeds all-powerful;
   wars will cease across the world when he
      shatters the spear!
   Be still and know your creator,
   uplift him in the nations –
   God the Lord of hosts is with us
      evermore!

2. That Word of Life, before all things
   in primal darkness spoken,
   became for us the Word made flesh
   for our redemption broken.
   His glory set aside,
   for us he lived and died,
   obedient to the death,
   renewed in life and breath,
   to endless glory woken!

3. That Breath of God, who brooded first
   upon the new creation,
   who lit with light the Virgin's womb
   to bear the world's salvation;
   that Dove whose shadow graced
   th'anointed Saviour's face,
   now challenges us all
   to recognise the call
   to hope and liberation.

4. O great Creator, Spirit, Word,
   the well-spring of creation,
   our Alpha and our Omega,
   our hope and our salvation;
   to Father, Spirit, Son,
   the Three for ever One,
   and One for ever Three,
   mysterious Trinity,
   be praise and adoration.

220

Michael Forster (b. 1946)
© 1996 Kevin Mayhew Ltd.

1. God is our strength from days of old,
   the hope of ev'ry nation;
   whose pow'r conceived the universe
   and set the earth's foundation.
   Though hidden from our sight
   in uncreated light,
   his presence yet is known,
   his wondrous purpose shown,
   resplendent in creation!

221

Arthur Campbell Ainger (1841-1919)
adapted by Michael Forster (b. 1946)
© This version 1996 Kevin Mayhew Ltd.

1. God is working his purpose out
   as year succeeds to year.
   God is working his purpose out,
   and the day is drawing near.
   Nearer and nearer draws the time,
   the time that shall surely be,
   when the earth shall be filled
   with the glory of God
   as the waters cover the sea.

2. From the east to the utmost west
   wherever foot has trod,
   through the mouths of his messengers
   echoes forth the voice of God:
   'Listen to me, ye continents,
   ye islands, give ear to me,
   that the earth shall be filled
   with the glory of God
   as the waters cover the sea.'

3. How can we do the work of God,
   how prosper and increase
   harmony in the human race,
   and the reign of perfect peace?
   What can we do to urge the time,
   the time that shall surely be,
   when the earth shall be filled
   with the glory of God
   as the waters cover the sea?

4. March we forth in the strength of God,
   his banner is unfurled;
   let the light of the gospel shine
   in the darkness of the world:
   strengthen the weary, heal the sick
   and set ev'ry captive free,
   that the earth shall be filled
   with the glory of God
   as the waters cover the sea.

5. All our efforts are nothing worth
   unless God bless the deed;
   vain our hopes for the harvest tide
   till he brings to life the seed.
   Yet ever nearer draws the time,
   the time that shall surely be,
   when the earth shall be filled
   with the glory of God
   as the waters cover the sea.

222 William Cowper (1731-1800)

1. God moves in a mysterious way
   his wonders to perform;
   he plants his footsteps in the sea,
   and rides upon the storm.

2. Deep in unfathomable mines
   of never-failing skill,
   he treasures up his bright designs,
   and works his sov'reign will.

3. Ye fearful saints, fresh courage take;
   the clouds ye so much dread
   are big with mercy, and shall break
   in blessings on your head.

4. Judge not the Lord by feeble sense,
   but trust him for his grace;
   behind a frowning providence
   he hides a shining face.

5. His purposes will ripen fast,
   unfolding ev'ry hour;
   the bud may have a bitter taste,
   but sweet will be the flow'r.

6. Blind unbelief is sure to err,
   and scan his work in vain;
   God is his own interpreter,
   and he will make it plain.

223 Christopher Idle (b. 1938)
© Christopher Idle/Jubilate Hymns

1. God of all human history,
   of time long fled and faded,
   yours is the secret mastery
   by which the years are guided:
   King of unchanging glory
   from ages unrecorded.

2. God of the hidden future
   unfolding life for ever,
   hope of each ransomed creature
   as time speeds ever faster:
   raise us to our full stature
   in Christ, our one Redeemer.

3. God of this present moment
   requiring our decision,
   now is the hour of judgement
   for ruin or salvation:
   give us complete commitment
   to your most urgent mission.

224

Shirley Erena Murray (b.1931)
© 1992 Hope Publishing Company

1. God of freedom, God of justice,
   you whose love is strong as death,
   you who saw the dark of prison,
   you who knew the price of faith:
   touch our world of sad oppression
   with your Spirit's healing breath.

2. Rid the earth of torture's terror,
   you whose hands were nailed to wood:
   hear the cries of pain and protest,
   you who shed the tears and blood;
   move in us the pow'r of pity,
   restless for the common good.

3. Make in us a captive conscience
   quick to hear, to act, to plead;
   make us truly sisters, brothers,
   of whatever race or creed:
   teach us to be fully human,
   open to each other's need.

225

Harry Emerson Fosdick (1878-1969) alt.
© The Estate of the late H.E. Fosdick
Used by permission of Dr. Elinor Fosdick Downs

1. God of grace and God of glory,
   on thy people pour thy pow'r;
   now fulfil thy Church's story;
   bring her bud to glorious flow'r.
   Grant us wisdom, grant us courage,
   for the facing of this hour.

2. Lo, the hosts of evil round us
   scorn thy Christ, assail his ways;
   from the fears that long have bound us
   free our hearts to faith and praise.
   Grant us wisdom, grant us courage,
   for the living of these days.

3. Cure thy children's warring madness,
   bend our pride to thy control;
   shame our wanton selfish gladness,
   rich in goods and poor in soul.
   Grant us wisdom, grant us courage,
   lest we miss thy kingdom's goal.

4. Set our feet on lofty places,
   gird our lives that they may be
   armoured with all Christlike graces
   as we set your people free.
   Grant us wisdom, grant us courage,
   lest we fail the world or thee.

226

Jean Holloway (b. 1939)
© 1999 Kevin Mayhew Ltd

1. God of love, you freely give us
   blessings more than we deserve;
   be our light in times of darkness,
   be our strength when fears unnerve.
   In this age when proof convinces,
   help us see where wisdom lies;
   more enduring than persuasion
   is your truth which never dies.

2. Son incarnate, yours the presence
   which can heal an aching heart;
   over death you reign triumphant,
   you alone new life impart.
   From your birth so long awaited,
   to the cross on Calvary,
   you will serve as our example,
   let us, Lord, your servants be.

3. Holy Spirit, inspiration
   day by day, yet mystery;
   with the Son and the Creator
   you form mystic unity.
   Draw us into your communion,
   with the love that sets us free;
   bind our hearts to you for ever,
   holy, blessèd Trinity.

227

Henry Francis Lyte (1793-1847)
based on Psalm 67, alt.

1. God of mercy, God of grace,
   show the brightness of thy face;
   shine upon us, Saviour, shine,
   fill thy Church with light divine;
   and thy saving health extend
   unto earth's remotest end.

2. Let the people praise thee, Lord;
   be by all that live adored;
   let the nations shout and sing
   glory to their Saviour King;
   at thy feet their tribute pay,
   and thy holy will obey.

3. Let the people praise thee, Lord;
   earth shall then her fruits afford;
   God to us his blessing give,
   we to God devoted live;
   all below, and all above,
   one in joy and light and love.

228 Michael Forster (b. 1946)
© 1993 Kevin Mayhew Ltd.

1. God of the Passover,
   Author and Lord of salvation,
   gladly we gather to bring
   you our heart's adoration;
   ransomed and free,
   called and commissioned to be
   signs of your love for creation.

2. Here we remember that evening
   of wonder enthralling,
   myst'ry of passion divine,
   and betrayal appalling.
   Breaking the bread,
   'This is my body,' he said,
   'do this, my passion recalling.'

3. God of the Eucharist,
   humbly we gather before you
   and, at your table,
   for pardon and grace we implore you.
   Under the cross,
   counting as profit our loss,
   safe in its shade, we adore you.

229 Traditional

1. God rest you merry, gentlemen,
   let nothing you dismay,
   for Jesus Christ our Saviour
   was born on Christmas day,
   to save us all from Satan's pow'r
   when we were gone astray:

O tidings of comfort and joy,
comfort and joy,
O tidings of comfort and joy.

2. In Bethlehem, in Jewry,
   this blessèd babe was born,
   and laid within a manger,
   upon this blessèd morn;
   at which his mother Mary
   did nothing take in scorn.

3. From God, our heav'nly Father,
   a blessèd angel came,
   and unto certain shepherds
   brought tidings of the same,
   how that in Bethlehem was born
   the Son of God by name.

4. 'Fear not,' then said the angel,
   'let nothing you affright,
   this day is born a Saviour,
   of virtue, pow'r and might;
   by him the world is overcome
   and Satan put to flight.'

5. The shepherds at those tidings
   rejoicèd much in mind,
   and left their flocks a-feeding,
   in tempest, storm and wind,
   and went to Bethlehem straightway
   this blessèd babe to find.

6. But when to Bethlehem they came,
   whereat this infant lay,
   they found him in a manger,
   where oxen feed on hay;
   his mother Mary kneeling,
   unto the Lord did pray.

7. Now to the Lord sing praises,
   all you within this place,
   and with true love and fellowship
   each other now embrace;
   this holy tide of Christmas
   all others doth deface.

230 vs. 1 & 2: unknown (17th or 18th century)
v.3: William E. Hickson (1803-1870) alt.

1. God save our gracious Queen,
   long live our noble Queen,
   God save the Queen.
   Send her victorious,
   happy and glorious,
   long to reign over us:
   God save the Queen.

2. Thy choicest gifts in store
   on her be pleased to pour,
   long may she reign:
   may she defend our laws,
   and ever give us cause
   to sing with heart and voice
   God save the Queen!

3. Not on this land alone,
   but be God's mercies known
   on ev'ry shore.
   Lord, make the nations see
   that all humanity
   should form one family
   the wide world o'er.

231 Alan Dale and Hubert J. Richards (b. 1921)
© 1982 Kevin Mayhew Ltd.

1. God's Spirit is in my heart.
   He has called me and set me apart.
   This is what I have to do,
   what I have to do.

   He sent me to give
   the Good News to the poor,
   tell pris'ners that they are pris'ners no more,
   tell blind people that they can see,
   and set the down trodden free,
   and go tell ev'ry one the news
   that the kingdom of God has come,
   and go tell ev'ryone the news
   that God's kingdom has come.

2. Just as the Father sent me,
   so I'm sending you out to be
   my witnesses throughout the world,
   the whole of the world.

3. Don't carry a load in your pack,
   you don't need two shirts on your back.
   A workman can earn his own keep,
   can earn his own keep.

4. Don't worry what you have to say,
   don't worry because on that day
   God's Spirit will speak in your heart,
   will speak in your heart.

232 v. 1: Reginald Heber (1783-1826)
v. 2: Richard Whately (1787-1863)

1. God that madest earth and heaven,
   darkness and light;
   who the day for toil hast given,
   for rest the night;
   may thine angel-guards defend us,
   slumber sweet thy mercy send us,
   holy dreams and hopes attend us,
   this live-long night.

2. Guard us waking, guard us sleeping,
   and, when we die,
   may we in thy mighty keeping
   all peaceful lie:
   when the last dread call shall wake us,
   do not thou our God forsake us,
   but to reign in glory take us
   with thee on high.

233 Ronald H Green
© Copyright control

1. God, the source and goal of being,
   in whose love we trust our lives,
   help us seek, and so discover
   pathways new which faith provides;
   give us knowledge, give us insight
   and fresh visions of your light.

2. God, whose touch brings hope to people,
   who are lost without your love,
   hear the prayers and praise we offer
   from our dark to light above;
   teach us how to share your glory
   that your presence all may see.

3. God of love, of pow'r and action
   from our bondage set us free;
   take our lives and in them fashion
   what you destine each shall be:
   live in us who stand before you
   and through us your world renew.

4. God the Father, God the Saviour,
   God the Holy Spirit - One;
   while we sing your praise to heav'nward
   may on earth your will be done:
   let the world accept our off'ring
   of your song of love we bring.

234 Fred Kaan (b 1929)
© 1989 Stainer & Bell Ltd

1. God! When human bonds are broken
   and we lack the love or skill
   to restore the hope of healing,
   give us grace and make us still.

2. Through that stillness, with your Spirit
   come into our world of stress,
   for the sake of Christ forgiving
   all the failures we confess.

3. You in us are bruised and broken:
   hear us as we seek release
   from the pain of earlier living;
   set us free and grant us peace.

4. Send us, God of new beginnings,
   humbly hopeful into life.
   Use us as a means of blessing:
   make us stronger, give us faith.

5. Give us faith to be more faithful,
   give us hope to be more true,
   give us love to go on learning:
   God! Encourage and renew!

235 Sarah Betts Rhodes (1824-1904)

1. God who made the earth,
   the air, the sky, the sea,
   who gave the light its birth,
   careth for me.

2. God who made the grass,
   the flow'r, the fruit, the tree,
   the day and night to pass,
   careth for me.

3. God who made the sun,
   the moon, the stars, is he
   who, when life's clouds come on,
   careth for me.

4. God who sent his Son
   to die on Calvary,
   he, if I lean on him,
   will care for me.

236 John Arlott (1914-1991) alt.
© The Estate of the late L. T. J. Arlott

1. God, whose farm is all creation,
   take the gratitude we give;
   take the finest of our harvest,
   crops we grow that all may live.

2. Take our ploughing, seeding, reaping,
   hopes and fears of sun and rain,
   all our thinking, planning, waiting,
   ripened in this fruit and grain.

3. All our labour, all our watching,
   all our calendar of care,
   in these crops of your creation,
   take, O God: they are our prayer.

237 Glen W. Baker
© Used by permission

1. God, you meet us in our weakness
   giving strength beyond our own,
   by your Spirit, by your people,
   showing we are not alone.

2. God, you meet us in our sorrows
   with the comfort of your voice,
   by your Spirit, by your people,
   helping crying hearts rejoice.

3. God, you meet us in our neighbours,
   when your strength and voice we need.
   Yours the Spirit, we your people,
   sharing love in word and deed!

238
James Edward Seddon (1915-1983)
© Mrs. M. Seddon/Jubilate Hymns

1. Go forth and tell!
   O Church of God, awake!
   God's saving news
   to all the nations take:
   proclaim Christ Jesus,
   Saviour, Lord and King,
   that all the world
   his worthy praise may sing.

2. Go forth and tell!
   God's love embraces all;
   he will in grace
   respond to all who call;
   how shall they call
   if they have never heard
   the gracious invitation
   of his word?

3. Go forth and tell!
   where still the darkness lies;
   in wealth or want,
   the sinner surely dies:
   give us, O Lord,
   concern of heart and mind,
   a love like yours
   which cares for humankind.

4. Go forth and tell!
   the doors are open wide:
   share God's good gifts –
   let no-one be denied;
   live out your life
   as Christ your Lord shall choose,
   your ransomed pow'rs
   for his sole glory use.

5. Go forth and tell!
   O Church of God, arise!
   Go in the strength
   which Christ your Lord supplies;
   go till all nations
   his great name adore
   and serve him, Lord and King,
   for evermore.

239
Michael Forster, (b. 1949)
© 1999 Kevin Mayhew Ltd

1. Going home, moving on,
   through God's open door;
   hush, my soul, have no fear,
   Christ has gone before.
   Parting hurts, love protests,
   pain is not denied;
   yet, in Christ, life and hope
   span the great divide.
   Going home, moving on,
   through God's open door;
   hush, my soul, have no fear,
   Christ has gone before,
   Christ has gone before.

2. No more guilt, no more fear,
   all the past is healed:
   broken dreams now restored,
   perfect grace revealed.
   Christ has died, Christ is ris'n,
   Christ will come again:
   death destroyed, life restored,
   love alone shall reign.
   Going home, moving on,
   through God's open door;
   hush, my soul, have no fear,
   Christ has gone before,
   Christ has gone before.

240
John Mason Neale (1818-1866)

1. Good Christians, all, rejoice
   with heart and soul and voice!
   Give ye heed to what we say:
   News! News! Jesus Christ is born today;
   ox and ass before him bow,
   and he is in the manger now:
   Christ is born today, Christ is born today!

2. Good Christians all, rejoice
   with heart and soul and voice!
   Now ye hear of endless bliss:
   Joy! Joy! Jesus Christ was born for this.
   He hath opened heaven's door,
   and we are blest for evermore:
   Christ was born for this,
   Christ was born for this.

3. Good Christians all, rejoice
   with heart and soul and voice!
   Now ye need not fear the grave:
   Peace! Peace! Jesus Christ was born to save;
   calls you one, and calls you all,
   to gain his everlasting hall:
   Christ was born to save,
   Christ was born to save.

241 Cyril Argentine Alington (1872-1955) alt.
         © Hymns Ancient & Modern

1. Good Christians all, rejoice and sing.
   Now is the triumph of our King.
   To all the world glad news we bring:
   Alleluia!

2. The Lord of Life is ris'n for ay:
   bring flow'rs of song to strew his way;
   let all mankind rejoice and say:
   Alleluia!

3. Praise we in songs of victory
   that Love, that Life, which cannot die
   and sing with hearts uplifted high:
   Alleluia!

4. Thy name we bless, O risen Lord,
   and sing today with one accord
   the life laid down, the life restored:
   Alleluia!

242 John Mason Neale (1818-1866) alt.

1. Good King Wenceslas looked out
   on the feast of Stephen,
   when the snow lay round about,
   deep, and crisp, and even;
   brightly shone the moon that night,
   though the frost was cruel,
   when a poor man came in sight,
   gath'ring winter fuel.

2. 'Hither, page, and stand by me,
   if thou know'st it, telling,
   yonder peasant, who is he,
   where and what his dwelling?'
   'Sire, he lives a good league hence,
   underneath the mountain,
   right against the forest fence,
   by Saint Agnes' fountain.'

3. 'Bring me flesh, and bring me wine,
   bring me pine logs hither:
   thou and I will see him dine,
   when we bring him thither.'
   Page and monarch, forth they went,
   forth they went together;
   through the rude wind's wild lament,
   and the bitter weather.

4. 'Sire, the night is darker now,
   and the wind blows stronger;
   fails my heart, I know not how;
   I can go no longer.'
   'Mark my footsteps good, my page;
   tread thou in them boldly:
   thou shalt find the winter's rage
   freeze thy blood less coldly.'

5. In his master's steps he trod,
   where the snow lay dinted;
   heat was in the very sod
   which the Saint had printed.
   Therefore, Christians all, be sure,
   wealth or rank possessing,
   ye who now will bless the poor,
   shall yourselves find blessing.

243 Traditional

*Go, tell it on the mountain,
over the hills and ev'rywhere.
Go, tell it on the mountain
that Jesus Christ is born.*

1. While shepherds kept their watching
   o'er wand'ring flocks by night,
   behold, from out of heaven,
   there shone a holy light.

2. And lo, when they had seen it,
   they all bowed down and prayed;
   they travelled on together
   to where the babe was laid.

3. When I was a seeker,
   I sought both night and day:
   I asked my Lord to help me
   and he showed me the way.

4. He made me a watchman
   upon the city wall,
   and, if I am a Christian,
   I am the least of all.

244 Basil Bridge (b. 1927)
© 1999 Kevin Mayhew Ltd.

1. Gracious God, in adoration
   saints with joy before you fall;
   only when our hearts are leaden
   can we fail to hear their call:
   'Come with wonder, serve with
       gladness
   God whose pow'r created all.'

2. Earth and sky in silent praises
   speak to those with eyes to see;
   all earth's living creatures echo
   'God has made us!' So may we
   come with wonder, serve with gladness
   him through whom they came to be.

3. You have made us in your image,
   breathed your Spirit, given us birth;
   Jesus calls, whose cross has given
   ev'ry life eternal worth,
   'Come with wonder, serve with
       gladness,
   let God's will be done on earth!'

4. Earth by war and want is threatened;
   deep the roots of fear and greed;
   let your mercy be our measure
   as we see our neighbour's need,
   come with wonder, serve with
       gladness,
   share your gift of daily bread.

5. Holy Spirit, urging, striving,
   give us love that casts out fear,
   courage, seeking peace with justice,
   faith to make this message clear –
   'Come with wonder, serve with
       gladness,
   live in hope; the Lord is near!'

245 Christopher Wordsworth (1807-1885)

1. Gracious Spirit, Holy Ghost,
   taught by thee, we covet most
   of thy gifts at Pentecost,
   holy, heav'nly love.

2. Love is kind, and suffers long,
   love is meek, and thinks no wrong,
   love than death itself more strong;
   therefore give us love.

3. Prophecy will fade away,
   melting in the light of day;
   love will ever with us stay;
   therefore give us love.

4. Faith will vanish into sight;
   hope be emptied in delight;
   love in heav'n will shine more bright;
   therefore give us love.

5. Faith and hope and love we see
   joining hand in hand agree;
   but the greatest of the three,
   and the best, is love.

6. From the overshadowing
   of thy gold and silver wing
   shed on us, who to thee sing,
   holy, heav'nly love.

246
Brian Wren (b. 1936)
© 1975, 1995 Stainer & Bell Ltd.

1. Great God, your love has called us here
   as we, by love, for love were made.
   Your living likeness still we bear,
   though marred, dishonoured, disobeyed.
   We come, with all our heart and mind
   your call to hear, your love to find.

2. We come with self-inflicted pains
   of broken trust and chosen wrong,
   half-free, half-bound by inner chains,
   by social forces swept along,
   by pow'rs and systems close confined
   yet seeking hope for humankind.

3. Great God, in Christ you call our name
   and then receive us as your own,
   not through some merit, right or claim
   but by your gracious love alone.
   We strain to glimpse your mercy-seat
   and find you kneeling at our feet.

4. Then take the tow'l, and break the bread,
   and humble us, and call us friends.
   Suffer and serve till all are fed,
   and show how grandly love intends
   to work till all creation sings,
   to fill all worlds, to crown all things.

5. Great God, in Christ you set us free
   your life to live, your joy to share.
   Give us your Spirit's liberty
   to turn from guilt and dull despair
   and offer all that faith can do
   while love is making all things new.

247
Aniceto Nazareth, based on the Psalms
© 1984 Kevin Mayhew Ltd.

*Great indeed are your works, O Lord,
now and evermore!* (Repeat)

1. The universe, night and day,
   tells of all your wonders.
   You are our life and our light:
   we shall praise you always.

2. You are the path which we tread,
   you will lead us onward.
   From ev'ry corner of earth
   all the nations gather.

3. You lead them all by the hand
   to the heav'nly kingdom.
   Then, at the end of all times,
   you will come in glory.

248
Steve McEwan
© 1985 Body Songs/CopyCare

1. Great is the Lord and most worthy of
      praise,
   the city of God, the holy place,
   the joy of the whole earth.
   Great is the Lord in whom we have the
      victory.
   He aids us against the enemy,
   we bow down on our knees.

2. And, Lord, we want to lift your name
      on high,
   and, Lord, we want to thank you
   for the works you've done in our lives;
   and, Lord, we trust in your unfailing
      love,
   for you alone are God eternal,
   throughout earth and heaven above.

249

Thomas Obadiah Chisholm (1866-1960)
© 1951 Hope Publishing Co.

1. Great is thy faithfulness,
   O God my Father,
   there is no shadow
   of turning with thee;
   thou changest not,
   thy compassions, they fail not;
   as thou hast been
   thou for ever wilt be.

   Great is thy faithfulness!
   Great is thy faithfulness!
   Morning by morning
   new mercies I see;
   all I have needed
   thy hand hath provided,
   great is thy faithfulness,
   Lord, unto me!

2. Summer and winter,
   and springtime and harvest,
   sun, moon and stars
   in their courses above,
   join with all nature
   in manifold witness
   to thy great faithfulness,
   mercy and love.

3. Pardon for sin
   and a peace that endureth,
   thine own dear presence
   to cheer and to guide;
   strength for today
   and bright hope for tomorrow,
   blessings all mine,
   with ten thousand beside!

250

John Newton (1725-1807)

1. Great Shepherd of thy people, hear,
   thy presence now display;
   as thou hast giv'n a place for pray'r,
   so give us hearts to pray.

2. Within these walls let holy peace
   and love and concord dwell;
   here give the troubled conscience ease,
   the wounded spirit heal.

3. May we in faith receive thy word,
   in faith present our pray'rs,
   and in the presence of our Lord
   unburden all our cares.

4. The hearing ear, the seeing eye,
   the contrite heart, bestow;
   and shine upon us from on high,
   that we in grace may grow.

251

Edwin Le Grice (1911-1992)
© 1995 Kevin Mayhew Ltd.

1. Great Son of God,
   you once on Cal'vry's cross
   fought the long fight
   for truth and freedom's sake,
   endured the scourge,
   the crown of thorns,
   the nails that fixed
   your youthful body to a stake.
   For six long hours
   you suffered searing pain
   to set your captive
   people free again.

2. 'Give us a sign from heav'n,'
   the people cried.
   'If you are Christ,
   leap down, alive and free.
   Who could accept as Saviour
   one who died
   like some poor miscreant
   skewered to a tree?'
   Lord Christ, our Saviour,
   you would not descend
   until your glorious work
   achieved its end.

3. 'My God, my God,
where have you gone?' you called,
alone and helpless,
willing still to share
through all the gath'ring
gloom of Calvary,
the depth of dying sinners'
deep despair.
But then triumphant,
ready now to die,
'The work is finished!'
was your glorious cry.

252 William Williams (1717-1791)
trans. Peter Williams (1727-1796) and others

1. Guide me, O thou great Redeemer,
pilgrim through this barren land;
I am weak, but thou art mighty,
hold me with thy pow'rful hand:
Bread of Heaven, Bread of Heaven,
feed me till I want no more,
feed me till I want no more.

2. Open now the crystal fountain,
whence the healing stream doth flow;
let the fire and cloudy pillar
lead me all my journey through;
strong deliv'rer, strong deliv'rer,
be thou still my strength and shield,
be thou still my strength and shield.

3. When I tread the verge of Jordan,
bid my anxious fears subside;
death of death, and hell's destruction,
land me safe on Canaan's side;
songs of praises, songs of praises,
I will ever give to thee,
I will ever give to thee.

253 Greek (3rd century or earlier)
trans. John Keble (1792-1866)

1. Hail, gladdening Light,
of his pure glory poured
from th' immortal Father,
heav'nly, blest,
holiest of holies,
Jesus Christ our Lord.

2. Now we are come
to the sun's hour of rest,
the lights of evening
round us shine,
we hymn the Father,
Son and Holy Spirit divine.

3. Worthiest art thou at all times
to be sung with undefilèd tongue,
Son of our God,
giver of life, alone:
therefore in all the world thy glories,
Lord, they own.

254 Latin (c. 9th century)
trans. Athelstan Riley (1858-1945)
© Oxford University Press

1. Hail, O Star that pointest
t'wards the port of heaven,
thou to whom as maiden
God for Son was given.

2. When the salutation
Gabriel had spoken,
peace was shed upon us,
Eva's bonds were broken.

3. Bound by Satan's fetters,
health and vision needing,
God will aid and light us
at thy gentle pleading.

4. Jesu's tender mother,
make the supplication
unto him who chose thee
at his incarnation.

Continued overleaf

5. That, O matchless maiden,
   passing meek and lowly,
   thy dear son may make us
   blameless, chaste and holy.

6. So, as now we journey,
   aid our weak endeavour
   till we gaze on Jesus,
   and rejoice for ever.

7. Father, Son and Spirit,
   Three in One confessing,
   give we equal glory,
   equal praise and blessing.

6. Still for us he intercedes,
   his prevailing death he pleads;
   near himself prepares our place,
   he the first-fruits of our race.

7. Lord, though parted from our sight,
   far above the starry height,
   grant our hearts may thither rise,
   seeking thee above the skies.

8. Ever upward let us move,
   wafted on the wings of love;
   looking when our Lord shall come,
   longing, sighing after home.

255
Charles Wesley (1707-1788)
Thomas Cotterill (1779-1823) and others, alt.

1. Hail the day that sees him rise, *alleluia!*
   to his throne above the skies; *alleluia!*
   Christ the Lamb, for sinners giv'n, *alleluia!*
   enters now the highest heav'n! *alleluia!*

2. There for him high triumph waits;
   lift your heads, eternal gates!
   He hath conquered death and sin;
   take the King of Glory in!

3. Circled round with angel-pow'rs,
   their triumphant Lord and ours;
   wide unfold the radiant scene,
   take the King of Glory in!

4. Lo, the heav'n its Lord receives,
   yet he loves the earth he leaves;
   though returning to his throne,
   calls the human race his own.

5. See, he lifts his hands above;
   see, he shows the prints of love;
   hark, his gracious lips bestow
   blessings on his Church below.

256
Based on the Latin of Venantius Fortunatus
(530-609) The Editors of *The New English Hymnal*
© Hymns Ancient & Modern

Hail thee, Festival Day, blest day that are
   hallowed for ever;
day when the Lord ascends, high in the
   heavens to reign.

1. Lo, the fair beauty of earth,
   from the death of the winter arising,
   ev'ry good gift of the year,
   now with its Master returns.

2. Daily the loveliness grows,
   adorned with the glory of blossom;
   green is the woodland with leaves,
   bright are the meadows with flowers.

3. He who was nailed to the cross
   is Lord and the ruler of all things;
   all things created on earth,
   worship the Maker of all.

4. He who has conquered the grave
    now rises to heavenly splendour;
    fitly the light gives him praise -
    meadows and ocean and sky.

5. Christ, in thy triumph ascend:
    thou hast led captivity captive;
    heaven her gates unbars,
    flinging her increase of light.

6. Thence shall the Spirit descend
    on them that await his appearing;
    flame from the heart of our God,
    life-giving Spirit of peace.

7. Jesus, thou health of the world,
    enlighten our minds, O Redeemer,
    Son of the Father supreme,
    only-begotten of God.

8. So shalt thou bear in thine arms
    an immaculate people to heaven,
    bearing them pure unto God,
    pledge of thy victory here.

9. Equal art thou, co-eternal,
    in fellowship One with the Father,
    and with the Spirit of truth,
    God evermore to be blest!

257 Based on the Latin of Venantius Fortunatus (530-609)
The Editors of *The New English Hymnal*
© *Hymns Ancient & Modern*

Hail thee, Festival Day,
  blest day that art hallowed for ever;
day wherein Christ arose,
  breaking the kingdom of death.

1. Lo, the fair beauty of earth,
    from the death of the winter arising,
    ev'ry good gift of the year,
    now with its Master returns.

2. Daily the loveliness grows,
    adorned with the glory of blossom;
    green is the woodland with leaves,
    bright are the meadows with flowers.

3. He who was nailed to the cross
    is Lord and the ruler of all things;
    all things created on earth,
    worship the Maker of all.

4. Ill it beseemeth that thou,
    by whose hand all things are
        encompassed,
    captive and bound should remain,
    deep in the gloom of the rock.

5. Rise now, O Lord from the grave
    and cast off the shroud that enwrapped
        thee;
    leaving the caverns of death,
    show us the light of thy face.

6. God of all pity and pow'r,
    let thy word be assured to the doubting;
    lo, he breaks from the tomb!
    See, he appears to his own!

7. Jesus, thou health of the world,
    enlighten our minds, O redeemer,
    Son of the Father supreme,
    only-begotten of God.

8. So shalt thou bear in thine arms
    an immaculate people to heaven,
    bearing them pure unto God,
    pledge of thy victory here.

9. Equal art thou, co-eternal,
    in fellowship One with the Father,
    and with the Spirit of truth,
    God evermore to be blest!

258
John Bakewell (1721-1819) alt.

1. Hail, thou once despisèd Jesus,
   hail, thou Galilean King!
   Thou didst suffer to release us;
   thou didst free salvation bring.
   Hail, thou universal Saviour,
   bearer of our sin and shame;
   by thy merits we find favour;
   life is given through thy name.

2. Paschal Lamb, by God appointed,
   all our sins on thee were laid;
   by almighty love anointed,
   thou hast full atonement made.
   All thy people are forgiven
   through the virtue of thy blood;
   opened is the gate of heaven,
   we are reconciled to God.

3. Jesus, hail! enthroned in glory,
   there for ever to abide;
   all the heav'nly hosts adore thee,
   seated at thy Father's side:
   there for sinners thou art pleading,
   there thou dost our place prepare;
   ever for us interceding,
   till in glory we appear.

4. Worship, honour, pow'r and blessing,
   thou art worthy to receive;
   loudest praises, without ceasing,
   it is right for us to give:
   help, ye bright angelic spirits!
   bring your sweetest, noblest lays;
   help to sing our Saviour's merits,
   help to chant Immanuel's praise.

259
Paraphase of Psalm 71 by James Montgomery (1771-1854)

1. Hail to the Lord's anointed,
   great David's greater son!
   Hail, in the time appointed,
   his reign on earth begun!
   He comes to break oppression,
   to set the captive free;
   to take away transgression,
   and rule in equity.

2. He comes with succour speedy
   to those who suffer wrong;
   to help the poor and needy,
   and bid the weak be strong;
   to give them songs for sighing,
   their darkness turn to light,
   whose souls, condemned and dying,
   were precious in his sight.

3. He shall come down like showers
   upon the fruitful earth,
   and love, joy, hope, like flowers,
   spring in his path to birth:
   before him on the mountains
   shall peace the herald go;
   and righteousness in fountains
   from hill to valley flow.

4. Kings shall fall down before him,
   and gold and incense bring;
   all nations shall adore him,
   his praise all people sing;
   to him shall prayer unceasing
   and daily vows ascend;
   his kingdom still increasing,
   a kingdom without end.

5. O'er ev'ry foe victorious,
   he on his throne shall rest,
   from age to age more glorious,
   all-blessing and all-blest;
   the tide of time shall never
   his covenant remove;
   his name shall stand for ever;
   that name to us is love.

260

Latin 14th century
trans. by H. N. Oxenham (1852-1941)
© Copyright control

1. Hail, true Body, born of Mary,
   by a wondrous virgin birth.
   You who on the cross were offered
   to redeem us all on earth.

2. You whose side became a fountain
   pouring forth your precious blood,
   give us now, and at our dying,
   your own self to be our food.

   O kindest Jesu, O gracious Jesu,
   O Jesu, blessed Mary's Son.

261

Tim Cullen, alt.
© 1975 Celebration/Kingsway's Thankyou Music

Hallelujah, my Father,
for giving us your Son;
sending him into the world
to be given up for all,
knowing we would bruise him
and smite him from the earth!
Hallelujah, my Father,
in his death is my birth.
Hallelujah, my Father,
in his life is my life.

262

Robert Bridges (1844-1930)
based on 'O quam juvat',
Charles Coffin (1676-1749) alt.
© Oxford University Press

1. Happy are they, they that love God,
   whose hearts have Christ confessed,
   who by his cross have found their life,
   and 'neath his yoke their rest.

2. Glad is the praise, sweet are the songs,
   when they together sing;
   and strong the prayers that bow the ear
   of heav'n's eternal King.

3. Christ to their homes giveth his peace,
   and makes their loves his own:
   but ah, what tares the evil one
   hath in his garden sown!

4. Sad were our lot, evil this earth,
   did not its sorrows prove
   the path whereby the sheep may find
   the fold of Jesus' love.

5. Then shall they know, they that love him,
   how hope is wrought through pain;
   their fellowship, through death itself,
   unbroken will remain.

263

'Vox clara ecce intonat' 6th century,
trans. Edward Caswall (1814-1878)

1. Hark! a herald voice is calling:
   'Christ is nigh!' it seems to say;
   'Cast away the dreams of darkness,
   O ye children of the day!'

2. Startled at the solemn warning,
   let the earth-bound soul arise;
   Christ, her sun, all sloth dispelling,
   shines upon the morning skies.

3. Lo, the Lamb, so long expected,
   comes with pardon down from heav'n;
   let us haste, with tears of sorrow,
   one and all to be forgiv'n.

4. So when next he comes with glory,
   wrapping all the earth in fear,
   may he then, as our defender,
   on the clouds of heav'n appear.

5. Honour, glory, virtue, merit,
   to the Father and the Son,
   with the co-eternal Spirit,
   while unending ages run.

264

William Cowper (1731-1800) based on John 21:16

1. Hark, my soul, it is the Lord;
   'tis thy Saviour, hear his word;
   Jesus speaks, and speaks to thee,
   'Say, poor sinner, lov'st thou me?

2. 'I delivered thee when bound,
   and, when wounded, healed thy wound;
   sought thee wand'ring, set thee right,
   turned thy darkness into light.

Continued overleaf

3. 'Can a woman's tender care
   cease towards the child she bare?
   yes, she may forgetful be,
   yet will I remember thee.

4. 'Mine is an unchanging love,
   higher than the heights above,
   deeper than the depths beneath,
   free and faithful, strong as death.

5. 'Thou shalt see my glory soon,
   when the work of grace is done;
   partner of my throne shalt be:
   say, poor sinner, lov'st thou me?'

6. Lord, it is my chief complaint
   that my love is weak and faint;
   yet I love thee, and adore;
   O for grace to love thee more!

265 Philip Doddridge (1702-1751) based on Luke 4:18-19

1. Hark the glad sound! the Saviour comes,
   the Saviour promised long:
   let ev'ry heart prepare a throne,
   and ev'ry voice a song.

2. He comes, the pris'ners to release
   in Satan's bondage held;
   the gates of brass before him burst,
   the iron fetters yield.

3. He comes, the broken heart to bind,
   the bleeding soul to cure,
   and with the treasures of his grace
   to bless the humble poor.

4. Our glad hosannas, Prince of Peace,
   thy welcome shall proclaim;
   and heav'n's eternal arches ring
   with thy belovèd name.

266 Charles Wesley (1707-1788), George Whitefield (1714-1770), Martin Madan (1726-1790) and others, alt.

1. Hark, the herald-angels sing
   glory to the new-born King;
   peace on earth and mercy mild,
   God and sinners reconciled:
   joyful, all ye nations rise,
   join the triumph of the skies,
   with th'angelic host proclaim,
   'Christ is born in Bethlehem.'

Hark, the herald-angels sing
glory to the new-born King.

2. Christ, by highest heav'n adored,
   Christ, the everlasting Lord,
   late in time behold him come,
   offspring of a virgin's womb!
   Veiled in flesh the Godhead see,
   hail, th'incarnate Deity!
   Pleased as man with us to dwell,
   Jesus, our Emmanuel.

3. Hail, the heav'n-born Prince of Peace!
   Hail, the Sun of Righteousness!
   Light and life to all he brings,
   ris'n with healing in his wings;
   mild he lays his glory by,
   born that we no more may die,
   born to raise us from the earth,
   born to give us second birth.

267 Christopher Wordsworth (1807-1885) alt.

1. Hark! the sound of holy voices,
   chanting at the crystal sea:
   Alleluia, alleluia,
   alleluia, Lord, to thee;
   multitude, which none can number,
   like the stars in glory stands,
   clothed in white apparel,
   holding palms of vict'ry in their hands.

2. Patriarch and holy prophet,
who prepared the way of Christ,
king, apostle, saint, confessor,
martyr and evangelist,
saintly maiden, godly matron,
widows who have watched in prayer,
joined in holy concert, singing
to the Lord of all, are there.

3. They have come from tribulation,
and have washed their robes in blood,
washed them in the blood of Jesus;
tried they were, and firm they stood;
gladly, Lord, with thee they suffered;
gladly, Lord, with thee they died,
and by death to life immortal
they were born and glorified.

4. Now they reign in heav'nly glory,
now they walk in golden light,
now they drink, as from a river,
holy bliss and infinite;
love and peace they taste for ever,
and all truth and knowledge see
in the beatific vision
of the blessèd Trinity.

5. God of God, the one-begotten,
Light of Light, Emmanuel,
in whose body joined together
all the saints for ever dwell;
pour upon us of thy fullness,
that we may for evermore
Father, Son and Holy Spirit
truly worship and adore.

268 Bryn Austin Rees (1911-1983)
© *Alexander Scott*

1. Have faith in God, my heart,
trust and be unafraid;
God will fulfil in ev'ry part
each promise he has made.

2. Have faith in God, my mind,
though oft thy light burns low;
God's mercy holds a wiser plan
than thou canst fully know.

3. Have faith in God, my soul,
his Cross for ever stands;
and neither life nor death can pluck
his children from his hands.

4. Lord Jesus, make me whole;
grant me no resting-place,
until I rest, heart, mind and soul,
the captive of thy grace.

269 Susan Sayers (b. 1946), based on Psalm 51
© *1989 Kevin Mayhew Ltd.*

*Have mercy on us,
O Lord, for we have sinned.* (Repeat)

1. O God, in your kindness,
have mercy on me,
and in your compassion
blot out my offence.
O wash me, O wash me
from all of my guilt,
until you have cleansed me from sin.

2. For all my offences
I know very well,
I cannot escape from
the sight of my sin.
Against you, O Lord,
only you, have I sinned,
and done what is wrong in your eyes.

3. A pure heart create
in your servant, O Lord;
a steadfast and trustworthy
spirit in me.
O cast me not out
from your presence, I pray,
and take not your spirit from me.

4. Restore to me, Lord,
all the joy of your help;
sustain me with fervour,
sustain me with zeal.
Then open my lips,
and my mouth shall declare
the praise of my Lord and my God.

270 Francesca Leftley (b. 1955)
© 1999 Kevin Mayhew Ltd.

1. Healer of the sick,
   Lord Jesus, Son of God;
   Lord, how we long for you:
   walk here among us.

   Bind up our broken lives,
   comfort our broken hearts,
   banish our hidden fears.
   Lord, come with power,
   bring new light to the blind,
   bring peace to troubled minds,
   hold us now in your arms, set us free now.

2. Bearer of our pain,
   Lord Jesus, Lamb of God;
   Lord, how we cry to you:
   walk here among us.

3. Calmer of our fears,
   Lord Jesus, Prince of Peace;
   Lord, how we yearn for you:
   walk here among us.

4. Saviour of the world,
   Lord Jesus, mighty God;
   Lord, how we sing to you:
   walk here among us.

271 Michael Forster (b. 1946)
© 1993 Kevin Mayhew Ltd.

1. Heaven is open wide,
   and Christ in glory stands,
   with all authority endowed
   and set at God's right hand.
   Above the world of noise
   extends his reign of peace,
   and all the blood of martyrs calls
   our angry ways to cease.

2. Heaven is open wide,
   and perfect love we see
   in God's eternal self revealed:
   the blessèd Trinity.
   Christ for the church has prayed,
   that we may all be one,
   and share the triune grace whereby
   creation was begun.

3. Heaven is open wide,
   and Christ in glory stands:
   the Source and End, the First and Last,
   with justice in his hands.
   Let all the thirsty come
   where life is flowing free,
   and Christ, in splendour yet unknown,
   our morning star will be.

272 John L. Bell (b. 1949) and Graham Maule (b. 1958)
© 1987 WGRG, Iona Community

1. Heav'n shall not wait
   for the poor to lose their patience,
   the scorned to smile,
   the despised to find a friend:
   Jesus is Lord,
   he has championed the unwanted;
   in him injustice
   confronts its timely end.

2. Heav'n shall not wait
   for the rich to share their fortunes,
   the proud to fall,
   the élite to tend the least:
   Jesus is Lord;
   he has shown the masters' privilege –
   to kneel and wash
   servants' feet before they feast.

3. Heav'n shall not wait
   for the dawn of great ideas,
   thoughts of compassion
   divorced from cries of pain:
   Jesus is Lord;
   he has married word and action;
   his cross and company
   make his purpose plain.

4. Heav'n shall not wait
for our legalised obedience,
defined by statute,
to strict conventions bound:
Jesus is Lord;
he has hallmarked true allegiance –
goodness appears
where his grace is sought and found.

5. Heav'n shall not wait
for triumphant hallelujahs,
when earth has passed
and we reach another shore:
Jesus is Lord
in our present imperfection;
his pow'r and love
are for now and then for evermore.

273 Twila Paris
© 1985 Straightway Music/Mountain Spring/EMI
Christian Music Publishing

He is exalted,
the King is exalted on high;
I will praise him.
He is exalted,
for ever exalted
and I will praise his name!
He is the Lord;
for ever his truth shall reign.
Heaven and earth rejoice
in his holy name.
He is exalted,
the King is exalted on high.

274 Unknown

1. He is Lord, he is Lord.
He is risen from the dead and he is Lord.
Ev'ry knee shall bow, ev'ry tongue confess
that Jesus Christ is Lord.

2. He is King, he is King,
He is risen from the dead and he is King.
Ev'ry knee shall bow, ev'ry tongue confess
that Jesus Christ is King.

3. He is love, he is love.
He is risen from the dead and he is love.
Ev'ry knee shall bow, ev'ry tongue confess
that Jesus Christ is love.

275 After Charles Wesley (1707-1788) alt.

1. Help us to help each other, Lord,
each other's cross to bear;
let each a helping hand afford,
and feel each other's care.

2. Up into thee, our living head,
let us in all things grow,
and by thy sacrifice be led
the fruits of love to show.

3. Drawn by the magnet of thy love
let all our hearts agree;
and ever t'wards each other move,
and ever move t'wards thee.

4. This is the bond of perfectness,
thy spotless charity.
O let us still we pray, possess
the mind that was in thee.

276 Brian Wren (b. 1936)
© 1975, 1995 Stainer & Bell Ltd.

1. Here hangs a man discarded,
a scarecrow hoisted high,
a nonsense pointing nowhere
to all who hurry by.

2. Can such a clown of sorrows
still bring a useful word
when faith and love seem phantoms
and ev'ry hope absurd?

3. Yet here is help and comfort
for lives by comfort bound,
when drums of dazzling progress
give strangely hollow sound:

4. Life, emptied of all meaning,
drained out in bleak distress,
can share in broken silence
our deepest emptiness;

Continued overleaf

5. And love that freely entered
   the pit of life's despair
   can name our hidden darkness
   and suffer with us there.

6. Christ, in our darkness risen,
   help all who long for light
   to hold the hand of promise,
   till faith receives its sight.

277 Graham Kendrick (b. 1950)
© 1991 Make Way Music

1. Here is bread, here is wine,
   Christ is with us, he is with us.
   Break the bread, taste the wine,
   Christ is with us here.

   In this bread there is healing,
   in this cup is life for ever.
   In this moment, by the Spirit,
   Christ is with us here.

2. Here is grace, here is peace.
   Christ is with us, he is with us;
   know his grace, find his peace,
   feast on Jesus here.

3. Here we are, joined in one,
   Christ is with us, he is with us;
   we'll proclaim, till he comes,
   Jesus crucified.

278 Charles Venn Pilcher (1879-1961)
© 1935 Mrs I.E.V. Pilcher. Used by permission

1. Here, Lord, we take the broken bread
   and drink the wine, believing
   that by your life our souls are fed,
   your parting gifts receiving.

2. As you have giv'n, so we would give
   ourselves for others' healing;
   and as you lived, so we would live,
   the Father's love revealing.

279 Honatius Bonar (1808-1889)

1. Here, O my Lord, I see thee face to face;
   here faith would touch and handle things
   unseen;
   here grasp with firmer hand th' eternal
   grace,
   and all my weariness upon thee lean.

2. Here would I feed upon the bread of
   God;
   here drink with thee the royal wine of
   heav'n;
   here would I lay aside each earthly load;
   here taste afresh the calm of sin forgiv'n.

3. I have no help but thine; nor do I need
   another arm save thine to lean upon:
   it is enough, my Lord, enough indeed,
   my strength is in thy might, thy might
   alone.

280 Timothy Dudley-Smith (b. 1926)
© Timothy Dudley-Smith

1. Here on the threshold of a new
      beginning,
   by grace forgiven, now we leave behind
   our long-repented selfishness and
      sinning,
   and all our blessings call again to mind:
   Christ to redeem us, ransom and restore
      us,
   the love that holds us in a Saviour's care,
   faith strong to welcome all that lies
      before us,
   our unknown future, knowing God is
      there.

2. May we, your children, feel with Christ's compassion
   an earth disordered, hungry and in pain;
   then, at your calling, find the will to fashion
   new ways where freedom, truth and justice reign;
   where wars are ended, ancient wrongs are righted,
   and nations value human life and worth;
   where in the darkness lamps of hope are lighted
   and Christ is honoured over all the earth.

3. So may your wisdom shine from scripture's pages
   to mould and make us stones with which to build
   God's holy temple, through eternal ages,
   one church united, strong and Spirit-filled;
   heirs to the fullness of your new creation
   in faith we follow, pledged to be your own;
   yours is the future, ours the celebration,
   for Christ is risen! God is on the throne!

281 Percy Dearmer (1867-1936)
after John Bunyan (1628-1688)
© Oxford University Press

1. He who would valiant be
   'gainst all disaster,
   let him in constancy
   follow the Master.
   There's no discouragement
   shall make him once relent
   his first avowed intent
   to be a pilgrim.

2. Who so beset him round
   with dismal stories,
   do but themselves confound –
   his strength the more is.
   No foes shall stay his might,
   though he with giants fight:
   he will make good his right
   to be a pilgrim.

3. Since, Lord, thou dost defend
   us with thy Spirit,
   we know we at the end
   shall life inherit.
   Then fancies flee away!
   I'll fear not what men say,
   I'll labour night and day
   to be a pilgrim.

282 Charles Edward Oakley (1832-1865), adapted

1. Hills of the north, rejoice,
   echoing songs arise,
   hail with united voice
   him who made earth and skies:
   he comes in righteousness and love,
   he brings salvation from above.

2. Isles of the southern seas
   sing to the list'ning earth,
   carry on ev'ry breeze
   hope of a world's new birth:
   in Christ shall all be made anew,
   his word is sure, his promise true.

3. Lands of the east, arise,
   he is your brightest morn,
   greet him with joyous eyes,
   praise shall his path adorn:
   the God whom you have longed to know
   in Christ draws near, and calls you now.

4. Shores of the utmost west,
   lands of the setting sun,
   welcome the heav'nly guest
   in whom the dawn has come:
   he brings a never-ending light
   who triumphed o'er our darkest night.

5. Shout, as you journey on,
   songs be in ev'ry mouth,
   lo, from the north they come,
   from east and west and south:
   in Jesus all shall find their rest,
   in him the longing earth be blest.

283 Richard Robinson (1842-1892)

1. Holy Father, cheer our way
   with thy love's perpetual ray;
   grant us ev'ry closing day
   light at evening time.

2. Holy Saviour, calm our fears
   when earth's brightness disappears;
   grant us in our latter years
   light at evening time.

3. Holy Spirit, be thou nigh
   when in mortal pains we lie;
   grant us, as we come to die,
   light at evening time.

4. Holy, blessed Trinity,
   darkness is not dark with thee;
   those thou keepest always see
   light at evening time.

284 Jimmy Owens
© 1972 Bud John Songs/EMI Christian Music
Publishing. Administered by CopyCare

1. Holy, holy, holy, holy.
   Holy, holy, holy Lord God almighty;
   and we lift our hearts before you
   as a token of our love,
   holy, holy, holy, holy.

2. Gracious Father, gracious Father,
   we are glad to be your children,
       gracious Father;
   and we lift our heads before you
   as a token of our love,
   gracious Father, gracious Father.

3. Risen Jesus, risen Jesus,
   we are glad you have redeemed us,
       risen Jesus;
   and we lift our hands before you
   as a token of our love,
   risen Jesus, risen Jesus.

4. Holy Spirit, Holy Spirit,
   come and fill our hearts anew, Holy Spirit;
   and we lift our voice before you
   as a token of our love,
   Holy Spirit, Holy Spirit.

5. Hallelujah, hallelujah,
   hallelujah, hallelujah, hallelujah;
   and we lift our hearts before you
   as a token of our love,
   hallelujah, hallelujah.

285 Unknown

1. Holy, holy, holy is the Lord,
   holy is the Lord God almighty.
   Holy, holy, holy is the Lord,
   holy is the Lord God almighty:
   who was, and is, and is to come;
   holy, holy, holy is the Lord.

2. Jesus, Jesus, Jesus is the Lord,
   Jesus is the Lord God almighty: *(Repeat)*
   who was, and is, and is to come;
   Jesus, Jesus, Jesus is the Lord.

3. Worthy, worthy, worthy is the Lord,
   worthy is the Lord God almighty: *(Repeat)*
   who was, and is and is to come;
   worthy, worth, worthy is the Lord.

4. Glory, glory, glory to the Lord,
   glory to the Lord God almighty: *(Repeat)*
   who was, and is, and is to come;
   glory, glory, glory to the Lord.

286 Reginald Heber (1783-1826)

1. Holy, holy, holy!
   Lord God almighty!
   Early in the morning
   our song shall rise to thee;
   holy, holy, holy!
   Merciful and mighty!
   God in three persons,
   blessed Trinity!

2.* Holy, holy, holy!
All the saints adore thee,
casting down their golden crowns
around the glassy sea;
cherubim and seraphim
falling down before thee,
which wert, and art,
and evermore shall be.

3. Holy, holy, holy!
Though the darkness hide thee,
though the sinful mortal eye
thy glory may not see,
only thou art holy,
there is none beside thee,
perfect in pow'r,
in love, and purity.

4. Holy, holy, holy!
Lord God almighty!
All thy works shall praise thy name,
in earth and sky and sea;
holy, holy, holy!
Merciful and mighty!
God in three persons,
blessèd Trinity!
  May be omitted

287 William John Sparrow-Simpson (1859-1952)
© *Novello & Co. Ltd.*

1. Holy Jesu, by thy passion,
by the woes which none can share,
borne in more than kingly fashion,
by thy love beyond compare:

Crucified, I turn to thee,
Son of Mary, plead for me.

2. By the treachery and trial,
by the blows and sore distress,
by desertion and denial,
by thine awful loneliness:

3. By thy look so sweet and lowly,
while they smote thee on the face,
by thy patience, calm and holy,
in the midst of keen disgrace:

4. By the hour of condemnation,
by the blood which trickled down,
when, for us and our salvation,
thou didst wear the robe and crown:

5. By the path of sorrows dreary,
by the cross, thy dreadful load,
by the pain, when, faint and weary,
thou didst sink upon the road:

6. By the Spirit which could render
love for hate and good for ill,
by the mercy, sweet and tender,
poured upon thy murd'rers still:

288 Brian Foley (b. 1919)
© *1971 Faber Music Ltd.*

1. Holy Spirit, come, confirm us
in the truth that Christ makes known;
we have faith and understanding
through your promised light alone.

2. Holy Spirit, come, console us,
come as Advocate to plead;
loving Spirit from the Father,
grant in Christ the help we need.

3. Holy Spirit, come, renew us,
come yourself to make us live;
holy through your loving presence,
holy through the gifts you give.

4. Holy Spirit, come, possess us,
you the love of Three in One,
Holy Spirit of the Father,
Holy Spirit of the Son.

289
Samuel Longfellow (1819-1892)

1. Holy Spirit, truth divine,
   dawn upon this soul of mine:
   voice of God, and inward light,
   wake my spirit, clear my sight.

2. Holy Spirit, love divine,
   glow within this heart of mine:
   kindle every high desire,
   purify me with your fire.

3. Holy Spirit, pow'r divine,
   fill and nerve this will of mine:
   boldly may I always live,
   bravely serve and gladly give.

4. Holy Spirit, law divine,
   reign within this soul of mine:
   be my law, and I shall be
   firmly bound, for ever free.

5. Holy Spirit, peace divine,
   still this restless heart of mine:
   speak to calm this tossing sea,
   grant me your tranquillity.

6. Holy Spirit, joy divine,
   gladden now this heart of mine:
   in the desert ways I sing -
   spring, O living water, spring!

290
Carl Tuttle
© 1985 Mercy/Vineyard Publishing
Administered by CopyCare

1. Hosanna, hosanna,
   hosanna in the highest! *(Repeat)*

   Lord, we lift up your name,
   with hearts full of praise;
   be exalted, O Lord, my God!
   Hosanna in the highest!

2. Glory, glory, glory
   to the King of kings! *(Repeat)*

291
Philipp Nicolai (1556-1608)
trans. William Mercer (1811-1873)

1. How brightly shines the Morning Star!
   The nations see and hail afar
   the light in Judah shining.
   Thou David's son of Jacob's race,
   the Bridegroom, and the King of grace,
   for thee our hearts are pining!
   Lowly, holy,
   great and glorious, thou victorious
   Prince of graces,
   filling all the heavenly places!

2. Though circled by the hosts on high,
   he deigns to cast a pitying eye
   upon his helpless creature;
   the whole creation's Head and Lord,
   by highest seraphim adored,
   assumes our very nature.
   Jesu, grant us,
   through thy merit, to inherit
   thy salvation;
   hear, O hear our supplication.

3. Rejoice, ye heav'ns; thou earth, reply;
   with praise, ye sinners, fill the sky,
   for this his incarnation.
   Incarnate God, put forth thy pow'r,
   ride on, ride on, great Conqueror,
   till all know thy salvation.
   Amen, amen!
   Alleluya, alleluya!
   Praise be given
   evermore by earth and heaven.

292
Richard Keen (c. 1787)

1. How firm a foundation,
   ye saints of the Lord,
   is laid for your faith
   in his excellent word;
   what more can he say
   than to you he hath said,
   you who unto Jesus
   for refuge have fled?

2. Fear not, he is with thee,
   O be not dismayed;
   for he is thy God,
   and will still give thee aid:
   he'll strengthen thee, help thee,
   and cause thee to stand,
   upheld by his righteous,
   omnipotent hand.

3. In ev'ry condition,
   in sickness, in health,
   in poverty's vale,
   or abounding in wealth;
   at home and abroad,
   on the land, on the sea,
   as thy days may demand
   shall thy strength ever be.

4. When through the deep waters
   he calls thee to go,
   the rivers of grief
   shall not thee overflow;
   for he will be with thee
   in trouble to bless,
   and sanctify to thee
   thy deepest distress.

5. When through fiery trials
   thy pathway shall lie,
   his grace all-sufficient
   shall be thy supply;
   the flame shall not hurt thee,
   his only design
   thy dross to consume
   and thy gold to refine.

6. The soul that on Jesus
   has leaned for repose
   he will not, he cannot,
   desert to its foes;
   that soul, though all hell
   should endeavour to shake,
   he never will leave,
   he will never forsake.

293 Joseph Hart (1712-1768)

1. How good is the God we adore!
   Our faithful, unchangeable friend:
   his love is as great as his pow'r
   and knows neither measure nor end.

2. For Christ is the first and the last;
   his Spirit will guide us safe home;
   we'll praise him for all that is past
   and trust him for all that's to come.

294 Arlo D. Duba, based on Psalm 84
© 1986 Hope Publishing Co

1. How lovely, Lord, how lovely
   is your abiding place;
   my soul is longing, fainting
   to feast upon your grace.
   The sparrow finds a shelter,
   a place to build her nest;
   and so your temple calls us
   within its walls to rest.

2. In your blest courts to worship,
   O God, a single day
   is better than a thousand
   if I from you should stray.
   I'd rather keep the entrance
   and claim you as my Lord,
   than revel in the riches
   the ways of sin afford.

3. A sun and shield for ever
   are you, O God most high;
   you shower us with blessings,
   no good will you deny.
   The saints, your grace receiving,
   from strength to strength shall go,
   and from their life shall rivers
   of blessing overflow.

295

v 1 Leonard E. Smith Jnr (b. 1942)
based on Isaiah 52, 53; vs 2-4 unknown.
© 1974 Kingsway's Thankyou Music

1. How lovely on the mountains
   are the feet of him
   who brings good news, good news,
   announcing peace,
   proclaiming news of happiness:
   our God reigns, our God reigns.

   Our God reigns. (x4)

2. You watchmen, lift your voices
   joyfully as one,
   shout for your King, your King!
   See eye to eye,
   the Lord restoring Zion:
   our God reigns, our God reigns.

3. Wasteplaces of Jerusalem,
   break forth with joy!
   We are redeemed, redeemed.
   The Lord has saved
   and comforted his people:
   our God reigns, our God reigns.

4. Ends of the earth, see
   the salvation of our God!
   Jesus is Lord, is Lord!
   Before the nations,
   he has bared his holy arm:
   our God reigns, our God reigns.

296 John Mason (c 1645-1694)

1. How shall I sing that majesty
   which angels do admire?
   Let dust in dust and silence lie;
   sing, sing, ye heavenly choir.
   Thousands of thousands stand around
   thy throne, O god most high;
   ten thousand times ten thousand sound
   thy praise; but who am I?

2. Thy brightness unto them appears,
   whilst I thy footsteps trace;
   a sound of God comes to my ears,
   but they behold thy face.
   They sing because thou art their Sun;
   Lord, send a beam on me;
   for where heav'n is but once begun
   there alleluias be.

3. How great a being, Lord, is thine,
   which doth all beings keep!
   Thy knowledge is the only line
   to sound so vast a deep.
   Thou art a sea without a shore,
   a sun without a sphere;
   thy time is now and evermore,
   thy place is ev'rywhere.

297 John Newton (1725-1807)

1. How sweet the name of Jesus sounds
   in a believer's ear!
   It soothes our sorrows, heals our
   wounds,
   and drives away our fear.

2. It makes the wounded spirit whole,
   and calms the troubled breast;
   'tis manna to the hungry soul,
   and to the weary rest.

3. Dear name! the rock on which I build,
   my shield and hiding-place,
   my never-failing treas'ry filled
   with boundless stores of grace.

4. Jesus! my shepherd, brother, friend,
   my prophet, priest, and king,
   my Lord, my life, my way, my end,
   accept the praise I bring.

5. Weak is the effort of my heart,
   and cold my warmest thought;
   but when I see thee as thou art,
   I'll praise thee as I ought.

6. Till then I would thy love proclaim
with ev'ry fleeting breath;
and may the music of thy name
refresh my soul in death.

298
Dave Bilbrough
© 1983 Kingsway's Thankyou Music

I am a new creation,
no more in condemnation,
here in the grace of God I stand.

My heart is overflowing,
my love just keeps on growing,
here in the grace of God I stand.

And I will praise you, Lord,
yes, I will praise you, Lord,
and I will sing of all that you have done.

A joy that knows no limit,
a lightness in my spirit,
here in the grace of God I stand.

299
Suzanne Toolan (b. 1927)
© 1966 GIA Publications Inc.

1. I am the bread of life.
   You who come to me shall not hunger;
   and who believe in me shall not thirst.
   No one can come to me
   unless the Father beckons.

   And I will raise you up,
   and I will raise you up,
   and I will raise you up on the last day.

2. The bread that I will give
   is my flesh for the life of the world,
   and if you eat of this bread,
   you shall live for ever,
   you shall live for ever.

3. Unless you eat
   of the flesh of the Son of Man,
   and drink of his blood,
   and drink of his blood,
   you shall not have life within you.

4. I am the resurrection,
   I am the life.
   If you believe in me,
   even though you die,
   you shall live for ever.

5. Yes, Lord, I believe
   that you are the Christ,
   the Son of God,
   who has come
   into the world.

300
Frances Ridley Havergal (1836-1879)

1. I am trusting thee, Lord Jesus,
   trusting only thee;
   trusting thee for full salvation,
   great and free.

2. I am trusting thee for pardon,
   at thy feet I bow;
   for thy grace and tender mercy,
   trusting now.

3. I am trusting thee for cleansing
   in the crimson flood;
   trusting thee to make me holy
   by thy blood.

4. I am trusting thee to guide me;
   thou alone shalt lead,
   ev'ry day and hour supplying
   all my need.

5. I am trusting thee for power,
   thine can never fail;
   words which thou thyself shalt give me
   must prevail.

6. I am trusting thee, Lord Jesus;
   never let me fall;
   I am trusting thee for ever,
   and for all.

301

Marc Nelson
© 1987 Mercy Vineyard Music Publishing
Administered by CopyCare

1. I believe in Jesus;
   I believe he is the Son of God.
   I believe he died and rose again.
   I believe he paid for us all.
   And I believe he's here now
   standing in our midst;
   here with the power to heal now,
   and the grace to forgive.

2. I believe in you, Lord;
   I believe you are the Son of God.
   I believe you died and rose again.
   I believe you paid for us all.
   And I believe you're here now
   standing in our midst;
   here with the power to heal now,
   and the grace to forgive.

302

Ascribed to St. Patrick (373-463),
trans. Cecil Frances Alexander (1818-1895) alt.

1. I bind unto myself today
   the strong name of the Trinity,
   by invocation of the same,
   the Three in One and One in Three.

2. I bind this day to me for ever,
   by pow'r of faith, Christ's incarnation,
   his baptism in the Jordan river,
   his death on cross for my salvation;
   his bursting from the spicèd tomb,
   his riding up the heav'nly way,
   his coming at the day of doom,
   I bind unto myself today.

3. I bind unto myself the pow'r
   of the great love of cherubim;
   the sweet 'Well done!' in judgement hour;
   the service of the seraphim,
   confessors' faith, apostles' word,
   the patriarchs' prayers, the prophets' scrolls,
   all good deeds done unto the Lord,
   and purity of faithful souls.

PART TWO

4. Christ be with me, Christ within me,
   Christ behind me, Christ before me.
   Christ beside me, Christ to win me,
   Christ to comfort and restore me.
   Christ beneath me, Christ above me,
   Christ in quiet, Christ in danger,
   Christ in hearts of all that love me,
   Christ in mouth of friend and stranger.

DOXOLOGY

5. I bind unto myself the name,
   the strong name of the Trinity,
   by invocation of the same,
   the Three in One and One in Three,
   of whom all nature hath creation,
   eternal Father, Spirit, Word.
   Praise to the Lord of my salvation:
   salvation is of Christ the Lord.
   Amen.

303

William Young Fullerton (1857-1932), alt.
© Copyright control

1. I cannot tell
   how he whom angels worship
   should stoop to love
   the peoples of the earth,
   or why as shepherd
   he should seek the wand'rer
   with his mysterious promise
   of new birth.
   But this I know,
   that he was born of Mary,
   when Bethl'em's manger
   was his only home,
   and that he lived at
   Nazareth and laboured,
   and so the Saviour,
   Saviour of the world, is come.

2. I cannot tell
how silently he suffered,
as with his peace
he graced this place of tears,
or how his heart
upon the cross was broken,
the crown of pain
to three and thirty years.
But this I know,
he heals the broken-hearted,
and stays our sin,
and calms our lurking fear,
and lifts the burden
from the heavy laden,
for yet the Saviour,
Saviour of the world, is here.

3. I cannot tell
how he will win the nations,
how he will claim
his earthly heritage,
how satisfy
the needs and aspirations
of east and west,
of sinner and of sage.
But this I know,
all flesh shall see his glory,
and he shall reap
the harvest he has sown,
and some glad day
his sun shall shine in splendour
when he the Saviour,
Saviour of the world, is known.

4. I cannot tell
how all the lands shall worship,
when, at his bidding,
ev'ry storm is stilled,
or who can say
how great the jubilation
when ev'ry heart
with perfect love is filled.

But this I know,
the skies will thrill with rapture,
and myriad, myriad
human voices sing,
and earth to heav'n,
and heav'n to earth, will answer:
'At last the Saviour,
Saviour of the world, is King!'

304 Brian A. Wren (b. 1936)
© 1971, 1995 Stainer & Bell Ltd.

1. I come with joy, a child of God,
forgiven, loved and free,
the life of Jesus to recall,
in love laid down for me.

2. I come with Christians far and near
to find, as all are fed,
the new community of love
in Christ's communion bread.

3. As Christ breaks bread, and bids us share,
each proud division ends.
The love that made us, makes us one,
and strangers now are friends.

4. The Spirit of the risen Christ,
unseen, but ever near,
is in such friendship better known,
alive among us here.

5. Together met, together bound
by all that God has done,
we'll go with joy, to give the world
the love that makes us one.

305 Sydney Carter (b. 1915)
© 1963 Stainer & Bell Ltd.

1. I danced in the morning
when the world was begun,
and I danced in the moon
and the stars and the sun,
and I came down from heaven
and I danced on the earth,
at Bethlehem I had my birth.

Continued overleaf

Dance then, wherever you may be,
I am the Lord of the Dance, said he,
and I'll lead you all, wherever you may be,
and I'll lead you all in the dance, said he.

2. I danced for the scribe
   and the Pharisee,
   but they would not dance
   and they wouldn't follow me.
   I danced for the fishermen,
   for James and John –
   they came with me
   and the dance went on.

3. I danced on the Sabbath
   and I cured the lame;
   the holy people,
   they said it was a shame.
   They whipped and they stripped
   and they hung me on high,
   and they left me there
   on a cross to die.

4. I danced on a Friday
   when the sky turned black –
   it's hard to dance
   with the devil on your back.
   They buried my body,
   and they thought I'd gone,
   but I am the dance,
   and I still go on.

5. They cut me down
   and I leapt up high;
   I am the life
   that'll never, never die;
   I'll live in you
   if you'll live in me –
   I am the Lord
   of the Dance, said he.

306 Michael Forster (b. 1946)
© 1992 Kevin Mayhew Ltd.

1. 'I do not know the man,'
   the fearful Peter said.
   No sharper nail could pierce the hand
   by which the world is fed,
   by which the world is fed!

2. The great disciple failed;
   his weakness we may own,
   and stand with him where judgement
      meets
   with grace, at Calv'ry's throne,
   with grace, at Calv'ry's throne.

3. Christ stands among us still,
   in those the world denies,
   and in the faces of the poor,
   we see his grieving eyes,
   we see his grieving eyes.

4. We cannot cleanse our hands
   of that most shameful spot,
   since of our brother we have said,
   'His keeper, I am not!'
   'His keeper, I am not!'

5. And yet, what love is this?
   Forgiveness all divine!
   Christ says of our poor faithless souls,
   'I know them, they are mine.'
   'I know them, they are mine.'

307 Susan Sayers (b. 1946)
© 1984 Kevin Mayhew Ltd

1. If we only seek peace
   when it's to our advantage,
   if we fail to release
   the down-trodden and poor,
   then let the gen'rous, caring, boundless
      sharing
   of the God
   who walked this earth
   nourish our roots until we fruit
   in the joy of the Lord.

The story of love he came to tell us,
bound in the making of the world.
We are the pages still unwritten:
let the story be told.

2. If we try to avoid
   inconvenient giving,
   or if love is destroyed
   by our failure to serve,
   then let the wide, unflinching, selfless
     giving
   of the God who walked this earth
   nourish our roots until we fruit
   in the joy of the Lord.

3. If we start to object
   to the path we are given
   and decide to select
   other ways of our own,
   then let the full acceptance, firm
     obedience
   of the God who walked this earth
   nourish our roots until we fruit
   in the joy of the Lord.

308

Carl Tuttle
© 1982 Mercy/Vineyard Publishing
Administered by CopyCare

1. I give you all the honour
   and praise that's due your name,
   for you are the King of Glory,
   the Creator of all things.

   And I worship you,
   I give my life to you,
   I fall down on my knees.
   Yes, I worship you,
   I give my life to you,
   I fall down on my knees.

2. As your Spirit moves upon me now,
   you meet my deepest need,
   and I lift my hands up to your throne,
   your mercy I've received.

3. You have broken chains that bound me,
   you've set this captive free,
   I will lift my voice to praise your name
   for all eternity.

309

Michael Forster (b. 1946)
based on the Good Friday Reproaches.
© 1996 Kevin Mayhew Ltd.

1. I give you love, and how do you repay?
   When you were slaves I strove to set
     you free;
   I led you out from under Pharaoh's yoke,
   but you led out your Christ to Calvary.

   My people, tell me, what is my offence?
   What have I done to harm you? Answer me!

2. For forty years I was your constant guide.
   I fed you with my manna from on high.
   I led you out to live in hope and peace,
   but you led out my only Son to die.

3. With cloud and fire I marked the
     desert way,
   I heard your cries of rage and calmed
     your fear.
   I opened up the sea and led you through,
   but you have opened Christ with nail
     and spear.

4. When in distress you cried to me for food,
   I sent you quails in answer to your call,
   and saving water from the desert rock,
   but to my Son you offered bitter gall.

5. I gave you joy when you were in despair,
   with songs of hope, I set your hearts
     on fire;
   crowned you with grace, the people of
     my choice,
   but you have crowned my Christ with
     thorny briar.

6. When you were weak, exploited and
     oppressed,
   I heard you cry and listened to your plea.
   I raised you up to honour and renown,
   but you have raised me on a shameful tree.

310
Horatius Bonar (1808-1889)

1. I heard the voice of Jesus say,
   'Come unto me and rest;
   lay down, thou weary one, lay down
   thy head upon my breast.'
   I came to Jesus as I was,
   so weary, worn and sad;
   I found in him a resting-place,
   and he has made me glad.

2. I heard the voice of Jesus say,
   'Behold, I freely give
   the living water, thirsty one;
   stoop down and drink and live.'
   I came to Jesus, and I drank
   of that life-giving stream;
   my thirst was quenched, my soul revived,
   and now I live in him.

3. I heard the voice of Jesus say,
   'I am this dark world's light;
   look unto me, thy morn shall rise,
   and all thy day be bright.'
   I looked to Jesus, and I found
   in him my star, my sun;
   and in that light of life I'll walk
   till trav'lling days are done.

311
Samuel Medley (1738-1799) alt.

1. I know that my Redeemer lives!
   What joy the blest assurance gives!
   He lives, he lives, who once was dead;
   he lives, my everlasting Head!

2. He lives, to bless me with his love;
   he lives, to plead for me above;
   he lives, my hungry soul to feed;
   he lives, to help in time of need.

3. He lives, and grants me daily breath;
   he lives – for me he conquered death;
   he lives, my mansion to prepare;
   he lives, to lead me safely there.

4. He lives, all glory to his name;
   he lives, my Saviour, still the same;
   what joy the blest assurance gives!
   I know that my Redeemer lives!

312
Timothy Dudley-Smith based on Psalm 121
© Timothy Dudley Smith

1. I lift my eyes
   to the quiet hills
   in the press of a busy day;
   as green hills stand
   in a dusty land
   so God is my strength and stay.

2. I lift my eyes
   to the quiet hills
   to a calm that is mine to share;
   secure and still
   in the Father's will
   and kept by the Father's care.

3. I lift my eyes
   to the quiet hills
   with a prayer as I turn to sleep;
   by day, by night,
   through the dark and light
   my Shepherd will guard his sheep.

4. I lift my eyes
   to the quiet hills
   and my heart to the Father's throne;
   in all my ways
   to the end of days
   the Lord will preserve his own.

313
Laurie Klein
© 1978 Maranatha! Music. Administered byCopyCare

I love you, Lord,
and I lift my voice to worship you,
O my soul rejoice.
Take joy, my King, in what you hear.
May it be a sweet, sweet sound in your
    ear.

314
Walter Chalmers Smith (1824-1908)
based on 1 Timothy 1:17

1. Immortal, invisible,
   God only wise,
   in light inaccessible hid
   from our eyes,
   most blessed, most glorious,
   the Ancient of Days,
   almighty, victorious,
   thy great name we praise.

2. Unresting, unhasting,
   and silent as light,
   nor wanting, nor wasting,
   thou rulest in might;
   thy justice like mountains
   high soaring above
   thy clouds which are fountains
   of goodness and love.

3. To all life thou givest,
   to both great and small;
   in all life thou livest,
   the true life of all;
   we blossom and flourish
   as leaves on the tree,
   and wither and perish;
   but naught changeth thee.

4. Great Father of glory,
   pure Father of light,
   thine angels adore thee,
   all veiling their sight;
   all laud we would render,
   O help us to see
   'tis only the splendour
   of light hideth thee.

315
John Greenleaf Whittier (1807-1892)

1. Immortal love, for ever full,
   for ever flowing free,
   for ever shared, for ever whole,
   a never-ebbing sea.

2. Our outward lips confess the name
   all other names above;
   love only knoweth whence it came
   and comprehendeth love.

3. O warm, sweet, tender, even yet
   a present help is he;
   and faith has still its Olivet,
   and love its Galilee.

4. The healing of his seamless dress
   is by our beds of pain;
   we touch him in life's throng and press,
   and we are whole again.

5. Through him the first fond prayers are said
   our lips of childhood frame;
   the last low whispers of our dead
   are burdened with his name.

6. Alone, O love ineffable,
   thy saving name is giv'n;
   to turn aside from thee is hell,
   to walk with thee is heav'n.

316
Isaac Watts (1674-1748)

1. I'm not ashamed to own my Lord,
   or to defend his cause;
   maintain the honour of his word,
   the glory of his cross.

2. Jesus, my God, I know his name;
   his name is all my trust;
   nor will he put my soul to shame,
   nor let my hope be lost.

3. Firm as his throne his promise stands;
   and he can well secure
   what I've committed to his hands,
   till the decisive hour.

4. Then will he own my worthless name
   before his Father's face;
   and in the new Jerusalem
   appoint my soul a place.

317
Martin E. Leckebusch (b. 1962)
© 1999 Kevin Mayhew Ltd

1. In an age of twisted values
   we have lost the truth we need;
   in sophisticated language
   we have justified our greed;
   by our struggle for possessions
   we have robbed the poor and weak –
   hear our cry and heal our nation:
   your forgiveness, Lord, we seek.

2. We have built discrimination
   on our prejudice and fear;
   hatred swiftly turns to cruelty
   if we hold resentments dear.
   For communities divided
   by the walls of class and race
   hear our cry and heal our nation:
   show us, Lord, your love and grace.

3. When our families are broken;
   when our homes are full of strife;
   when our children are bewildered,
   when they lose their way in life;
   when we fail to give the aged
   all the care we know we should –
   hear our cry and heal our nation
   with your tender fatherhood.

4. We who hear your word so often
   choose so rarely to obey;
   turn us from our wilful blindness,
   give us truth to light our way.
   In the power of your Spirit
   come to cleanse us, make us new:
   hear our cry and heal our nation
   till our nation honours you.

318
Kevin Nichols (b. 1929)
© 1976 Kevin Mayhew Ltd.

1. In bread we bring you, Lord,
   our bodies' labour.
   In wine we offer you our spirits' grief.
   We do not ask you, Lord,
   who is my neighbour,
   but stand united now, one in belief.

O we have gladly heard
your Word, your holy Word,
and now in answer, Lord,
our gifts we bring.
Our selfish hearts make true,
our failing faith renew,
our lives belong to you, our Lord and King.

2. The bread we offer you
   is blessed and broken,
   and it becomes for us our spirits' food.
   Over the cup we bring
   your Word is spoken;
   make it your gift to us,
   your healing blood.
   Take all that daily toil
   plants in our hearts' poor soil,
   take all we start and spoil,
   each hopeful dream,
   the chances we have missed,
   the graces we resist,
   Lord, in thy Eucharist, take and redeem.

319
John Oxenham (1852-1941) alt.
© Copyright control

1. In Christ there is no east or west,
   in him no south or north,
   but one great fellowship of love
   throughout the whole wide earth.

2. In him shall true hearts ev'rywhere
   their high communion find;
   his service is the golden cord,
   close binding humankind.

3. Join hands, united in the faith,
   whate'er your race may be;
   who serve my Father as their own
   are surely kin to me.

4. In Christ now meet both east and west,
   in him meet south and north;
   all Christlike souls are one in him,
   throughout the whole wide earth.

320 Annie Sherwood Hawks (1835-1918)

1. I need thee ev'ry hour,
   most gracious Lord;
   no tender voice like thine
   can peace afford.

   I need thee, O I need thee!
   ev'ry hour I need thee;
   O bless me now,
   my Saviour! I come to thee.

2. I need thee ev'ry hour;
   stay thou near by;
   temptations lose their pow'r
   when thou art nigh.

3. I need thee ev'ry hour,
   in joy or pain;
   come quickly and abide,
   or life is vain.

4. I need thee ev'ry hour;
   teach me thy will,
   and thy rich promises
   in me fulfil.

5. I need thee ev'ry hour,
   most Holy One;
   O make me thine indeed,
   thou blessèd Son!

321 Trans. from the Polish by Edith Margaret Gellibrand Reed (1885-1933). © *Copyright control*

1. Infant holy, infant lowly,
   for his bed a cattle stall;
   oxen lowing, little knowing
   Christ the babe is Lord of all.
   Swift are winging angels singing,
   nowells ringing, tidings bringing,
   Christ the babe is Lord of all,
   Christ the babe is Lord of all.

2. Flocks were sleeping, shepherds keeping
   vigil till the morning new;
   saw the glory, heard the story,
   tidings of a gospel true.
   Thus rejoicing, free from sorrow,
   praises voicing, greet the morrow,
   Christ the babe was born for you,
   Christ the babe was born for you.

322 Frances Ridley Havergal (1836-1879)

1. In full and glad surrender,
   I give myself to thee,
   thine utterly and only
   and evermore to be.

2. O Son of God, who lov'st me,
   I will be thine alone;
   and all I have and am, Lord,
   shall henceforth be thine own!

3. Reign over me, Lord Jesus,
   O make my heart thy throne;
   it shall be thine, dear Saviour,
   it shall be thine alone.

4. O come and reign, Lord Jesus,
   rule over ev'rything!
   And keep me always loyal
   and true to thee, my King.

323 Anna Laetitia Waring (1820-1910) based on Psalm 23

1. In heav'nly love abiding,
   no change my heart shall fear;
   and safe is such confiding,
   for nothing changes here.
   The storm may roar without me,
   my heart may low be laid,
   but God is round about me,
   and can I be dismayed?

Continued overleaf

2. Wherever he may guide me,
no want shall turn me back;
my Shepherd is beside me,
and nothing can I lack.
His wisdom ever waketh,
his sight is never dim,
he knows the way he taketh,
and I will walk with him.

3. Green pastures are before me,
which yet I have not seen;
bright skies will soon be o'er me,
where the dark clouds have been.
My hope I cannot measure,
my path to life is free,
my Saviour has my treasure,
and he will walk with me.

324 William Henry Draper (1855-1993) alt.
© J. Curwen & Sons

1. In our day of thanksgiving
one psalm let us offer
for the saints who before us
have found their reward;
when the shadow of death
fell upon them, we sorrowed,
but now we rejoice
that they rest in the Lord.

2. In the morning of life,
and at noon, and at even,
he called them away
from our worship below;
but not till his love,
at the font and the altar,
supplied them with grace
for the way they should go.

3. These stones that have echoed
their praises are holy,
and dear is the ground
where their feet have once trod;
yet here they confessed
they were strangers and pilgrims,
and still they were seeking
the city of God.

4. Sing praise, then, for all who
here sought and here found him,
whose journey is ended,
whose perils are past:
they believed in the light;
and its glory is round them,
where the clouds of earth's sorrow
are lifted at last.

325 John L. Bell (b. 1949) and Graham Maule (b. 1958)
© 1987 WGRG, Iona Community

1. Inspired by love and anger,
disturbed by endless pain,
aware of God's own bias,
we ask him once again:
'How long must some folk suffer?
How long can few folk mind?
How long dare vain self-int'rest
turn prayer and pity blind?'

2. From those for ever victims
of heartless human greed,
their cruel plight composes
a litany of need:
'Where are the fruits of justice?
Where are the signs of peace?
When is the day when pris'ners
and dreams find their release?'

3. From those for ever shackled
to what their wealth can buy,
the fear of lost advantage
provokes the bitter cry:
'Don't query our position!
Don't criticise our wealth!
Don't mention those exploited
by politics and stealth!'

4. To God, who through the prophets
proclaimed a diff'rent age,
we offer earth's indiff'rence,
its agony and rage:
'When will the wronged be righted?
When will the kingdom come?
When will the world be gen'rous
to all instead of some?'

5. God asks: 'Who will go for me?
   Who will extend my reach?
   And who, when few will listen,
   will prophesy and preach?
   And who, when few bid welcome,
   will offer all they know?
   And who, when few dare follow,
   will walk the road I show?'

6. Amused in someone's kitchen,
   asleep in someone's boat,
   attuned to what the ancients
   exposed, proclaimed and wrote,
   a Saviour without safety,
   a tradesman without tools
   has come to tip the balance
   with fishermen and fools.

4. Angels and archangels
   may have gathered there,
   cherubim and seraphim
   thronged the air;
   but only his mother
   in her maiden bliss
   worshipped the beloved with a kiss.

5. What can I give him,
   poor as I am?
   If I were a shepherd
   I would bring a lamb;
   if I were a wise man
   I would do my part,
   yet what I can I give him:
   give my heart.

326 Christina Georgina Rossetti (1830-1894)

1. In the bleak mid-winter
   frosty wind made moan,
   earth stood hard as iron,
   water like a stone;
   snow had fallen, snow on snow,
   snow on snow,
   in the bleak mid-winter, long ago.

2. Our God, heav'n cannot hold him
   nor earth sustain;
   heav'n and earth shall flee away
   when he comes to reign.
   In the bleak mid-winter
   a stable place sufficed
   the Lord God almighty, Jesus Christ.

3. Enough for him, whom cherubim
   worship night and day,
   a breastful of milk,
   and a mangerful of hay:
   enough for him, whom angels
   fall down before,
   the ox and ass and camel which adore.

327 John Bowring (1792-1872) based on Galatians 6:14

1. In the Cross of Christ I glory,
   tow'ring o'er the wrecks of time;
   all the light of sacred story
   gathers round its head sublime.

2. When the woes of life o'ertake me,
   hopes deceive, and fears annoy,
   never shall the Cross forsake me;
   Lo! it glows with peace and joy.

3. When the sun of bliss is beaming
   light and love upon my way,
   from the Cross the radiance streaming
   adds more lustre to the day.

4. Bane and blessing, pain and pleasure,
   by the Cross are sanctified;
   peace is there that knows no measure,
   joys that through all time abide.

328 Francesca Leftley (b. 1955)
© 1978 Kevin Mayhew Ltd.

1. In you, my God,
   may my soul find its peace;
   you are my refuge,
   my rock and my strength,
   calming my fears
   with the touch of your love.
   Here in your presence
   my troubles will cease.

2. In you, my God,
   may my soul find its joy;
   you are the radiance,
   the song of my heart,
   drying my tears
   with the warmth of your love.
   Here in your presence
   my troubles will cease.

3. In you, my God,
   may my soul find its rest;
   you are the meaning,
   the purpose of life,
   drawing me near
   to the fire of your love,
   safe in your presence
   my yearning will cease.

329 Charles H. Gabriel
© The Rodeheaver Company/Word Music/CopyCare

1. I stand amazed in the presence
   of Jesus the Nazarene,
   and wonder how he could love me,
   a sinner, condemned, unclean.

   O, how marvellous! O, how wonderful,
   and my song shall ever be:
   O, how marvellous! O, how wonderful!
   is my Saviour's love for me.

2. For me it was in the garden
   he prayed – 'Not my will, but thine';
   he had no tears for his own griefs,
   but sweat drops of blood for mine.

3. In pity angels beheld him,
   and came from the world of light,
   to comfort him in the sorrows
   he bore for my soul that night.

4. He took my sins and my sorrows,
   he made them his very own;
   he bore the burden to Calvary,
   and suffered, and died alone.

5. When with the ransomed in glory
   his face I at last shall see,
   'twill be my joy through the ages
   to sing of his love for me.

330 Edmund Hamilton Sears (1810-1876), alt.

1. It came upon the midnight clear,
   that glorious song of old,
   from angels bending near the earth
   to touch their harps of gold:
   'Peace on the earth, goodwill to all,
   from heav'n all gracious King!'
   The world in solemn stillness lay
   to hear the angels sing.

2. Still through the cloven skies they come,
   with peaceful wings unfurled;
   and still their heav'nly music floats
   o'er all the weary world:
   above its sad and lowly plains
   they bend on hov'ring wing;
   and ever o'er its Babel-sounds
   the blessèd angels sing.

3. Yet with the woes of sin and strife
   the world has suffered long;
   beneath the angel-strain have rolled
   two thousand years of wrong;
   and warring humankind hears not
   the love-song which they bring;
   O hush the noise of mortal strife,
   and hear the angels sing!

4. And ye, beneath life's crushing load,
   whose forms are bending low,
   who toil along the climbing way
   with painful steps and slow:
   look now! for glad and golden hours
   come swiftly on the wing;
   O rest beside the weary road,
   and hear the angels sing.

5. For lo, the days are hast'ning on,
   by prophets seen of old,
   when with the ever-circling years
   comes round the age of gold;
   when peace shall over all the earth
   its ancient splendours fling,
   and all the world give back the song
   which now the angels sing.

331 Stopford Augustus Brooke (1832-1916) alt.

1. It fell upon a summer day,
   when Jesus walked in Galilee,
   the mothers from a village
   brought their children to his knee.

2. He took them in his arms, and laid
   his hands on each remembered head;
   'Allow these little ones to come
   to me,' he gently said.

3. 'Forbid them not: unless ye bear
   the childlike heart your hearts within,
   unto my kingdom ye may come,
   but may not enter in.'

4. My Lord, I fain would enter there;
   O let me follow thee, and share
   thy meek and lowly heart, and be
   freed from all worldly care.

5. O happy thus to live and move,
   and sweet this world, where I shall find
   God's beauty everywhere, his love,
   his good in humankind.

6. Then, Father, grant this childlike heart,
   that I may come to Christ, and feel
   his hands on me in blessing laid,
   love-giving, strong to heal.

332 Dan Schutte, based on Isaiah 6
© 1981 Daniel L. Schutte and New Dawn Music

1. I, the Lord of sea and sky,
   I have heard my people cry.
   All who dwell in dark and sin
   my hand will save.
   I who made the stars of night,
   I will make their darkness bright.
   Who will bear my light to them?
   Whom shall I send?

   Here I am, Lord. Is it I, Lord?
   I have heard you calling in the night.
   I will go, Lord, if you lead me.
   I will hold your people in my heart.

2. I, the Lord of snow and rain,
   I have borne my people's pain.
   I have wept for love of them.
   They turn away.
   I will break their hearts of stone,
   give them hearts for love alone.
   I will speak my word to them.
   Whom shall I send?

3. I, the Lord of wind and flame,
   I will tend the poor and lame.
   I will set a feast for them.
   My hand will save.
   Finest bread I will provide
   till their hearts be satisfied.
   I will give my life to them.
   Whom shall I send?

333

William Walsham How (1823-1897)

1. It is a thing most wonderful,
almost too wonderful to be,
that God's own Son should come from
  heav'n,
and die to save a child like me.

2. And yet I know that it is true:
he chose a poor and humble lot,
and wept and toiled, and mourned and
  died,
for love of those who loved him not.

3. I cannot tell how he could love
a child so weak and full of sin;
his love must be most wonderful,
if he could die my love to win.

4. I sometimes think about the cross,
and shut my eyes, and try to see
the cruel nails and crown of thorns,
and Jesus crucified for me.

5. But even could I see him die,
I could but see a little part
of that great love which, like a fire,
is always burning in his heart.

6. It is most wonderful to know
his love for me so free and sure;
but 'tis more wonderful to see
my love for him so faint and poor.

7. And yet I want to love thee, Lord;
O light the flame within my heart,
and I will love thee more and more,
until I see thee as thou art.

334

John Glynn (b. 1948)
© 1976 Kevin Mayhew Ltd.

1. I watch the sunrise lighting the sky,
casting its shadows near.
And on this morning, bright though it be,
I feel those shadows near me.

But you are always close to me,
following all my ways.
May I be always close to you,
following all your ways, Lord.

2. I watch the sunlight shine through
  the clouds,
warming the earth below.
And at the mid-day, life seems to say:
'I feel your brightness near me.'
For you are always . . .

3. I watch the sunset fading away,
lighting the clouds with sleep.
And as the evening closes its eyes,
I feel your presence near me.
For you are always . . .

4. I watch the moonlight guarding the night,
waiting till morning comes.
The air is silent, earth is at rest –
only your peace is near me.
Yes, you are always . . .

335

Susan Sayers (b. 1946), based on Psalm 33
© 1996 Kevin Mayhew Ltd.

I will bless the Lord at all times. (x2)

1. Ev'rywhere I am, ev'rywhere I go,
I will praise the living God.
In ev'ryone I meet,
in ev'rything I see,
I will sing your praise, O Lord.

2. When I was in pain, when I lived in fear,
I was calling out to him.
He rescued me from death,
he wiped my tears away,
I will sing your praise, O Lord.

3. Trust him with your life,
  trust him with today,
come and praise the Lord with me;
O come and know his love,
O taste and understand,
let us sing your praise, O Lord.

336 Leona von Brethorst
© 1976 Maranatha! Music/CopyCare

I will enter his gates
with thanksgiving in my heart,
I will enter his courts with praise,
I will say this is the day
that the Lord has made,
I will rejoice for he has made me glad.
He has made me glad, he has made me glad,
I will rejoice for he has made me glad.
He has made me glad, he had made me glad,
I will rejoice for he has made me glad.

337 Francis Harold Rawley (1854-1952)
© HarperCollins Religious/CopyCare

1. I will sing the wondrous story
   of the Christ who died for me,
   how he left the realms of glory
   for the cross on Calvary.
   Yes, I'll sing the wondrous story
   of the Christ who died for me –
   sing it with his saints in glory,
   gathered by the crystal sea.

2. I was lost but Jesus found me,
   found the sheep that went astray,
   raised me up and gently led me
   back into the narrow way.
   Days of darkness still may meet me,
   sorrow's path I oft may tread;
   but his presence still is with me,
   by his guiding hand I'm led.

3. He will keep me till the river
   rolls its waters at my feet:
   then he'll bear me safely over,
   made by grace for glory meet.
   Yes, I'll sing the wondrous story
   of the Christ who died for me –
   sing it with his saints in glory,
   gathered by the crystal sea.

338 John L. Bell (b. 1949) and Graham Maule (b. 1958)
© 1987 WGRG, Iona Community

1. 'James and Andrew, Peter and John,
   men of temper, talent and tide,
   your nets are empty, empty and bare.
   Cast them now on the opposite side.'

2. 'Jesus, you're only a carpenter's son:
   joints and joists are part of your trade,
   but ours the skill to harvest the deep.
   Why presume to come to our aid?'

3. 'Friends of mine and brothers thro'
      love,
   I mean more than fishing for food.
   I call your skill to service my will,
   call your lives to harvest the good.'

4. 'Cast your nets where you think is right;
   spend your lives where you think is need;
   but if you long for that which is best,
   let it be on my word you feed.'

5. 'Stir then the waters, Lord, stir up the
      wind;
   stir the hope that needs to be stretched;
   stir up the love that needs to be ground;
   stir the faith that needs to be fetched.'

6. James and Andrew, Peter and John,
   and the women close by his side,
   hear how the Lord calls each by their
      name,
   asking all to turn like the tide.

339 Based on verses by F. B. P.,
an unknown author (c. 1600)

1. Jerusalem, my happy home,
   name ever dear to me,
   when shall my labours have an end?
   thy joys when shall I see?

2. Apostles, martyrs, prophets, there
   around my Saviour stand;
   and all I love in Christ below
   will join the glorious band.

Continued overleaf

3. Jerusalem, my happy home,
   when shall I come to thee?
   when shall my labours have an end?
   thy joys when shall I see?

4. O Christ, do thou my soul prepare
   for that bright home of love;
   that I may see thee and adore
   with all thy saints above.

340 'De Contemptu Mundi' by St. Bernard of Cluny,
12th century, trans. John Mason Neale (1818-1866), alt.

1. Jerusalem the golden,
   with milk and honey blest,
   beneath thy contemplation
   sink heart and voice oppressed.
   I know not, ah, I know not
   what joys await us there,
   what radiancy of glory,
   what bliss beyond compare.

2. They stand, those halls of Zion,
   all jubilant with song,
   and bright with many angels,
   and all the martyr throng;
   the prince is ever with them,
   the daylight is serene;
   the pastures of the blessèd
   are decked in glorious sheen.

3. There is the throne of David;
   and there, from care released,
   the shout of them that triumph,
   the song of them that feast;
   and they, who with their leader
   have fully run the race,
   are robed in white for ever
   before their Saviour's face.

4. O sweet and blessèd country,
   the home of God's elect!
   O sweet and blessèd country,
   that eager hearts expect!
   Jesus, in mercy, bring us
   to that dear land of rest;
   who art, with God the Father
   and Spirit, ever blest.

341 George Ratcliffe Woodward (1848-1934)
© Copyright control

1. Jesus, all holy, gentle and lowly,
   snow white lily of the vale:
   thou art our Master, Monarch and
       Pastor,
   Priest, Interceder, Prophet and Leader,
   Refuge, Defender, loving and strong:
   Sovran supernal, Son of th' Eternal,
   born of Mary maiden hail!
   Fountain of gladness, solace in sadness,
   more than brother, father or mother,
   to thee we render tribute of song.

2. Jesu, we bless thee, worship, confess thee:
   Shepherd of the sheep thou art:
   shelter, protect us, tend and direct us,
   strong of arm, and kind of heart:
   shadow and moonlight turn into
       noonlight;
   soften the scorner, comfort the mourner,
   rule our behaviour, order our way:
   bide with us, giving grace to the living,
   shrift to the dying freely supplying,
   be thou our Saviour ever and aye.

342 Latin (17th century)
trans. Henry Williams Baker (1821-1877)

1. Jesu, grant me this, I pray,
   ever in thy heart to stay;
   let me evermore abide
   hidden in thy wounded side.

2. If the world or Satan lay
   tempting snares about my way,
   I am safe when I abide
   in thy heart and wounded side.

3. If the flesh, more dang'rous still,
   tempt my soul to deeds of ill,
   naught I fear when I abide
   in thy heart and wounded side.

4. Death will come one day to me;
   Jesu, cast me not from thee:
   dying let me still abide
   in thy heart and wounded side.

343 Charles Wesley (1707-1788) alt.

1. Jesu, lover of my soul,
   let me to thy bosom fly,
   while the gath'ring waters roll,
   while the tempest still is high:
   hide me, O my Saviour, hide,
   till the storm of life is past;
   safe into the haven guide,
   O receive my soul at last.

2. Other refuge have I none,
   hangs my helpless soul on thee;
   leave, ah, leave me not alone,
   still support and comfort me.
   All my trust on thee is stayed,
   all my help from thee I bring;
   cover my defenceless head
   with the shadow of thy wing.

3. Plenteous grace with thee is found,
   grace to cleanse from ev'ry sin;
   let the healing streams abound,
   make and keep me pure within.
   Thou of life the fountain art,
   freely let me take of thee,
   spring thou up within my heart,
   rise to all eternity.

344 Johann Franck (1618-1677) alt.

1. Jesu, priceless treasure,
   source of purest pleasure,
   truest friend to me;
   ah, how long I've panted,
   and my heart hath fainted,
   thirsting, Lord, for thee!
   Thine I am, O spotless Lamb,
   I will let no other hide thee,
   naught I ask beside thee.

2. Hence, all fears and sadness,
   for the Lord of gladness,
   Jesus, enters in;
   they who love the Father,
   though the storms may gather,
   still have peace within;
   yea, whate'er I here must bear,
   still in thee lies purest pleasure,
   Jesu, priceless treasure.

345 Chris Bowater
© 1982 Sovereign Lifestyle Music

Jesus, at your name we bow the knee.
Jesus, at your name we bow the knee.
Jesus, at your name we bow the knee,
and acknowledge you as Lord.
(Repeat)
You are the Christ, you are the Lord.
Through your Spirit in our lives
we know who you are.
(Repeat)

346 John L. Bell (b. 1949) and Graham Maule (b. 1958)
© 1989 WGRG, Iona Community

1. Jesus calls us here to meet him as,
   through word and song and prayer,
   we affirm God's promised presence
   where his people live and care.
   Praise the God who keeps his promise;
   praise the Son who calls us friends;
   praise the Spirit who, among us,
   to our hopes and fears attends.

Continued overleaf

2. Jesus calls us to confess him
Word of life and Lord of All,
sharer of our flesh and frailness
saving all who fail or fall.
Tell his holy human story;
tell his tales that all may hear;
tell the world that Christ in glory
came to earth to meet us here.

3. Jesus calls us to each other:
found in him are no divides.
Race and class and sex and language –
such are barriers he derides.
Join the hand of friend and stranger;
join the hands of age and youth;
join the faithful and the doubter
in their common search for truth.

4. Jesus calls us to his table,
rooted firm in time and space,
where the Church in earth and heaven
finds a common meeting place.
Share the bread and wine, his body;
share the love of which we sing;
share the feast for saints and sinners
hosted by our Lord and King.

347 Cecil Frances Alexander (1818-1895)

1. Jesus calls us: o'er the tumult
of our life's wild, restless sea;
day by day his sweet voice soundeth,
saying, 'Christian, follow me.'

2. As of old Saint Andrew heard it
by the Galilean lake,
turned from home and toil and kindred,
leaving all for his dear sake.

3. Jesus calls us from the worship
of the vain world's golden store,
from each idol that would keep us,
saying, 'Christian, love me more.'

4. In our joys and in our sorrows,
days of toil and hours of ease,
still he calls, in cares and pleasures,
that we love him more than these.

5. Jesus call us: by thy mercies,
Saviour, make us hear thy call,
give our hearts to thine obedience,
serve and love thee best of all.

348 v.1: 'Surrexit hodie (14th Century) trans. anon.
as in 'Lyra Davidica' (1708) vs. 2-3 from J. Arnold's
Compleat Psalmodist (1749)

1. Jesus Christ is ris'n today, alleluia!
our triumphant holy day, alleluia!
who did once, upon the cross, alleluia!
suffer to redeem our loss, alleluia!

2. Hymns of praise then let us sing, alleluia!
unto Christ, our heav'nly King, alleluia!
who endured the cross and grave, alleluia!
sinners to redeem and save, alleluia!

3. But the pains that he endured, alleluia!
our salvation have procured; alleluia!
now above the sky he's King, alleluia!
where the angels ever sing, alleluia!

349 John L. Bell (b. 1949) and Graham Maule (b. 1958)
© 1988 WGRG. Iona Community, from the 'Enemy of
Apathy' collection Wild Goose Publications, 1988.

1. Jesus Christ is waiting,
waiting in the streets:
no one is his neighbour,
all alone he eats.
Listen, Lord Jesus,
I am lonely too;
make me, friend or stranger,
fit to wait on you.

2. Jesus Christ is raging,
raging in the streets
where injustice spirals
and all hope retreats.
Listen, Lord Jesus,
I am angry too;
in the kingdom's causes
let me rage with you.

3. Jesus Christ is healing,
   healing in the streets
   curing those who suffer,
   touching those he greets.
   Listen, Lord Jesus,
   I have pity too;
   let my care be active,
   healing just like you.

4. Jesus Christ is dancing,
   dancing in the streets,
   where each sign of hatred
   his strong love defeats.
   Listen, Lord Jesus,
   I feel triumph too;
   on suspicion's graveyard,
   let me dance with you.

5. Jesus Christ is calling,
   calling in the streets,
   'Come and walk faith's tightrope,
   I will guide your feet.'
   Listen, Lord Jesus,
   let my fears be few;
   walk one step before me,
   I will follow you.

350 Percy Dearmer (1867-1936)
after John Mason Neale (1818-1866) alt.
© *Oxford University Press*

1. Jesus, good above all other,
   gentle child of gentle mother,
   in a stable born our brother,
   give us grace to persevere.

2. Jesus, cradled in a manger,
   for us facing ev'ry danger,
   living as a homeless stranger,
   make we thee our King most dear.

3. Jesus, for thy people dying,
   risen Master, death defying,
   Lord in heav'n thy grace supplying,
   keep us to thy presence near.

4. Jesus, who our sorrows bearest,
   all our thoughts and hopes thou sharest,
   thou to us the truth declarest;
   help us all thy truth to hear.

5. Lord, in all our doings guide us;
   pride and hate shall ne'er divide us;
   we'll go on with thee beside us,
   and with joy we'll persevere.

351 Margaret Rizza (b. 1929)
© *1999 Kevin Mayhew Ltd*

1. Jesus, in the new dawn, guide our way,
   lead us to your light;
   Jesus, in the new dawn, guide our way,
   free us from our strife;
   Jesus, in the new dawn, fill our world,
   bless us with your joy;
   Jesus, in the new dawn, fill our world,
   bring us to your truth.

2. Spirit, in the new dawn, sing to us,
   play for us your song;
   Spirit, in the new dawn, sing to us,
   we will join your dance;
   Spirit, in the new dawn, take our hearts,
   birth in us your peace;
   Spirit, in the new dawn, take our hearts,
   make them one with yours.

3. Father, in the new dawn, speak to us,
   plant in us your love;
   Father, in the new dawn, speak to us,
   teach us to forgive;
   Father, in the new dawn, hold us fast,
   bring us to new life;
   Father, in the new dawn, hold us fast,
   bind us to your heart.

352

David J. Mansell
© 1982 Word's Spirit of Praise Music
Administered by CopyCare

1. Jesus is Lord!
   Creation's voice proclaims it,
   for by his pow'r each tree and flow'r
   was planned and made.
   Jesus is Lord! The universe declares it;
   sun, moon and stars in heaven cry:
   Jesus is Lord!

   Jesus is Lord! Jesus is Lord!
   Praise him with alleluias
   for Jesus is Lord!

2. Jesus is Lord!
   Yet from his throne eternal
   in flesh he came to die in pain
   on Calv'ry's tree.
   Jesus is Lord! From him all life proceeding,
   yet gave his life as ransom
   thus setting us free.

3. Jesus is Lord!
   O'er sin the mighty conqu'ror,
   from death he rose and all his foes
   shall own his name.
   Jesus is Lord! God sends his Holy Spirit
   to show by works of power
   that Jesus is Lord.

353

John Barnett
© 1980 Mercy/Vineyard Publishing/CopyCare

Jesus, Jesus,
holy and anointed One, Jesus.
Jesus, Jesus,
risen and exalted One, Jesus.

Your name is like honey on my lips,
your Spirit like water to my soul.
Your word is a lamp unto my feet.
Jesus, I love you, I love you.

354

Christian Fürchtegott Gellert (1715-1769)
trans. Frances Elizabeth Cox (1812-1897) alt.

1. Jesus lives! thy terrors now
   can no more, O death, appal us;
   Jesus lives! by this we know
   thou, O grave, canst not enthral us.
   Alleluia.

2. Jesus lives! henceforth is death
   but the gate of life immortal:
   this shall calm our trembling breath,
   when we pass its gloomy portal.
   Alleluia.

3. Jesus lives! for us he died;
   then, alone to Jesus living,
   pure in heart may we abide,
   glory to our Saviour giving.
   Alleluia.

4. Jesus lives! our hearts know well
   naught from us his love shall sever;
   life nor death nor pow'rs of hell
   tear us from his keeping ever.
   Alleluia.

5. Jesus lives! to him the throne
   over all the world is given:
   may we go where he is gone,
   rest and reign with him in heaven.
   Alleluia.

355

Nadia Hearn (b. 1940)
© 1974 Scripture in Song, a division of Integrity Music
Administered by Kingsway's Thankyou Music

Jesus, Name above all names,
beautiful Saviour, glorious Lord,
Emmanuel, God is with us,
blessed Redeemer, living Word.

356

From the Swahili
trans. Edmund S. Palmer (1856-1931)
© Oxford University Press. Used by permission

1. Jesu, Son of Mary,
   fount of life alone,
   here we hail thee present
   on thine altar-throne.

2. Humbly we adore thee,
   Lord of endless might,
   in the mystic symbols
   veiled from earthly sight.

3. Think, O Lord, in mercy
   on the souls of those
   who, in faith gone from us,
   now in death repose.

4. Here 'mid stress and conflict
   toils can never cease;
   there, the warfare ended,
   bid them rest in peace.

5. Often were they wounded
   in the deadly strife;
   heal them, good Physician,
   with the balm of life.

6. Ev'ry taint of evil,
   frailty and decay,
   good and gracious Saviour,
   cleanse and purge away.

7. Rest eternal grant them,
   after weary fight;
   shed on them the radiance
   of thy heav'nly light.

8. Lead them onward, upward,
   to the holy place,
   where thy saints made perfect
   gaze upon thy face.

357

Brian A Wren (b. 1936)
© 1977, 1995 Stainer & Bell Ltd

1. Jesus, on the mountain peak,
   stands alone in glory blazing.
   Let us, if we dare to speak,
   join the saints and angels praising:
   Alleluia!

2. Trembling at his feet we saw
   Moses and Elijah speaking.
   All the Prophets and the Law
   shout through them their joyful greeting:
   Alleluia!

3. Swift the cloud of glory came,
   God, proclaiming in the thunder,
   Jesus as the Son by name!
   Nations, cry aloud in wonder:
   Alleluia!

4. Jesus is the chosen One,
   living hope of ev'ry nation,
   hear and heed him, everyone;
   sing, with earth and all creation.
   Alleluia!

358

Timothy Dudley-Smith (b. 1926)
© Timothy Dudley-Smith

1. Jesus, Prince and Saviour,
   Lord of life who died;
   Christ, the friend of sinners,
   mocked and crucified;
   for a world's salvation,
   he his body gave,
   lay at last death's victim,
   lifeless in the grave.

   Lord of life triumphant,
   risen now to reign!
   King of endless ages,
   Jesus lives again!

Continued overleaf

2. In his pow'r and Godhead
ev'ry vict'ry won;
pain and passion ended,
all his purpose done.
Christ the Lord is risen!
sighs and sorrows past,
death's dark night is over,
morning comes at last!

Lord of life triumphant,
risen now to reign!
King of endless ages,
Jesus lives again!

3. Resurrection morning!
sinners' bondage freed;
Christ the Lord is risen –
he is ris'n indeed!
Jesus, Prince and Saviour,
Lord of Life who died,
Christ the King of Glory
now is glorified!

359 Isaac Watts (1674-1748)

1. Jesus shall reign where'er the sun
does his successive journeys run;
his kingdom stretch from shore to shore,
till moons shall wax and wane no more.

2. People and realms of ev'ry tongue
dwell on his love with sweetest song,
and infant voices shall proclaim
their early blessings on his name.

3. Blessings abound where'er he reigns:
the pris'ners leap to lose their chains;
the weary find eternal rest,
and all the humble poor are blest.

4. To him shall endless prayer be made,
and praises throng to crown his head;
his name like incense shall arise
with ev'ry morning sacrifice.

5. Let ev'ry creature rise and bring
peculiar honours to our King;
angels descend with songs again,
and earth repeat the loud amen.

360 Chris Bowater
© 1988 Sovereign Lifestyle Music Ltd.

Jesus shall take the highest honour,
Jesus shall take the highest praise;
let all earth join heav'n in exalting
the Name which is above all other names.
Let's bow the knee in humble adoration,
for at his name ev'ry knee must bow.
Let ev'ry tongue confess
he is Christ, God's only Son,
Sov'reign Lord, we give you glory now.

For all honour and blessing and power
belongs to you, belongs to you.
All honour and blessing and power
belongs to you, belongs to you,
Lord Jesus Christ, Son of the living God.

361 Graham Kendrick (b. 1950)
© 1977 Kingsway's Thankyou Music

1. Jesus, stand among us
at the meeting of our lives,
be our sweet agreement
at the meeting of our eyes.

O Jesus, we love you,
so we gather here,
join our hearts in unity
and take away our fear.

2. So to you we're gath'ring
out of each and ev'ry land,
Christ the love between us
at the joining of our hands.

Optional verse for Communion

3. Jesus stand among us
at the breaking of the bread;
join us as one body
as we worship you, our Head.

362
William Pennefather (1816-1873)

1. Jesus, stand among us
   in thy risen pow'r;
   let this time of worship
   be a hallowed hour.

2. Breathe the Holy Spirit
   into ev'ry heart;
   bid the fears and sorrows
   from each soul depart.

3. Thus with quickened footsteps
   we'll pursue our way,
   watching for the dawning
   of eternal day.

4. Jesus, the risen Lord, we come with
      praise;
   gladly, we sing of you, our hearts ablaze.
   Teach us to glimpse new life beyond
      the grave,
   reach out in love, we pray, to heal
      and save.

5. Jesus, the living one, we come with joy,
   truly, no evil can your love destroy.
   Teach us to walk in faith, though hope
      seems vain,
   reach out in love, we pray, renew again.

6. Jesus, the King of kings, we come to
      serve,
   freely give all for you as you deserve.
   Teach us to share the love you daily
      show,
   reach out in love, we pray, and bid us go.

363
Nick Fawcett (b. 1957)
© 1999 Kevin Mayhew Ltd.

1. Jesus, the broken bread, we come to you;
   empty, we would be fed – meet us anew.
   Teach us to hunger after righteousness,
   reach out in love, we pray, to guide
      and bless.

2. Jesus, the poured out wine, we come
      with awe;
   thirsty, we take the cup – quench and
      restore.
   Teach us to seek your kingdom and
      your will,
   reach out in love, we pray, our lives
      to fill.

3. Jesus, the crucified, we come with shame;
   greedy, we've sought reward – made
      that our aim.
   Teach us to worship now through
      word and deed,
   reach out in love, we pray, to all in need.

364
Charles Wesley (1707-1788)

1. Jesus, the name high over all,
   in hell, or earth, or sky;
   angels and mortals prostrate fall
   and devils fear and fly.

2. Jesus, the name to sinners dear,
   the name to sinners giv'n;
   it scatters all their guilty fear,
   it turns their hell to heav'n.

3. Jesus, the pris'ner's fetters breaks,
   and bruises Satan's head;
   pow'r into strengthless souls he speaks,
   and life into the dead,

4. O, that the world might taste and see
   the riches of his grace!
   The arms of love that compass me,
   hold all the human race.

Continued overleaf

5. His only righteousness I show,
   his saving grace proclaim:
   'tis all my business here below
   to cry: 'Behold the Lamb!'

6. Happy, if with my latest breath
   I may but gasp his name:
   preach him to all, and cry in death:
   'Behold, behold the Lamb!'

365 Ray Palmer (1808-1887)
based on John 20:29 and 1 Peter 1:8

1. Jesus, these eyes have never seen
   the radiant form of thine;
   the veil of sense hangs dark between
   thy blessed face and mine.

2. I see thee not, I hear thee not,
   yet thou art oft with me;
   and earth hath ne'er so dear a spot
   as where I meet with thee.

3. Yet, though I have not seen, and still
   must rest in faith alone,
   I love thee, dearest Lord, and will,
   unseen, but not unknown.

4. When death these mortal eyes shall seal,
   and still this throbbing heart,
   the rending veil shall thee reveal
   all glorious as thou art.

366 Michael Forster (b. 1946)
© 1996 Kevin Mayhew Ltd.

Jesus took a piece of bread,
he shared a cup of wine.
'Eat and drink with me,' he said,
'because you're friends of mine!'

1. We eat and drink with Jesus
   because we are his friends,
   remembering his promise
   of life that never ends.

2. We share with one another
   the bread and wine he gives,
   and celebrate together
   the special life he lives.

3. We rise up from the table,
   and go where Jesus sends,
   to tell the world the gospel
   of love that never ends.

367 William Cowper (1731-1800)

1. Jesus, where'er thy people meet,
   there they behold thy mercy seat;
   where'er they seek thee thou art found,
   and ev'ry place is hallowed ground.

2. For thou, within no walls confined,
   inhabitest the humble mind;
   such ever bring thee when they come,
   and, going, take thee to their home.

3. Dear Shepherd of thy chosen few,
   thy former mercies here renew;
   here to our waiting hearts proclaim
   the sweetness of thy saving name.

4. Here may we prove the pow'r of prayer
   to strengthen faith and sweeten care,
   to teach our faint desires to rise,
   and bring all heav'n before our eyes.

5. Lord, we are few, but thou art near;
   nor short thine arm, nor deaf thine ear;
   O rend the heav'ns, come quickly down,
   and make a thousand hearts thine own.

368 St. Bernard of Clairvaux (1091-1153)
trans. Edward Caswall (1814-1878) alt.

1. Jesu, the very thought of thee
   with sweetness fills the breast;
   but sweeter far thy face to see,
   and in thy presence rest.

2. No voice can sing, no heart can frame,
   nor can the mem'ry find,
   a sweeter sound than Jesu's name,
   the Saviour of mankind.

3. O hope of ev'ry contrite heart,
   O joy of all the meek,
   to those who ask how kind thou art,
   how good to those who seek!

4. But what to those who find? Ah, this
   nor tongue nor pen can show;
   the love of Jesus, what it is
   his true disciples know.

5. Jesu, our only joy be thou,
   as thou our prize wilt be;
   in thee be all our glory now,
   and through eternity.

369 'Jesu, dulcis memoria' (12th century) trans. Ray Palmer (1808-1887) alt.

1. Jesu, thou joy of loving hearts,
   thou fount of life, thou perfect grace;
   from the best bliss that earth imparts
   we turn unfilled to seek thy face.

2. Thy truth unchanged hath ever stood;
   thou savest those that on thee call;
   to them that seek thee thou art good,
   to them that find thee, all in all.

3. We taste thee, O thou living bread,
   and long to feast upon thee still;
   we drink of thee, the fountain-head,
   and thirst our souls from thee to fill.

4. Our restless spirits yearn for thee,
   where'er our changeful lot is cast,
   glad when thy gracious smile we see,
   blest when our faith is holding fast.

5. O Jesu, ever with us stay;
   make all our moments calm and bright;
   chase the dark night of sin away;
   shed o'er the world thy holy light.

370 Isaac Watts (1674-1748), based on Psalm 97, alt.

1. Joy to the world! The Lord is come;
   let earth receive her King;
   let ev'ry heart prepare him room,
   and heav'n and nature sing,
   and heav'n and nature sing,
   and heav'n and heav'n and nature sing.

2. Joy to the earth! The Saviour reigns;
   let us our songs employ;
   while fields and floods, rocks,
       hills and plains
   repeat the sounding joy,
   repeat the sounding joy,
   repeat, repeat the sounding joy.

3. He rules the world with truth and grace,
   and makes the nations prove
   the glories of his righteousness,
   and wonders of his love,
   and wonders of his love,
   and wonders, and wonders of his love.

371 Fred Dunn (1707-1779) © 1977 Kingsway's Thankyou Music

Jubilate, ev'rybody,
serve the Lord in all your ways and
come before his presence singing;
enter now his courts with praise.
For the Lord our God is gracious,
and his mercy everlasting.
Jubilate, jubilate, jubilate, Deo!

372 Henry Scott Holland (1847-1918) alt.

1. Judge eternal, throned in splendour,
   Lord of lords and King of kings,
   with thy living fire of judgement
   purge this realm of bitter things:
   solace all its wide dominion
   with the healing of thy wings.

Continued overleaf

2. Still the weary folk are pining
for the hour that brings release:
and the city's crowded clangour
cries aloud for sin to cease;
and the homesteads and the woodlands
plead in silence for their peace.

3. Crown, O God, thine own endeavour;
cleave our darkness with thy sword;
feed thy people's hungry spirits
with the richness of thy word:
cleanse the body of this nation
through the glory of the Lord.

373 Traditional

1. Just a closer walk with thee,
grant it, Jesus, if you please;
daily walking close to thee,
let it be, dear Lord, let it be.

2. Through the day of toil that's near,
if I fall, dear Lord, who cares?
Who with me my burden shares?
None but thee, dear Lord, none but thee.

3. When my feeble life is o'er,
time for me will be no more.
Guide me gently, safely on
to the shore, dear Lord, to the shore.

374 Charlotte Elliott (1789-1871)

1. Just as I am, without one plea
but that thy blood was shed for me,
and that thou bidst me come to thee,
O Lamb of God, I come.

2. Just as I am, though tossed about
with many a conflict, many a doubt,
fightings and fears within, without,
O Lamb of God, I come.

3. Just as I am, poor, wretched, blind;
sight, riches, healing of the mind,
yea, all I need, in thee to find,
O Lamb of God, I come.

4. Just as I am, thou wilt receive,
wilt welcome, pardon, cleanse, relieve:
because thy promise I believe,
O Lamb of God, I come.

5. Just as I am, thy love unknown
has broken ev'ry barrier down,
now to be thine, yea, thine alone,
O Lamb of God, I come.

6. Just as I am, of that free love
the breadth, length, depth and height
   to prove,
here for a season, then above,
O Lamb of God, I come.

*When the tune 'Maunder' is used this
Refrain is added to each verse:*

*Just as I am, just as I am,
just as I am, I come.*

375 George Herbert (1593-1633)

1. King of glory, King of peace,
I will love thee;
and, that love may never cease,
I will move thee.
Thou hast granted my appeal,
thou hast heard me;
thou didst note my ardent zeal,
thou hast spared me.

2. Wherefore with my utmost art,
I will sing thee,
and the cream of all my heart
I will bring thee.
Though my sins against me cried,
thou didst clear me,
and alone, when they replied,
thou didst hear me.

3. Sev'n whole days, not one in sev'n,
   I will praise thee;
   in my heart, though not in heav'n,
   I can raise thee.
   Small it is, in this poor sort
   to enrol thee:
   e'en eternity's too short
   to extol thee.

376 Naomi Batya and Sophie Conty
© 1980 Maranatha! Music/CopyCare

King of kings and Lord of lords,
glory, hallelujah.
King of kings and Lord of lords,
glory, hallelujah.
Jesus, Prince of Peace,
glory, hallelujah.
Jesus, Prince of Peace,
glory, hallelujah.

377 Chris Bowater
© 1988 Sovereign Lifestyle Music Ltd.

Lamb of God, Holy One,
Jesus Christ, Son of God,
lifted up willingly to die;
that I the guilty one may know
the blood once shed
still freely flowing,
still cleansing, still healing.
I exalt you, Jesus, my sacrifice,
I exalt you, my Redeemer and my Lord.
I exalt you, worthy Lamb of God,
and in honour I bow down before
  your throne.

378 John Henry Newman (1801-1890)

1. Lead, kindly light,
   amid th'encircling gloom,
   lead thou me on;
   the night is dark,
   and I am far from home;
   lead thou me on.

Keep thou my feet;
I do not ask to see
the distant scene;
one step enough for me.

2. I was not ever thus,
   nor prayed that thou
   shouldst lead me on;
   I loved to choose
   and see my path; but now
   lead thou me on.
   I loved the garish day,
   and, spite of fears,
   pride ruled my will:
   remember not past years.

3. So long thy pow'r
   hath blest me, sure it still
   will lead me on,
   o'er moor and fen,
   o'er crag and torrent, till
   the night is gone;
   and with the morn
   those angel faces smile,
   which I have loved long since,
   and lost awhile.

379 James Edmeston (1791-1867)

1. Lead us, heav'nly Father, lead us
   o'er the world's tempestuous sea;
   guard us, guide us, keep us, feed us,
   for we have no help but thee;
   yet possessing ev'ry blessing
   if our God our Father be.

2. Saviour, breathe forgiveness o'er us,
   all our weakness thou dost know,
   thou didst tread this earth before us,
   thou didst feel its keenest woe;
   lone and dreary, faint and weary,
   through the desert thou didst go.

Continued overleaf

3. Spirit of our God, descending,
   fill our hearts with heav'nly joy,
   love with ev'ry passion blending,
   pleasure that can never cloy;
   thus provided, pardoned, guided,
   nothing can our peace destroy.

380
Graham Kendrick (b. 1950)
© 1983 Kingsway's Thankyou Music

1. Led like a lamb to the slaughter,
   in silence and shame,
   there on your back you carried a world
   of violence and pain.
   Bleeding, dying, bleeding, dying.

   You're alive, you're alive,
   you have risen!
   Alleluia! And the pow'r
   and the glory is given,
   alleluia! Jesus to you.

2. At break of dawn, poor Mary,
   still weeping she came,
   when through her grief she heard your
     voice
   now speaking her name.
   Mary, Master, Mary, Master.

3. At the right hand of the Father
   now seated on high
   you have begun your eternal reign
   of justice and joy.
   Glory, glory, glory, glory.

381
George Herbert, trans. G. Moultrie (1829-1885)

Liturgy of St James, trans. G. Moultrie (1829-1885)

1. Let all mortal flesh keep silence
   and with fear and trembling stand;
   ponder nothing earthly-minded,
   for with blessing in his hand
   Christ our God on earth descendeth,
   our full homage to demand.

2. King of kings, yet born of Mary,
   as of old on earth he stood,
   Lord of lords, in human vesture,
   in the body and the blood.
   He will give to all the faithful
   his own self for heav'nly food.

3. Rank on rank the host of heaven
   spreads its vanguard on the way,
   as the Light of light descendeth
   from the realms of endless day,
   that the pow'rs of hell may vanish
   as the darkness clears away.

4. At his feet the six-winged seraph;
   cherubim, with sleepless eye,
   veil their faces to the Presence,
   as with ceaseless voice they cry,
   alleluia, alleluia,
   alleluia, Lord most high.

382
George Herbert (1593-1633)

1. Let all the world in ev'ry corner sing,
   my God and King!
   The heav'ns are not too high,
   his praise may thither fly;
   the earth is not too low,
   his praises there may grow.
   Let all the world in ev'ry corner sing,
   my God and King!

2. Let all the world in ev'ry corner sing,
   my God and King!
   The Church with psalms must shout,
   no door can keep them out;
   but, above all, the heart
   must bear the longest part.
   Let all the world in ev'ry corner sing,
   my God and King!

383

Michael Forster (b. 1946)
© 1995 Kevin Mayhew Ltd.

1. Let love be real, in giving and receiving,
   without the need to manage and to own;
   a haven free from posing and pretending,
   where ev'ry weakness may be safely known.
   Give me your hand,
   along the desert pathway,
   give me your love
   wherever we may go.

   As God loves us,
   so let us love each other:
   with no demands,
   just open hands and space to grow.

2. Let love be real, not grasping or confining,
   that strange embrace that holds yet sets
       us free;
   that helps us face the risk of truly living,
   and makes us brave to be what we
       might be.
   Give me your strength
   when all my words are weakness;
   give me your love
   in spite of all you know.

3. Let love be real, with no manipulation,
   no secret wish to harness or control;
   let us accept each other's incompleteness,
   and share the joy of learning to be whole.
   Give me your hope
   through dreams and disappointments;
   give me your trust
   when all my failings show.

384

Charles Wesley (1707-1788) and others, alt.

1. Let saints on earth in concert sing
   with those whose work is done;
   for all the servants of our King
   in heav'n and earth are one.

2. One family, we dwell in him,
   one Church, above, beneath;
   though now divided by the stream,
   the narrow stream of death.

3. The people of the living God,
   to his command we bow:
   part of the host have crossed the flood,
   and part are crossing now.

4. E'en now to their eternal home
   there pass some spirits blest;
   while others to the margin come,
   waiting their call to rest.

5. Jesu, be thou our constant guide;
   then, when the word is giv'n,
   bid Jordan's narrow stream divide,
   and bring us safe to heav'n.

385

Mike Anderson (b. 1950)
© 1999 Kevin Mayhew Ltd.

Let the heavens declare,
let the mountains sing,
let the oceans roar
that Jesus lives and is our King.
Lift your hands in praise,
let your spirits soar,
let the heavens declare,
let the mountains sing,
let the oceans roar.

1. All the sins we've ever sinned
   died upon the cross with him,
   but we know he lives again:
   the vict'ry is won, the vict'ry is won,
   the vict'ry is won, the vict'ry is won.

2. Hanging on the cross for me
   Jesus died in agony.
   Blood and tears he shed for me,
   that I might have life. *(x4)*

3. In the kingdom he revealed
   broken hearts can all be healed,
   through the covenant he sealed
   with his holy blood. *(x4)*

386 Dave Bilbrough
© 1979 Kingsway's Thankyou Music

Let there be love shared among us,
let there be love in our eyes.
May now your love sweep this nation;
cause us, O Lord, to arise.
Give us a fresh understanding,
brotherly love that is real.
Let there be love shared among us,
let there be love.

387 Unknown

1. Let us break bread together
   on our knees,
   let us break bread together
   on our knees.
   When I fall on my knees
   with my face to the rising sun,
   O Lord, have mercy on me.

2. Let us share wine together
   on our knees,
   let us share wine together
   on our knees.
   When I fall on my knees
   with my face to the rising sun,
   O Lord, have mercy on me.

3. Let us praise God together
   on our knees,
   let us praise God together
   on our knees.
   When I fall on my knees
   with my face to the rising sun,
   O Lord, have mercy on me.

388 James Edward Seddon (1915-1983)
© Mrs. M. Seddon/Jubilee Hymns

1. Let us praise God together, let us praise;
   let us praise God together all our days.
   He is faithful in all his ways,
   he is worthy of all our praise,
   his name be exalted on high.

2. Let us seek God together, let us pray;
   let us seek his forgiveness as we pray.
   He will cleanse us from all our sin,
   he will help us the fight to win,
   his name be exalted on high.

3. Let us serve God together, him obey;
   let our lives show his goodness
     through each day.
   Christ the Lord is the world's true light,
   let us serve him with all our might,
   his name be exalted on high.

389 Martin E. Leckebusch (b. 1962)
based on Romans 5:1-5
© 1999 Kevin Mayhew Ltd.

1. Let us rejoice: God's gift to us is peace!
   Here is the calm which bids our
     strivings cease,
   for God's acceptance brings a true
     release:
   alleluia!

2. We can be strong, for now we stand
     by grace,
   held in his loving, fatherly embrace;
   his care remains, whatever trials
     we face:
   alleluia!

3. We trust in God – and shall not
     be dismayed,
   nor find our hopes of glory are
     betrayed,
   for all his splendour we shall see
     displayed:
   alleluia!

4. And come what may, we never need
     despair –
   God is at work through all the griefs
     we bear,
   that in the end his likeness we may
     share:
   alleluia!

5. Deep in our hearts the love of God
   is found;
   his precious gifts of life and joy
   abound –
   so let our finest songs of praise
   resound:
   alleluia!

390 Marie Lydia Pereira (b. 1920)
© 1999 Kevin Mayhew Ltd.

1. Let us sing your glory, Lord, alleluia,
   let us praise your name adored, alleluia.
   Joy and beauty come from you, alleluia,
   and each hour your love shines through,
   alleluia.

   Alleluia, alleluia, allelu, alleluia. (x2)

2. Leaf that quivers on the tree, alleluia,
   flowers that we delight to see, alleluia.
   Planets as they reel in space, alleluia,
   tell us of your pow'r and grace, alleluia.

3. All creation sings your praise, alleluia,
   young and old their voices raise, alleluia.
   Children as they laugh and sing, alleluia,
   to your goodness homage bring, alleluia.

391 Fred Kaan (b. 1929)
© 1975 Stainer & Bell Ltd.

1. Let us talents and tongues employ,
   reaching out with a shout of joy:
   bread is broken, the wine is poured,
   Christ is spoken and seen and heard.

   Jesus lives again,
   earth can breathe again,
   pass the word around:
   loaves abound!

2. Christ is able to make us one,
   at his table he sets the tone,
   teaching people to live to bless,
   love in word and in deed express.

3. Jesus calls us in, sends us out
   bearing fruit in a world of doubt,
   gives us love to tell, bread to share:
   God-Immanuel everywhere!

392 John Milton (1608-1674), based on Psalm 136

1. Let us, with a gladsome mind,
   praise the Lord, for he is kind;

   for his mercies ay endure,
   ever faithful, ever sure.

2. Let us blaze his name abroad,
   for of gods he is the God;

3, He, with all-commanding might,
   filled the new-made world with light;

4. He the golden-tressèd sun
   caused all day his course to run;

5. And the moon to shine at night,
   'mid her starry sisters bright;

6. All things living he doth feed,
   his full hand supplies their need;

7. Let us, with a gladsome mind,
   praise the Lord, for he is kind;

393 Brian A Wren (b. 1936)
© 1974, 1995 Stainer & Bell Ltd.

1. Life is great! So sing about it,
   as we can and as we should -
   shops and buses, towns and people,
   village, farmland, field and wood.
   Life is great and life is given.
   Life is lovely, free and good.

2. Life is great! - whatever happens,
   snow or sunshine, joy or pain,
   hardship, grief or disillusion,
   suff'ring that I can't explain.
   Life is great if someone loves me,
   holds my hand and calls my name.

Continued overleaf

3. Love is great! - the love of lovers,
   whispered words and longing eyes;
   love that gazes at the cradle
   where a child of loving lies;
   love that lasts when youth has faded,
   bends with age, but never dies.

4. Love is giving and receiving -
   boy and girl, or friend with friend.
   Love is bearing and forgiving
   all the hurts that hate can send.
   Love's the greatest way of living:
   hoping, trusting to the end.

5. Great is God, who lived among us:
   truth in Jesus seen and done,
   healing, teaching, hate resisting,
   loving where we scoff and shun,
   dying, rising, joy surprising
   reaching out to everyone.

394 George William Kitchin (1827-1912) and
Michael Robert Newbolt (1874-1956), alt.
© *Hymns Ancient & Modern Ltd.*

Lift high the Cross,
the love of Christ proclaim
till all the world adore his sacred name!

1. Come, Christians,
   follow where our Saviour trod,
   o'er death victorious,
   Christ the Son of God.

2. Led on their way by this
   triumphant sign,
   the hosts of God in joyful
   praise combine:

3. Each new disciple
   of the Crucified
   is called to bear the seal
   of him who died:

4. Saved by the Cross
   whereon their Lord was slain,
   now Adam's children
   their lost home regain:

5. From north and south,
   from east and west they raise
   in growing harmony
   their song of praise:

6. O Lord, once lifted
   on the glorious tree,
   as thou hast promised,
   draw us unto thee:

7. Let ev'ry race
   and ev'ry language tell
   of him who saves
   from fear of death and hell:

8. From farthest regions,
   let them homage bring,
   and on his Cross
   adore their Saviour King:

9. Set up thy throne,
   that earth's despair may cease
   beneath the shadow
   of its healing peace:

10. For thy blest Cross
    which doth for all atone,
    creation's praises rise
    before thy throne:

11. So let the world
    proclaim with one accord
    the praise of our
    ever-living Lord.

395 Henry Montagu Butler (1833-1918) alt.

1. 'Lift up your hearts!'
   We lift them, Lord, to thee;
   here at thy feet
   none other may we see:
   'Lift up your hearts!'
   E'en so, with one accord,
   we lift them up,
   we lift them to the Lord.

2. Above the swamps
   of subterfuge and shame,
   the deeds, the thoughts,
   that honour may not name,
   the halting tongue
   that dares not tell the whole,
   O Lord of truth,
   lift ev'ry human soul.

3. Lift ev'ry gift
   that thou thyself hast giv'n:
   low lies the best
   till lifted up to heav'n;
   low lie the pounding heart,
   the teeming brain,
   till, sent from God,
   they mount to God again.

4. Then, as the trumpet-call,
   in after years,
   'Lift up your hearts!'
   rings pealing in our ears,
   still shall those hearts respond,
   with full accord,
   'We lift them up,
   we lift them to the Lord.'

396 David Mowbray (b. 1938)
© David Mowbray/Jubilate Hymns

1. Light a candle for thanksgiving!
   Sing to God for Christ the Lord!
   Born to Mary, dying, living;
   still the Spirit speaks his word.
   Welcome ev'ry tower pealing,
   celebrate two thousand years!
   Years of grace and years revealing
   Christ where Christlike love appears.

2. Light a candle for achievers!
   Marvel at their range of thought:
   artists, scientists, believers
   famed for what their hands have wrought.
   For the feats of engineering,
   for each fresh, creative probe;
   ev'ry benefit appearing,
   spread across a shrinking globe.

3. Light a candle for the nation
   and the future of its youth!
   Build with them on this foundation:
   love, security and truth.
   Christ the Lord, by patience winning
   many a household, many a heart,
   set ablaze their faith's beginning,
   journey with them from the start.

4. Light a candle for tomorrow!
   Ask that countries may walk free:
   truly free, not bound to borrow,
   but released for jubilee.
   One has come among us bearing
   news that prisoners are restored:
   let his voice move us to sharing –
   sing to God for Christ the Lord!

397 Timothy Dudley-Smith (b. 1926)
based on a prayer of St Augustine of Hippo
© Timothy Dudley-Smith

1. Light of the minds that know him:
   may Christ be light to mine!
   my sun in risen splendour,
   my light of truth divine;
   my guide in doubt and darkness,
   my true and living way,
   my clear light ever shining,
   my dawn of heaven's day.

2. Life of the souls that love him:
   may Christ be ours indeed!
   the living bread from heaven
   on whom our spirits feed;
   who died for love of sinners
   to bear our guilty load,
   and make of life's brief journey
   a new Emmaus road.

3. Strength of the wills that serve him:
   may Christ be strength to me,
   who stilled the storm and tempest,
   who calmed the tossing sea;
   his Spirit's pow'r to move me,
   his will to master mine,
   his cross to carry daily
   and conquer in his sign.

Continued overleaf

4. May it be ours to know him
   that we may truly love,
   and loving, fully serve him
   as serve the saints above;
   till in that home of glory
   with fadeless splendour bright,
   we serve in perfect freedom
   our strength, our life, our light.

398
Ascribed to Thomas à Kempis (c. 1379-1471)
trans. John Mason Neale (1818-1866)

1. Light's abode, celestial Salem,
   vision whence true peace doth spring,
   brighter than the heart can fancy,
   mansion of the highest King;
   O how glorious are the praises
   which of thee the prophets sing!

2. There for ever and for ever
   alleluia is outpoured;
   for unending, for unbroken
   is the feast-day of the Lord;
   all is pure and all is holy
   that within thy walls is stored.

3. There no cloud or passing vapour
   dims the brightness of the air;
   endless noon-day, glorious noon-day,
   from the Sun of suns is there;
   there no night brings rest from labour,
   for unknown are toil and care.

4. O how glorious and resplendent,
   fragile body, shalt thou be,
   when endued with so much beauty,
   full of health and strong and free,
   full of vigour, full of pleasure
   that shall last eternally.

5. Now with gladness, now with courage,
   bear the burden on thee laid,
   that hereafter these thy labours
   may with endless gifts be paid;
   and in everlasting glory
   thou with brightness be arrayed.

6. Laud and honour to the Father,
   laud and honour to the Son,
   laud and honour to the Spirit,
   ever Three and ever One,
   consubstantial, co-eternal,
   while unending ages run.

399
Graham Kendrick (b. 1950)
© Copyright 1988 Make Way Music

1. Like a candle flame,
   flick'ring small
   in our darkness,
   uncreated light
   shines through infant eyes.

   God is with us,
   alleluia,
   come to save us,
   alleluia,
   alleluia!

2. Stars and angels sing,
   yet the earth
   sleeps in shadows;
   can this tiny spark
   set a world on fire?

3. Yet his light shall shine
   from our lives,
   spirit blazing,
   as we touch the flame
   or his holy fire.

400
Michael Perry (1942-96)
© Mrs B Perry/Jubilate Hymns

1. Like a mighty river flowing,
   like a flow'r in beauty growing,
   far beyond all human knowing
   is the perfect peace of God.

2. Like the hills serene and even,
   like the coursing clouds of heaven,
   like the heart that's been forgiven
   is the perfect peace of God.

3. Like the summer breezes playing,
   like the tall trees softly swaying,
   like the lips of silent praying
   is the perfect peace of God.

4. Like the morning sun ascended,
   like the scents of evening blended,
   like a friendship never ended
   is the perfect peace of God.

5. Like the azure ocean swelling,
   like the jewel all-excelling,
   far beyond our human telling
   is the perfect peace of God.

401 Aniceto Nazareth
© 1984 Kevin Mayhew Ltd.

Listen, let your heart keep seeking;
listen to his constant speaking;
listen to the Spirit calling you.
Listen to his inspiration;
listen to his invitation;
listen to the Spirit calling you.

1. He's in the sound of the thunder,
   in the whisper of the breeze.
   He's in the might of the whirlwind,
   in the roaring of the seas.

2. He's in the laughter of children,
   in the patter of the rain.
   Hear him in cries of the suff'ring,
   in their moaning and their pain.

3. He's in the noise of the city,
   in the singing of the birds.
   And in the night-time the stillness
   helps you listen to his word.

402 Mike Anderson (b. 1950), based on Psalm 86
© 1999 Kevin Mayhew Ltd.

Listen to me, Yahweh, answer me,
poor and needy as I am.
Listen to me, Yahweh, answer me,
I rely on you.

1. Lord, I invoke you in my trouble;
   give me reason to rejoice.

2. Lord, in your goodness, please forgive me;
   listen to me, hear my plea.

3. Lord, you are merciful and faithful;
   turn to me now in my need.

4. Lord, give me strength, I am your servant;
   show me that you really care.

403 Francesca Leftley (b. 1955)
© 1999 Kevin Mayhew Ltd.

1. Listen to my voice,
   and then turn back to me:
   I will heal your heart,
   and I will set you free.
   Oh, my dearest child,
   how much you mean to me:
   let me fill your life
   and love you tenderly.

2. Rest within my arms
   and let your fears depart,
   feel my peace and joy
   bind up your broken heart.
   I will wipe your tears
   and make you whole again:
   come to me, my child,
   and turn away from sin.

3. Take my hand, and now
   we will begin once more,
   I will walk beside you
   as I did before.
   I have never left you,
   though your eyes were dim:
   walk with me in light,
   and turn away from sin.

404

Jan Berry (b. 1953)
© 1999 Kevin Mayhew Ltd

1. Living God, your word has called us,
   summoned us to live by grace,
   make us one in hope and vision,
   as we gather in this place.
   Take our searching, take our praising,
   take the silence of our prayer,
   offered up in joyful worship,
   springing from the love we share.

2. Living God, your love has called us
   in the name of Christ your Son,
   forming us to be his body,
   by your Spirit making one.
   Working, laughing, learning, growing,
   old and young and black and white,
   gifts and skills together sharing,
   in your service all unite.

3. Living God, your hope has called us
   to the world that you have made,
   teaching us to live for others,
   humble, joyful, unafraid.
   Give us eyes to see your presence,
   joy in laughter, hope in pain.
   In our loving, in our living,
   give us strength that Christ may reign.

405

Charles Wesley (1707-1788), John Cennick
(1718-1755) and Martin Madan (1728-1790)

1. Lo, he comes with clouds descending,
   once for mortal sinners slain;
   thousand thousand saints attending
   swell the triumph of his train.
   Alleluia! Alleluia! Alleluia!
   Christ appears on earth to reign.

2. Ev'ry eye shall now behold him
   robed in dreadful majesty;
   we who set at naught and sold him,
   pierced and nailed him to the tree,
   deeply grieving, deeply grieving,
      deeply grieving,
   shall the true Messiah see.

3. Those dear tokens of his passion
   still his dazzling body bears,
   cause of endless exultation
   to his ransomed worshippers:
   with what rapture, with what rapture,
      with what rapture
   gaze we on those glorious scars!

4. Yea, amen, let all adore thee,
   high on thine eternal throne;
   Saviour, take the pow'r and glory,
   claim the kingdom for thine own.
   Alleluia! Alleluia! Alleluia!
   Thou shalt reign, and thou alone.

406

Fred Pratt Green (b. 1903)
© 1971 Stainer & Bell Ltd

1. Long ago, prophets knew
   Christ would come, born a Jew,
   come to make all things new,
   bear his people's burden,
   freely love and pardon.

   Ring, bells, ring, ring, ring!
   Sing, choirs, sing, sing, sing!
   When he comes, when he comes,
   who will make him welcome?

2. God in time, God in man,
   this is God's timeless plan:
   he will come, as a man,
   born himself of woman,
   God divinely human:

3. Mary, hail! Though afraid,
   she believed, she obeyed.
   In her womb God is laid:
   till the time expected,
   nurtured and protected:

4. Journey ends! Where afar
   Bethlem shines, like a star,
   stable door stands ajar.
   Unborn Son of Mary,
   Saviour, do not tarry.

407

Arnold Thomas (1848-1924) alt.

1. Lord Christ, who on thy heart didst bear
   the burden of our shame and sin,
   and now on high dost stoop to share
   the fight without, the fear within;

2. Thy patience cannot know defeat,
   thy pity will not be denied,
   thy loving-kindness still is great,
   thy tender mercies still abide.

3. O brother Man, for this we pray,
   thou brother Man and sov'reign Lord,
   that we thy brethren, day by day,
   may follow thee and keep thy word;

4. That we may care, as thou hast cared,
   for sick and lame, for deaf and blind,
   and freely share, as thou hast shared,
   in all the woes of humankind;

5. That ours may be the holy task
   to help and bless, to heal and save;
   this is the happiness we ask,
   and this the service that we crave.
   Amen.

408

George Hugh Bourne (1840-1925)

1. Lord, enthroned in heav'nly splendour,
   first begotten from the dead,
   thou alone, our strong defender,
   liftest up thy people's head.
   Alleluia, alleluia,
   Jesu, true and living bread.

2. Here our humblest homage pay we,
   here in loving rev'rence bow;
   here for faith's discernment pray we,
   lest we fail to know thee now.
   Alleluia, alleluia,
   thou art here, we ask not how.

3. Though the lowliest form doth veil thee
   as of old in Bethlehem,
   here as there thine angels hail thee,
   Branch and Flow'r of Jesse's Stem.
   Alleluia, alleluia,
   we in worship join with them.

4. Paschal Lamb, thine off'ring, finished
   once for all when thou wast slain,
   in its fulness undiminished
   shall for evermore remain.
   Alleluia, alleluia,
   cleansing souls from ev'ry stain.

5. Life-imparting heav'nly manna,
   stricken rock with streaming side,
   heav'n and earth with loud hosanna
   worship thee, the Lamb who died.
   Alleluia, alleluia,
   ris'n, ascended, glorified!

409

Timothy Dudley-Smith (b. 1926)
© Timothy Dudley-Smith

1. Lord for the years
   your love has kept and guided,
   urged and inspired us,
   cheered us on our way,
   sought us and saved us,
   pardoned and provided:
   Lord of the years,
   we bring our thanks today.

2. Lord, for that word,
   the word of life which fires us,
   speaks to our hearts
   and sets our souls ablaze,
   teaches and trains,
   rebukes us and inspires us:
   Lord of the word,
   receive your people's praise.

Continued overleaf

3. Lord, for our land
   in this our generation,
   spirits oppressed by pleasure,
   wealth and care:
   for young and old,
   for commonwealth and nation,
   Lord of our land,
   be pleased to hear our prayer.

4. Lord, for our world;
   when we disown and doubt you,
   loveless in strength,
   and comfortless in pain,
   hungry and helpless,
   lost indeed without you:
   Lord of the world,
   we pray that Christ may reign.

5. Lord for ourselves;
   in living power remake us –
   self on the cross
   and Christ upon the throne,
   past put behind us,
   for the future take us:
   Lord of our lives,
   to live for Christ alone.

410 Sister M. Xavier

1. Lord, for tomorrow and its needs
   I do not pray;
   keep me, my God, from stain of sin,
   just for today.

2. Let me both diligently work
   and duly pray;
   let me be kind in word and deed,
   just for today.

3. Let me no wrong or idle word
   unthinking say;
   set thou a seal upon my lips,
   just for today.

4. And if today my tide of life
   should ebb away,
   give me thy sacraments divine,
   sweet Lord, today.

5. So, for tomorrow and its needs
   I do not pray;
   but keep me, guide me, love me, Lord,
   just for today.

411 Patrick Appleford (b. 1925)
© 1960 Josef Weinberger Ltd.

1. Lord Jesus Christ, you have come to us,
   you are one with us, Mary's Son.
   Cleansing our souls from all their sin,
   pouring your love and goodness in,
   Jesus, our love for you we sing,
   living Lord.

2. Lord Jesus Christ, now and ev'ry day
   teach us how to pray, Son of God.
   You have commanded us to do
   this in remembrance, Lord, of you.
   Into our lives your pow'r breaks through,
   living Lord.

3. Lord Jesus Christ, you have come to us,
   born as one of us, Mary's Son.
   Led out to die on Calvary,
   risen from death to set us free,
   living Lord Jesus, help us see
   you are Lord.

4. Lord Jesus Christ, I would come to you,
   live my life for you, Son of God.
   All your commands I know are true,
   your many gifts will make me new,
   into my life your pow'r breaks through,
   living Lord.

412 Bishop Synesius (375-430)
trans. Allen William Chatfield (1808-1896)

1. Lord Jesus, think on me,
   and purge away my sin;
   from earth-born passions set me free,
   and make me pure within.

2. Lord Jesus, think on me,
   with care and woe opprest;
   let me thy loving servant be
   and taste thy promised rest.

3. Lord Jesus, think on me
   amid the battle's strife;
   in all my pain and misery
   be thou my health and life.

4. Lord Jesus, think on me,
   nor let me go astray;
   through darkness and perplexity
   point thou the heav'nly way.

5. Lord Jesus, think on me,
   when flows the tempest high:
   when on doth rush the enemy,
   O Saviour, be thou nigh.

6. Lord Jesus, think on me,
   that, when the flood is past,
   I may th'eternal brightness see,
   and share thy joy at last.

413 Jan Struther (1901-1953)
© Oxford University Press

1. Lord of all hopefulness,
   Lord of all joy,
   whose trust, ever childlike,
   no cares could destroy,
   be there at our waking,
   and give us, we pray,
   your bliss in our hearts, Lord,
   at the break of the day.

2. Lord of all eagerness,
   Lord of all faith,
   whose strong hands were skilled
   at the plane and the lathe,
   be there at our labours,
   and give us, we pray,
   your strength in our hearts, Lord,
   at the noon of the day.

3. Lord of all kindliness,
   Lord of all grace,
   your hands swift to welcome,
   your arms to embrace,
   be there at our homing,
   and give us, we pray,
   your love in our hearts, Lord,
   at the eve of the day.

4. Lord of all gentleness,
   Lord of all calm,
   whose voice is contentment,
   whose presence is balm,
   be there at our sleeping,
   and give us, we pray,
   your peace in our hearts, Lord,
   at the end of the day.

414 Timothy Dudley-Smith (b. 1926)
© Timothy Dudley-Smith

1. Lord of all life and power
   at whose creative word
   in nature's first primeval hour
   our formless being stirred,
   you made the light to shine,
   O shine on us, we pray,
   renew with light and life divine
   your church in this our day.

2. Lord of the fertile earth
   who caused the world to be,
   whose life alone can bring to birth
   the fruits of land and sea,
   teach us to use aright
   and share the gifts you give,
   to tend the earth as in your sight
   that all the world may live.

3. Lord of the cross and grave
   who died and lives again,
   who came in love to seek and save
   and then to rise and reign,
   we share, as once you shared,
   in mortal birth and breath,
   and ours the risen life that dared
   to vanquish sin and death.

Continued overleaf

4. Lord of the wind and flame,
   the promised Spirit's sign,
   possess our hearts in Jesus' name,
   come down, O Love divine!
   Help us in Christ to grow,
   from sin and self to cease,
   and daily in our lives to show
   your love and joy and peace.

5. Lord of the passing years
   whose changeless purpose stands,
   our lives and loves, our hopes and fears,
   we place within your hands;
   we bring you but your own,
   forgiven, loved and free,
   to follow Christ, and Christ alone,
   through all the days to be.

415 Cyril Argentine Alington (1872-1955)
    © Hymns Ancient & Modern

1. Lord of beauty, thine the splendour
   shown in earth and sky and sea,
   burning sun and moonlight tender,
   hill and river, flow'r and tree:
   lest we fail our praise to render
   touch our eyes that they may see.

2. Lord of wisdom, whom obeying
   mighty waters ebb and flow,
   while unhasting, undelaying,
   planets on their courses go:
   in thy laws thyself displaying,
   teach our minds thyself to know.

3. Lord of life, alone sustaining
   all below and all above,
   Lord of love, by whose ordaining
   sun and stars sublimely move:
   in our earthly spirits reigning,
   lift our hearts that we may love.

4. Lord of beauty, bid us own thee,
   Lord of truth, our footsteps guide,
   till as Love our hearts enthrone thee,
   and, with vision purified,
   Lord of all, when all have known thee,
   thou in all art glorified.

416 Mike Anderson (b. 1956)
    © 1999 Kevin Mayhew Ltd.

Lord of life, Lord of love,
come, fill me with your love.
Lord of life, Lord of love,
come, live now in my heart.

1. You are clothed in majesty,
   you set the waves upon the sea,
   come, wash me anew with your love.

2. You are wrapped in radiant light,
   you are the Lord of day and night,
   come, lighten my life with your love.

3. All my sins you will forgive,
   for you alone I want to live,
   come, take me and fill me again.

417 Philip Pusey (1799-1855), based on the German of
    Matthäus Apelles von Löwenstern (1594-1648) alt.

1. Lord of our life,
   and God of our salvation,
   star of our night,
   and hope of ev'ry nation,
   hear and receive
   thy Church's supplication,
   Lord God almighty.

2. Lord, thou canst help
   when earthly armour faileth,
   Lord, thou canst save
   when deadly sin assaileth;
   Christ, o'er thy rock
   nor death nor hell prevaileth;
   grant us thy peace, Lord.

3. Peace in our hearts,
   our evil thoughts assuaging;
   peace in thy Church,
   where people are engaging;
   peace, when the world
   its busy war is waging:
   calm all our raging.

4. Grant us thy grace
through trial and temptation,
grant us thy truth,
thy promise of salvation,
grant us thy peace
in ev'ry heart and nation,
and in thy heaven.

418 James Montgomery (1771-1854) alt.
© This version 1996 Kevin Mayhew Ltd.

1. Lord, teach us how to pray aright
with rev'rence and with fear;
though fallen sinners in thy sight,
we may, we must, draw near.

2. Our spirits fail through lack of prayer:
O grant us pow'r to pray;
and, when to meet thee we prepare,
Lord, meet us by the way.

3. God of all grace, we bring to thee
a broken, contrite heart;
give what thine eye delights to see,
truth in the inward part;

4. Faith in the only sacrifice
that can for sin atone,
to cast our hopes, to fix our eyes,
on Christ, on Christ alone;

5. Patience to watch and wait and weep,
though mercy long delay;
courage our fainting souls to keep,
and trust in thee alway.

6. Give these, and then thy will be done;
thus, strengthened with all might,
we, through thy Spirit and thy Son,
shall pray, and pray aright.

419 Graham Kendrick (b. 1950)
© 1987 Make Way Music

1. Lord, the light of your love is shining,
in the midst of the darkness, shining;
Jesus, Light of the World, shine upon us,
set us free by the truth you now bring us.
Shine on me, shine on me.

Shine, Jesus, shine,
fill this land with the Father's glory;
blaze, Spirit, blaze,
set our hearts on fire.
Flow, river, flow,
flood the nations with grace and mercy;
send forth your word, Lord,
and let there be light.

2. Lord, I come to your awesome presence,
from the shadows into your radiance;
by the blood I may enter your brightness,
search me, try me, consume all
my darkness.
Shine on me, shine on me.

3. As we gaze on your kingly brightness,
so our faces display your likeness,
ever changing from glory to glory;
mirrored here may our lives tell your story.
Shine on me, shine on me.

420 Henry Williams Baker (1821-1877)

1. Lord, thy word abideth,
and our footsteps guideth;
who its truth believeth
light and joy receiveth.

2. When our foes are near us,
then thy word doth cheer us,
word of consolation,
message of salvation.

3. When the storms are o'er us,
and dark clouds before us,
then its light directeth,
and our way protecteth.

4. Who can tell the pleasure,
who recount the treasure,
by thy word imparted
to the simple-hearted?

5. Word of mercy, giving
succour to the living;
word of life, supplying
comfort to the dying.

Continued overleaf

6. O that we, discerning
   its most holy learning,
   Lord, may love and fear thee,
   evermore be near thee.

421
Marie Lydia Pereira (b. 1920)
© 1999 Kevin Mayhew Ltd.

Lord, unite all nations in your love.
Bless us with your bounty from above.
And may all in heaven one day sing
at the banquet of their Lord and King.

1. Draw us in love, grant us your peace
   that ev'rywhere your Spirit may increase.
   Help us proclaim that all are one in you:
   Lord, unite all nations in your love.

2. Fill us with love, give us your peace,
   let grace abound and charity increase.
   From East to West may all be one in love:
   Lord, unite all nations in your love.

3. Teach us your love, teach us your peace,
   that joy may grow and happiness increase.
   Help us to work to make all nations one;
   Lord, unite all nations in your love.

422
Jean Holloway (b. 1939)
© 1995 Kevin Mayhew Ltd.

1. Lord, we come to ask your healing,
   teach us of love;
   all unspoken shame revealing,
   teach us of love.
   Take our selfish thoughts and actions,
   petty feuds, divisive factions,
   hear us now to you appealing,
   teach us of love.

2. Soothe away our pain and sorrow,
   hold us in love;
   grace we cannot buy or borrow,
   hold us in love.
   Though we see but dark and danger,
   though we spurn both friend and stranger,
   though we often dread tomorrow,
   hold us in love.

3. When the bread is raised and broken,
   fill us with love;
   words of consecration spoken,
   fill us with love.
   As our grateful prayers continue,
   make the faith that we have in you
   more than just an empty token,
   fill us with love.

4. Help us live for one another,
   bind us in love;
   stranger, neighbour, father, mother –
   bind us in love.
   All are equal at your table,
   through your Spirit make us able
   to embrace as sister, brother,
   bind us in love.

423
Nick Fawcett (b. 1957)
© 1999 Kevin Mayhew Ltd

1. Lord, we know that we have failed you,
   false and foolish in so much,
   loath to listen to your guidance,
   slow to recognise your touch.
   Though we keep you at a distance,
   by our side, Lord, still remain;
   cleanse our hearts, renew our spirits,
   give us grace to start again.

2. Lord, we know that we have failed you
   through the things we do and say,
   though we claim to care for others
   we have thrust their needs away.
   Too concerned with our own comfort
   we have added to their pain;
   teach us to show faith in action,
   give us grace to start again.

3. Lord, we know that we have failed you,
   full of doubt when life's been hard;
   suffering has sapped our vision,
   sorrow left our spirits scarred.
   Faced by bitter disappointment
   faith has buckled under strain;
   help us know your hand upon us,
   give us grace to start again.

4. Lord, we know that we have failed you,
   too familiar with your word,
   even though you've spoken clearly
   all too often we've not heard.
   Closed to truths which stretch horizons
   or which go against the grain –
   teach us, Lord, to stop and listen,
   give us grace to start again.

5. Lord, we know that we have failed you,
   lives too fraught to stop and stare;
   dwelling always on the present –
   what to eat or drink or wear.
   Teach us first to seek your kingdom,
   in our hearts for ever reign;
   send us out, restored, forgiven,
   give us grace to start again.

424 Martin E. Leckebusch (b. 1962)

1. Lord, we thank you for the promise
   seen in ev'ry human birth:
   you have planned each new beginning –
   who could hope for greater worth?
   Hear our pray'r for those we cherish;
   claim our children as your own:
   in the fertile ground of childhood
   may eternal seed be sown.

2. Lord, we thank you for the vigour
   burning in the years of youth:
   strength to face tomorrow's challenge,
   zest for life and zeal for truth.
   In the choice of friends and partners,
   when ideas and values form,
   may the message of your kingdom
   be the guide, the goal, the norm.

3. Lord, we thank you for the harvest
   of the settled, middle years:
   times when work and home can prosper,
   when life's richest fruit appears;
   but when illness, stress and hardship
   fill so many days with dread,
   may your love renew the vision
   of a clearer road ahead.

4. Lord, we thank you for the beauty
   of a heart at last mature:
   crowned with peace and rich in wisdom,
   well-respected and secure;
   but to those who face the twilight
   frail, bewildered, lacking friends,
   Lord, confirm your gracious offer:
   perfect life which never ends.

425 Susan Sayers (b. 1946)

1. Lord, when I turn my back on you
   the fears and darkness grow.
   I need you, oh I need you, Lord,
   to show me where to go.

2. With you beside me, Lord, I find
   the evils that I face
   become instead a joyfulness,
   a fountain of your grace.

3. So shape me to your purpose, Lord,
   and tell me what to do;
   and if I start to turn away,
   then turn me back to you.

4. And when the world is over Lord,
   or over just for me,
   there is nowhere but with you, Lord,
   that I would rather be.

426 Edwin Le Grice (1911-1992)

1. Lord, your voice in Eden's garden
   in the cool of ev'ry day
   echoes still, among the olives,
   calling us to watch and pray.
   Christ, our glorious Easter gard'ner,
   list'ning daily to your voice,
   in the life of resurrection may we here
   and now rejoice.

Continued overleaf

2. Here we meet you, risen Saviour,
   in the marvels of your earth:
   in the trust of little children
   see the wonder of your birth:
   here in sweat of daily labour,
   here in love of man and wife,
   here in strength of mind and body
   share your resurrection life.

3. In unlimited forgiveness
   ready to receive and give,
   open handed, open hearted,
   show your servants how to live,
   bearing sin, enduring suff'ring,
   sharing joy, accepting pain,
   learning, risen Lord and Master,
   how to die and rise again.

4. From this earth to heav'n ascending
   by the ladder of our love,
   here your angels, Lord, surround us,
   op'ning doors to realms above.
   Here, in stillness of your presence,
   knowing that we are your own,
   may the dawn of resurrection
   break upon us, Love Unknown.

427 Christina Georgina Rossetti (1830-1894)

1. Love came down at Christmas,
   Love all lovely Love divine;
   Love was born at Christmas,
   star and angels gave the sign.

2. Worship we the Godhead,
   Love incarnate, Love divine;
   worship we our Jesus:
   but wherewith for sacred sign?

3. Love shall be our token,
   love be yours and love be mine,
   love to God and all men,
   love for plea and gift and sign.

428 Charles Wesley (1707-1788)

1. Love divine, all loves excelling,
   joy of heav'n, to earth come down,
   fix in us thy humble dwelling,
   all thy faithful mercies crown.

2. Jesu, thou art all compassion,
   pure unbounded love thou art;
   visit us with thy salvation,
   enter ev'ry trembling heart.

3. Breathe, O breathe thy loving Spirit
   into ev'ry troubled breast;
   let us all in thee inherit,
   let us find thy promised rest.

4. Take away the love of sinning,
   Alpha and Omega be;
   end of faith, as its beginning,
   set our hearts at liberty.

5. Come, almighty to deliver,
   let us all thy grace receive;
   suddenly return, and never,
   never more thy temples leave.

6. Thee we would be always blessing,
   serve thee as thy hosts above;
   pray, and praise thee without ceasing,
   glory in thy perfect love.

7. Finish then thy new creation,
   pure and spotless let us be;
   let us see thy great salvation
   perfectly restored in thee.

8. Changed from glory into glory,
   till in heav'n we take our place,
   till we cast our crowns before thee,
   lost in wonder, love, and praise.

429 Luke Connaughton (1917-1979)
© *McCrimmon Publishing Co. Ltd.*

1. Love is his word, love is his way,
   feasting with all, fasting alone,
   living and dying, rising again,
   love only love, is his way.

   Richer than gold is the love of my Lord:
   better than splendour and wealth.

2. Love is his way, love is his mark,
   sharing his last Passover feast,
   Christ at the table, host to the twelve,
   love, only love, is his mark.

3. Love is his mark, love is his sign,
   bread for our strength, wine for our joy,
   'This is my body, this is my blood.'
   Love, only love, is his sign.

4. Love is his sign, love is his news,
   'Do this,' he said, 'lest you forget
   all my deep sorrow, all my dear blood.'
   Love, only love, is his news.

5. Love is his news, love is his name,
   we are his own, chosen and called,
   family, brethren, cousins and kin.
   Love, only love, is his name.

6. Love is his name, love is his law,
   hear his command, all who are his,
   'Love one another, I have loved you.'
   Love, only love, is his law.

7. Love is his law, love is his word:
   love of the Lord, Father and Word,
   love of the Spirit, God ever one,
   love, only love, is his word.

430 Michael Forster (b. 1946)
© *1997 Kevin Mayhew Ltd.*

1. Love is the only law
   for God and humankind,
   love your God with all your heart,
   your strength and soul and mind.
   Love your neighbour as yourself,

of ev'ry creed and race,
turn the water of endless laws
into the wine of grace.

Love is God's only law,
love is God's only law;
love is God's wisdom,
love is God's strength,
love of such height,
such depth, such length,
love is God's only law.

2. Give to the poor a voice
   and help the blind to see,
   feed the hungry, heal the sick
   and set the captive free.
   All that God requires of you
   will then fall into place,
   turn the water of endless laws
   into the wine of grace.

3. Let love like fountains flow
   and justice like a stream,
   faith become reality
   and hope your constant theme.
   Then shall freedom, joy and peace
   with righteousness embrace,
   turn the water of endless laws
   into the wine of grace.

431 Pamela Hayes
© *1998 Kevin Mayhew Ltd.*

1. Lovely in your littleness,
   longing for our lowliness,
   longing for our lowliness,
   searching for our meekness:
   Jesus is our joy, Jesus is our joy.

2. Peace within our powerlessness,
   hope within our helplessness,
   hope within our helplessness,
   love within our loneliness:
   Jesus is our joy, Jesus is our joy.

Continued overleaf

3. Held in Mary's tenderness,
   tiny hands are raised to bless,
   tiny hands are raised to bless,
   touching us with God's caress:
   Jesus is our joy, Jesus is our joy.

4. Joy, then, in God's graciousness,
   peace comes with gentleness,
   peace comes with gentleness,
   filling hearts with gladness:
   Jesus is our joy, Jesus is our joy.

432 Robert Bridges (1844-1930)
based on 'Amor Patris et Filii' (12th century) alt.
© *Copyright control*

1. Love of the Father,
   love of God the Son,
   from whom all came,
   in whom was all begun;
   who formest heav'nly
   beauty out of strife,
   creation's whole desire
   and breath of life.

2. Thou the all-holy,
   thou supreme in might,
   thou dost give peace,
   thy presence maketh right;
   thou with thy favour
   all things dost enfold,
   with thine all-kindness
   free from harm wilt hold.

3. Hope of all comfort,
   splendour of all aid,
   that dost not fail
   nor leave the heart afraid:
   to all that cry thou dost
   all help accord,
   the angels' armour,
   and the saints' reward.

4. Purest and highest,
   wisest and most just,
   there is no truth save
   only in thy trust;
   thou dost the mind
   from earthly dreams recall,
   and bring, through Christ,
   to him for whom are all.

5. Eternal glory,
   let the world adore,
   who art and shalt be
   worshipped evermore:
   us whom thou madest,
   comfort with thy might,
   and lead us to enjoy
   thy heav'nly light.

433 Charles Wesley (1707-1788)

1. Love's redeeming work is done;
   fought the fight, the battle won:
   lo, our Sun's eclipse is o'er,
   lo, he sets in blood no more.

2. Vain the stone, the watch, the seal;
   Christ has burst the gates of hell;
   death in vain forbids his rise;
   Christ has opened paradise.

3. Lives again our glorious King;
   where, O death, is now thy sting?
   Dying once, he all doth save;
   where thy victory, O grave?

4. Soar we now where Christ has led,
   foll'wing our exalted Head;
   made like him, like him we rise;
   ours the cross, the grave, the skies.

5. Hail the Lord of earth and heav'n!
   praise to thee by both be giv'n;
   thee we greet triumphant now;
   hail, the Resurrection thou!

434
Jane Elizabeth Leeson (1809-1881)

1. Loving shepherd of thy sheep,
   keep me, Lord, in safety keep;
   nothing can thy pow'r withstand,
   none can pluck me from thy hand.

2. Loving shepherd, thou didst give
   thine own life that I might live;
   may I love thee day by day,
   gladly thy sweet will obey.

3. Loving shepherd, ever near,
   teach me still thy voice to hear;
   suffer not my steps to stray
   from the straight and narrow way.

4. Where thou leadest may I go,
   walking in thy steps below;
   then, before thy Father's throne,
   Jesu, claim me for thine own.

435
Robert Lowry (1826-1899)

1. Low in the grave he lay,
   Jesus, my Saviour;
   waiting the coming day,
   Jesus, my Lord.

   Up from the grave he arose,
   with a mighty triumph o'er his foes;
   he arose a victor
   from the dark domain,
   and he lives for ever
   with his saints to reign.
   He arose! He arose!
   Hallelujah! Christ arose!

2. Vainly they watch his bed,
   Jesus, my Saviour;
   vainly they seal the dead,
   Jesus, my Lord.

3. Death cannot keep its prey,
   Jesus, my Saviour;
   he tore the bars away,
   Jesus, my Lord.

436
Jack W. Hayford (b. 1934)
© Rocksmith Music Inc./Leosong Copyright Service Ltd.

Majesty, worship his majesty;
unto Jesus be glory, honour and praise.
Majesty, kingdom authority
flow from his throne unto his own:
his anthem raise.
So exalt, lift up on high the name of Jesus;
magnify, come glorify Christ Jesus the King.
Majesty, worship his majesty,
Jesus who died, now glorified,
King of all kings.

437
Sebastian Temple (1928-1997)
based on the Prayer of St Francis
© 1967 OCP Publications

1. Make me a channel of your peace.
   Where there is hatred, let me bring
      your love.
   Where there is injury, your pardon, Lord;
   and where there's doubt, true faith in you.

   O, Master, grant that I may never seek
   so much to be consoled as to console,
   to be understood as to understand,
   to be loved as to love with all my soul.

2. Make me a channel of your peace.
   Where there's despair in life, let me
      bring hope.
   Where there is darkness, only light,
   and where there's sadness, ever joy.

3. Make me a channel of your peace.
   It is in pardoning that we are pardoned,
   in giving of ourselves that we receive,
   and in dying that we're born to eternal life.

438
Graham Kendrick (b. 1950)
© 1986 Kingsway's Thankyou Music

1. Make way, make way, for Christ the King
   in splendour arrives;
   fling wide the gates and welcome him
   into your lives.

Continued overleaf

Make way (make way), make way (make way),
for the King of kings (for the King of kings);
make way (make way), make way (make way),
and let his kingdom in!

2. He comes the broken hearts to heal,
   the pris'ners to free;
   the deaf shall hear, the lame shall dance,
   the blind shall see.

3. And those who mourn with heavy hearts,
   who weep and sigh,
   with laughter, joy and royal crown
   he'll beautify.

4. We call you now to worship him
   as Lord of all,
   to have no gods before him,
   their thrones must fall.

439 Philipp Bliss (1838-1876) alt.

1. Man of sorrows! What a name
   for the Son of God who came
   ruined sinners to reclaim!
   Alleluia! What a Saviour!

2. Bearing shame and scoffing rude,
   in my place condemned he stood;
   sealed my pardon with his blood;
   Alleluia! What a Saviour!

3. Guilty, vile and helpless we;
   spotless Lamb of God was he:
   full atonement – can it be?
   Alleluia! What a Saviour!

4. Lifted up was he to die:
   'It is finished!' was his cry;
   now in heav'n exalted high;
   Alleluia! What a Saviour!

5. When he comes, our glorious King,
   all his ransomed home to bring,
   then anew this song we'll sing:
   Alleluia! what a Saviour!

440 William Wright (1859-1924)

1. March on, my soul, with strength,
   march forward void of fear;
   he who has led will lead
   while year succeeds to year;
   and as you travel on your way,
   his hand shall hold you day by day.

2. March on, my soul, with strength;
   in ease you dare not dwell;
   high duty calls you forth;
   then up, and serve him well!
   Take up your cross, take your sword,
   and fight the battles of your Lord!

3. March on, my soul, with strength,
   with strength, but not your own;
   the conquest you will gain
   through Christ your Lord alone;
   his grace shall nerve your feeble arm,
   his love preserve you safe from harm.

4. March on, my soul, with strength,
   from strength to strength march on;
   warfare shall end at length,
   all foes be overthrown.
   And then, my soul, if faithful now,
   the crown of life awaits your brow.

441 Michael Forster (b. 1946)
© 1996 Kevin Mayhew Ltd.

1. Mary, blessed grieving mother,
   waiting by the cross of shame,
   through your patient, prayerful vigil,
   kindle hope's eternal flame;
   crying in the pains of earth,
   singing of redemption's birth.

2. Where the crosses of the nations
   darken still the noon-day skies,
   see the sad madonna weeping
   through a million mothers' eyes.
   Holy Mary, full of grace,
   all our tears with yours embrace.

3. Standing with the suff'ring Saviour,
   still oppressed by hate and fear,
   where the gentle still are murdered
   and protestors disappear:
   mother of the crucified,
   call his people to your side!

4. Holy mother, watching, waiting,
   for the saving of the earth;
   in the loneliness of dying,
   speak of hope and human worth,
   there for all the world to see,
   lifted up at Calvary!

442
Michael Forster (b. 1946)
© 1996 Kevin Mayhew Ltd.

1. Mary, blessed teenage mother,
   with what holy joy you sing!
   Humble, yet above all other,
   from your womb shall healing spring.
   Out of wedlock pregnant found,
   full of grace with blessing crowned.

2. Mother of the homeless stranger
   only outcasts recognise,
   point us to the modern manger;
   not a sight for gentle eyes!
   Oh the joyful news we tell:
   'Even here, Immanuel!'

3. Now, throughout the townships ringing,
   hear the black madonna cry,
   songs of hope and freedom singing,
   poor and humble lifted high.
   Here the Spirit finds a womb
   for the breaker of the tomb!

4. Holy mother, for the nations
   bring to birth the child divine:
   Israel's strength and consolation,
   and the hope of Palestine!
   All creation reconciled
   in the crying of a child!

443
West Indian Spiritual
© 1999 Kevin Mayhew Ltd.

1. Mary had a baby, yes, Lord,
   Mary had a baby, yes, my Lord,
   Mary had a baby, yes, Lord,
   the people came to Bethlehem
   to see her son.

2. What did she name him, yes, Lord? *(x3)*

3. Mary named him Jesus, yes, Lord *(x3)*

4. Where was he born, yes, Lord? *(x3)*

5. Born in a stable, yes, Lord *(x3)*

6. Where did she lay him, yes, Lord? *(x3)*

7. Laid him in a manger, yes, Lord *(x3)*

444
Cliff Barrows
© 1982 Cliff Barrows. Used by permission

May God's blessing surround you *each
day,
as you trust him and walk in his way.
May his presence within guard and keep
you from sin,
go in peace, go in joy, go in love.

 * *Alternative - tonight*

445
Graham Kendrick (b. 1950)
© 1986 Kingsway's Thankyou Music

1. May the fragrance of Jesus fill this place
   (may the fragrance of Jesus fill this place).
   May the fragrance of Jesus fill this place.
   (Lovely fragrance of Jesus),
   rising from the sacrifice
   of lives laid down in adoration.

2. May the glory of Jesus fill his church
   (may the glory of Jesus fill his church).
   May the glory of Jesus fill his church.
   (Radiant glory of Jesus),
   shining from our faces
   as we gaze in adoration.

3. May the beauty of Jesus fill my life.
(may the beauty of Jesus fill my life).
May the beauty of Jesus fill my life
(Perfect beauty of Jesus),
fill my thoughts, my words, my deeds;
may I give in adoration.
Fill my thoughts, my words, my deeds;
may I give in adoration.

446
John Newton (1725-1807)
based on 2 Corinthians 13:14

1. May the grace of Christ our Saviour,
and the Father's boundless love,
with the Holy Spirit's favour,
rest upon us from above.

2. Thus may we abide in union
with each other and the Lord,
and possess, in sweet communion,
joys which earth cannot afford.

447
Kate Barclay Wilkinson (1859-1928)

1. May the mind of Christ my Saviour
live in me from day to day,
by his love and pow'r controlling
all I do and say.

2. May the word of God dwell richly
in my heart from hour to hour,
so that I may triumph only
in his saving pow'r.

3. May the peace of God my Father
rule my life in ev'rything,
that I may be calm to comfort
sick and sorrowing.

4. May the love of Jesus fill me,
as the waters fill the sea;
him exalting, self abasing,
this is victory.

5. May I run the race before me,
strong and brave to face the foe,
looking only unto Jesus,
as I onward go.

448
Graham Kendrick (b. 1950)
© 1986 Kingsway's Thankyou Music

1. Meekness and majesty,
manhood and deity,
in perfect harmony, the Man who is God.
Lord of eternity dwells in humanity,
kneels in humility and washes our feet.

O what a mystery, meekness and majesty.
Bow down and worship for this is your God,
this is your God.

2. Father's pure radiance,
perfect in innocence,
yet learns obedience to death on a cross.
Suff'ring to give us life,
conqu'ring through sacrifice,
and as they crucify prays: 'Father forgive.'

3. Wisdom unsearchable,
God the invisible,
love indestructible in frailty appears.
Lord of infinity, stooping so tenderly,
lifts our humanity to the heights of
his throne.

449
Julia Ward Howe (1819-1910) alt.
© 1992, 1994 Kevin Mayhew Ltd.

1. Mine eyes have seen the glory
of the coming of the Lord.
He is tramping out the vintage
where the grapes of wrath are stored.
He has loosed the fateful lightning
of his terrible swift sword.
His truth is marching on.

Glory, glory hallelujah!
Glory, glory hallelujah!
Glory, glory hallelujah!
His truth is marching on.

2. I have seen him in the watchfires
of a hundred circling camps.
They have gilded him an altar
in the evening dews and damps.
I can read his righteous sentence
by the dim and flaring lamps.
His day is marching on.

3. He has sounded forth the trumpet
   that shall never sound retreat.
   He is sifting out all human hearts
   before his judgement seat.
   O, be swift my soul to answer him,
   be jubilant my feet!
   Our God is marching on.

4. In the beauty of the lilies
   Christ was born across the sea,
   with a glory in his bosom
   that transfigures you and me.
   As he died to make us holy,
   let us live that all be free,
   whilst God is marching on.

Eleanor Farjeon (1881-1965)
© David Higham Associates. Used by permission from
'The Children's Bells' published by Oxford University Press

450

1. Morning has broken like the first morning,
   blackbird has spoken like the first bird.
   Praise for the singing!
       Praise for the morning!
   Praise for them, springing
       fresh from the Word!

2. Sweet the rain's new fall, sunlit from heaven,
   like the first dew-fall on the first grass.
   Praise for the sweetness of the wet garden,
   sprung in completeness where his feet pass.

3. Mine is the sunlight! Mine is the morning
   born of the one light Eden saw play!
   Praise with elation, praise ev'ry morning,
   God's re-creation of the new day!

451 Estelle White (b. 1925)
© McCrimmon Publishing Co. Ltd.

1. 'Moses, I know you're the man,'
   the Lord said.
   'You're going to work out my plan,'
   the Lord said.
   'Lead all the Israelites out of slavery,
   and I shall make them a wandering race
   called the people of God.'

So ev'ry day we're on our way,
for we're a travelling, wandering race
called the people of God.

2. 'Don't get too set in your ways,'
   the Lord said.
   'Each step is only a phase,'
   the Lord said.
   'I'll go before you and I shall be a sign
   to guide my travelling, wandering race.
   You're the people of God.'

3. 'No matter what you may do,'
   the Lord said,
   'I shall be faithful and true,'
   the Lord said.
   'My love will strengthen you as you go along,
   for you're my travelling, wandering race.
   You're the people of God.'

4. 'Look at the birds in the air,'
   the Lord said.
   'They fly unhampered by care,'
   the Lord said.
   'You will move easier if you're trav'lling
       light,
   for you're a wandering, vagabond race.'
   You're the people of God.'

5. 'Foxes have places to go,'
   the Lord said.
   'but I've no home here below,'
   the Lord said.
   'So if you want to be with me all
       your days,
   keep up the moving and travelling on.
   You're the people of God.'

452 Edmund Spenser (1552-1599)

1. Most glorious Lord of life, that on
       this day
   didst make thy triumph over death
       and sin,
   and having harrowed hell, didst
       bring away
   captivity thence captive, us to win:

Continued overleaf

2. This joyous day, dear Lord, with
     joy begin,
   and grant that we for whom thou
     didst die,
   being with thy dear blood clean washed
     from sin,
   May live for ever in felicity:

3. And that thy love we weighing worthily,
   may likewise love thee for the same again;
   and for thy sake, that all like dear
     didst buy,
   with love may one another entertain;

4. So let us love, dear Love, like as we
     ought;
   love is the lesson which the Lord
     us taught.

453 Ray Palmer (1808-1887)

1. My faith looks up to thee,
   thou Lamb of Calvary,
   Saviour divine!
   Now hear me while I pray,
   take all my guilt away,
   O let me from this day
   be wholly thine.

2. May thy rich grace impart
   strength to my fainting heart,
   my zeal inspire.
   As thou hast died for me,
   O may my love to thee
   pure, warm and changeless be,
   a living fire.

3. While life's dark maze I tread,
   and griefs around me spread,
   be thou my guide;
   bid darkness turn to day,
   wipe sorrow's tears away,
   nor let me ever stray
   from thee aside.

4. When ends life's transient dream,
   when death's cold sullen stream
   shall o'er me roll,
   blest Saviour, then in love,
   fear and distrust remove;
   O bear me safe above,
   a ransomed soul.

454 Henry Williams Baker (1821-1877)

1. My Father, for another night
   of quiet sleep and rest,
   for all the joy of morning light,
   thy holy name be blest.

2. Now with the new-born day I give
   myself anew to thee,
   that as thou willest I may live,
   and what thou willest be.

3. Whate'er I do, things great or small,
   whate'er I speak or frame,
   thy glory may I seek in all,
   do all in Jesus' name.

4. My Father, for his sake, I pray,
   thy child accept and bless;
   and lead me by thy grace today
   in paths of righteousness.

455 Matthew Bridges (1800-1894)

1. My God, accept my heart this day,
   and make it wholly thine,
   that I from thee no more may stray,
   no more from thee decline.

2. Before the cross of him who died,
   behold, I prostrate fall;
   let ev'ry sin be crucified,
   and Christ be all in all.

3. Anoint me with thy heav'nly grace,
   and seal me for thine own,
   that I may see thy glorious face,
   and worship at thy throne.

4. Let ev'ry thought and work and word
   to thee be ever giv'n.
   then life shall be thy service, Lord,
   and death the gate of heav'n.

5. All glory to the Father be,
   all glory to the Son,
   all glory, Holy Ghost, to thee,
   while endless ages run.

456 Philip Doddridge (1702-1751), alt.
v 3 Michael Forster (b. 1946)
© 1996 Kevin Mayhew Ltd.

1. My God, and is thy table spread,
   and does thy cup with love o'erflow?
   Thither be all thy children led,
   and let them all thy sweetness know.

2. Hail, sacred feast, which Jesus makes!
   Rich banquet of his flesh and blood!
   Thrice happy all, who here partake
   that sacred stream, that heav'nly food.

3. What wondrous love! What perfect grace,
   for Jesus, our exalted host,
   invites us to this special place
   who offer least and need the most.

4. O let thy table honoured be,
   and furnished well with joyful guests;
   and may each soul salvation see,
   that here its sacred pledges tastes.

457 Frederick William Faber (1814-1863), alt.
© Jubilate Hymns

1. My God, how wonderful you are,
   your majesty how bright;
   how beautiful your mercy-seat,
   in depths of burning light!

2. Creator from eternal years
   and everlasting Lord,
   by holy angels day and night
   unceasingly adored!

3. How wonderful, how beautiful
   the sight of you must be –
   your endless wisdom, boundless power,
   and awesome purity!

4. O how I fear you, living God,
   with deepest, tenderest fears,
   and worship you with trembling hope
   and penitential tears!

5. But I may love you too, O Lord,
   though you are all-divine,
   for you have stooped to ask of me
   this feeble love of mine.

6. Father of Jesus, love's reward,
   great King upon your throne,
   what joy to see you as you are
   and know as I am known.

458 Latin (17th century)
trans. Edward Caswall (1814-1878)

1. My God, I love thee; not because
   I hope for heav'n thereby,
   nor yet because who love thee not
   are lost eternally.

2. Thou, O my Jesus, thou didst me
   upon the cross embrace;
   for me didst bear the nails and spear,
   and manifold disgrace.

3. And griefs and torments numberless,
   and sweat of agony;
   yea, death itself – and all for me
   who was thine enemy.

4. Then why, O blessèd Jesu Christ,
   should I not love thee well?
   Not for the sake of winning heav'n,
   nor of escaping hell.

5. Not from the hope of gaining aught,
   not seeking a reward;
   but as thyself hast lovèd me,
   O ever-loving Lord.

6. So would I love thee, dearest Lord,
   and in thy praise will sing;
   solely because thou art my God,
   and my most loving King.

459

Philip Doddridge (1702-1751)

1. My gracious Lord, I own thy right
   to every service I can pay;
   and call it my supreme delight
   to hear thy dictates and obey.

2. What is my being but for thee,
   its sure support, its noblest end,
   thy ever-smiling face to see
   and serve the cause of such a friend?

3. I would not breathe for worldly joy,
   or to increase my worldly good,
   nor future days or powers employ
   to spread a sounding name abroad;

4. But to my Saviour I would live,
   to him who for my ransom died;
   nor could untainted Eden give
   such bliss as blossoms at his side.

5. His work my later years shall bless,
   when youthful vigour is no more,
   and my last hour of life confess
   his love has animating pow'r.

460

Robin Mark
© 1996 Daybreak Music Ltd.

1. My heart will sing to you
   because of your great love,
   a love so rich, so pure,
   a love beyond compare;
   the wilderness, the barren place,
   become a blessing
   in the warmth of your embrace.

   May my heart sing your praise for ever,
   may my voice lift your name, my God;
   may my soul know no other treasure
   than your love, than your love.

2. When earthly wisdom dims
   the light of knowing you,
   or if my search for understanding
   clouds your way,
   to you I fly, my hiding-place,
   where revelation
   is beholding face to face.

461

Darlene Zschech
© 1993 Darlene Zschech /Hillsong Music
Australia/Kingsway's Thankyou Music

1. My Jesus, my Saviour,
   Lord, there is none like you.
   All of my days I want to praise
   the wonders of your mighty love.

2. My comfort, my shelter,
   tower of refuge and strength,
   let ev'ry breath, all that I am,
   never cease to worship you.

3. Shout to the Lord,
   all the earth, let us sing
   power and majesty,
   praise to the King.
   Mountains bow down
   and the seas will roar
   at the sound of your name.

4. I sing for joy
   at the work of your hands.
   Forever I'll love you,
   forever I'll stand.
   Nothing compares to the promise
   I have in you.

462

Graham Kendrick (b. 1950)
© 1989 Make Way Music

1. My Lord, what love is this,
   that pays so dearly,
   that I, the guilty one,
   may go free!

   Amazing love, O what sacrifice,
   the Son of God, giv'n for me.
   My debt he pays, and my death he dies,
   that I might live,
   that I might live.

2. And so they watched him die,
   despised, rejected;
   but O, the blood he shed
   flowed for me!

3. And now this love of Christ
   shall flow like rivers;
   come, wash your guilt away,
   live again!

463

Samuel Crossman (c. 1624-1684) alt.

1. My song is love unknown,
   my Saviour's love to me,
   love to the loveless shown,
   that they might lovely be.
   O who am I, that for my sake,
   my Lord should take frail flesh and die?

2. He came from his blest throne,
   salvation to bestow;
   but man refused, and none
   the longed-for Christ would know.
   But O, my friend, my friend indeed,
   who at my need his life did spend!

3. Sometimes they strew his way,
   and his sweet praises sing:
   resounding all the day
   hosannas to their King:
   then 'Crucify'! is all their breath,
   and for his death they thirst and cry.

4. Why what hath my Lord done?
   What makes this rage and spite?
   He made the lame to run,
   he gave the blind their sight.
   Sweet injuries! Yet they at these
   themselves displease,
       and 'gainst him rise.

5. They rise, and needs will have
   my dear Lord made away;
   a murderer they save,
   the Prince of Life they slay.
   Yet cheerful he to suff'ring goes,
   that he his foes from thence might free.

6. Here might I stay and sing,
   no story so divine;
   never was love, dear King,
   never was grief like thine.
   This is my friend in whose sweet praise
   I all my days could gladly spend.

464

Henry Vaughan (1622-1695)

1. My soul, there is a country
   far beyond the stars,
   where stands a wingèd sentry
   all skilful in the wars.

2. There above noise, and danger,
   sweet peace sits crowned with smiles,
   and one born in a manger
   commands the beauteous files.

3. He is thy gracious Friend,
   and - O my soul, awake! -
   did in pure love descend,
   to die here for thy sake.

4. If thou canst get but thither,
   there grows the flow'r of peace,
   the Rose that cannot wither,
   thy fortress and thy ease.

5. Leave then thy foolish ranges,
   for none can thee secure
   but one who never changes,
   thy God, thy life, thy cure.

465

Timothy Dudley-Smith (b. 1926)
© Timothy Dudley-Smith

1. Name of all majesty,
   fathomless mystery,
   King of the ages
   by angels adored;
   power and authority,
   splendour and dignity,
   bow to his mastery –
   Jesus is Lord!

2. Child of our destiny,
   God from eternity,
   love of the Father
   on sinners outpoured;
   see now what God has done
   sending his only Son,
   Christ the beloved One,
   Jesus is Lord!

Continued overleaf

3. Saviour of Calvary,
   costliest victory,
   darkness defeated
   and Eden restored;
   born as a man to die,
   nailed to a cross on high,
   cold in the grave to lie,
   Jesus is Lord!

4. Source of all sovereignty,
   light, immortality,
   life everlasting
   and heaven assured;
   so with the ransomed, we
   praise him eternally,
   Christ in his majesty,
   Jesus is Lord!

466 Sarah Flower Adams (1805-1848)

1. Nearer, my God, to thee,
   nearer to thee!
   E'en though it be a cross
   that raiseth me:
   still all my song would be,
   'Nearer, my God, to thee,
   nearer to thee.'

2. Though, like the wanderer,
   the sun gone down,
   darkness be over me,
   my rest a stone;
   yet in my dreams I'd be
   nearer, my God, to thee,
   nearer to thee!

3. There let the way appear,
   steps unto heav'n;
   all that thou sendest me
   in mercy giv'n:
   angels to beckon me
   nearer, my God, to thee,
   nearer to thee!

4. Then, with my waking thoughts
   bright with thy praise,
   out of my stony griefs
   Bethel I'll raise;
   so by my woes to be
   nearer, my God, to thee,
   nearer to thee!

5. Or if on joyful wing
   cleaving the sky,
   sun, moon and stars forgot,
   upwards I fly,
   still all my song shall be,
   'Nearer, my God, to thee,
   nearer to thee.'

467 John Keble (1792-1866) based on Lamentations 3:23

1. New ev'ry morning is the love
   our wak'ning and uprising prove;
   through sleep and darkness safely
     brought,
   restored to life and pow'r and thought.

2. New mercies, each returning day,
   hover around us while we pray;
   new perils past, new sins forgiv'n,
   new thoughts of God, new hopes of
     heav'n.

3. If on our daily course our mind
   be set to hallow all we find,
   new treasures still, of countless price,
   God will provide for sacrifice.

4. Old friends, old scenes, will lovelier be,
   as more of heav'n in each we see;
   some soft'ning gleam of love and prayer
   shall dawn on ev'ry cross and care.

5. The trivial round, the common task,
   will furnish all we need to ask,
   room to deny ourselves, a road
   to bring us daily nearer God.

6. Only, O Lord, in thy dear love
   fit us for perfect rest above;
   and help us, this and ev'ry day,
   to live more nearly as we pray.

468
Erik Routley (1917-1982)
© 1974 Hope Publishing Co

1. New songs of celebration render
   to him who has great wonders done.
   Love sits enthroned in ageless
      splendour:
   come and adore the mighty one.
   He has made known his great salvation
   which all his friends with joy confess:
   he has revealed to ev'ry nation
   his everlasting righteousness.

2. Joyfully, heartily resounding,
   let ev'ry instrument and voice
   peal out the praise of grace abounding,
   calling the whole world to rejoice.
   Trumpets and organs, set in motion
   such sounds as make the heavens ring;
   all things that live in earth and ocean,
   make music for your mighty King.

3. Rivers and seas and torrents roaring,
   honour the Lord with wild acclaim;
   mountains and stones look up adoring
   and find a voice to praise his name.
   Righteous, commanding, ever glorious,
   praises be his that never cease:
   just is our God, whose truth victorious
   establishes the world in peace.

469
Mike Anderson (b. 1956)
© 1999 Kevin Mayhew Ltd.

Now I know what love is,
now I know your Spirit is here,
living deep within me,
now I know love is real.

1. Death could never hide your love:
   your love lifts me high.

2. Darkness will not hide your love,
   shining like a star.

3. What could ever quench your love,
   love that changes hearts.

470
George Wallace Briggs (1875-1959) alt.
© Oxford University Press

1. Now is eternal life,
   if ris'n with Christ we stand,
   in him to life reborn,
   and held within his hand;
   no more we fear death's ancient dread,
   in Christ arisen from the dead.

2. The human mind so long
   brooded o'er life's brief span;
   was it, O God, for naught,
   for naught that life began?
   Thou art our hope, our vital breath;
   shall hope undying end in death?

3. And God, the living God,
   stooped down to share our state;
   by death destroying death,
   Christ opened wide life's gate.
   He lives, who died; he reigns on high;
   who lives in him shall never die.

4. Unfathomed love divine,
   reign thou within my heart;
   from thee nor depth nor height,
   nor life nor death can part;
   my life is hid in God with thee,
   now and through all eternity.

5. Thee will I love and serve
   now in time's passing day;
   thy hand shall hold me fast
   when time is done away,
   in God's unknown eternal spheres
   to serve him through eternal years.

471
Fred Kaan (1929)
© 1968 Stainer & Bell Ltd

1. Now join we, to praise the Creator,
   our voices in worship and song;
   we stand to recall with thanksgiving
   that to God all seasons belong.

2. We thank you, O Source of all goodness,
   for the joy and abundance of crops,
   for food that is stored in our larders,
   for all we can buy in the shops.

3. But also of need and starvation
   we sing with concern and despair,
   of skills that are used for destruction,
   of land that is burnt and laid bare.

4. We cry for the plight of the hungry
   while harvests are left on the field,
   for orchards neglected and wasting,
   for produce from markets withheld.

5. The song grows in depth and in
      wideness;
   the earth and its people are one.
   There can be no thanks without giving,
   no words without deeds that are done.

6. Then teach us, O God of the harvest,
   to be humble in all that we claim,
   to share what we have with the nations,
   to care for the world in your name.

472
Fred Kaan (b. 1929)
© 1968 Stainer & Bell Ltd.

1. Now let us from this table rise,
   renewed in body, mind and soul;
   with Christ we die and live again,
   his selfless love has made us whole.

2. With minds alert, upheld by grace,
   to spread the Word in speech and
      deed,
   we follow in the steps of Christ,
   at one with all in hope and need.

3. To fill each human house with love,
   it is the sacrament of care;
   the work that Christ began to do
   we humbly pledge ourselves to share.

4. Then give us courage, living God,
   to choose again the pilgrim way,
   and help us to accept with joy
   the challenge of tomorrow's day.

473
St. Thomas Aquinas (1227-1274)
trans. John Mason Neale (1818-1866),
Edward Caswall (1814-1878) and others

1. Now, my tongue, the myst'ry telling
   of the glorious body sing,
   and the blood, all price excelling,
   which the Gentiles' Lord and King,
   in a virgin's womb once dwelling,
   shed for this world's ransoming.

2. Giv'n for us, for us descending
   of a virgin to proceed,
   he, with us in converse blending,
   scattered here the gospel seed,
   till his sojourn drew to ending
   which he closed with wondrous deed.

3. At the last great supper lying,
   circled by his chosen band,
   meekly with the law complying,
   first he finished its command.
   Then, immortal food supplying,
   gave himself with his own hand.

4. Word made flesh, by word he maketh
   very bread his flesh to be;
   we, in wine, Christ's blood partaketh,
   and if senses fail to see,
   faith alone the true heart waketh,
   to behold the mystery.

5. Therefore we, before him bending,
   this great sacrament revere:
   types and shadows have their ending,
   for the newer rite is here;
   faith, our outward sense befriending,
   makes our inward vision clear.

6. Glory let us give and blessing
   to the Father and the Son,
   honour, might and praise addressing,
   while eternal ages run;
   ever too his love confessing,
   who, from both, with both is one.
   (Amen.)

474 Martin Rinkart (1586-1649)
trans. Catherine Winkworth (1827-1878)

1. Now thank we all our God,
   with hearts and hands and voices,
   who wondrous things hath done,
   in whom his world rejoices;
   who from our mother's arms
   hath blessed us on our way
   with countless gifts of love,
   and still is ours today.

2. O may this bounteous God
   through all our life be near us,
   with ever joyful hearts
   and blessèd peace to cheer us;
   and keep us in his grace,
   and guide us when perplexed,
   and free us from all ills
   in this world and the next.

3. All praise and thanks to God
   the Father now be given,
   the Son and him who reigns
   with them in highest heaven,
   the one eternal God,
   whom earth and heav'n adore;
   for thus it was, is now,
   and shall be evermore.

475 John Macleod Campbell Crum (1872-1958), alt.
© 1928 Oxford University Press

1. Now the green blade riseth
   from the buried grain,
   wheat that in the dark earth
   many days has lain;
   Love lives again,
   that with the dead has been:
   Love is come again,
   like wheat that springeth green.

2. In the grave they laid him,
   Love by hatred slain,
   thinking that never
   he would wake again,
   laid in the earth
   like grain that sleeps unseen:
   Love is come again,
   like wheat that springeth green.

3. Forth he came at Easter,
   like the risen grain,
   he that for three days
   in the grave had lain;
   quick from the dead,
   my risen Lord is seen:
   Love is come again,
   like wheat that springeth green.

4. When our hearts are wintry,
   grieving or in pain,
   thy touch can call us
   back to life again;
   fields of our hearts,
   that dead and bare have been:
   Love is come again,
   like wheat that springeth green.

476 Elizabeth Ann Porter Head (1850-1936)
© Copyright control

1. O Breath of Life,
      come sweeping through us,
   revive your Church with life and pow'r;
   O Breath of Life, come cleanse,
      renew us,
   and fit your Church to meet this hour.

Continued overleaf

2. O Breath of Love,
   come breathe within us,
   renewing thought and will and heart;
   come, love of Christ, afresh to win us,
   revive your Church in ev'ry part!

3. O Wind of God,
   come bend us, break us,
   till humbly we confess our need;
   then, in your tenderness remake us,
   revive, restore – for this we plead.

4. Revive us, Lord; is zeal abating
   while harvest fields are vast and white?
   Revive us, Lord, the world is waiting –
   equip thy Church to spread the light.

477 Timothy Dudley-Smith (b. 1926)
© Timothy Dudley-Smith

1. O Christ the same through all our story's
      pages,
   our loves and hopes, our failures and our
      fears;
   eternal Lord, the King of all the ages,
   unchanging still, amid the passing years:
   O living word, the source of all creation,
   who spread the skies, and set the stars
      ablaze,
   O Christ the same, who wrought our
      whole salvation,
   we bring our thanks for all our yesterdays.

2. O Christ the same, the friend of sinners,
      sharing
   our inmost thoughts, the secrets none
      can hide,
   still as of old upon your body bearing
   the marks of love, in triumph glorified:
   O Son of Man, who stooped for us from
      heaven,
   O Prince of life, in all your saving pow'r,
   O Christ the same, to whom our hearts
      are given,
   we bring our thanks for this the present
      hour.

3. O Christ the same, secure within whose
      keeping
   our lives and loves, our days and years
      remain,
   our work and rest, our waking and our
      sleeping,
   our calm and storm, our pleasure and
      our pain:
   O Lord of love, for all our joys and
      sorrows,
   for all our hopes, when earth shall fade
      and flee,
   O Christ the same, for all our brief
      tomorrows,
   we bring our thanks for all that is to be.

478 6th Century Latin
trans. by William Copeland (1804-1885) and others

1. O Christ, who art the Light and Day,
   thou drivest darksome night away!
   We know thee as the Light of light,
   illuminating mortal sight.

2. All-holy Lord, we pray to thee,
   keep us to-night from danger free;
   grant us, dear Lord, in thee to rest,
   so be our sleep in quiet blest.

3. And while the eyes soft slumber take,
   still be the heart to thee awake;
   be thy right hand upheld above
   thy servants resting in thy love.

4. O strong defender, be thou nigh
   to bid the pow'rs of darkness fly;
   keep us from sin, and guide for good
   thy servants purchased by the blood.

5. Remember us, dear Lord, we pray
   while in this mortal flesh we stay:
   'tis thou who dost the soul defend-
   be present with us to the end.

6. Blest Three in One and One in Three,
   almighty God, we pray to thee
   that thou wouldst now vouchsafe to bless
   our fast with fruits of righteousness.
      Amen.

479
Attributed to John Francis Wade (1711-1786)
trans. Frederick Oakeley (1802-1880) and others

1. O come, all ye faithful,
   joyful and triumphant,
   O come ye, O come ye to Bethlehem;
   come and behold him,
     born the king of angels:

   O come, let us adore him,
   O come let us adore him,
   O come, let us adore him,
   Christ the Lord.

2. God of God,
   Light of Light,
   lo, he abhors not the Virgin's womb;
   very God, begotten not created:

3. See how the shepherds,
   summoned to his cradle,
   leaving their flocks, draw nigh with lowly
     fear;
   we too will thither bend our joyful
     footsteps:

4. Lo, star-led chieftains,
   Magi, Christ adoring,
   offer him incense, gold and myrrh;
   we to the Christ-child bring our hearts'
     oblations:

5. Child, for us sinners
   poor and in the manger,
   fain we embrace thee, with love and awe;
   who would not love thee, loving us so
     dearly?

6. Sing, choirs of angels,
   sing in exultation,
   sing, all ye citizens of heav'n above;
   glory to God in the highest:

7. Yea, Lord, we greet thee,
   born this happy morning,
   Jesu, to thee be glory giv'n;
   Word of the Father, now in flesh
     appearing:

480
from the 'Great O Antiphons' (12th - 13th century)
trans. John Mason Neale (1818-1866)

1. O come, O come, Emmanuel,
   and ransom captive Israel,
   that mourns in lonely exile here,
   until the Son of God appear.

   Rejoice, rejoice!
   Emmanuel shall come to thee,
   O Israel.

2. O come, thou rod of Jesse, free
   thine own from Satan's tyranny;
   from depths of hell thy people save,
   and give them vict'ry o'er the grave.

3. O come, thou dayspring, come and
     cheer
   our spirits by thine advent here;
   disperse the gloomy clouds of night,
   and death's dark shadows put to flight.

4. O come, thou key of David, come
   and open wide our heav'nly home;
   make safe the way that leads on high,
   and close the path to misery.

5. O come, O come, thou Lord of might,
   who to thy tribes on Sinai's height
   in ancient times didst give the Law,
   in cloud and majesty and awe.

481
Chrysogonus Waddell, based on Isaiah 40
© *Chrysogonus Waddell*

1. O comfort my people
   and calm all their fear,
   and tell them the time
   of salvation draws near.
   O tell them I come
   to remove all their shame.
   Then they will forever
   give praise to my name.

Continued overleaf

2. Proclaim to the cities
   of Judah my word;
   that 'gentle yet strong
   is the hand of the Lord.
   I rescue the captives,
   my people defend,
   and bring them to justice
   and joy without end.'

3. 'All mountains and hills
   shall become as a plain,
   for vanished are mourning
   and hunger and pain.
   And never again shall
   these war against you.
   Behold I come quickly
   to make all things new.'

482 Henry Ernest Hardy (Father Andrew S.D.C.) (1869-1946) © Coyright control

1. O dearest Lord, thy sacred head
   with thorns was pierced for me;
   O pour thy blessing on my head
   that I may think for thee.

2. O dearest Lord, thy sacred hands
   with nails were pierced for me;
   O shed thy blessing on my hands
   that they may work for thee.

3. O dearest Lord, thy sacred feet
   with nails were pierced for me;
   O pour thy blessing on my feet
   that they may follow thee.

4. O dearest Lord, thy sacred heart
   with spear was pierced for me;
   O pour thy Spirit in my heart
   that I may live for thee.

483 William Cowper (1731-1800)

1. O for a closer walk with God,
   a calm and heav'nly frame;
   a light to shine upon the road
   that leads me to the Lamb.

2. What peaceful hours I once enjoyed,
   how sweet their mem'ry still!
   But they have left an aching void
   the world can never fill.

3. The dearest idol I have known,
   whate'er that idol be,
   help me to tear it from thy throne,
   and worship only thee.

4. So shall my walk be close with God,
   calm and serene my frame;
   so purer light shall mark the road
   that leads me to the Lamb.

484 Charles Wesley (1707-1788)

1. O for a heart to praise my God,
   a heart from sin set free;
   a heart that's sprinkled with the blood
   so freely shed for me.

2. A heart resigned, submissive, meek,
   my great Redeemer's throne;
   where only Christ is heard to speak,
   where Jesus reigns alone.

3. A humble, lowly, contrite heart,
   believing, true and clean,
   which neither life nor death can part
   from him that dwells within.

4. A heart in ev'ry thought renewed,
   and full of love divine;
   perfect and right and pure and good –
   a copy, Lord, of thine.

5. Thy nature, gracious Lord, impart,
   come quickly from above;
   write thy new name upon my heart,
   thy new best name of love.

485

Charles Wesley (1707-1788)

When the tune 'Lyngham' is used

1. O for a thousand tongues to sing
   my dear Redeemer's praise,
   my dear Redeemer's praise,
   the glories of my God and King,
   the triumphs of his grace,
   the triumphs of his grace,
   the triumphs of his grace!

2. Jesus! the name that charms our fears,
   that bids our sorrows cease,
   that bids our sorrows cease;
   'tis music in the sinner's ears,
   'tis life and health and peace. (x3)

3. He breaks the pow'r of cancelled sin,
   he sets the pris'ner free,
   he sets the pris'ner free;
   his blood can make the foulest clean;
   his blood availed for me. (x3)

4. He speaks; and, list'ning to his voice,
   new life the dead receive,
   new life the dead receive,
   the mournful broken hearts rejoice,
   the humble poor believe. (x3)

5. Hear him, ye deaf; his praise, ye dumb,
   your loosened tongues employ,
   your loosened tongues employ;
   ye blind, behold your Saviour come;
   and leap, ye lame, for joy! (x3)

6. My gracious Master and my God,
   assist me to proclaim,
   assist me to proclaim
   and spread through all the earth abroad
   the honours of thy name. (x3)

When another tune is used

1. O for a thousand tongues to sing
   my dear Redeemer's praise,
   the glories of my God and King,
   the triumphs of his grace!

2. Jesus! the name that charms our fears,
   that bids our sorrows cease;
   'tis music in the sinner's ears,
   'tis life and health and peace.

3. He breaks the pow'r of cancelled sin,
   he sets the pris'ner free;
   his blood can make the foulest clean;
   his blood availed for me.

4. He speaks; and, list'ning to his voice,
   new life the dead receive,
   the mournful broken hearts rejoice,
   the humble poor believe,

5. Hear him, ye deaf; his praise, ye dumb,
   your loosened tongues employ;
   ye blind, behold your Saviour come;
   and leap, ye lame, for joy!

6. My gracious Master and my God,
   assist me to proclaim
   and spread through all the earth abroad
   the honours of thy name.

486

Aurelius Clemens Prudentius (348-413)
trans. John Mason Neale (1818-1866), alt.

1. Of the Father's love begotten,
   ere the worlds began to be,
   he is Alpha and Omega,
   he the source, the ending he,
   of the things that are, and have been,
   and that future years shall see,
   evermore and evermore.

2. At his word they were created;
   he commanded; it was done:
   heav'n and earth and depths of ocean
   in their threefold order one;
   all that grows beneath the shining
   of the light of moon and sun,
   evermore and evermore.

Continued overleaf

3. O that birth for ever blessèd,
   when the Virgin, full of grace,
   by the Holy Ghost conceiving,
   bore the Saviour of our race,
   and the babe, the world's Redeemer,
   first revealed his sacred face,
   evermore and evermore.

4. O ye heights of heav'n, adore him;
   angel hosts, his praises sing;
   pow'rs, dominions, bow before him,
   and extol our God and King:
   let no tongue on earth be silent,
   ev'ry voice in concert ring,
   evermore and evermore.

5. This is he whom seers and sages
   sang of old with one accord;
   whom the writings of the prophets
   promised in their faithful word;
   now he shines, the long-expected;
   let our songs declare his worth,
   evermore and evermore.

6. Christ, to thee, with God the Father,
   and, O Holy Ghost, to thee,
   hymn and chant and high thanksgiving,
   and unwearied praises be;
   honour, glory, and dominion,
   and eternal victory,
   evermore and evermore.

487 Henry Kirke White (1785-1806) and others

1. Oft in danger, oft in woe,
   onward, Christians, onward go;
   bear the toil, endure the strife,
   strengthened with the bread of life.

2. Onward through the desert night,
   keeping faith and vision bright;
   face the challenge of the hour
   trusting in your Saviour's pow'r.

3. Let not sorrow dim your eye,
   soon shall ev'ry tear be dry;
   let not fears your course impede,
   great your strength if great your need.

4. Let your drooping hearts be glad;
   march in faith and honour clad;
   march, nor think the journey long,
   march to hope's eternal song.

5. Onward then, undaunted, move;
   more than faithful God will prove;
   though the raging waters flow,
   Christian pilgrims, onward go.

488 Graham Kendrick (b. 1950)
© 1991 Make Way Music

O give thanks to the Lord,
for his love will never end.
O give thanks to the Lord,
for his love it never will end.
(Repeat)

1. Sing to him, sing your praise to him,
   tell the world of all he has done.
   Fill the nations with celebrations
   to welcome him as he comes.

2. Give him thanks for the fruitful earth,
   for the sun, the seasons, the rain.
   For the joys of his good creation,
   the life and breath he sustains.

3. Let the heavens rejoice before him,
   the earth and all it contains.
   All creation in jubilation,
   join in the shout, 'The Lord reigns!'

4. Let the hearts of those who seek him
   be happy now in his love.
   Let their faces look up and gaze
   at his gracious smile from above.

489

Michael Perry (1942-1996)
© Mrs B. Perry/Jubilee Hymns

1. O God beyond all praising,
   we worship you today,
   and sing the love amazing
   that songs cannot repay;
   for we can only wonder
   at ev'ry gift you send,
   at blessings without number
   and mercies without end:
   we lift our hearts before you
   and wait upon your word,
   we honour and adore you,
   our great and mighty Lord.

2. Then hear, O gracious Saviour,
   accept the love we bring,
   that we who know your favour
   may serve you as our King;
   and whether our tomorrows
   be filled with good or ill,
   we'll triumph through our sorrows
   and rise to bless you still:
   to marvel at your beauty
   and glory in your ways,
   and make a joyful duty
   our sacrifice of praise.

490

Michael Forster (b. 1946)
© 1999 Kevin Mayhew Ltd

1. O God, enthroned in majesty
   and crowned with mortal pain,
   inspired by your amazing love
   we turn to you again;
   for grace and judgement here combine
   to meet our deepest need,
   no cheap and easy formula,
   but costly grace, indeed!

2. Confronted by the awesome truth,
   we shrink away in fear:
   all sin is death, the cross proclaims,
   and none stands blameless here.
   Yet through the pain, amazing love
   assures us of your grace,
   and gives us courage to return
   and stand before your face.

3. Now give us grace to stand beneath
   the crosses of the world,
   that all may judge the power of sin,
   yet see your love unfurled.
   Let no more lives be crucified
   by poverty or war,
   but grace and judgement, hand in hand,
   unite to cry, 'No more!'

4. Then let the world be freed from fear
   to seek love's open way,
   to journey from untimely night
   toward a greater day:
   to justice, hope and liberty,
   the kingdom of your choice,
   when all our praise is gathered up
   in one united voice.

491

Philip Doddridge (1702-1751) and
John Logan (1748-1788) alt.

1. O God of Bethel, by whose hand
   thy people still are fed,
   who through this earthly pilgrimage
   has all our forebears led.

2. Our vows, our prayers, we now present
   before thy throne of grace;
   God of our forebears, be the God
   of their succeeding race.

3. Through each mysterious path of life
   be thou our constant guide;
   give us each day our daily bread,
   and raiment fit provide.

Continued overleaf

4. O spread thy cov'ring wings around,
   till all our journeys cease,
   and at our Father's loved abode
   our souls arrive in peace.

492 Gilbert Keith Chesterton (1874-1936)
© Copyright control

1. O God of earth and altar,
   bow down and hear our cry,
   our earthly rulers falter,
   our people drift and die;
   the walls of gold entomb us,
   the swords of scorn divide,
   take not thy thunder from us,
   but take away our pride.

2. From all that terror teaches,
   from lies of tongue and pen,
   from all the easy speeches
   that comfort cruel men,
   from sale and profanation
   of honour and the sword,
   from sleep and from damnation,
   deliver us, good Lord!

3. Tie in a living tether
   the prince and priest and thrall,
   bind all our lives together,
   smite us and save us all;
   in ire and exultation
   aflame with faith and free,
   lift up a living nation,
   a single sword to thee.

493 Basil E. Bridge (b. 1927)
© 1999 Kevin Mayhew Ltd

1. O God of hope, your prophets spoke
   of days when war would cease:
   when, taught to see each person's worth,
   and faithful stewards of the earth,
   we all would live in peace.

2. We pray that our divided world
   may hear their words anew:
   then lift for good the curse of war,
   let bread with justice bless the poor,
   and turn in hope to you.

3. Earth's fragile web of life demands
   our reverence and our care,
   lest in our folly, sloth and greed,
   deaf both to you and others' need,
   we lay our planet bare.

4. Earth's rich resources give us power
   to build or to destroy:
   your Spirit urges us to turn
   from selfish, fear-bound ways, and learn
   his selfless trust and joy.

5. The Prince of Peace is calling us
   to shun the way of strife:
   he brings us healing through his pain;
   our shattered hope is born again
   through his victorious life.

494 Isaac Watts (1674-1748) alt.

1. O God, our help in ages past,
   our hope for years to come,
   our shelter from the stormy blast,
   and our eternal home.

2. Beneath the shadow of thy throne,
   thy saints have dwelt secure;
   sufficient is thine arm alone,
   and our defence is sure.

3. Before the hills in order stood,
   or earth received her frame,
   from everlasting thou art God,
   to endless years the same.

4. A thousand ages in thy sight
   are like an evening gone;
   short as the watch that ends the night
   before the rising sun.

5. Time, like an ever-rolling stream,
   will bear us all away;
   we fade and vanish, as a dream
   dies at the op'ning day.

6. O God, our help in ages past,
   our hope for years to come,
   be thou our guard while troubles last,
   and our eternal home.

495
Frances M. Kelly, based on Psalm 55
© 1999 Kevin Mayhew Ltd.

1. O God, please listen to my cry,
   and give me answer.
   I am afraid of what the future
   holds for me, O Lord.

   Let me hide, Lord,
   in the shadow of your wings. (Repeat)

2. If only I had wings to fly
   I would escape, Lord:
   I'd fly as far as I could go
   to find some peace of mind.

3. I feel defeated by life's trials
   and disappointments.
   My days and nights are spent in fear,
   with no one I can trust.

4. But all of this I can survive
   if you are with me:
   my life is here, my life is now,
   and I must carry on.

5. Within the shadow of your wings
   I find my refuge.
   You are the only one I have;
   I count on you, O Lord.

496
Edward Osler (1798-1863)

1. O God, unseen yet ever near,
   thy presence may we feel;
   and, thus inspired with holy fear,
   before thine altar kneel.

2. Here may thy faithful people know
   the blessings of thy love,
   the streams that through the desert flow,
   the manna from above.

3. We come, obedient to thy word,
   to feast on heav'nly food;
   our meat the body of the Lord,
   our drink his precious blood.

4. Thus may we all thy word obey,
   for we, O God, are thine;
   and go rejoicing on our way,
   renewed with strength divine.

497
John Mason Neale (1818-1866) alt
© v6:1996 Kevin Mayhew Ltd.

1. O happy band of pilgrims,
   if onward ye will tread,
   with Jesus as your fellow,
   to Jesus as your head.

2. The cross that Jesus carried
   he carried as your due:
   the crown that Jesus weareth
   he weareth it for you.

3. The faith by which ye see him,
   the hope in which ye yearn,
   the love that through all troubles
   to him alone will turn.

4. What are they but forerunners
   to lead you to his sight,
   the longed-for distant dawning
   of uncreated light?

5. The trials that beset you,
   the sorrows ye endure,
   are known to Christ your Saviour,
   whose perfect grace will cure.

6. O happy band of pilgrims,
   let fear not dim your eyes,
   remember, your afflictions
   shall lead to such a prize!

498

Philip Doddridge (1702-1751) alt.

1. O happy day! that fixed my choice
   on thee, my Saviour and my God!
   Well may this glowing heart rejoice,
   and tell its raptures all abroad.

2. 'Tis done, the work of grace is done!
   I am my Lord's, and he is mine!
   He drew me, and I followed on,
   glad to confess the voice divine.

3. Now rest, my long-divided heart,
   fixed on this blissful centre, rest;
   nor ever from thy Lord depart,
   with him of ev'ry good possessed.

4. High heav'n, that heard the solemn vow,
   that vow renewed shall daily hear;
   till in life's latest hour I bow,
   and bless in death a bond so dear.

   When a tune with a Refrain is used this is
   sung after each verse:

   O happy day! O happy day!
   When Jesus washed my sins away;
   he taught me how to watch and pray,
   and live rejoicing ev'ry day;
   O happy day! O happy day!
   When Jesus washed my sins away.

499

Graham Kendrick (b. 1950)
© 1991 Make Way Music

O, heaven is in my heart.
O, heaven is in my heart.
(Repeat)

1. Leader The kingdom of our God is here,
   All   **heaven is in my heart.**
   Leader The presence of his majesty,
   All   **heaven is in my heart.**
   Leader And in his presence joy abounds,
   All   **heaven is in my heart.**
   Leader The light of holiness surrounds,
   All   **heaven is in my heart.**

2. Leader His precious life on me he spent,
   All   **heaven is in my heart.**
   Leader To give me life without an end,
   All   **heaven is in my heart.**
   Leader In Christ is all my confidence,
   All   **heaven is in my heart.**
   Leader The hope of my inheritance,
   All   **heaven is in my heart.**

3. Leader We are a temple for his throne,
   All   **heaven is in my heart.**
   Leader And Christ is the foundation
          stone,
   All   **heaven is in my heart.**
   Leader He will return to take us home,
   All   **heaven is in my heart.**
   Leader The Spirit and the Bride say,
          'Come!',
   All   **heaven is in my heart.**

500

Henry Williams Baker (1821-1877)

1. O Holy Ghost, thy people bless
   who long to feel thy might,
   and fain would grow in holiness
   as children of the light.

2. To thee we bring, who art the Lord,
   ourselves to be thy throne;
   let ev'ry thought and deed and word
   thy pure dominion own.

3. Life-giving Spirit, o'er us move,
   as on the formless deep;
   give life and order, light and love,
   where now is death or sleep.

4. Great gift of our ascended King,
   his saving truth reveal;
   our tongues inspire his praise to sing,
   our hearts his love to feel.

5. True wind of heav'n, from south or north,
   for joy or chast'ning, blow;
   the garden-spices shall spring forth
   if thou wilt bid them flow.

6. O Holy Ghost, of sev'nfold might,
   all graces come from thee;
   grant us to know and serve aright
   One God in Persons Three.

501 Charles Coffin (1676-1749)
trans. John Chandler (1808-1876) alt.

1. O Holy Spirit, Lord of grace,
   eternal fount of love,
   inflame, we pray, our inmost hearts
   with fire from heav'n above.

2. As thou dost join with holiest bonds
   the Father and the Son,
   so fill thy saints with mutual love
   and link their hearts in one.

3. To God the Father, God the Son
   and God the Holy Ghost,
   be praise eternal from the earth,
   and from the angel-host.

502 Traditional

O, how good is the Lord! (x3)
I never will forget what he has done for me.

1. He gives us salvation,
   how good is the Lord. *(x3)*
   I never will forget
   what he has done for me.

2. He gives us his Spirit . . .

3. He gives us healing . . .

4. He gives us his body . . .

5. He gives us his freedom . . .

6. He gives us each other . . .

7. He gives us his glory . . .

503 John Ernest Bode (1816-1874)

1. O Jesus, I have promised
   to serve thee to the end;
   be thou for ever near me,
   my Master and my friend:
   I shall not fear the battle
   if thou art by my side,
   nor wander from the pathway
   if thou wilt be my guide.

2. O let me feel thee near me;
   the world is ever near;
   I see the sights that dazzle,
   the tempting sounds I hear;
   my foes are ever near me,
   around me and within;
   but, Jesus, draw thou nearer,
   and shield my soul from sin.

3. O let me hear thee speaking
   in accents clear and still,
   above the storms of passion,
   the murmurs of self-will;
   O speak to reassure me,
   to hasten or control;
   O speak and make me listen,
   thou guardian of my soul.

4. O Jesus, thou hast promised,
   to all who follow thee,
   that where thou art in glory
   there shall thy servant be;
   and, Jesus, I have promised
   to serve thee to the end:
   O give me grace to follow,
   my Master and my friend.

5. O let me see thy foot-marks,
   and in them plant mine own;
   my hope to follow duly
   is in thy strength alone:
   O guide me, call me, draw me,
   uphold me to the end;
   and then in heav'n receive me,
   my Saviour and my friend.

504
Greek hymn (8th century)
trans. John Brownlie (1857-1925)

1. O King enthroned on high,
thou Comforter divine,
blest Spirit of all truth, be nigh
and make us thine.

2. Thou art the source of life,
thou art our treasure-store;
give us thy peace, and end our strife
for evermore.

3. Descend, O heav'nly Dove,
abide with us alway;
and in the fullness of thy love
cleanse us, we pray.

505
Michael Forster (b. 1946) based on the German
© 1996 Kevin Mayhew Ltd.

1. O Lamb of God, most holy,
salvation's perfect sign,
by your redeeming passion,
we share the life divine.
The cost of our deliv'rance
in flowing blood is shown,
and life in all its fullness
is found in you alone.

2. Upon the cross you carried
a universe of shame,
your dying breath atoning
for centuries of blame.
So now accept your servant,
who on your love relied,
to rest in peace eternal
redeemed and purified.

3. O draw us to your presence,
beyond the sundered veil,
to stand in silent wonder,
where words and senses fail.
In fellowship unbroken
with all who went before,
we join with saints and angels
to worship and adore.

506
John Wimber
© 1979 Mercy/Vineyard Publishing/Music
Services/CopyCare

1. O let the Son of God enfold you
with his Spirit and his love,
let him fill your heart and satisfy your
soul.
O let him have the things that hold you,
and his Spirit like a dove
will descend upon your life and make
you whole.

Jesus, O Jesus,
come and fill your lambs.
Jesus, O Jesus,
come and fill your lambs.

2. O come and sing this song with gladness
as your hearts are filled with joy,
lift your hands in sweet surrender to his
name.
O give him all your tears and sadness,
give him all your years of pain,
and you'll enter into life in Jesus' name.

507
Samuel Scheidt (1650)
trans. Percy Dearmer (1867-1936) alt.
© Oxford University Press. Used by permission

1. O little one sweet, O little one mild,
thy Father's purpose thou hast fulfilled;
thou cam'st from heav'n to dwell below,
to share the joys and tears we know.
O little one sweet, O little one mild.

2. O little one sweet, O little one mild,
with joy thou hast the whole world filled;
thou camest here from heav'n's domain,
to bring us comfort in our pain,
O little one sweet, O little one mild.

3. O little one sweet, O little one mild,
in thee Love's beauties are all distilled;
then light in us thy love's bright flame,
that we may give thee back the same,
O little one sweet, O little one mild.

508
Philip Brooks (1835-1893) alt.

1. O little town of Bethlehem,
   how still we see thee lie!
   Above thy deep and dreamless sleep
   the silent stars go by.
   Yet in thy dark streets shineth
   the everlasting light;
   the hopes and fears of all the years
   are met in thee tonight.

2. O morning stars, together
   proclaim the holy birth,
   and praises sing to God the King,
   and peace to all the earth.
   For Christ is born of Mary;
   and, gathered all above,
   while mortals sleep, the angels keep
   their watch of wond'ring love;

3. How silently, how silently,
   the wondrous gift is giv'n!
   So God imparts to human hearts
   the blessings of his heav'n.
   No ear may hear his coming;
   but in this world of sin,
   where meek souls will receive him still,
   the dear Christ enters in.

4. O holy child of Bethlehem,
   descend to us, we pray;
   cast out our sin, and enter in,
   be born in us today.
   We hear the Christmas angels
   the great glad tidings tell:
   O come to us, abide with us,
   our Lord Emmanuel.

509
Patrick Appleford
© 1965 Josef Weinberger Ltd.

1. O Lord, all the world belongs to you,
   and you are always making all things new.
   What is wrong you forgive,
   and the new life you give
   is what's turning the world upside down.

2. The world's only loving to its friends,
   but you have brought us love that
      never ends;
   loving enemies too,
   and this loving with you
   is what's turning the world upside down.

3. This world lives divided and apart.
   You draw us all together and we start,
   in your body, to see
   that in a fellowship we
   can be turning the world upside down.

4. The world wants the wealth to live
      in state,
   but you show us a new way to be great:
   like a servant you came,
   and if we do the same,
   we'll be turning the world upside down.

5. O Lord, all the world belongs to you,
   and you are always making all things new.
   Send your Spirit on all
   in your Church, whom you call
   to be turning the world upside down.

510
John Ryland (1753-1825)

1. O Lord, I would delight in thee
   and on thy care depend;
   to thee in every trouble flee,
   my best, my only friend.

2. When all created streams are dried
   thy fullness is the same:
   may I with this be satisfied,
   and glory in thy name.

3. No good in creatures can be found
   but may be found in thee;
   I must have all things and abound,
   while God is God to me.

Continued overleaf

4. He that has made my heav'n secure
will here all good provide;
while Christ is rich can I be poor?
What can I want beside?

5. O Lord, I cast my care on thee;
I triumph and adore;
henceforth my great concern shall be
to love and please thee more.

Karl Boberg (1859-1940)
trans. Stuart K. Hine (1899-1989)
© 1953 Stuart K. Hine
Administered by Kingsway's Thankyou Music

511

1. O Lord, my God,
when I in awesome wonder
consider all the works
thy hand has made,
I see the stars,
I hear the rolling thunder,
thy pow'r throughout
the universe displayed.

*Then sings my soul,
my Saviour God, to thee:
how great thou art, how great thou art.
Then sings my soul,
my Saviour God, to thee;
how great thou art, how great thou art.*

2. When through the woods
and forest glades I wander
and hear the birds sing
sweetly in the trees;
when I look down
from lofty mountain grandeur,
and hear the brook,
and feel the gentle breeze.

3. And when I think that God,
his Son not sparing,
sent him to die,
I scarce can take it in
that on the cross,
my burden gladly bearing,
he bled and died
to take away my sin.

4. When Christ shall come
with shout of acclamation
and take me home,
what joy shall fill my heart;
when I shall bow
in humble adoration,
and there proclaim:
my God, how great thou art.

512

Albert F Bayly (1901-1984)
© 1988 Oxford University Press

1. O Lord of every shining constellation
that wheels in splendour through the
midnight sky,
grant us your Spirit's true illumination
to read the secrets of our work on high.

2. You, Lord, have made the atom's hidden
forces,
your laws its mighty energies fulfil;
teach us, to whom you give such rich
resources,
in all we use, to serve your holy will.

3. O Life, awaking life in cell and tissue,
from flow'r to bird, from beast to brain of
man;
help us to trace, from birth to final issue,
the sure unfolding of your age-long plan.

4. You, Lord, have stamped your image on
your creatures,
and, though they mar that image, love
them still;
lift up our eyes to Christ, that in his
features
we may discern the beauty of your will.

5. Great Lord of nature, shaping and
renewing,
you made us more than nature's sons to be;
you help us tread, with grace our souls
enduring,
the road to life and immortality.

513

Michael Forster (b. 1946)
© 1996 Kevin Mayhew Ltd.

1. O Lord of our salvation,
   the pains of all creation
   are borne upon your cross:
   the failure of compassion,
   revealed in starkest fashion,
   exposes all our gold as dross.

2. We hear your voice protesting,
   to love and hope attesting,
   where justice is denied.
   Where innocents are dying,
   where hate is crucifying,
   you call us to your bleeding side.

3. O give us faith to stay here,
   to wait, to watch and pray here,
   and witness to your cry;
   in scarred and tearful faces,
   in countless painful places,
   you give us hope that will not die.

514

John Raphael Peacey (1896-1971)
© The Revd. Mary J. Hancock. Used by kind permission

1. O Lord, we long to see your face,
   to know you risen from the grave,
   but we have missed the joy and grace
   of seeing you, as others have.
   Yet in your company we'll wait,
   and we shall see you, soon or late.

2. O Lord, we do not know the way,
   nor clearly see the path ahead;
   so often, therefore, we delay
   and doubt your pow'r to raise the dead.
   Yet with you we will firmly stay;
   you are the Truth, the Life, the Way.

3. We find it hard, Lord, to believe;
   all habit makes us want to prove;
   we would with eye and hand perceive
   the truth and person whom we love.
   Yet, as in fellowship we meet,
   you come yourself each one to greet.

4. You come to us, our God, our Lord;
   you do not show your hands and side;
   but faith has its more blest reward;
   in love's assurance we confide.
   Now we believe, that we may know,
   and in that knowledge daily grow.

515

Graham Kendrick (b. 1950)
© 1986 Kingsway's Thankyou Music

O Lord, your tenderness,
melting all my bitterness,
O Lord, I receive your love.
O Lord, your loveliness,
changing all my ugliness,
O Lord, I receive your love.
O Lord, I receive your love.
O Lord, I receive your love.

516

Benjamin Webb (1819-1885) alt.,
from Thomas à Kempis (c. 1379-1471)

1. O love, how deep, how broad, how high!
   It fills the heart with ecstasy,
   that God, the Son of God, should take
   our mortal form for mortals' sake.

2. He sent no angel to our race
   of higher or of lower place,
   but wore the robe of human frame
   himself, and to this lost world came.

3. For us he was baptised and bore
   his holy fast, and hungered sore;
   for us temptations sharp he knew;
   for us the tempter overthrew.

4. For us to wicked pow'rs betrayed,
   scourged, mocked, in purple robe
     arrayed,
   he bore the shameful cross and death;
   for us at length gave up his breath.

Continued overleaf

5. For us he rose from death again,
for us he went on high to reign,
for us he sent his Spirit here
to guide, to strengthen and to cheer.

6. To him whose boundless love has won
salvation for us through his Son,
to God the Father glory be,
both now and through eternity.

517 George Matheson (1842-1906)

1. O Love that wilt not let me go,
I rest my weary soul in thee;
I give thee back the life I owe,
that in thine ocean depths its flow
may richer, fuller be.

2. O Light that follow'st all my way,
I yield my flick'ring torch to thee;
my heart restores its borrowed ray,
that in thy sunshine's blaze its day
may brighter, fairer be.

3. O Joy that seekest me through pain,
I cannot close my heart to thee;
I trace the rainbow through the rain,
and feel the promise is not vain
that morn shall tearless be.

4. O Cross that liftest up my head,
I dare not ask to fly from thee:
I lay in dust life's glory dead,
and from the ground there blossoms red
life that shall endless be.

518 Reginald Heber (1783-1826)

O most merciful!
O most bountiful!
God the Father almighty!
By the Redeemer's
sweet intercession,
hear us, help us when we cry.

519 William Walsham How (1823-1897)

1. O my Saviour, lifted
from the earth for me,
draw me, in thy mercy,
nearer unto thee.

2. Lift my earth-bound longings,
fix them, Lord, above;
draw me with the magnet
of thy mighty love.

3. Lord, thine arms are stretching
ever far and wide,
to enfold thy children
to thy loving side.

4. And I come, O Jesus:
dare I turn away?
No, thy love hath conquered,
and I come today.

5. Bringing all my burdens,
sorrow, sin and care;
at thy feet I lay them,
and I leave them there.

520 George Bennard (1873-1958)
© The Rodeheaver Co./ Word Music
Administered by CopyCare

1. On a hill far away
stood an old rugged cross,
the emblem of suff'ring and shame;
and I loved that old cross
where the dearest and best
for a world of lost sinners was slain.

So I'll cherish the old rugged cross,
till my trophies at last I lay down;
I will cling to the old rugged cross
and exchange it some day for a crown.

2. O that old rugged cross,
so despised by the world,
has a wondrous attraction for me:
for the dear Lamb of God
left his glory above
to bear it to dark Calvary.

3. In the old rugged cross,
   stained with blood so divine,
   a wondrous beauty I see.
   For t'was on that old cross
   Jesus suffered and died
   to pardon and sanctify me.

4. To the old rugged cross
   I will ever be true,
   its shame and reproach gladly bear.
   Then he'll call me some day
   to my home far away;
   there his glory for ever I'll share.

521 Cecil Frances Alexander (1818-1895) alt.
© *This version 1996 Kevin Mayhew Ltd.*

1. Once in royal David's city
   stood a lowly cattle shed,
   where a mother laid her baby
   in a manger for his bed;
   Mary was that mother mild,
   Jesus Christ her little child.

2. He came down to earth from heaven,
   who is God and Lord of all,
   and his shelter was a stable,
   and his cradle was a stall;
   with the needy, poor and lowly,
   lived on earth our Saviour holy.

3. For he is our childhood's pattern,
   day by day like us he grew;
   he was little, weak and helpless,
   tears and smiles like us he knew;
   and he feeleth for our sadness,
   and he shareth in our gladness.

4. And our eyes at last shall see him
   through his own redeeming love,
   for that child so dear and gentle
   is our Lord in heav'n above;
   and he leads his children on
   to the place where he is gone.

522 William Bright (1824-1901)

1. Once, only once, and once for all,
   his precious life he gave;
   before the Cross our spirits fall,
   and own it strong to save.

2. 'One off'ring, single and complete,'
   with lips and heart we say;
   but what he never can repeat
   he shows forth day by day.

3. For, as the priest of Aaron's line
   within the holiest stood,
   and sprinkled all the mercy-shrine
   with sacrificial blood;

4. So he who once atonement wrought,
   our Priest of endless pow'r,
   presents himself for those he bought
   in that dark noontide hour.

5. And so we show thy death, O Lord,
   till thou again appear;
   and feel, when we approach thy board,
   we have an altar here.

6. All glory to the Father be,
   all glory to the Son,
   all glory, Holy Ghost, to thee,
   while endless ages run.

523 Traditional English carol, alt.

1. On Christmas night all Christians sing,
   to hear the news the angels bring,
   on Christmas night all Christians sing,
   to hear the news the angels bring.
   news of great joy, news of great mirth,
   news of our merciful King's birth.

2. Then why should we on earth be so sad,
   since our Redeemer made us glad,
   then why should we on earth be so sad,
   since our Redeemer made us glad,
   when from our sin he set us free,
   all for to gain our liberty?

Continued overleaf

3. When sin departs before his grace,
   then life and health come in its place,
   when sin departs before his grace,
   then life and health come in its place,
   angels and earth with joy may sing,
   all for to see the new-born King.

4. All out of darkness we have light,
   which made the angels sing this night:
   all out of darkness we have light,
   which made the angels sing this night:
   'Glory to God and peace to men,
   now and for evermore. Amen.'

524
Gerard Markland (b. 1953)
© 1998 Kevin Mayhew Ltd.

One Father who's giving me life,
one Saviour who's conquered my fears,
one Spirit changing my heart,
O my God, I rejoice in you.

1. Creator Lord, almighty Father,
   what God is this who carves my name
   upon his hand?

2. Lord Jesus, now enthroned in glory,
   what God is this who gives his life
   to set me free?

3. O loving breath of God almighty,
   what God is this who through
      my weakness
   sings his praise?

525
Sydney Carter (b. 1915)
© 1971 Stainer & Bell Ltd.

1. One more step along the world I go,
   one more step along the world I go.
   From the old things to the new
   keep me travelling along with you.

   And it's from the old
   I travel to the new,
   keep me travelling
   along with you.

2. Round the corners of the world I turn,
   more and more about the world
      I learn.
   All the new things that I see
   you'll be looking at along with me.

3. As I travel through the bad and good,
   keep me travelling the way I should.
   Where I see no way to go,
   you'll be telling me the way, I know.

4. Give me courage when the world
      is rough,
   keep me loving though the world
      is tough.
   Leap and sing in all I do,
   keep me travelling along with you.

5. You are older than the world can be,
   you are younger than the life in me.
   Ever old and ever new,
   keep me travelling along with you.

526
Graham Kendrick (b. 1950)
© 1981 Kingsway's Thankyou Music

1. One shall tell another,
   and he shall tell his friend,
   husbands, wives and children
   shall come following on.
   From house to house in families
   shall more be gathered in,
   and lights will shine in every street,
   so warm and welcoming.

   Come on in and taste the new wine,
   the wine of the kingdom,
   the wine of the kingdom of God.
   Here is healing and forgiveness,
   the wine of the kingdom,
   the wine of the kingdom of God.

2. Compassion of the Father
is ready now to flow,
through acts of love and mercy
we must let it show.
He turns now from his anger
to show a smiling face,
and longs that all should stand beneath
the fountain of his grace.

3. He longs to do much more than
our faith has yet allowed,
to thrill us and surprise us
with his sovereign power.
Where darkness has been darkest
the brightest light will shine;
his invitation comes to us,
it's yours and it is mine.

527 Charles Coffin (1676-1749)
trans. John Chandler (1806-1876), alt.

1. On Jordan's bank the Baptist's cry
announces that the Lord is nigh;
awake, and hearken, for he brings
glad tidings of the King of kings.

2. Then cleansed be ev'ry breast from sin;
make straight the way for God within;
prepare we in our hearts a home,
where such a mighty guest may come.

3. For thou art our salvation, Lord,
our refuge and our great reward;
without thy grace we waste away,
like flow'rs that wither and decay.

4. To heal the sick stretch out thine hand,
and bid the fallen sinner stand;
shine forth and let thy light restore
earth's own true loveliness once more.

5. All praise, eternal Son, to thee
whose advent doth thy people free,
whom with the Father we adore
and Holy Ghost for evermore.

528 Gerrit Gustafson
© 1990 Integrity's Hosanna! Music/Kingsway's
Thankyou Music

Only by grace can we enter,
only by grace can we stand;
not by our human endeavour,
but by the blood of the Lamb.
Into your presence you call us,
you call us to come.
Into your presence you draw us,
and now by your grace we come,
now by your grace we come.

Lord, if you mark our transgressions,
who would stand?
Thanks to your grace we are cleansed
by the blood of the Lamb.
(Repeat)

529 Marie Lydia Pereira (b. 1920)
© 1999 Kevin Mayhew Ltd.

On this day of joy, on this day of hope,
we come to you in love, O Lord,
on this day of joy, on this day of hope,
we come to you in love.

1. With this bread and wine we come
to this eucharistic feast.
On this day of joy, on this day of hope,
we come to you in love.

2. Bread to be your body, Lord,
wine to be your saving blood;
on this day of joy, on this day of hope,
we come to you in love.

530 18th century trans. Henry Williams Baker
(1821-1877) adapted by the editors of 'English Praise'
© Oxford University Press

1. On this day, the first of days,
God the Father's name we praise,
who, creation's Lord and spring,
did the world from darkness bring.

2. On this day his only Son
over death the triumph won;
on this day the Spirit came
with his gifts of living flame.

Continued overleaf

3. On this day his people raise
   one pure sacrifice of praise,
   and, with all the saints above,
   tell of Christ's redeeming love.

4. Praise, O God, to thee be giv'n,
   praise on earth and praise in heav'n,
   praise to thy eternal Son,
   who this day our vict'ry won.

531 Michael Forster (b. 1946)
© 1996 Kevin Mayhew Ltd.

1. Onward, Christian pilgrims,
   Christ will be our light;
   see, the heav'nly vision
   breaks upon our sight!
   Out of death's enslavement
   Christ has set us free,
   on then to salvation,
   hope and liberty.

   Onward, Christian pilgrims,
   Christ will be our light;
   see, the heav'nly vision
   breaks upon our sight!

2. Onward, Christian pilgrims,
   up the rocky way,
   where the dying Saviour
   bids us watch and pray.
   Through the darkened valley
   walk with those who mourn,
   share the pain and anger,
   share the promised dawn!

3. Onward, Christian pilgrims,
   in the early dawn;
   death's great seal is broken,
   life and hope reborn!
   Faith in resurrection
   strengthens pilgrim's hearts,
   ev'ry load is lightened,
   ev'ry fear departs.

4. Onward, Christian pilgrims,
   hearts and voices raise,
   till the whole creation
   echoes perfect praise;
   swords are turned to ploughshares,
   pride and envy cease,
   truth embraces justice,
   hope resolves in peace.

532 Robert Cull (b. 1949)
© 1976 Maranatha! Music/CopyCare

Open our eyes, Lord, we want to see Jesus,
to reach out and touch him
and say that we love him;
open our ears, Lord, and help us to listen;
O, open our eyes, Lord,
we want to see Jesus!

533 Dorothy Francis Gurney (1858-1932)
© Copyright control

1. O perfect love,
   all human thought transcending,
   lowly we kneel
   in prayer before thy throne,
   that theirs may be
   the love which knows no ending,
   whom thou for evermore
   dost join in one.

2. O perfect life,
   be thou their full assurance
   of tender charity
   and steadfast faith,
   of patient hope
   and quiet, brave endurance,
   with childlike trust that fears
   not pain nor death.

3. Grant them the joy
   which brightens earthly sorrow,
   grant them the peace
   which calms all earthly strife;
   and to life's day
   the glorious unknown morrow
   that dawns upon
   eternal love and life.

534 Henry Williams Baker (1821-1877)
based on Psalms 148 and 150, alt.

1. O praise ye the Lord!
   praise him in the height;
   rejoice in his word, ye angels of light;
   ye heavens, adore him,
   by whom ye were made,
   and worship before him,
   in brightness arrayed.

2. O praise ye the Lord!
   praise him upon earth,
   in tuneful accord, all you of new birth;
   praise him who hath brought you
   his grace from above,
   praise him who hath taught you
   to sing of his love.

3. O praise ye the Lord!
   all things that give sound;
   each jubilant chord re-echo around;
   loud organs his glory
   forth tell in deep tone,
   and, sweet harp, the story
   of what he hath done.

4. O praise ye the Lord!
   thanksgiving and song
   to him be outpoured all ages along:
   for love in creation,
   for heaven restored,
   for grace of salvation,
   O praise ye the Lord!

535 Paul Gerhardt (1607-1676)
based on 'Salve caput cruentatum'
trans. Henry Williams Baker (1821-1877)

1. O sacred head, surrounded
   by crown of piercing thorn!
   O bleeding head, so wounded,
   so shamed and put to scorn!
   Death's pallid hue comes o'er thee,
   the glow of life decays;
   yet angel-hosts adore thee,
   and tremble as they gaze.

2. Thy comeliness and vigour
   is withered up and gone,
   and in thy wasted figure
   I see death drawing on.
   O agony and dying!
   O love to sinners free!
   Jesu, all grace supplying,
   turn thou thy face on me.

3. In this thy bitter passion,
   good Shepherd, think of me
   with thy most sweet compassion,
   unworthy though I be:
   beneath thy cross abiding
   for ever would I rest,
   in thy dear love confiding,
   and with thy presence blest.

536 Louis F Benson (1855-1930)
© Copyright control

1. O sing a song of Bethlehem,
   of shepherds watching there,
   and of the news that came to them
   from angels in the air:
   the light that shone on Bethlehem
   fills all the world today;
   of Jesus' birth and peace on earth
   the angels sing alway.

2. O sing a song of Nazareth,
   of sunny days of joy,
   O sing of fragrant flowers' breath
   and of the sinless Boy:
   for now the flow'rs of Nazareth
   in ev'ry heart may grow;
   now spreads the fame of his dear name
   on all the winds that blow.

3. O sing a song of Galilee,
   of lake and woods and hill,
   of him who walked upon the sea
   and bade its waves be still:
   for though, like waves on Galilee,
   dark seas of trouble roll,
   when faith has heard the Master's word,
   falls peace upon the soul.

Continued overleaf

4. O sing a song of Calvary,
   its glory and dismay;
   of him who hung upon the tree,
   and took our sins away;
   for he who died on Calvary
   is risen from the grave,
   and Christ our Lord, by heaven adored,
   is mighty now to save.

537 St. Ambrose (c. 340-397) trans. John Ellerton (1826-1893) and Fenton John Anthony Hort (1828-1892)

1. O strength and stay upholding all
      creation,
   who ever dost thyself unmoved abide,
   yet day by day the light in due gradation
   from hour to hour through all its changes
      guide.

2. Grant to life's day a calm unclouded
      ending,
   an eve untouched by shadows of decay,
   the brightness of a holy death-bed
      blending
   with dawning glories of th'eternal day.

3. Hear us, O Father, gracious and
      forgiving,
   through Jesus Christ thy co-eternal
      Word,
   who with the Holy Ghost by all things
      living
   now and to endless ages art adored.

538 Samuel Trevor Francis (1834-1925)

1. O the deep, deep love of Jesus!
   Vast, unmeasured, boundless, free;
   rolling as a mighty ocean
   in its fullness over me.
   Underneath me, all around me,
   is the current of thy love;
   leading onward, leading homeward,
   to my glorious rest above.

2. O the deep, deep love of Jesus!
   Spread his praise from shore to shore,
   how he loveth, ever loveth,
   changeth never, nevermore;
   how he watches o'er his loved ones,
   died to call them all his own;
   how for them he intercedeth,
   watcheth o'er them from the throne.

3. O the deep, deep love of Jesus!
   Love of ev'ry love the best;
   'tis an ocean vast of blessing,
   'tis a haven sweet of rest.
   O the deep, deep love of Jesus!
   'Tis a heav'n of heav'ns to me;
   and it lifts me up to glory,
   for its lifts me up to thee.

539 Estelle White (b. 1925)
© McCrimmon Publishing Co. Ltd.

1. O, the love of my Lord is the essence
   of all that I love here on earth.
   All the beauty I see he has given to me,
   and his giving is gentle as silence.

2. Ev'ry day, ev'ry hour, ev'ry moment
   have been blessed by the strength of
      his love.
   At the turn of each tide he is there at
      my side,
   and his touch is as gentle as silence.

3. There've been times when I've turned
      from his presence,
   and I've walked other paths, other ways;
   but I've called on his name in the dark of
      my shame,
   and his mercy was gentle as silence.

540 William Harry Turton (1856-1938), based on John 17

1. O thou, who at thy Eucharist didst pray
   that all thy Church might be for
     ever one,
   grant us at ev'ry eucharist to say,
   with longing heart and soul,
   'Thy will be done.'
   O may we all one bread, one body be,
   through this blest sacrament of unity.

2. For all thy Church, O Lord, we intercede;
   make thou our sad divisions soon
     to cease;
   draw us the nearer each to each,
     we plead,
   by drawing all to thee, O Prince of Peace:
   thus may we all one bread, one body be,
   through this blest sacrament of unity.

3. We pray thee too for wand'rers from
     thy fold;
   O bring them back, good Shepherd of
     the sheep,
   back to the faith which saints believed
     of old,
   back to the Church which still that faith
     doth keep;
   soon may we all one bread, one body be,
   through this blest sacrament of unity.

4. So, Lord, at length when sacraments
     shall cease,
   may we be one with all thy Church above,
   one with thy saints in one unbroken peace,
   one with thy saints in one unbounded love;
   more blessèd still, in peace and love to be
   one with the Trinity in unity.

541 Charles Wesley (1707-1788) based on Leviticus 6:13

1. O thou who camest from above
   the fire celestial to impart,
   kindle a flame of sacred love
   on the mean altar of my heart.

2. There let it for thy glory burn
   with inextinguishable blaze,
   and trembling to its source return
   in humble prayer and fervent praise.

3. Jesus, confirm my heart's desire
   to work and speak and think for thee;
   still let me guard the holy fire
   and still stir up the gift in me.

4. Ready for all thy perfect will,
   my acts of faith and love repeat,
   till death thy endless mercies seal,
   and make the sacrifice complete.

542 John Mason Neale (1818-1866) alt.

1. O Trinity, most blessèd light,
   O Unity of sovereign might,
   as now the fiery sun departs
   shed thou thy beams within our hearts.

2. To thee our morning song of praise,
   to thee our evening prayer we raise;
   thee may our souls for evermore
   in lowly reverence adore.

3. All praise to God the Father be,
   all praise, eternal Son, to thee,
   whom with the Spirit we adore,
   for ever and evermore. Amen.

543 Harriet Auber (1773-1862)

1. Our blest Redeemer, ere he breathed
   his tender last farewell,
   a Guide, a Comforter, bequeathed
   with us to dwell.

2. He came in tongues of living flame,
   to teach, convince, subdue;
   all-pow'rful as the wind he came,
   as viewless too.

Continued overleaf

3. He came sweet influence to impart,
   a gracious, willing guest,
   while he can find one humble heart
   wherein to rest.

4. And his that gentle voice we hear,
   soft as the breath of ev'n,
   that checks each fault, that calms each fear,
   and speaks of heav'n.

5. And ev'ry virtue we possess,
   and ev'ry vict'ry won,
   and ev'ry thought of holiness,
   are his alone.

6. Spirit of purity and grace,
   our weakness, pitying, see:
   O make our hearts thy dwelling-place,
   and worthier thee.

544 Traditional Caribbean,
based on Matthew 6:9-13 and Luke 11:2-4

1. Our Father, who art in heaven,
   hallowed be thy name.
   Thy kingdom come, thy will be done,
   hallowed be thy name. (x2)

2. On earth as it is in heaven.
   hallowed be thy name.
   Give us this day our daily bread,
   hallowed be thy name. (x2)

3. Forgive us our trespasses,
   hallowed be thy name.
   as we forgive those who trespass against us.
   hallowed be thy name. (x2)

4. Lead us not into temptation,
   hallowed be thy name.
   but deliver us from all that is evil.
   hallowed be thy name. (x2)

5. For thine is the kingdom,
   the power, and the glory,
   hallowed be thy name.
   for ever, and for ever and ever.
   hallowed be thy name. (x2)

6. Amen, amen, it shall be so.
   hallowed be thy name.
   Amen, amen, it shall be so.
   hallowed be thy name. (x2)

545 Our Father (Estelle White)

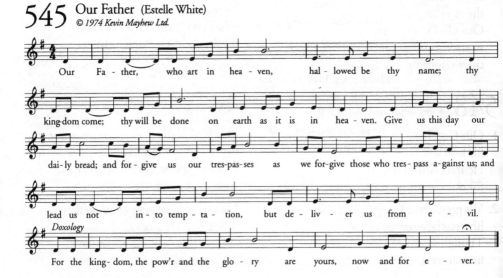

Our Father, who art in hea-ven, hal-lowed be thy name; thy king-dom come; thy will be done on earth as it is in hea-ven. Give us this day our dai-ly bread; and for-give us our tres-pas-ses as we for-give those who tres-pass a-gainst us; and lead us not in-to temp-ta-tion, but de-liv-er us from e-vil.

Doxology

For the king-dom, the pow'r and the glo-ry are yours, now and for e-ver.

546 Our Father (Julian Wiener)

Our Fa - ther, who art in hea - ven, hal - lowed be thy name;

thy king-dom come; thy will be done on earth as it is in hea -

ven. Give us this day our dai - ly bread; and for-give us our tres-pas - ses

as we for - give those who tres-pass a - gainst us; and lead us not in - to temp-

Doxology

ta - tion, but de-li - ver us from all that is e - vil. For the king - dom,

the pow'r and the glo - ry are yours, now and for e -ver. A - men.

547 Unknown

Our God is so great,
so strong and so mighty,
there's nothing that he cannot do.
(Repeat)
The rivers are his,
the mountains are his,
the stars are his handiwork too.
Our God is so great,
so strong and so mighty,
there's nothing that he cannot do.

548 v 1 unknown, vs 2-5 Sandra Joan Billington (b. 1946)

1. Our God loves us,
his love will never end.
He rests within our hearts
for our God loves us.

2. His gentle hand
he stretches over us.
Though storm-clouds threaten the day,
he will set us free.

3. He comes to us
in sharing bread and wine.
He brings us life that will reach
past the end of time.

4. Our God loves us,
his faithful love endures,
and we will live like his child
held in love secure.

5. The joys of love
as off'rings now we bring.
The pains of love will be lost
in the praise we sing.

549 Fred Kaan (b. 1929)

1. Out of our failure to create
a world of love and care:
out of the depths of human life
we cry to God in pray'r.

2. Out of the darkness of our time,
of days forever gone,
our souls are longing for the light,
like watchers for the dawn.

Continued overleaf

3. Out of the depths we cry to God
whose mercy ends our night.
Our human hole-and-corner ways
by God are brought to light.

4. Hope in the Lord whose timeless love
gives laughter where we wept;
who at every time, at every point
his word has giv'n and kept.

550 Peter Abelard (1079-1142)
trans. John Mason Neale (1818-1866) alt.

1. O what their joy and their glory must be,
those endless sabbaths the blessèd ones see;
crown for the valiant, to weary ones rest;
God shall be all, and in all ever blest.

2. What are the Monarch, his court, and
his throne?
What are the peace and the joy that
they own?
O that the blest ones, who in it have
share,
all that they feel could as fully declare.

3. Truly Jerusalem name we that shore,
'Vision of peace,' that brings joy
evermore.
Wish and fulfilment can severed be ne'er,
nor the thing prayed for come short of
the prayer.

4. There, where no troubles distraction can
bring,
we the sweet anthems of Sion shall sing,
while for they grace, Lord, their voices
of praise
thy blessèd people eternally raise.

5. There dawns no sabbath, no sabbath
is o'er,
those sabbath-keepers have one
evermore;
one and unending is that triumph-song
which to the angels and us shall belong.

6. Now in the meanwhile, with hearts
raised on high,
we for that country must yearn and
must sigh;
seeking Jerusalem, dear native land,
through our long exile on Babylon's stran

7. Low before him with our praises we fal
of whom, and in whom, and through
whom are all:
of whom, the Father; and in whom,
the Son;
through whom, the Spirit, with them
ever One.

551 Robert Grant (1779-1838), based on Psalm 104

1. O worship the King
all glorious above;
O gratefully sing
his pow'r and his love:
our shield and defender,
the Ancient of Days,
pavilioned in splendour,
and girded with praise.

2. O tell of his might,
O sing of his grace,
whose robe is the light,
whose canopy space;
his chariots of wrath
the deep thunder-clouds form,
and dark in his path
on the wings of the storm.

3. This earth, with its store
of wonders untold,
almighty, thy pow'r
hath founded of old:
hath stablished it fast
by a changeless decree,
and round it hath cast,
like a mantle, the sea.

4. Thy bountiful care
   what tongue can recite?
   It breathes in the air,
   it shines in the light;
   it streams from the hills,
   it descends to the plain,
   and sweetly distils
   in the dew and the rain.

5. Frail children of dust,
   and feeble as frail,
   in thee do we trust,
   nor find thee to fail;
   thy mercies how tender,
   how firm to the end!
   Our maker, defender,
   redeemer, and friend.

6. O measureless might,
   ineffable love,
   while angels delight
   to hymn thee above,
   thy humbler creation,
   though feeble their lays,
   with true adoration
   shall sing to thy praise.

552 John Samuel Bewley Monsell (1811-1875)

1. O worship the Lord
   in the beauty of holiness;
   bow down before him,
   his glory proclaim;
   with gold of obedience
   and incense of lowliness,
   kneel and adore him:
   the Lord is his name.

2. Low at his feet lay
   thy burden of carefulness:
   high on his heart
   he will bear it for thee,
   comfort thy sorrows,
   and answer thy prayerfulness,
   guiding thy steps
   as may best for thee be.

3. Fear not to enter
   his courts in the slenderness
   of the poor wealth
   thou wouldst reckon as thine:
   truth in its beauty,
   and love in its tenderness,
   these are the off'rings
   to lay on his shrine.

4. These, though we bring them
   in trembling and fearfulness,
   he will accept
   for the name that is dear;
   mornings of joy give
   for evenings of tearfulness,
   trust for our trembling
   and hope for our fear.

553 v 1-4 unknown, v 5 the Editors
v 5 © 1999 Kevin Mayhew Ltd.

1. Peace is flowing like a river,
   flowing out through you and me,
   spreading out into the desert,
   setting all the captives free.

   (This refrain is not always sung.)

   Let it flow through me,
   let it flow through me,
   let the mighty peace of God
   flow out through me. (Repeat)

2. Love is flowing like a river,
   flowing out through you and me,
   spreading out into the desert,
   setting all the captives free.

3. Joy is flowing like a river,
   flowing out through you and me,
   spreading out into the desert,
   setting all the captives free.

4. Hope is flowing like a river,
   flowing out through you and me,
   spreading out into the desert,
   setting all the captives free.

Continued overleaf

5. Christ brings peace to all creation,
   flowing out through you and me,
   love, joy, hope and true salvation,
   setting all the captives free.

554 Edward Henry Bickersteth (1825-1906)

1. Peace, perfect peace,
   in this dark world of sin?
   The blood of Jesus
   whispers peace within.

2. Peace, perfect peace,
   by thronging duties pressed?
   To do the will of Jesus,
   this is rest.

3. Peace, perfect peace,
   with sorrows surging round?
   In Jesus' presence
   naught but calm is found.

4. Peace, perfect peace,
   with loved ones far away?
   In Jesus' keeping
   we are safe, and they.

5. Peace, perfect peace,
   our future all unknown?
   Jesus we know,
   and he is on the throne.

6. Peace, perfect peace,
   death shad'wing us and ours?
   Jesus has vanquished death
   and all its pow'rs.

7. It is enough: earth's struggles
   soon shall cease,
   and Jesus call us
   to heav'n's perfect peace.

555 Kevin Mayhew (b. 1942)
© 1976 Kevin Mayhew Ltd.

1. Peace, perfect peace
   is the gift of Christ our Lord.
   Peace, perfect peace,
   is the gift of Christ our Lord.
   Thus says the Lord,
   will the world know my friends.
   Peace, perfect peace,
   is the gift of Christ our Lord.

2. Love, perfect love . . .

3. Faith, perfect faith . . .

4. Hope, perfect hope . . .

5. Joy, perfect joy . . .

556 Graham Kendrick (b. 1950)
© 1988 Make Way Music

Peace to you.
We bless you now
in the name of the Lord.
Peace to you.
We bless you now
in the name of the Prince of Peace.
Peace to you.

557 Eleanor Farjeon (1881-1965)
© David Higham Associates Ltd.

1. People, look east. The time is near
   of the crowning of the year.
   Make your house fair as you are able,
   trim the hearth, and set the table.
   People, look east, and sing today:
   Love the guest is on the way.

2. Furrows, be glad. Though the earth is
   bare,
   one more seed is planted there:
   give up your strength the seed to nourish,
   that in course the flower may flourish.
   People, look east, and sing today:
   love the rose is on the way.

3. Birds, though ye long have ceased to
     build,
   guard the nest that must be filled.
   Even the hour when wings are frozen
   he for fledging-time has chosen.
   People, look east, and sing today:
   love the bird is on the way.

4. Stars, keep the watch. When night is dim
   one more light the bowl shall brim,
   shining beyond the frosty weather,
   bright as sun and moon together.
   People, look east, and sing today:
   love the star is on the way.

5. Angels, announce to man and beast
   him who cometh from the east.
   Set ev'ry peak and valley humming
   with the word, the Lord is coming.
   People, look east, and sing today:
   love the lord is on the way.

558 Albert F Bayly (1901-1984) alt.
© Oxford University Press

1. Praise and thanksgiving, Father, we offer,
   for all things living you have made good;
   harvest of sown fields, fruits of the
     orchard,
   hay from the mown fields, blossom and
     wood.

2. Lord, bless the labour we bring to serve
     you,
   that with our neighbour we may be fed.
   Sowing or tilling, we would work with
     you;
   harvesting milling, for daily bread

3. Father, providing food for your children,
   your wisdom guiding teaches us share
   one with another, so that, rejoicing,
   sister and brother may know your care.

4. Then will your blessing reach ev'ry
     people;
   each one confessing your gracious hand:
   where you are reigning no one will
     hunger,
   your love sustaining fruitful the land.

559 Brian Wren (b. 1936)
© 1974, 1996 *Stainer & Bell Ltd.*

1. Praise God for the harvest of orchard
     and field,
   praise God for the people who gather
     their yield,
   the long hours of labour, the skills of a
     team,
   the patience of science, the pow'r
     of machine.

2. Praise God for the harvest that comes
     from afar,
   from market and harbour, the sea and
     the shore:
   foods packed and transported, and
     gathered and grown
   by God-given neighbours, unseen
     and unknown.

3. Praise God for the harvest that's quarried
     and mined,
   then sifted, and smelted, or shaped and
     refined:
   for oil and for iron, for copper and coal,
   praise God, who in love has provided
     them all.

4. Praise God for the harvest of science
     and skill,
   the urge to discover, create and fulfil:
   for dreams and inventions that promise
     to gain
   a future more hopeful, a world more
     humane.

Continued overleaf

5. Praise God for the harvest of mercy and
     love
   from leaders and peoples who struggle
     and serve
   with patience and kindness, that all may
     be led
   to freedom and justice, and all may
     be fed.

560 Thomas Ken (1637-1710)

Praise God, from whom all blessings flow,
praise him, all creatures here below,
praise him above ye heav'nly host,
praise Father, Son and Holy Ghost.

561 John Kennett, based on Psalm 150
© 1981 Kingsway's Thankyou Music

Praise him on the trumpet,
the psalt'ry and harp;
praise him on the timbrel and the dance;
praise him with stringed instruments
     too;
praise him on the loud cymbals,
praise him on the loud cymbals;
let ev'rything that has breath praise
     the Lord!

Hallelujah, praise the Lord;
hallelujah, praise the Lord:
let ev'rything that has breath
praise the Lord!
Hallelujah, praise the Lord;
hallelujah, praise the Lord:
let ev'rything that has breath
praise the Lord!

562 Frances Jane van Alstyne
(Fanny J. Crosby) (1820-1915)

1. Praise him, praise him!
   Jesus, our blessèd Redeemer!
   Sing, O earth,
   his wonderful love proclaim!
   Hail him, hail him!
   highest archangels in glory;
   strength and honour
   give to his holy name!
   Like a shepherd,
   Jesus will guard his children,
   in his arms he carries
   them all day long.
   Praise him, praise him!
   tell of his excellent greatness;
   praise him, praise him
   ever in joyful song!

2. Praise him, praise him!
   Jesus, our blessèd Redeemer!
   For our sins
   he suffered, and bled, and died!
   He – our rock,
   our hope of eternal salvation,
   hail him, hail him!
   Jesus the crucified!
   Sound his praises
   – Jesus who bore our sorrows,
   love unbounded, wonderful,
   deep and strong.

3. Praise him, praise him!
   Jesus, our blessèd Redeemer!
   Heav'nly portals,
   loud with hosannas ring!
   Jesus, Saviour,
   reigneth for ever and ever:
   crown him, crown him!
   Prophet, and Priest, and King!
   Christ is coming,
   over the world victorious,
   pow'r and glory
   unto the Lord belong.

563

Percy Dearmer (1867-1936)
based on Carey Bonner (1859-1938)
© Oxford University Press. Used by permission

1. Praise him, praise him,
   all his children praise him!
   He is love, he is love.
   Praise him, praise him,
   all his children praise him!
   He is love, he is love.

2. Thank him, thank him,
   all his children thank him!
   He is love, he is love.
   Thank him, thank him,
   all his children thank him!
   He is love, he is love.

3. Love him, love him,
   all his children love him!
   He is love, he is love.
   Love him, love him,
   all his children love him!
   He is love, he is love.

4. Crown him, crown him,
   all his children crown him!
   He is love, he is love.
   Crown him, crown him,
   all his children crown him!
   He is love, he is love.

564 Unknown

1. Praise him, praise him,
   praise him in the morning,
   praise him in the noontime.
   Praise him, praise him,
   praise him when the sun goes down.

2. Love him, love him, . . .

3. Trust him, trust him, . . .

4. Serve him, serve him, . . .

5. Jesus, Jesus, . . .

565 Henry Francis Lyte (1793-1847), based on Psalm 103

1. Praise, my soul, the King of heaven!
   To his feet thy tribute bring;
   ransomed, healed, restored, forgiven,
   who like me his praise should sing?
   Praise him! Praise him!
   Praise him! Praise him!
   Praise the everlasting King!

2. Praise him for his grace and favour
   to our fathers in distress;
   praise him still the same as ever,
   slow to chide and swift to bless.
   Praise him! Praise him!
   Praise him! Praise him!
   Glorious in his faithfulness!

3. Father-like, he tends and spares us;
   well our feeble frame he knows;
   in his hands he gently bears us,
   rescues us from all our foes.
   Praise him! Praise him!
   Praise him! Praise him!
   Widely as his mercy flows!

4. Angels, help us to adore him;
   ye behold him face to face;
   sun and moon, bow down before him,
   dwellers all in time and space.
   Praise him! Praise him!
   Praise him! Praise him!
   Praise with us the God of grace!

566 Henry Williams Baker (1821-1877)

1. Praise, O praise our God and King;
   hymns of adoration sing:

   for his mercies still endure
   ever faithful, ever sure.

2. Praise him that he made the sun
   day by day his course to run:

3. And the silver moon by night,
   shining with her gentle light:

Continued overleaf

4. Praise him that he gave the rain
to mature the swelling grain:

for his mercies still endure
ever faithful, ever sure.

5. And hath bid the fruitful field
crops of precious increase yield:

6. Praise him for our harvest-store;
he hath filled the garner-floor:

7. And for richer food than this,
pledge of everlasting bliss:

8. Glory to our bounteous King;
glory let creation sing:
glory to the Father, Son
and blest Spirit, Three in One.

567 Mike Anderson (b. 1956), based on Psalm 47
© 1999 Kevin Mayhew Ltd.

Praise the Lord, all of you peoples,
praise the Lord, shout for joy!
Praise the Lord, sing him a new song,
praise the Lord and bless his name!

1. Clap your hands, now, all of you nations.
shout for joy, acclaim the Lord.

2. He goes up to shouts which acclaim him,
he goes up to trumpet blast.

3. Let the music sound for the Lord, now;
let your chords resound in praise.

4. He is King of all the nations;
honour him by singing psalms.

568 Timothy Dudley-Smith (b. 1926), based on Psalm 148
© Timothy Dudley-Smith

1. Praise the Lord of heaven,
praise him in the height;
praise him, all his angels,
praise him, hosts of light.
Sun and moon together,
shining stars aflame,
planets in their courses,
magnify his name!

2. Earth and ocean praise him;
mountains, hills and trees;
fire and hail and tempest,
wind and storm and seas.
Praise him, fields and forests,
birds on flashing wings,
praise him, beasts and cattle,
all created things.

3. Now by prince and people
let his praise be told;
praise him, men and maidens,
praise him, young and old.
He, the Lord of glory!
We, his praise proclaim!
High above all heavens
magnify his name!

569 Howard Charles Adie Gaunt (1902-1983)
© Oxford University Press

1. Praise the Lord, rise up rejoicing,
worship, thanks, devotion voicing:
glory be to God on high!
Christ, your cross and passion sharing,
by this Eucharist declaring
yours th'eternal victory.

2. Scattered flock, one Shepherd sharing,
lost and lonely, one voice hearing,
ears are open to your word;
by your blood new life receiving,
in your body firm, believing,
we are yours, and you the Lord.

3. Send us forth alert and living,
sins forgiven, wrongs forgiving,
in your Spirit strong and free.
Finding love in all creation,
bringing peace in ev'ry nation,
may we faithful foll'wers be.

570 vs 1 and 2 from 'Foundling Hospital Collection' (1796)
vs 3 Edward Osler (1798-1863)

1. Praise the Lord, ye heav'ns, adore him!
Praise him, angels, in the height;
sun and moon, rejoice before him,
praise him, all ye stars and light.
Praise the Lord, for he hath spoken;
worlds his mighty voice obeyed:
laws, which never shall be broken,
for their guidance he hath made.

2. Praise the Lord, for he is glorious:
never shall his promise fail.
God hath made his saints victorious;
sin and death shall not prevail.
Praise the God of our salvation,
hosts on high, his pow'r proclaim;
heav'n and earth and all creation,
laud and magnify his name!

3. Worship, honour, glory, blessing,
Lord, we offer to thy name;
young and old, thy praise expressing,
join their Saviour to proclaim.
As the saints in heav'n adore thee,
we would bow before thy throne;
as thine angels serve before thee,
so on earth thy will be done.

571 Michael Forster (b. 1946)
© 1999 Kevin Mayhew Ltd.

1. Praise to God for saints and martyrs
inspiration to us all;
in the presence of our Saviour,
their example we recall:
lives of holy contemplation,
sacrifice or simple love,
witnesses to truth and justice,
honoured here and crowned above.

2. How we long to share their story,
faithful in response to grace,
signs of God's eternal presence
in the realm of time and space.
Now, their pilgrimage completed,
cross of Christ their only boast,
they unite their own rejoicing
with the great angelic host.

3. Saints and martyrs, now in glory,
robed before your Saviour's face,
let us join your intercession
for God's holy human race.
Let us join with you in singing
Mary's liberation song,
till a just and free creation sings,
with the angelic throng:

4. Praise and honour to the Father,
adoration to the Son,
with the all-embracing Spirit
wholly Three and holy One.
All the universe, united
in complete diversity,
sings as one your endless praises,
ever blessèd Trinity!

572 John Henry Newman (1801-1890)

1. Praise to the Holiest in the height,
and in the depth be praise;
in all his words most wonderful,
most sure in all his ways.

2. O loving wisdom of our God!
when all was sin and shame,
a second Adam to the fight,
and to the rescue came.

3. O wisest love! that flesh and blood,
which did in Adam fail,
should strive afresh against the foe,
should strive and should prevail.

Continued overleaf

4. And that a higher gift than grace
   should flesh and blood refine,
   God's presence and his very self,
   and essence all-divine.

5. And in the garden secretly,
   and on the cross on high,
   should teach his brethren, and inspire
   to suffer and to die.

6. Praise to the Holiest in the height,
   and in the depth be praise;
   in all his words most wonderful,
   most sure in all his ways.

573 Joachim Neander (1650-1680)
trans. Catherine Winkworth (1827-1878)

1. Praise to the Lord,
   the Almighty, the King of creation!
   O my soul, praise him,
   for he is thy health and salvation.
   All ye who hear,
   now to his temple draw near;
   joining in glad adoration.

2. Praise to the Lord,
   who o'er all things so wondrously reigneth,
   shieldeth thee gently from harm,
   or when fainting sustaineth:
   hast thou not seen
   how thy heart's wishes have been
   granted in what he ordaineth?

3. Praise to the Lord,
   who doth prosper thy work and defend thee,
   surely his goodness and mercy
   shall daily attend thee:
   ponder anew
   what the Almighty can do,
   if to the end he befriend thee.

4. Praise to the Lord,
   O let all that is in us adore him!
   All that hath life and breath,
   come now with praises before him.
   Let the 'Amen'
   sound from his people again,
   gladly for ay we adore him.

574 Brian Doerksen
© 1990 Mercy/Vineyard Publishing/CopyCare

1. Purify my heart,
   let me be as gold and precious silver.
   Purify my heart,
   let me be as gold, pure gold.

   Refiner's fire,
   my heart's one desire
   is to be holy,
   set apart for you, Lord.
   I choose to be holy,
   set apart for you, my master,
   ready to do your will.

2. Purify my heart,
   cleanse me from within and make me
      holy.
   Purify my heart,
   cleanse me from my sin, deep within.

575 Fred Kaan (b. 1929)
© 1989 Stainer & Bell Ltd.

1. Put peace into each other's hands
   and like a treasure hold it,
   protect it like a candle-flame,
   with tenderness enfold it.

2. Put peace into each other's hands
   with loving expectation;
   be gentle in your words and ways,
   in touch with God's creation.

3. Put peace into each other's hands
   like bread we break for sharing;
   look people warmly in the eye:
   our life is meant for caring.

4. As at communion, shape your hands
   into a waiting cradle;
   the gift of Christ receive, revere,
   united round the table.

5. Put Christ into each other's hands,
   he is love's deepest measure;
   in love make peace, give peace a chance
   and share it like a treasure.

576 Paul Gerhardt (1607-1676)
trans. John Wesley (1703-1791) and others

1. Put thou thy trust in God,
   in duty's path go on;
   walk in his strength with faith and hope,
   so shall thy work be done.

2. Commit thy ways to him,
   thy works into his hands,
   and rest on his unchanging word,
   who heav'n and earth commands.

3. Though years on years roll on,
   his cov'nant shall endure;
   though clouds and darkness hide his path,
   the promised grace is sure.

4. Give to the winds thy fears;
   hope, and be undismayed:
   God hears thy sighs and counts thy tears;
   God shall lift up thy head.

5. Through waves and clouds and storms
   his pow'r will clear thy way:
   wait thou his time; the darkest night
   shall end in brightest day.

6. Leave to his sov'reign sway
   to choose and to command;
   so shalt thou, wond'ring, own his way,
   how wise, how strong his hand.

577 Mike Anderson (b. 1956), based on the Exsultet,
© 1999 Kevin Mayhew Ltd

*Rejoice, heavenly powers, sing, choirs of
    angels,
exult, all creation, around God's throne.
Jesus is risen, sound the trumpet of salvation.
Sing, dance and rejoice for Jesus lives.*

1. Rejoice, O Mother Church and sing,
   (Rejoice! Rejoice!)
   bathed in the brightness of your King!
   (Rejoice! Rejoice!)
   Enjoy the victory he brings! (Rejoice!
   Rejoice!)
   rejoice, rejoice, rejoice!

2. The price for Adam's sin is paid,
   (Rejoice! Rejoice!)
   by Jesus' blood we have been saved;
   (Rejoice! Rejoice!)
   he rose triumphant from the grave,
   (Rejoice! Rejoice!)
   rejoice, rejoice, rejoice!

3. This night will be as clear as day,
   (Rejoice! Rejoice!)
   the morning star is here to stay;
   (Rejoice! Rejoice!)
   and he has washed all guilt away,
   (Rejoice! Rejoice!)
   rejoice, rejoice, rejoice!

4. And now this Easter candle's light
   (Rejoice! Rejoice!)
   dispels the darkness of the night;
   (Rejoice! Rejoice!)
   rejoice in justice, peace and right,
   (Rejoice! Rejoice!)
   rejoice, rejoice, rejoice!

578 Unknown
Based on Philippians 4:4

Rejoice in the Lord always and again
I say rejoice. *(Repeat)*
Rejoice, rejoice and again I say rejoice.
(Repeat)

579 Robert Bridges (1844-1930)
© 1996 Oxford University Press. Used by permission

1. Rejoice, O land, in God thy might;
   his will obey, him serve aright;
   for thee the saints uplift their voice:
   fear not, O land, in God rejoice.

2. Glad shalt thou be, with blessing
      crowned,
   with joy and peace thou shalt abound;
   yea, love with thee shall make his home
   until thou see God's kingdom come.

Continued overleaf

3. He shall forgive thy sins untold:
   remember thou his love of old;
   walk in his way, his word adore,
   and keep his truth for evermore.

580 Charles Wesley (1707-1788)

1. Rejoice the Lord is King!
   Your Lord and King adore;
   mortals, give thanks and sing,
   and triumph evermore.

   Lift up your heart, lift up your voice;
   rejoice, again I say, rejoice.

2. Jesus the Saviour reigns,
   the God of truth and love;
   when he had purged our stains,
   he took his seat above.

3. His kingdom cannot fail;
   he rules o'er earth and heav'n;
   the keys of death and hell
   are to our Jesus giv'n.

4. He sits at God's right hand
   till all his foes submit,
   and bow to his command,
   and fall beneath his feet.

581 Based on the Latin (c. 4th century)
trans. the Editors of 'The New English Hymnal'
© *The Canterbury Press*

1. Rejoice, the year upon its way
   has brought again that blessèd day
   when on the Church by Christ our Lord
   the Holy Spirit was outpoured.

2. From out the heav'ns a rushing noise
   came like the tempest's sudden voice,
   and mingled with th'Apostles' prayer,
   proclaiming loud that God was there.

3. Like quiv'ring tongues of light and flame,
   upon each one the Spirit came:
   tongues, that the earth might hear
       their call,
   and fire, that love might burn in all.

4. And so to all were spread abroad
   the wonders of the works of God;
   they knew the prophet's word fulfilled,
   and owned the gift which God had
       willed.

5. Look down, most gracious God, this day
   upon thy people as we pray;
   and Christ the Lord upon us pour
   the Spirit's gift for evermore.
   Amen.

582 Graham Kendrick (b. 1950) and Chris Rolinson
© *1981 Kingsway's Thankyou Music*

1. Restore, O Lord,
   the honour of your name,
   in works of sov'reign power
   come shake the earth again,
   that all may see,
   and come with rev'rent fear
   to the living God,
   whose kingdom shall outlast the years.

2. Restore, O Lord,
   in all the earth your fame,
   and in our time revive
   the church that bears your name.
   And in your anger,
   Lord, remember mercy,
   O living God,
   whose mercy shall outlast the years.

3. Bend us, O Lord,
   where we are hard and cold,
   in your refiner's fire:
   come purify the gold.
   Though suff'ring comes
   and evil crouches near,
   still our living God
   is reigning, he is reigning here.

4. *As verse 1*

583

583 Henry Hart Milman (1791-1868), alt.

1. Ride on, ride on in majesty!
   Hark all the tribes hosanna cry;
   thy humble beast pursues his road
   with palms and scattered garments
   strowed.

2. Ride on, ride on in majesty!
   In lowly pomp ride on to die;
   O Christ, thy triumphs now begin
   o'er captive death and conquered sin.

3. Ride on, ride on in majesty!
   The wingèd squadrons of the sky
   look down with sad and wond'ring eyes
   to see th'approaching sacrifice.

4. Ride on, ride on in majesty!
   Thy last and fiercest strife is nigh;
   the Father, on his sapphire throne,
   awaits his own appointed Son.

5. Ride on, ride on in majesty!
   In lowly pomp ride on to die;
   bow thy meek head to mortal pain,
   then take, O God, thy pow'r, and reign.

584 Augustus Montague Toplady (1740-1778) alt.

1. Rock of ages, cleft for me,
   let me hide myself in thee;
   let the water and the blood,
   from thy riven side which flowed,
   be of sin the double cure:
   cleanse me from its guilt and pow'r.

2. Not the labours of my hands
   can fulfil thy law's demands;
   could my zeal no respite know,
   could my tears for ever flow,
   all for sin could not atone:
   thou must save, and thou alone.

3. Nothing in my hands I bring,
   simply to thy cross I cling;
   naked, come to thee for dress;
   helpless, look to thee for grace;
   tainted, to the fountain fly;
   wash me, Saviour, or I die.

4. While I draw this fleeting breath,
   when mine eyelids close in death,
   when I soar through tracts unknown,
   see thee on thy judgement throne;
   Rock of ages, cleft for me,
   let me hide myself in thee.

585 William Romanis (1824-1889)

1. Round me falls the night;
   Saviour, be my light:
   through the hours in darkness shrouded
   let me see thy face unclouded:
   let thy glory shine
   in this heart of mine.

2. Earthly work is done,
   earthly sounds are none;
   rest in sleep and silence seeking,
   let me hear thee softly speaking;
   in my spirit's ear
   whisper, 'I am near.'

3. Blessèd, heavenly light,
   shining through earth's night;
   voice, that oft of love hast told me,
   arms, so strong to clasp and hold me;
   thou thy watch wilt keep,
   Saviour, o'er my sleep.

586 The Office of Night Prayer

Save us, O Lord, while we are awake,
and guard us while we sleep,
that awake we may watch with Christ,
and asleep we may rest in peace,
in Jesus' name, in Jesus' name.

587
John Ellerton (1826-1893)

1. Saviour, again
   to thy dear name we raise
   with one accord
   our parting hymn of praise;
   we stand to bless thee
   ere our worship cease;
   then, lowly kneeling,
   wait thy word of peace.

2. Grant us thy peace
   upon our homeward way;
   with thee began,
   with thee shall end, the day:
   guard thou the lips from sin,
   the hearts from shame,
   that in this house
   have called upon thy name.

3. Grant us thy peace,
   Lord, through the coming night;
   turn thou for us
   its darkness into light;
   from harm and danger
   keep thy children free,
   for dark and light
   are both alike to thee.

4. Grant us thy peace
   throughout our earthly life,
   our balm in sorrow,
   and our stay in strife;
   then, when thy voice
   shall bid our conflict cease,
   call us, O Lord,
   to thine eternal peace.

588
Edward Caswall (1814-1878)

1. See, amid the winter's snow,
   born for us on earth below,
   see, the tender Lamb appears,
   promised from eternal years.

   Hail, thou ever-blessèd morn,
   hail, redemption's happy dawn!
   Sing through all Jerusalem,
   Christ is born in Bethlehem.

2. Lo, within a manger lies
   he who built the starry skies;
   he, who, throned in heights sublime,
   sits amid the cherubim.

3. Say, you holy shepherds, say,
   what your joyful news today?
   Wherefore have you left your sheep
   on the lonely mountain steep?

4. 'As we watched at dead of night,
   there appeared a wondrous light;
   angels, singing peace on earth,
   told us of the Saviour's birth.'

5. Sacred infant, all divine,
   what a tender love was thine,
   thus to come from highest bliss,
   down to such a world as this!

6. Virgin mother, Mary, blest,
   by the joys that fill thy breast,
   pray for us, that we may prove
   worthy of the Saviour's love.

589
Michael Perry (1942-1996)
© 1965 Mrs B. Perry/Jubilate Hymns

1. See him lying on a bed of straw:
   a draughty stable with an open door.
   Mary cradling the babe she bore:
   the Prince of Glory is his name.

   O now carry me to Bethlehem
   to see the Lord of Love again:
   just as poor as was the stable then,
   the Prince of Glory when he came!

2. Star of silver, sweep across the skies,
   show where Jesus in the manger lies;
   shepherds, swiftly from your stupor rise
   to see the Saviour of the world!

3. Angels, sing again the song you sang,
   sing the glory of God's gracious plan;
   sing that Bethlehem's little baby can
   be the Saviour of us all.

4. Mine are riches, from your poverty;
   from your innocence, eternity;
   mine, forgiveness by your death for me,
   child of sorrow for my joy.

590
v 1 Karen Lafferty (b. 1948), vs 2 and 3 unknown, based on Matthew 6:33, 7:7
© 1972 Maranatha! Music/CopyCare

1. Seek ye first the kingdom of God,
   and his righteousness,
   and all these things shall be added
        unto you;
   allelu, alleluia.

   Alleluia, alleluia,
   alleluia, allelu, alleluia.

2. You shall not live by bread alone,
   but by ev'ry word
   that proceeds from the mouth of God;
   allelu, alleluia.

3. Ask and it shall be given unto you,
   seek and ye shall find;
   knock, and it shall be opened unto you;
   allelu, alleluia.

591 Christopher Wordsworth (1807-1885) alt.

1. See the conqu'ror mounts in triumph,
   see the King in royal state
   riding on the clouds his chariot
   to his heav'nly palace gate;
   hark, the choirs of angel-voices
   joyful alleluias sing,
   and the portals high are lifted
   to receive their heav'nly King.

2. Who is this that comes in glory
   with the trump of jubilee?
   Lord of battles, God of armies,
   he has gained the victory;
   he who on the cross did suffer,
   he who from the grave arose,
   he has vanquished sin and Satan,
   he by death has spoiled his foes.

3. Thou hast raised our human nature
   in the clouds of God's right hand;
   there we sit in heav'nly places,
   there with thee in glory stand;
   Jesus reigns, adored by angels,
   takes our flesh to heaven's throne;
   mighty Lord, in thine ascension,
   we by faith behold our own.

4. Glory be to God the Father;
   glory be to God the Son,
   dying, ris'n, ascending for us,
   who the heav'nly realm has won;
   glory to the Holy Spirit;
   to One God in persons Three;
   glory both in earth and heaven,
   glory, endless glory, be.

592
Michael Forster (b. 1946)
© 1993 Kevin Mayhew Ltd.

1. See the holy table,
   spread for our healing;
   hear the invitation
   to share in bread and wine.
   Catch the scent of goodness,
   taste and touch salvation;
   all mortal senses
   tell of love divine!

2. As the bread is broken,
   Christ is remembered;
   as the wine is flowing,
   his passion we recall;
   as redemption's story
   opens up before us,
   hope is triumphant,
   Christ is all in all.

Continued overleaf

3. Tell again the story,
   wonder of wonders:
   Christ, by grace eternal,
   transforms the simplest food!
   Sign of hope and glory,
   life in all its fullness,
   God's whole creation
   ransomed and renewed!

593 Michael Forster (b. 1946), based on Psalm 104
© 1997 Kevin Mayhew Ltd.

Send forth your Spirit, Lord,
renew the face of the earth. (Repeat)

1. Bless the Lord, O my soul,
   O Lord God, how great you are;
   you are clothed in honour and glory,
   you set the world on its foundations.

2. Lord, how great are your works,
   in wisdom you made them all;
   all the earth is full of your creatures,
   your hand always open to feed them.

3. May your wisdom endure,
   rejoice in your works, O Lord.
   I will sing for ever and ever,
   in praise of my God and my King.

594 Robert Lowry (1826-1899)

1. Shall we gather at the river,
   where bright angel feet have trod,
   with its crystal tide for ever
   flowing from the throne of God?

   Yes, we'll gather at the river,
   the beautiful, the beautiful river,
   gather with the saints at the river,
   that flows from the throne of God.

2. On the margin of the river,
   washing up its silver spray,
   we will walk and worship ever,
   all the happy golden day.

3. Ere we reach the shining river,
   lay we every burden down;
   grace our spirits will deliver,
   and provide a robe and crown.

4. At the smiling of the river,
   mirror of the Saviour's face,
   saints, whom death will never sever,
   lift their songs of saving grace.

5. Soon we'll reach the shining river,
   soon our pilgrimage will cease;
   soon our happy hearts will quiver
   with the melody of peace.

595 Henry Williams Baker (1821-1877)

1. Shall we not love thee, Mother dear,
   whom Jesus loves so well,
   and to his glory year by year
   thy praise and honour tell?

2. Thee did he choose from whom to take
   true flesh, his flesh to be;
   in it to suffer for our sake,
   and by it make us free.

3. O wondrous depth of love divine,
   that he should bend so low;
   and, Mary, O what joy was thine
   the Saviour's love to know.

4. Joy to be mother of the Lord,
   yet thine the truer bliss,
   in ev'ry thought and deed and word
   to be for ever his.

5. Now in the realm of life above
   close to thy Son thou art,
   while on thy soul glad streams of love
   flow from his sacred heart.

6. Jesu, the Virgin's holy Son,
   praise we thy mother blest;
   grant when our earthly course is run,
   life with the saints at rest.

596
David Fellingham
© 1988 Kingsway's Thankyou Music

Shout for joy and sing your praises to the
King,
lift your voice and let your hallelujahs
ring;
come before his throne to worship and
adore,
enter joyfully now the presence of the
Lord.

You are my Creator, you are my
Deliverer,
you are my Redeemer, you are Lord,
and you are my Healer.
You are my Provider,
you are now my Shepherd, and my
Guide,
Jesus, Lord and King, I worship you.

597
Joseph Mohr, (1792-1848)
trans. John Freeman Young (1820-1885)

1. Silent night, holy night.
   All is calm, all is bright,
   round yon virgin mother and child;
   holy infant, so tender and mild,
   sleep in heavenly peace,
   sleep in heavenly peace.

2. Silent night, holy night.
   Shepherds quake at the sight,
   glories stream from heaven afar,
   heav'nly hosts sing alleluia:
   Christ, the Saviour is born,
   Christ, the Saviour is born.

3. Silent night, holy night.
   Son of God, love's pure light,
   radiant beams from thy holy face,
   with the dawn of redeeming grace:
   Jesus, Lord, at thy birth,
   Jesus, Lord, at thy birth.

598
Kathy Galloway
© Kathy Galloway. Used by permission

1. Sing for God's glory
   that colours the dawn of creation,
   racing across the sky,
   trailing bright clouds of elation;
   sun of delight succeeds the velvet of
   night,
   warming the earth's exultation.

2. Sing for God's power
   that shatters the chains that would
   bind us,
   searing the darkness of
   fear and despair that could blind us,
   touching our shame with love that will
   not lay blame,
   reaching out gently to find us.

3. Sing for God's justice
   disturbing each easy illusion,
   tearing down tyrants
   and putting our pride to confusion:
   lifeblood of right, resisting evil and slight,
   offering freedom's transfusion.

4. Sing for God's saints who have
   travelled faith's journey before us,
   who in our weariness
   give us their hope to restore us;
   in them we see the new creation to be,
   spirit of love made flesh for us.

599
Michael Saward (b. 1932)
© Michael Saward/Jubilate Hymns

1. Sing glory to God the Father,
   the King of the universe, changelessly
   the same.
   Sing praise to the world's creator
   and magnify his holy name.

   *He made all that is round us and all that
   is beyond,
   his hands uphold the planets, to him they
   all respond.*

Continued overleaf

2. Sing glory to God the Saviour,
   the Lord of the galaxies, bearer of our
      shame.
   Sing praise to the world's redeemer
   and magnify his holy name.

   He suffered grief and torment, for sin he
      paid the price,
   he rose in glorious triumph, both priest
      and sacrifice.

3. Sing glory to God the Spirit,
   the power of the elements, setting
      hearts aflame.
   Sing praise to the world's life-giver
   and magnify his holy name.

   His gifts to all are given, his fruit
      transforms our hearts,
   his fellowship enriches, a grace which he
      imparts.

4. Sing glory, the whole creation!
   Give thanks to the Trinity, heaven's
      love proclaim.
   Sing praise to our God, almighty,
   and magnify his holy name.

600 Mike Anderson (b. 1956)
© 1999 Kevin Mayhew Ltd.

Sing it in the valleys,
shout it from the mountain tops,
Jesus came to save us,
and his saving never stops.
He is King of kings,
and new life he brings,
sing it in the valleys,
shout it from the mountain tops,
Oh, shout it from the mountain tops.

1. Jesus, you are by my side,
   you take all my fears.
   If I only come to you,
   you will heal the pain of years.

2. You have not deserted me,
   though I go astray.
   Jesus, take me in your arms,
   help me walk with you today.

3. Jesus, you are living now,
   Jesus, I believe.
   Jesus, take me, heart and soul,
   yours alone I want to be.

601 Sabine Baring-Gould (1834-1924)

1. Sing lullaby!
   Lullaby baby, now reclining,
   sing lullaby!
   Hush, do not wake the infant king.
   Angels are watching,
   stars are shining
   over the place where he is lying:
   sing lullaby!

2. Sing lullaby!
   Lullaby baby, now a-sleeping,
   sing lullaby!
   Hush, do not wake the infant king.
   Soon will come sorrow
   with the morning,
   soon will come bitter grief and weeping:
   sing lullaby!

3. Sing lullaby!
   Lullaby baby, now a-dozing,
   sing lullaby!
   Hush, do not wake the infant king.
   Soon comes the cross,
   the nails, the piercing,
   then in the grave at last reposing:
   sing lullaby!

4. Sing lullaby!
   Lullaby! is the babe awaking?
   Sing lullaby.
   Hush, do not stir the infant king.
   Dreaming of Easter,
   gladsome morning,
   conquering death, its bondage breaking:
   sing lullaby!

602
Venantius Fortunatus (c. 530-609)
trans. John Mason Neale (1818-1866)

1. Sing, my tongue, the glorious battle,
   sing the last the dread affray;
   o'er the Cross, the victor's trophy,
   sound the high triumphal lay;
   how, the pains of death enduring,
   earth's Redeemer won the day.

2. When at length th'appointed fullness
   of the sacred time was come,
   he was sent, the world's creator,
   from the Father's heav'nly home,
   and was found in human fashion,
   offspring of the Virgin's womb.

3. Now the thirty years are ended
   which on earth he willed to see,
   willingly he meets his Passion,
   born to set his people free;
   on the cross the Lamb is lifted,
   there the sacrifice to be.

4. There the nails and spear he suffers,
   vinegar and gall and reed;
   from his sacred body piercèd
   blood and water both proceed:
   precious flood, which all creation
   from the stain of sin hath freed.

PART TWO

5. Faithful Cross, above all other,
   one and only noble tree!
   None in foliage, none in blossom,
   none in fruit thy peer may be;
   sweetest wood and sweetest iron,
   sweetest weight is hung on thee!

6. Bend, O lofty tree, thy branches,
   thy too rigid sinews bend;
   and awhile the stubborn hardness,
   which thy birth bestowed, suspend;
   and the limbs of heav'n's high monarch
   gently on thine arms extend.

7. Thou alone wast counted worthy
   this world's ransom to sustain,
   that by thee a wrecked creation
   might its ark and haven gain,
   with the sacred blood anointed
   of the Lamb that hath been slain.

8. Praise and honour to the Father,
   praise and honour to the Son,
   praise and honour to the Spirit,
   ever Three and ever One,
   One in might and One in glory,
   while eternal ages run.
   (Amen.)

603
Michael Baughen (b. 1930) from Psalm 98
© Michael Baughen/Jubilate Hymns

1. Sing to God new songs of worship,
   all his deeds are marvellous;
   he has brought salvation to us
   with his hand and holy arm:
   he has shown to all the nations
   righteousness and saving pow'r;
   he recalled his truth and mercy
   to his people Israel.

2. Sing to God new songs of worship,
   earth has seen his victory;
   let the lands of earth be joyful
   praising him with thankfulness:
   sound upon the harp his praises,
   play to him with melody;
   let the trumpets sound his triumph,
   show your joy to God the king!

3. Sing to God new songs of worship,
   let the sea now make a noise;
   all on earth and in the waters
   sound your praises to the Lord:
   let the hills be joyful together,
   let the rivers clap their hands,
   for with righteousness and justice
   he will come to judge the earth.

604

Fred Kaan (b. 1929)
© 1968 Stainer & Bell

1. Sing we a song of high revolt;
   make great the Lord, his name exalt!
   sing we the song that Mary sang
   of God at war with human wrong.

2. Sing we of him who deeply cares
   and still with us our burden bears.
   He who with strength the proud
       disowns,
   brings down the mighty from their
       thrones.

3. By him the poor are lifted up;
   he satisfies with bread and cup
   the hungry ones of many lands;
   the rich must go with empty hands.

4. He calls us to revolt and fight
   with him for what is just and right,
   to sing and live Magnificat
   in crowded street and council flat.

605

George Bourne Timms (b. 1910)
© Oxford University Press, from 'English Praise'.
Used by permission

1. Sing we of the blessèd Mother
   who received the angel's word,
   and obedient to his summons
   bore in love the infant Lord;
   sing we of the joys of Mary
   at whose breast that child was fed,
   who is Son of God eternal
   and the everlasting Bread.

2. Sing we, too, of Mary's sorrows,
   of the sword that pierced her through,
   when beneath the cross of Jesus
   she his weight of suff'ring knew,
   looked upon her Son and Saviour
   reigning high on Calv'ry's tree,
   saw the price of our redemption
   paid to set the sinner free.

3. Sing again the joys of Mary
   when she saw the risen Lord,
   and, in prayer with Christ's apostles,
   waited on his promised word:
   from on high the blazing glory
   of the Spirit's presence came,
   heav'nly breath of God's own being,
   manifest through wind and flame.

4. Sing the greatest joy of Mary
   when on earth her work was done,
   and the Lord of all creation
   brought her to his heav'nly home:
   virgin mother, Mary blessèd,
   raised on high and crowned with grace,
   may your Son, the world's redeemer,
   grant us all to see his face.

606

Charles Wesley (1707-1788)
based on Ephesians 6:10-18

1. Soldiers of Christ, arise,
   and put your armour on,
   strong in the strength which God supplies
   through his eternal Son.

2. Strong in the Lord of hosts,
   and in his mighty pow'r;
   who in the strength of Jesus trusts
   is more than conqueror.

3. Stand then in his great might,
   with all his strength endued;
   and take, to arm you for the fight,
   the panoply of God.

4. To keep your armour bright,
   attend with constant care,
   still walking in your Captain's sight
   and watching unto prayer.

5. From strength to strength go on,
   wrestle and fight and pray;
   tread all the pow'rs of darkness down,
   and win the well-fought day.

6. That, having all things done,
   and all your conflicts past,
   ye may o'ercome, through Christ alone,
   and stand entire at last.

607
Latin hymn (18th century)
trans. John H. Clark (1839-1888) alt.

1. Soldiers who are Christ's below,
   strong in faith resist the foe:
   boundless is the pledged reward
   unto them who serve the Lord.
   Alleluia.

2. 'Tis no palm of fading leaves
   that the conqu'ror's hand receives;
   joys are ours, serene and pure,
   light that ever shall endure.
   Alleluia.

3. For the souls that overcome
   waits the beauteous heav'nly home,
   where the blessèd evermore
   tread on high the starry floor.
   Alleluia.

4. Passing soon and little worth
   are the things that tempt on earth;
   heav'nward lift thy soul's regard:
   God himself is thy reward.
   Alleluia.

5. Father, who the crown dost give,
   Saviour, by whose death we live,
   Spirit, who our hearts dost raise,
   Three in One, thy name we praise.
   Alleluia.

608
James Montgomery (1771-1854), alt.

1. Songs of praise the angels sang,
   heav'n with alleluias rang,
   when creation was begun,
   when God spake and it was done.

2. Songs of praise awoke the morn
   when the Prince of Peace was born;
   songs of praise arose when he
   captive led captivity.

3. Heav'n and earth must pass away,
   songs of praise shall crown that day;
   God will make new heav'ns and earth,
   songs of praise shall hail their birth.

4. And shall we alone be dumb
   till that glorious kingdom come?
   No, the Church delights to raise
   psalms and hymns and songs of praise.

5. Saints below, with heart and voice,
   still in songs of praise rejoice;
   learning here, by faith and love,
   songs of praise to sing above.

6. Hymns of glory, songs of praise,
   Father, unto thee we raise;
   Jesu, glory unto thee,
   ever with the Spirit be.

609
Christopher Wordsworth (1807-1885)

1. Songs of thankfulness and praise,
   Jesus, Lord to thee we raise,
   manifested by the star
   to the sages from afar;
   branch of royal David's stem,
   in thy birth at Bethlehem;
   anthems be to thee addressed:
   God in man made manifest.

2. Manifest at Jordan's stream,
   prophet, priest and King supreme,
   and at Cana wedding-guest,
   in thy Godhead manifest,
   manifest in pow'r divine,
   changing water into wine;
   anthems be to thee addressed:
   God in man made manifest.

Continued overleaf

3. Manifest in making whole,
   palsied limbs and fainting soul,
   manifest in valiant fight,
   quelling all the devil's might,
   manifest in gracious will,
   ever bringing good from ill;
   anthems be to thee addressed:
   God in man made manifest.

4. Sun and moon shall darkened be,
   stars shall fall, the heav'ns shall flee;
   Christ will then like lightning shine,
   all will see his glorious sign.
   All will then the trumpet hear,
   all will see the judge appear;
   thou by all wilt be confessed:
   God in man made manifest.

5. Grant us grace to see thee, Lord,
   mirrored in thy holy word;
   may we imitate thee now,
   and be pure, as pure art thou;
   that we like to thee may be
   at thy great Epiphany,
   and may praise thee, ever blest,
   God in man made manifest.

610 'Anima Christi'. Ascribed to John XXII (1249-1334) trans. unknown

1. Soul of my Saviour,
   sanctify my breast;
   Body of Christ,
   be thou my saving guest;
   Blood of my Saviour,
   bathe me in thy tide,
   wash me with water
   flowing from thy side.

2. Strength and protection
   may thy passion be;
   O blessèd Jesus,
   hear and answer me;
   deep in thy wounds, Lord,
   hide and shelter me;
   so shall I never,
   never part from thee.

3. Guard and defend me
   from the foe malign;
   in death's dread moments
   make me only thine;
   call me, and bid me
   come to thee on high,
   when I may praise thee
   with thy saints for aye.

611 Helen Kennedy
© St Mungo Music

1. Spirit of God, come dwell within me.
   Open my heart, O come set me free,
   fill me with love for Jesus, my Lord,
   O fill me with living water.

   Jesus is living, Jesus is here.
   Jesus, my Lord, come closer to me.
   Jesus, our Saviour dying for me,
   and rising to save his people.

2. Lord, how I thirst, O Lord, I am weak.
   Lord, come to me, you alone do I seek.
   Lord, you are life, and love and hope,
   O fill me with living water.

3. Lord, I am blind. O Lord, I can't see.
   Stretch out your hand, O Lord,
      comfort me.
   Lead me your way in light and in truth,
   O fill me with living water.

612 Timothy Dudley-Smith (b. 1926)
© Timothy Dudley-Smith

1. Spirit of God within me,
   possess my human frame;
   fan the dull embers of my heart,
   stir up the living flame.
   Strive till that image Adam lost,
   new minted and restored,
   in shining splendour brightly bears
   the likeness of the Lord.

2. Spirit of truth within me,
   possess my thought and mind;
   lighten anew the inward eye
   by Satan rendered blind;
   shine on the words that wisdom speaks,
   and grant me pow'r to see
   the truth made known to all in Christ,
   and in that truth be free.

3. Spirit of love within me,
   possess my hands and heart;
   break through the bonds of self-concern
   that seeks to stand apart;
   grant me the love that suffers long,
   that hopes, believes and bears,
   the love fulfilled in sacrifice,
   that cares as Jesus cares.

4. Spirit of life within me,
   possess this life of mine;
   come as the wind of heaven's breath,
   come as the fine divine!
   Spirit of Christ, the living Lord,
   reign in this house of clay,
   till from its dust with Christ I rise
   to everlasting day.

614 Paul Armstrong
© 1984 Restoration Music Ltd/Sovereign Music Ltd

Spirit of the living God,
fall afresh on me;
Spirit of the living God,
fall afresh on me;
fill me anew, fill me anew;
Spirit of the Lord,
fall afresh on me.

615 Daniel Iverson (1890-1972)
© 1963 Birdwing Music/EMI Christian Music
Publishing. Administered by CopyCare

1. Spirit of the living God, fall afresh on me.
   Spirit of the living God, fall afresh on me.
   Melt me, mould me, fill me, use me.
   Spirit of the living God, fall afresh on me.

2. Spirit of the living God, fall afresh on us.
   Spirit of the living God, fall afresh on us.
   Melt us, mould us, fill us, use us.
   Spirit of the living God, fall afresh on us.

*When appropriate a third verse may be
added, singing 'on them', for example,
before Confirmation, or at a service for the
sick.*

613 Foundling Hospital Collection' (1774) alt.

1. Spirit of mercy, truth and love,
   O shed thine influence from above,
   and still from age to age convey
   the wonders of this sacred day.

2. In ev'ry clime, by ev'ry tongue,
   be God's surpassing glory sung;
   let all the list'ning earth be taught
   the acts our great Redeemer wrought.

3. Unfailing comfort, heav'nly guide,
   still o'er thy holy Church preside;
   let humankind thy blessings prove,
   Spirit of mercy, truth and love.

616 James Montgomery (1771-1854)

1. Stand up and bless the Lord,
   ye people of his choice;
   stand up and bless the Lord your God
   with heart and soul and voice.

2. Though high above all praise,
   above all blessing high,
   who would not fear his holy name,
   and laud and magnify?

3. O for the living flame
   from his own altar brought,
   to touch our lips, our mind inspire,
   and wing to heav'n our thought.

Continued overleaf

4. God is our strength and song,
   and his salvation ours;
   then be his love in Christ proclaimed
   with all our ransomed pow'rs.

5. Stand up and bless the Lord,
   the Lord your God adore;
   stand up and bless his glorious name
   henceforth for evermore.

617 Jean Holloway (b. 1939)
© 1996 Kevin Mayhew Ltd.

1. Stand up, stand up for Jesus,
   stand up before his cross,
   an instrument of torture
   inflicting pain and loss;
   transformed by his obedience
   to God's redeeming plan,
   the cross was overpowered
   by Christ, both God and man.

2. Stand up, stand up for Jesus,
   be counted as his own;
   his gospel of forgiveness
   he cannot spread alone.
   The love which draws us to him,
   he calls us out to share;
   he calls us to the margins
   to be his presence there.

3. Stand up, stand up for Jesus,
   in faith and hope be strong,
   stand firm for right and justice,
   opposed to sin and wrong.
   Give comfort to the wounded,
   and care for those in pain,
   for Christ, in those who suffer,
   is crucified again.

4. Stand up, stand up for Jesus,
   who reigns as King of kings,
   be ready for the challenge
   of faith his kingship brings.
   He will not force obedience,
   he gives to each the choice
   to turn from all that's holy,
   or in his love rejoice.

5. Stand up, stand up for Jesus,
   give courage to the weak,
   be unashamed to praise him,
   be bold his name to speak.
   Confront the cross unflinching,
   Christ's love has set us free;
   he conquered death for ever
   and lives eternally.

618 Spiritual

Steal away, steal away,
steal away to Jesus.
Steal away, steal away home.
I ain't got long to stay here.

1. My Lord, he calls me,
   he calls me by the thunder.
   The trumpet sounds within my soul;
   I ain't got long to stay here.

2. Green trees are bending,
   the sinner stands a-trembling.
   The trumpet sounds within my soul;
   I ain't got long to stay here.

3. My Lord, he calls me,
   he calls me by the lightning.
   The trumpet sounds within my soul;
   I ain't got long to stay here.

619 Syriac Liturgy, perhaps by Ephraim the Syrian
(c. 306-373), trans. Charles William Humphreys
(1840-1921) and Percy Dearmer (1867-1936)
© Oxford University Press. Used by permission

1. Strengthen for service, Lord, the hands
   that holy things have taken;
   let ears that now have heard thy songs
   to clamour never waken.

2. Lord, may the tongues which
      'Holy' sang
   keep free from all deceiving;
   the eyes which saw thy love be bright,
   thy blessèd hope perceiving.

3. The feet that tread thy holy courts
   from light do thou not banish;
   the bodies by thy Body fed
   with thy new life replenish.

620 Graham Kendrick (b. 1950)
© 1988 Make Way Music

1. Such love, pure as the whitest snow;
   such love weeps for the shame I know;
   such love, paying the debt I owe;
   O Jesus, such love.

2. Such love, stilling my restlessness;
   such love, filling my emptiness;
   such love, showing me holiness;
   O Jesus, such love.

3. Such love springs from eternity;
   such love, streaming through history;
   such love, fountain of life to me;
   O Jesus, such love.

621 John Keble (1792-1866)

1. Sun of my soul, thou Saviour dear,
   it is not night if thou be near:
   O may no earth-born cloud arise
   to hide thee from thy servant's eyes.

2. When the soft dews of kindly sleep
   my wearied eyelids gently steep,
   be my last thought, how sweet to rest
   for ever on my Saviour's breast.

3. Abide with me from morn till eve,
   for without thee I cannot live;
   abide with me when night is nigh,
   for without thee I dare not die.

4. Watch by the sick; enrich the poor
   with blessings from thy boundless store;
   be ev'ry mourner's sleep tonight
   like infant's slumbers, pure and light.

622 Francis Stanfield (1835-1914), alt.

1. Sweet sacrament divine,
   hid in thy earthly home,
   lo, round thy lowly shrine,
   with suppliant hearts we come;
   Jesus, to thee our voice we raise,
   in songs of love and heartfelt praise,
   sweet sacrament divine,
   sweet sacrament divine.

2. Sweet sacrament of peace,
   dear home of ev'ry heart,
   where restless yearnings cease,
   and sorrows all depart,
   there in thine ear all trustfully
   we tell our tale of misery,
   sweet sacrament of peace,
   sweet sacrament of peace.

3. Sweet sacrament of rest,
   Ark from the ocean's roar,
   within thy shelter blest
   soon may we reach the shore;
   save us, for still the tempest raves;
   save, lest we sink beneath the waves,
   sweet sacrament of rest,
   sweet sacrament of rest.

4. Sweet sacrament divine,
   earth's light and jubilee,
   in thy far depths doth shine
   thy Godhead's majesty;
   sweet light, so shine on us, we pray,
   that earthly joys may fade away,
   sweet sacrament divine,
   sweet sacrament divine.

623 Francesca Leftley (b. 1955)
© 1984 Kevin Mayhew Ltd.

1. Take me, Lord, use my life
   in the way you wish to do.
   Fill me, Lord, touch my heart
   till it always thinks of you.
   Take me now, as I am,
   this is all I can offer.

Continued overleaf

Here today I, the clay,
will be moulded by my Lord.

2. Lord, I pray that each day
   I will listen to your will.
   Many times I have failed
   but I know you love me still.
   Teach me now, guide me,
   Lord, keep me close to you always.

3. I am weak, fill me now
   with your strength and set me free.
   Make me whole, fashion me
   so that you will live in me.
   Hold me now in your hands,
   form me now with your Spirit.

624
v 1 and 3 Margaret Rizza (b. 1929), v 2 unknown
© 1998 Kevin Mayhew Ltd.

1. Take my hands, Lord,
   to share in your labours,
   take my eyes, Lord, to see your needs,
   let me hear the voice of lonely people,
   let my love, Lord, bring riches to the poor.

2. Give me someone to feed
   when I'm hungry,
   when I'm thirsty give water for their thirst.
   When I stand in need of tenderness,
   give me someone to hold who longs
       for love.

3. Keep my heart
   ever open to others,
   may my time, Lord, be spent with those
       in need;
   may I tend to those who need your care.
   Take my life, Lord, and make it
       truly yours.

625
Frances Ridley Havergal (1836-1879)

1. Take my life, and let it be
   consecrated, Lord, to thee;
   take my moments and my days,
   let them flow in ceaseless praise.

2. Take my hands, and let them move
   at the impulse of thy love;
   take my feet, and let them be
   swift and beautiful for thee.

3. Take my voice, and let me sing
   always, only, for my King;
   take my lips, and let them be
   filled with messages from thee.

4. Take my silver and my gold;
   not a mite would I withhold;
   take my intellect, and use
   ev'ry pow'r as thou shalt choose.

5. Take my will, and make it thine:
   it shall be no longer mine;
   take my heart: it is thine own;
   it shall be thy royal throne.

6. Take my love; my Lord, I pour
   at thy feet its treasure-store;
   take myself, and I will be
   ever, only, all for thee.

626
Charles William Everest (1814-1877)
based on Mark 8, alt.

1. Take up thy cross, the Saviour said,
   if thou wouldst my disciple be;
   deny thyself, the world forsake,
   and humbly follow after me.

2. Take up thy cross – let not its weight
   fill thy weak spirit with alarm:
   his strength shall bear thy spirit up,
   and brace thy heart, and nerve thine arm.

3. Take up thy cross, nor heed the shame,
   nor let thy foolish pride rebel:
   thy Lord for thee the Cross endured,
   to save thy soul from death and hell.

4. Take up thy cross then in his strength,
   and calmly ev'ry danger brave;
   'twill guide thee to a better home,
   and lead to vict'ry o'er the grave.

5. Take up thy cross, and follow Christ,
   nor think till death to lay it down;
   for only those who bear the cross
   may hope to wear the glorious crown.

6. To thee, great Lord, the One in Three,
   all praise for evermore ascend:
   O grant us in our home to see
   the heav'nly life that knows no end.

627 Susan Sayers (b. 1946), based on Mark 8 and John 14
© 1984 Kevin Mayhew Ltd

*'Take up your cross,' he says, 'and follow me,
and in my love and comfort you shall hide.
I am the Way,' he says, ' so follow me;
do not fear, I am here at your side!'*

1. What if the wind is howling round
      my house
   'til the walls are trembling like a leaf?
   What if the windows rattle in the storm
   as doubts come battering belief?

2. What if the rocks are blistering my feet,
   and the sun's heat beats upon my head?
   Near me a grass path beckons with its
      flowers,
   I'm tempted to go that way instead.

3. What if the tiredness aches behind my eyes
   and my boat is impossible to steer?
   Out on an ocean, drifting and alone,
   am I still, even then, to persevere?

4. Strangest of wonders, wonderfully strange,
   that the cross can set me free.
   Nothing is stronger than the love of God:
   I know very well that he loves me.

628 Hubert J. Richards (b. 1921), based on Psalm 34
© 1996 Kevin Mayhew Ltd.

*Taste and see the goodness of the Lord,
the goodness of the Lord.*

1. I sing God's praises all my days,
   his name is always on my lips;
   he is my one and only boast,
   the pride and joy of all the poor.

2. So come with me to sing his praise,
   together let us praise his name.
   I seek the Lord, he answers me,
   rescues me from all my fears.

3. The Lord is quick to heed the poor
   and liberate them from their chains.
   The Lord is close to broken hearts,
   he rescues slaves and sets them free.

629 George Herbert (1593-1633)

1. Teach me, my God and King,
   in all things thee to see;
   and what I do in anything
   to do it as for thee.

2. A man that looks on glass,
   on it may stay his eye;
   or, if he pleaseth, through it pass,
   and then the heav'n espy.

3. All may of thee partake;
   nothing can be so mean
   which, with this tincture, 'For thy sake',
   will not grow bright and clean.

4. A servant with this clause
   makes drudgery divine;
   who sweeps a room, as for thy laws,
   makes that and the action fine.

5. This is the famous stone
   that turneth all to gold;
   for that which God doth touch and own
   cannot for less be told.

630 Timothy Dudley-Smith, based on Psalm 34
© Timothy Dudley-Smith

1. Tell his praise in song and story,
   bless the Lord with heart and voice;
   in my God is all my glory,
   come before him and rejoice.
   Join to praise his name together,
   he who hears his people's cry;
   tell his praise, come wind or weather,
   shining faces lifted high.

Continued overleaf

2. To the Lord whose love has found them
   cry the poor in their distress;
   swift his angels camped around them
   prove him sure to save and bless.
   God it is who hears our crying
   though the spark of faith be dim:
   taste and see! beyond denying
   blest are those who trust in him.

3. Taste and see! In faith draw near him,
   trust the Lord with all our pow'rs;
   seek and serve him, love and fear him,
   life and all its joys are ours-
   true delight in holy living,
   peace and plenty, length of days:
   come, my children, with thanksgiving
   bless the Lord in songs of praise.

4. In our need he walks beside us,
   ears alert to ev'ry cry;
   watchful eyes to guard and guide us,
   love that whispers, 'It is I'.
   Good shall triumph, wrong be righted,
   God has pledged his promised word;
   so with ransomed saints united
   join to praise our living Lord!

Timothy Dudley-Smith (b. 1926)
based on Luke 1:46-55
© 1961 Timothy Dudley-Smith
From 'Enlarged Songs of Praise'. Used by permission

631

1. Tell out, my soul, the greatness of the Lord:
   unnumbered blessings, give my
       spirit voice;
   tender to me the promise of his word;
   in God my Saviour shall my heart rejoice.

2. Tell out, my soul, the greatness of
   his name:
   make known his might, the deeds his
       arm has done;
   his mercy sure, from age to age the same;
   his holy name, the Lord, the mighty one.

3. Tell out, my soul, the greatness of
   his might:
   pow'rs and dominions lay their glory by;
   proud hearts and stubborn wills are put
       to flight,
   the hungry fed, the humble lifted high.

4. Tell out, my soul, the glories of his word:
   firm is his promise, and his mercy sure.
   Tell out, my soul, the greatness of
   the Lord
   to children's children and for evermore.

632 Jean Holloway (b. 1939)
© 1994 Kevin Mayhew Ltd.

Thanks for the fellowship found at this meal,
thanks for a day refreshed;
thanks to the Lord for his presence we feel,
thanks for the food he blessed.
Joyfully sing praise to the Lord,
praise to the risen Son,
alleluia, ever adored,
pray that his will be done.
As he was known in the breaking of bread,
now is he known again,
and by his hand have the hungry been fed,
thanks be to Christ. Amen!

633 Charles Coffin (1676-1749)
trans. John Chandler (1806-1876) alt.

1. The advent of our King
   our prayers must now employ,
   and we must hymns of welcome sing
   in strains of holy joy.

2. The everlasting Son
   incarnate deigns to be;
   himself a servant's form puts on,
   to set his servants free.

3. Daughter of Sion, rise
   to meet thy lowly King;
   nor let thy faithless heart despise
   the peace he comes to bring.

4. As Judge, on clouds of light,
   he soon will come again,
   and his true members all unite
   with him in heav'n to reign.

5. All glory to the Son
   who comes to set us free,
   with Father, Spirit, ever One,
   through all eternity.

634 Sabine Baring-Gould (1834-1924),
based on 'Birjina gaztettobat zegoen'

1. The angel Gabriel from heaven came,
   his wings as drifted snow, his eyes
      as flame.
   'All hail,' said he,
   'thou lowly maiden, Mary,
   most highly favoured lady.' Gloria!

2. 'For known a blessèd Mother thou
      shalt be.
   All generations laud and honour thee.
   Thy Son shall be Emmanuel,
   by seers foretold,
   most highly favoured lady.' Gloria!

3. Then gentle Mary meekly bowed
      her head.
   'To me be as it pleaseth God,' she said.
   'My soul shall laud and magnify
   his holy name.'
   Most highly favoured lady! Gloria!

4. Of her, Emmanuel, the Christ, was born
   in Bethlehem, all on a Christmas morn;
   and Christian folk throughout
   the world will ever say:
   'Most highly favoured lady.' Gloria!

635 Lionel Muirhead (1845-1925) alt.

1. The Church of God a kingdom is,
   where Christ in pow'r doth reign;
   where spirits yearn till, seen in bliss,
   their Lord shall come again.

2. Glad companies of saints possess
   this Church below, above;
   and God's perpetual calm doth bless
   their paradise of love.

3. An altar stands within the shrine
   whereon, once sacrificed,
   is set, immaculate, divine,
   the Lamb of God, the Christ.

4. There rich and poor, from countless
      lands,
   praise Christ on mystic rood;
   there nations reach forth holy hands
   to take God's holy food.

5. There pure life-giving streams o'erflow
   the sower's garden-ground;
   and faith and hope fair blossoms show,
   and fruits of love abound.

6. O King, O Christ, this endless grace
   to all your people bring,
   to see the vision of your face
   in joy, O Christ, our King.

636 Samuel John Stone (1839-1900)

1. The Church's one foundation
   is Jesus Christ, her Lord;
   she is his new creation,
   by water and the word;
   from heav'n he came and sought her
   to be his holy bride,
   with his own blood he bought her,
   and for her life he died.

2. Elect from ev'ry nation,
   yet one o'er all the earth,
   her charter of salvation,
   one Lord, one faith, one birth;
   one holy name she blesses,
   partakes one holy food,
   and to one hope she presses,
   with ev'ry grace endued.

Continued overleaf

3. 'Mid toil and tribulation,
   and tumult of her war,
   she waits the consummation
   of peace for evermore;
   till with the vision glorious
   her longing eyes are blest,
   and the great Church victorious
   shall be the Church at rest.

4. Yet she on earth hath union
   with God the Three in One,
   and mystic sweet communion
   with those whose rest is won:
   O happy ones and holy! Lord,
   give us grace that we
   like them, the meek and lowly,
   on high may dwell with thee.

637 St John of Damascus (c. 750) trans. John Mason Neale (1818-1866)

1. The day of resurrection!
   Earth, tell it out abroad;
   the passover of gladness,
   the passover of God!
   From death to life eternal,
   from earth unto the sky,
   our Christ hath brought us over
   with hymns of victory.

2. Our hearts be pure from evil,
   that we may see aright
   the Lord in rays eternal
   of resurrection-light;
   and list'ning to his accents,
   may hear so calm and plain
   his own 'All hail' and, hearing,
   may raise the victor strain.

3. Now let the heav'ns be joyful,
   and earth her song begin,
   the round world keep high triumph,
   and all that is therein;
   let all things, seen and unseen,
   their notes of gladness blend,
   for Christ the Lord hath risen,
   our joy that hath no end.

638 John Ellerton (1826-1893)

1. The day thou gavest, Lord, is ended:
   the darkness falls at thy behest;
   to thee our morning hymns ascended;
   thy praise shall sanctify our rest.

2. We thank thee that thy Church unsleeping,
   while earth rolls onward into light,
   through all the world her watch
       is keeping,
   and rests not now by day or night.

3. As o'er each continent and island
   the dawn leads on another day,
   the voice of prayer is never silent,
   nor dies the strain of praise away.

4. The sun that bids us rest is waking
   our brethren 'neath the western sky,
   and hour by hour fresh lips are making
   thy wondrous doings heard on high.

5. So be it, Lord; thy throne shall never,
   like earth's proud empires, pass away;
   thy kingdom stands, and grows for ever,
   till all thy creatures own thy sway.

639 St. Ambrose (c. 340-397) trans. John Mason Neale (1818-1866) alt.

1. Th'eternal gifts of Christ the King,
   th'apostles' glory, let us sing;
   and all, with hearts of gladness, raise
   due hymns of thankful love and praise.

2. Theirs is the steadfast faith of saints,
   and hope that never yields nor faints,
   and love of Christ in perfect glow
   that lays the prince of this world low.

3. In them the Father's glory shone,
   in them the will of God the Son,
   in them exults the Holy Ghost,
   through them rejoice the heav'nly host.

4. To thee, Redeemer, now we cry,
   that thou wouldst join to them on high
   thy servants, who this grace implore,
   for ever and for evermore.

640 St. Thomas Aquinas (1227-1274)
trans. James Russell Woodford (1820-1885) alt.

1. Thee we adore,
   O hidden Saviour, thee,
   who in thy sacrament
   art pleased to be;
   both flesh and spirit
   in thy presence fail,
   yet here thy presence
   we devoutly hail.

2. O blest memorial
   of our dying Lord,
   who living bread
   to all doth here afford;
   O may our souls
   for ever feed on thee,
   and thou, O Christ,
   for ever precious be.

3. Fountain of goodness,
   Jesus, Lord and God,
   cleanse us, unclean,
   with thy most cleansing blood;
   increase our faith and love,
   that we may know
   the hope and peace
   which from thy presence flow.

4. O Christ, whom now
   beneath a veil we see,
   may what we thirst for
   soon our portion be:
   to gaze on thee unveiled,
   and see thy face,
   the vision of thy glory
   and thy grace.

641 From William Sandys' 'Christmas Carols,
Ancient and Modern', alt.

1. The first Nowell the angel did say
   was to certain poor shepherds in fields as
       they lay:
   in fields where they lay keeping their sheep,
   on a cold winter's night that was so deep.

   Nowell, Nowell, Nowell, Nowell,
   born is the King of Israel!

2. They lookèd up and saw a star,
   shining in the east, beyond them far,
   and to the earth it gave great light,
   and so it continued both day and night.

3. And by the light of that same star,
   three wise men came from country far;
   to seek for a king was their intent,
   and to follow the star wherever it went.

4. This star drew nigh to the north-west,
   o'er Bethlehem it took its rest,
   and there it did both stop and stay
   right over the place where Jesus lay.

5. Then entered in those wise men three,
   full rev'rently upon their knee,
   and offered there in his presence,
   their gold and myrrh and frankincense.

6. Then let us all with one accord
   sing praises to our heav'nly Lord,
   who with the Father we adore
   and Spirit blest for evermore.

642 Thomas Olivers (1725-1799)
based on the Hebrew Yigdal alt.

1. The God of Abraham praise,
   who reigns enthroned above,
   Ancient of everlasting Days,
   and God of love:
   Jehovah, great I AM,
   by earth and heav'n confessed;
   we bow and bless the sacred name,
   for ever blest.

Continued overleaf

2. The God of Abraham praise,
   at whose supreme command
   from earth we rise, and seek the joys
   at his right hand:
   we all on earth forsake,
   its wisdom, fame and pow'r;
   and him our only portion make,
   our shield and tow'r.

3. The God of Abraham praise,
   whose all-sufficient grace
   shall guide us all our happy days,
   in all our ways:
   he is our faithful friend;
   he is our gracious God;
   and he will save us to the end,
   through Jesus' blood.

4. He by himself has sworn –
   we on his oath depend –
   we shall, on eagles' wings upborne,
   to heav'n ascend:
   we shall behold his face,
   we shall his pow'r adore,
   and sing the wonders of his grace
   for evermore.

5. The whole triumphant host
   give thanks to God on high:
   'Hail, Father, Son and Holy Ghost!'
   they ever cry:
   Hail, Abraham's God and ours!
   We join the heav'nly throng,
   and celebrate with all our pow'rs
   in endless song.

643 George Herbert (1593-1633) based on Psalm 23

1. The God of love my shepherd is,
   and he that doth me feed;
   while he is mine and I am his,
   what can I want or need?

2. He leads me to the tender grass,
   where I both feed and rest;
   then to the streams that gently pass:
   in both I have the best.

3. Or if I stray, he doth convert,
   and bring my mind in frame,
   and all this not for my desert,
   but for his holy name.

4. Yea, in death's shady black abode
   well may I walk, nor fear;
   for thou art with me, and thy rod
   to guide, thy staff to bear.

5. Surely thy sweet and wondrous love
   shall measure all my days;
   and, as it never shall remove,
   so neither shall my praise.

644 Thomas Kelly (1769-1855)

1. The head that once was crowned
      with thorns
   is crowned with glory now:
   a royal diadem adorns
   the mighty victor's brow.

2. The highest place that heav'n affords
   is his, is his by right.
   The King of kings and Lord of lords,
   and heav'ns eternal light.

3. The joy of all who dwell above,
   the joy of all below,
   to whom he manifests his love,
   and grants his name to know.

4. To them the cross, with all its shame,
   with all its grace is giv'n;
   their name an everlasting name,
   their joy the joy of heav'n.

5. They suffer with their Lord below,
   they reign with him above,
   their profit and their joy to know
   the myst'ry of his love.

6. The cross he bore is life and health,
   though shame and death to him;
   his people's hope, his people's wealth,
   their everlasting theme.

645 Traditional

1. The holly and the ivy,
   when they are both full grown,
   of all the trees that are in the wood
   the holly bears the crown.

   The rising of the sun
   and the running of the deer,
   the playing of the merry organ,
   sweet singing in the choir.

2. The holly bears a blossom,
   white as the lily flower,
   and Mary bore sweet Jesus Christ
   to be our sweet Saviour.

3. The holly bears a berry,
   as red as any blood,
   and Mary bore sweet Jesus Christ
   to do poor sinners good.

4. The holly bears a prickle,
   as sharp as any thorn,
   and Mary bore sweet Jesus Christ
   on Christmas day in the morn.

5. The holly bears a bark,
   as bitter as any gall,
   and Mary bore sweet Jesus Christ
   to redeem us all.

6. The holly and the ivy,
   when they are both full grown,
   of all the trees that are in the wood
   the holly bears the crown.

646 Bryn A Rees (1911-1983)
© Mr. Alexander Scott. Used by permission

1. The kingdom of God
   is justice and joy,
   for Jesus restores
   what sin would destroy;
   God's power and glory
   in Jesus we know,
   and here and hereafter
   the kingdom shall grow.

2. The kingdom of God
   is mercy and grace,
   the captives are freed,
   the sinners find place,
   the outcast are welcomed
   God's banquet to share,
   and hope is awakened
   in place of despair.

3. The kingdom of God
   is challenge and choice,
   believe the good news,
   repent and rejoice!
   His love for us sinners
   brought Christ to his cross,
   our crisis of judgement
   for gain or for loss.

4. God's kingdom is come,
   the gift and the goal,
   in Jesus begun,
   in heaven made whole;
   the heirs of the kingdom
   shall answer his call,
   and all things cry 'Glory!'
   to God all in all.

647

Mike Anderson (b. 1956), based on Matthew 5:3-10
© 1999 Kevin Mayhew Ltd.

The kingdom of heaven,
the kingdom of heaven is yours.
A new world in Jesus
a new world in Jesus is yours.

1. Blessed are you in sorrow and grief,
   for you shall all be consoled;
   blessed are you, the gentle of heart,
   you shall inherit the earth.

2. Blessed are you who hunger for right,
   for you shall be satisfied;
   blessed are you the merciful ones,
   for you shall be pardoned too.

3. Blessed are you whose hearts are pure,
   your eyes shall gaze on the Lord;
   blessed are you who strive after peace,
   the Lord will call you his own.

4. Blessed are you who suffer for right,
   the heav'nly kingdom is yours;
   blessed are you who suffer for me,
   for you shall reap your reward.

648

Graham Kendrick (b. 1950)
© 1981 Kingsway's Thankyou Music

1. The King is among us,
   his spirit is here,
   let's draw near and worship,
   let songs fill the air.

2. He looks down upon us,
   delight in his face,
   enjoying his children's love,
   enthralled by our praise.

3. For each child is special,
   accepted and loved,
   a love gift from Jesus
   to his Father above.

4. And now he is giving
   his gifts to us all,
   for no one is worthless
   and each one is called.

5. The Spirit's anointing
   on all flesh comes down,
   and we shall be channels
   for works like his own.

6. We come now believing
   your promise of pow'r,
   for we are your people
   and this is your hour.

7. The King is among us,
   his Spirit is here,
   let's draw near and worship,
   let songs fill the air.

649

Henry Williams Baker (1821-1877), based on Psalm 23

1. The King of love my shepherd is,
   whose goodness faileth never;
   I nothing lack if I am his
   and he is mine for ever.

2. Where streams of living water flow
   my ransomed soul he leadeth,
   and where the verdant pastures grow
   with food celestial feedeth.

3. Perverse and foolish oft I strayed,
   but yet in love he sought me,
   and on his shoulder gently laid,
   and home, rejoicing, brought me.

4. In death's dark vale I fear no ill
   with thee, dear Lord, beside me;
   thy rod and staff my comfort still,
   thy cross before to guide me.

5. Thou spread'st a table in my sight,
   thy unction grace bestoweth:
   and O what transport of delight
   from thy pure chalice floweth!

6. And so through all the length of days
thy goodness faileth never;
good Shepherd, may I sing thy praise
within thy house for ever.

650 Josiah Conder (1789-1855) alt.

1. The Lord is King! lift up thy voice,
O earth, and all ye heav'ns, rejoice;
from world to world the joy shall ring:
'The Lord omnipotent is King!'

2. He reigns! ye saints, exalt your strains;
your God is King, your Saviour reigns;
and he is at the Father's side,
the Man of Love, the Crucified.

3. Alike pervaded by his eye
all parts of his dominion lie:
this world of ours and worlds unseen,
and thin the boundary between.

4. One Lord one empire all secures;
he reigns, and endless life is yours;
through earth and heav'n one song
   shall ring:
'The Lord omnipotent is King!'

651 Taizé Community
© Ateliers et Presses de Taizé

The Lord is my song, the Lord is my praise:
all my hope comes from God.
The Lord is my song, the Lord is my praise:
God the well-spring of life

652 Thomas Kelly (1769-1855)

1. The Lord is ris'n indeed:
now is his work performed;
now is the mighty captive freed,
and death's strong castle stormed.

2. The Lord is ris'n indeed:
then hell has lost his prey;
with him is ris'n the ransomed seed
to reign in endless day.

3. The Lord is ris'n indeed:
he lives, to die no more;
he lives, the sinner's cause to plead,
whose curse and shame he bore.

4. The Lord is ris'n indeed:
attending angels, hear!
up to the courts of heav'n with speed
the joyful tidings bear.

5. Then take your golden lyres
and strike each cheerful chord;
join, all ye bright celestial choirs,
to sing our risen Lord.

653 Joseph Addison (1672-1719), based on Psalm 23

1. The Lord my pasture shall prepare,
and feed me with a shepherd's care;
his presence shall my wants supply,
and guard me with a watchful eye;
my noonday walks he shall attend,
and all my midnight hours defend.

2. When in the sultry glebe I faint,
or on the thirsty mountain pant,
to fertile vales and dewy meads
my weary wand'ring steps he leads,
where peaceful rivers, soft and slow,
amid the verdant landscape flow.

3. Though in a bare and rugged way
through devious lonely wilds I stray,
thy bounty shall my pains beguile;
the barren wilderness shall smile
with sudden greens and herbage crowned,
and streams shall murmur all around.

4. Though in the paths of death I tread,
with gloomy horrors overspread,
my steadfast heart shall fear no ill,
for thou, O Lord, art with me still:
thy friendly staff shall give me aid,
and guide me through the dreadful shade.

654
Psalm 23 from 'The Scottish Psalter' (1650)

1. The Lord's my shepherd, I'll not want.
   He makes me down to lie
   in pastures green.
   He leadeth me the quiet waters by.

2. My soul he doth restore again,
   and me to walk doth make
   within the paths of righteousness,
   e'en for his own name's sake.

3. Yea, though I walk in death's dark vale,
   yet will I fear no ill.
   For thou art with me, and thy rod
   and staff me comfort still.

4. My table thou hast furnishèd
   in presence of my foes,
   my head thou dost with oil anoint,
   and my cup overflows.

5. Goodness and mercy all my life
   shall surely follow me.
   And in God's house for evermore
   my dwelling-place shall be.

655
John Milton (1608-1674)
based on Psalms 82, 85 and 86, alt.

1. The Lord will come and not be slow,
   his footsteps cannot err;
   before him righteousness shall go,
   his royal harbinger.

2. Truth from the earth, like to a flow'r,
   shall bud and blossom free;
   and justice, from her heav'nly bow'r,
   bless all humanity.

3. The nations all whom thou hast made
   shall come, and all shall frame
   to bow them low before thee, Lord,
   and glorify thy name.

4. For great thou art, and wonders great
   by thy strong hand are done:
   thou in thy everlasting seat
   remainest God alone.

656
John Morrison (1750-1798), based on Isaiah 9:2-7

1. The race that long in darkness pined
   has seen a glorious light:
   the people dwell in day,
   who dwelt in death's surrounding night.

2. To hail thy rise, thou better sun,
   the gath'ring nations come,
   joyous as when the reapers bear
   the harvest treasures home.

3. To us a child of hope is born,
   to us a Son is giv'n;
   him shall the tribes of earth obey,
   him all the hosts of heav'n.

4. His name shall be the Prince of Peace
   for evermore adored,
   the Wonderful, the Counsellor,
   the great and mighty Lord.

5. His pow'r increasing still shall spread,
   his reign no end shall know;
   justice shall guard his throne above,
   and peace abound below.

657
Cecil Frances Alexander (1818-1895), alt.

1. There is a green hill far away,
   outside a city wall,
   where the dear Lord was crucified
   who died to save us all.

2. We may not know, we cannot tell
   what pains he had to bear,
   but we believe it was for us
   he hung and suffered there.

3. He died that we might be forgiv'n,
   he died to make us good;
   that we might go at last to heav'n,
   saved by his precious blood.

4. There was no other good enough
   to pay the price of sin;
   he only could unlock the gate
   of heav'n, and let us in.

5. O, dearly, dearly has he loved,
   and we must love him too,
   and trust in his redeeming blood,
   and try his works to do.

658
Melody Green, based on Scripture
© 1982 Birdwing/Music/BMG Songs Inc/
Ears to hear music/EMI Christian Music
Publishing/CopyCare Ltd

1. There is a Redeemer,
   Jesus, God's own Son,
   precious Lamb of God, Messiah,
   Holy One.

   Thank you, O my Father,
   for giving us your Son,
   and leaving your Spirit
   till the work on earth is done.

2. Jesus, my Redeemer,
   name above all names,
   precious Lamb of God, Messiah,
   O for sinners slain.

3. When I stand in glory,
   I will see his face,
   and there I'll serve my King for ever,
   in that holy place.

659
E R (Tedd) Smith
© 1973 Hope Publishing Company

1. There's a quiet understanding
   when we're gathered in the Spirit:
   it's a promise that he gives us
   when we gather in his name.
   There's a love we feel in Jesus,
   there's a manna that he feeds us:
   it's a promise that he gives us
   when we gather in his name.

2. And we know when we're together,
   sharing love and understanding,
   that our brothers and our sisters
   feel the oneness that he brings.
   Thank you, thank you, thank you Jesus
   for the way you love and feed us,
   for the many ways you lead us,
   thank you, thank you, Lord.

660
Michael Forster (b. 1946)
© 2000 Kevin Mayhew Ltd.

1. There's a song in the heart of creation:
   there's a song on the lips of the poor:
   there's a song that protests at injustice,
   with a faith and a hope that is sure.

   It's a song of freedom!
   A song of peace.
   God keeps his promise;
   justice, will increase.

2. There's a song in the hearts of the people;
   there's a song on the lips of the youth;
   there's a song that protests at the waiting
   for the coming of wholeness and truth.

3. There's a song in the heart of the Saviour;
   there's a song on the lips of his friends;
   there's a song that protests for the dying,
   while proclaiming that life never ends.

4. There's a song in the heart of creation;
   there's a song on the lips of the healed;
   there's a song in the graveyard proclaiming
   that the life of the world is revealed.

661
Brian A Wren (b. 1936)
© 1969, 1995 Stainer & Bell Ltd

1. There's a spirit in the air,
   telling Christians everywhere:
   'Praise the love that Christ revealed,
   living, working, in our world'.

2. Lose your shyness, find your tongue,
   tell the world what God has done:
   God in Christ has come to stay.
   Live tomorrow's life today!

3. When believers break the bread,
   when a hungry child is fed,
   praise the love that Christ revealed,
   living, working, in our world.

4. Still the Spirit gives us light,
   seeing wrong and setting right:
   God in Christ has come to stay.
   Live tomorrow's life today!

Continued overleaf

5. When a stranger's not alone,
   where the homeless find a home,
   praise the love that Christ revealed,
   living, working, in our world.

6. May his Spirit fill our praise,
   guide our thoughts and change our ways.
   God in Christ has come to stay.
   Live tomorrow's life today!

7. There's a Spirit in the air,
   calling people ev'rywhere:
   praise the love that Christ revealed,
   living, working, in our world.

662 Frederick William Faber (1814-1863) alt.

1. There's a wideness in God's mercy,
   like the wideness of the sea;
   there's a kindness in his justice,
   which is more than liberty.
   There is no place where earth's sorrows
   are more felt than up in heav'n;
   there is no place where earth's failings
   have such kindly judgement giv'n.

2. But we make his love too narrow
   by false limits of our own;
   and we magnify his strictness
   with a zeal he will not own.
   There is plentiful redemption
   in the blood that has been shed,
   there is joy for all the members
   in the sorrows of the Head.

3. For the love of God is broader
   than the scope of human mind,
   and the heart of the Eternal
   is most wonderfully kind.
   If our love were but more simple,
   we should take him at his word;
   and our hearts would find assurance
   in the promise of the Lord.

663 Venantius Fortunatus (530-609) trans. John Mason Neale (1818-1866) and others

1. The royal banners forward go,
   the cross shines forth in mystic glow;
   where he in flesh, our flesh who made,
   our sentence bore, our ransom paid.

2. There whilst he hung, his sacred side
   by soldier's spear was opened wide,
   to cleanse us in the precious flood
   of water mingled with his blood.

3. Fulfilled is now what David told
   in true prophetic song of old,
   how God the sinner's king should be;
   for God is reigning from the tree.

4. O tree of glory, tree most fair,
   ordained those holy limbs to bear,
   how bright in purple robe it stood,
   the purple of a Saviour's blood!

5. Upon its arms, like balance true,
   he weighed the price for sinners due,
   the price which none but he could pay:
   and spoiled the spoiler of his prey.

6. To thee, eternal Three in One,
   let homage meet by all be done,
   as by the cross thou dost restore,
   so rule and guide us evermore.
   Amen.

664 Michael Forster (b. 1946), based on Isaiah 35 © 1993 Kevin Mayhew Ltd.

1. The Saviour will come,
   resplendent in joy;
   the lame and the sick
   new strength will enjoy.
   The desert, rejoicing,
   shall burst into flower,
   the deaf and the speechless
   will sing in that hour!

2. The Saviour will come,
   like rain on the earth,
   to harvest at last
   his crop of great worth.

In patience await him,
with firmness of mind;
both mercy and judgement
his people will find.

3. The Saviour will come,
his truth we shall see:
where lepers are cleansed
and captives set free.
No finely clad princeling
in palace of gold,
but Christ with his people,
O wonder untold!

665 Joseph Addison (1672-1719)
based on Psalm 19:1-6, alt.

1. The spacious firmament on high,
with all the blue ethereal sky,
and spangled heav'ns, a shining frame,
their great Original proclaim.
The unwearied sun from day to day
does his Creator's pow'r display,
and publishes to ev'ry land
the works of an almighty hand,
the works of an almighty hand.

2. Soon as the evening shades prevail
the moon takes up the wondrous tale,
and nightly to the list'ning earth
repeats the story of her birth;
whilst all the stars that round her burn,
and all the planets in their turn,
confirm the tidings, as they roll,
and spread the truth from pole to pole,
and spread the truth from pole to pole.

3. What though in solemn silence all
move round the dark terrestrial ball;
what though nor lit'ral voice nor sound
amid their radiant orbs be found;
in reason's ear they all rejoice,
and utter forth a glorious voice,
for ever singing as they shine,
'The hand that made us is divine,
the hand that made us is divine.'

666 Damian Lundy (1944-1997)
© 1978, 1993 Kevin Mayhew Ltd.

1. The Spirit lives to set us free,
walk, walk in the light.
He binds us all in unity,
walk, walk in the light.

Walk in the light (x3)
walk in the light of the Lord.

2. Jesus promised life to all,
walk, walk in the light.
The dead were wakened by his call,
walk, walk in the light.

3. He died in pain on Calvary,
walk, walk in the light,
to save the lost like you and me,
walk, walk in the light.

4. We know his death was not the end,
walk, walk in the light.
He gave his Spirit to be our friend,
walk, walk in the light.

5. By Jesus' love our wounds are healed,
walk, walk in the light.
The Father's kindness is revealed,
walk, walk in the light.

6. The Spirit lives in you and me,
walk, walk in the light.
His light will shine for all to see,
walk, walk in the light.

667 Latin hymn (17th century)
trans. Francis Pott (1832-1909)

1. The strife is o'er, the battle done;
now is the Victor's triumph won;
O let the song of praise be sung:
Alleluia, alleluia, alleluia.

2. Death's mightiest pow'rs have done
their worst,
and Jesus hath his foes dispersed;
let shouts of praise and joy outburst:
Alleluia, alleluia, alleluia.

Continued overleaf

3. On the third morn he rose again
glorious in majesty to reign;
O let us swell the joyful strain:
Alleluia, alleluia, alleluia.

4. Lord, by the stripes which wounded thee
from death's dread sting thy servants free,
that we may live, and sing to thee:
Alleluia, alleluia, alleluia.

668
Robert B. Kelly (b. 1948)
© 1999 Kevin Mayhew Ltd.

1. The table's set, Lord, your people gathered;
around this table each finds their place.
Sign of the kingdom, the greatest gath'ring,
around Christ Jesus each has their place.

2. At this same table in other places,
so many people here in Christ's name.
Those gone before us, who will succeed us,
one single table throughout all time.

3. One Lord inviting, one Church
responding;
one single bread and one cup of wine.
May what we do here change and
transform us,
one single presence, Christ through
all time.

669
Michael Forster (b. 1946)
© 1999 Kevin Mayhew Ltd

1. The universe was waiting
in dark, chaotic night,
until the word was spoken:
'Let there be glorious light!'
From darkness and from chaos
were light and order born;
the God of new beginnings
rejoiced to see their dawn.

2. And as in that beginning,
in every age the same,
creation's Re-creator
is keeping hope aflame.
From Eden to the desert,
the manger to the tomb,
each fall becomes a rising,
and every grave a womb.

3. Wherever people languish
in darkness or despair,
the God of new beginnings
is pierced, and rises there.
We join with him, to listen,
to care, and to protest,
to see the mighty humbled
and all the humble blessed.

4. We join with our Creator
to keep the vision bright:
in places of oppression
we call for freedom's light:
a glorious new beginning,
a universe at peace,
where justice flows like fountains
and praises never cease.

670
Traditional West Indian

1. The Virgin Mary had a baby boy,
the Virgin Mary had a baby boy,
the Virgin Mary had a baby boy,
and they said that his name was Jesus.

He came from the glory,
he came from the glorious kingdom.
He came from the glory,
he came from the glorious kingdom.
O yes, believer. O yes, believer.
He came from the glory,
he came from the glorious kingdom.

2. The angels sang when the baby
was born, *(x3)*
and proclaimed him the Saviour Jesus.

3. The wise men saw where the baby
was born, *(x3)*
and they saw that his name was Jesus.

671

Edward Hayes Plumptre (1821-1891) alt.

1. Thine arm, O Lord, in days of old
was strong to heal and save;
it triumphed o'er disease and death,
o'er darkness and the grave:
to thee they went, the blind, the dumb,
the palsied and the lame,
the outcasts with their grievances,
the sick with fevered frame.

2. And lo, thy touch brought life and
health,
gave speech and strength and sight;
and youth renewed and frenzy calmed
owned thee, the Lord of light:
and now, O Lord, be near to bless,
almighty as before,
in crowded street, by restless couch,
as by that ancient shore.

3. Be thou our great deliv'rer still,
thou Lord of life and death;
restore and quicken, soothe and bless,
with thine almighty breath:
to hands that work, and eyes that see,
give wisdom's heav'nly lore,
that whole and sick, and weak and
strong,
may praise thee evermore.

672

'A toi la gloire' Edmond Louis Budry (1854-1932)
trans. Richard Birch Hoyle
© Copyright Control

1. Thine be the glory,
risen, conqu'ring Son,
endless is the vict'ry
thou o'er death hast won;
angels in bright raiment
rolled the stone away,
kept the folded grave-clothes
where thy body lay.

*Thine be the glory,
risen, conqu'ring Son,
endless is the vict'ry
thou o'er death has won.*

2. Lo! Jesus meets us,
risen from the tomb;
lovingly he greets us,
scatters fear and gloom.
Let the Church with gladness
hymns of triumph sing,
for her Lord now liveth;
death hath lost its sting.

3. No more we doubt thee,
glorious Prince of Life!
Life is naught without thee:
aid us in our strife.
Make us more than conqu'rors
through thy deathless love.
Bring us safe through Jordan
to thy home above.

673

Mary Fawler Maude (1819-1913) alt.

1. Thine for ever! God of love,
hear us from thy throne above;
thine for ever may we be
here and in eternity.

2. Thine for ever! Lord of life,
shield us through our earthly strife;
thou the life, the truth, the way,
guide us to the realms of day.

3. Thine for ever! O how blest
they who find in thee their rest!
Saviour, guardian, heav'nly friend,
O defend us to the end.

4. Thine for ever! Shepherd, keep
us thy frail and trembling sheep;
safe within thy tender care,
let us all thy goodness share.

5. Thine for ever! thou our guide,
all our wants by thee supplied,
all our sins by thee forgiv'n,
lead us, Lord, from earth to heav'n.

674

vs 1 & 2 Jimmy Owens
vs 3-5 Damian Lundy (1944-1997)
© 1978 Bud John Songs/EMI Christian Music
Publishing/CopyCare

1. This is my body, broken for you,
   bringing you wholeness, making you free.
   Take it and eat it, and when you do,
   do it in love for me.

2. This is my blood, poured out for you,
   bringing forgiveness, making you free.
   Take it and drink it, and when you do,
   do it in love for me.

3. Back to my Father soon I shall go.
   Do not forget me; then you will see
   I am still with you, and you will know
   you're very close to me.

4. Filled with my Spirit, how you will grow!
   You are my branches; I am the tree.
   If you are faithful, others will know
   you are alive in me.

5. Love one another; I have loved you,
   and I have shown you how to be free;
   serve one another, and when you do,
   do it in love for me.

675

James Quinn (b. 1919)
© Geoffrey Chapman, an imprint of Cassell plc

1. This is my will, my one command,
   that love should dwell among you all.
   This is my will that you should love
   as I have shown that I love you.

2. No greater love can be than this:
   to choose to die to save one's friends.
   You are my friends if you obey
   all I command that you should do.

3. I call you now no longer slaves;
   no slave knows all his master does.
   I call you friends, for all I hear
   my Father say, you hear from me.

4. You chose not me, but I chose you,
   that you should go and bear much fruit.
   I called you out that you in me
   should bear much fruit that will abide.

5. All that you ask my Father dear
   for my name's sake you shall receive.
   This is my will, my one command,
   that love should dwell in each, in all.

676

Les Garrett (b. 1944)
© 1967 Scripture in Song/Integrity Music/
Kingsway's Thankyou Music

1. This is the day, this is the day
   that the Lord has made,
   that the Lord has made;
   we will rejoice, we will rejoice
   and be glad in it, and be glad in it.
   This is the day that the Lord has made;
   we will rejoice and be glad in it.
   This is the day, this is the day
   that the Lord has made.

2. This is the day, this is the day
   when he rose again,
   when he rose again;
   we will rejoice, we will rejoice
   and be glad in it, and be glad in it.
   This is the day when he rose again;
   we will rejoice and be glad in it.
   This is the day, this is the day
   when he rose again.

3. This is the day, this is the day
   when the Spirit came,
   when the Spirit came;
   we will rejoice, we will rejoice
   and be glad in it, and be glad in it.
   This is the day when the Spirit came;
   we will rejoice and be glad in it.
   This is the day, this is the day
   when the Spirit came.

677

Isaac Watts (1674-1748) alt.

1. This is the day the Lord has made,
   he calls the hours his own:
   let heav'n rejoice, let earth be glad,
   and praise surround his throne.

2. Today he rose and left the dead,
   and Satan's empire fell;
   today the saints his triumphs spread,
   and all his wonders tell.

3. Hosanna to th'anointed King,
   to David's holy Son!
   Make haste to help us, Lord, and bring
   salvation from thy throne.

4. Blest be the Lord: let us proclaim
   his messages of grace;
   who comes, in God his Father's name,
   to save our sinful race.

5. Hosanna in the highest strains
   the Church on earth can raise;
   the highest heav'ns in which he reigns
   shall give him nobler praise.

678 English Traditional

1. This is the truth sent from above,
   the truth of God, the God of love;
   therefore don't turn me from the door,
   but hearken all, both rich and poor.

2. The first thing that I will relate,
   that God at first did man create;
   the next thing which to you I tell-
   woman was made with him to dwell.

3. Then after that 'twas God's own choice
   to place them both in paradise,
   there to remain from evil free
   except they ate of such a tree.

4. But they did eat, which was a sin,
   and thus their ruin did begin-
   ruined themselves, both you and me,
   and all of our posterity.

5. Thus we were heirs to endless woes
   till God the Lord did interpose;
   and so a promise soon did run:
   that he'd redeem us by his Son.

6. And at this season of the year
   our blest Redeemer did appear,
   and here did live, and here did preach,
   and many thousands he did teach.

7. Thus he in love to us behaved,
   to show us how we must be saved;
   and if you want to know the way,
   be pleased to hear what he did say:

8. 'Go preach the gospel,' now he said,
   'to all the nations that are made!
   And those that do believe on me,
   from all their sins I'll set them free.'

9. O seek! O seek of God above
   that saving faith that works by love!
   And, if he's pleased to grant thee this,
   thou'rt sure to have eternal bliss.

10. God grant to all within this place
    true saving faith, that special grace
    which to his people doth belong:
    and thus I close my Christmas song.

679
Graham Kendrick (b. 1950), based on Isaiah 61
and Luke 4: 18-19 from 'The Millennium Chorus'
© 1999 Ascent Music

1. This is the year when hearts go free, and
      broken lives are mended;
   I hear the sound of Jubilee, the song of
      sorrow ended.
   Love is the greatest story the world has
      known,
   the beacon in the darkness, the way back
      home.

2. This is the year of joy for tears, and
      beauty out of ashes,
   when skies will clear if we will share,
      forgive and learn what love is.
   Let's crown the year with kindness and
      live in peace,
   fill all the world with songs that never
      cease.

Continued overleaf

3. These are the days of heaven's grace, and
   favour smiling on us,
   two thousand years of hopes and prayers
   are met in one great chorus.
   A light has dawned upon us, and will
   increase,
   and countless captive souls will be
   released.

680
George Ratcliffe Woodward (1848-1934)
© Copyright control

1. This joyful Eastertide,
   away with sin and sorrow.
   My love, the Crucified,
   hath sprung to life this morrow.

   Had Christ, that once was slain,
   ne'er burst his three-day prison,
   our faith had been in vain:
   but now hath Christ arisen,
   arisen, arisen, arisen.

2. My flesh in hope shall rest,
   and for a season slumber;
   till trump from east to west
   shall wake the dead in number.

3. Death's flood hath lost its chill,
   since Jesus crossed the river:
   lover of souls, from ill
   my passing soul deliver.

681
Susan Sayers (b. 1946)
© 1991 Kevin Mayhew Ltd.

This world you have made
is a beautiful place;
it tells the pow'r of your love.
We rejoice in the beauty
of your world,
from the seas
to the heavens above.

1. The morning whispers of purity;
   the evening of your peace;
   the thunder booms your exuberance
   in the awesome pow'r you release.

2. The tenderness of a new-born child;
   the gentleness of the rain;
   simplicity in a single cell;
   and complexity in a brain.

3. Your stillness rests in a silent pool;
   infinity drifts in space;
   your grandeur straddles the mountain tops;
   and we see your face in each face.

682
George Washington Doane (1799-1859)
based on John 14

1. Thou art the Way: by thee alone
   from sin and death we flee;
   and all who would the Father seek
   must seek him, Lord, by thee.

2. Thou art the Truth: thy word alone
   true wisdom can impart;
   thou only canst inform the mind
   and purify the heart.

3. Thou art the Life: the rending tomb
   proclaims thy conqu'ring arm;
   and those who put their trust in thee
   nor death nor hell shall harm.

4. Thou art the Way, the Truth, the Life:
   grant us that Way to know,
   that Truth to keep, that Life to win,
   whose joys eternal flow.

683
Emily Elizabeth Steele Elliott (1836-1897)
based on Luke 2:7
adapted by Michael Forster (b. 1946)
© This version copyright 1996 Kevin Mayhew Ltd.

1. Thou didst leave thy throne
   and thy kingly crown
   when thou camest to earth for me,
   but in Bethlehem's home
   was there found no room
   for thy holy nativity.

   O come to my heart, Lord Jesus,
   there is room in my heart for thee.

2. Heaven's arches rang
   when the angels sang
   and proclaimed thee of royal degree,
   but in lowliest birth
   didst thou come to earth
   and in deepest humility.

3. Though the fox found rest,
   and the bird its nest
   in the shade of the cedar tree,
   yet the world found no bed
   for the Saviour's head
   in the desert of Galilee.

4. Though thou cam'st, Lord,
   with the living word
   that should set all thy people free,
   yet with treachery,
   scorn and a crown of thorn
   did they bear thee to Calvary.

5. When the heav'ns shall ring
   and the angels sing
   at thy coming to victory,
   let thy voice call me home,
   saying 'Heav'n has room,
   there is room at my side for thee.'

684 John Marriott (1780-1825) alt.

1. Thou, whose almighty word
   chaos and darkness heard,
   and took their flight;
   hear us, we humbly pray,
   and where the gospel day
   sheds not its glorious ray,
   let there be light.

2. Thou, who didst come to bring
   on thy redeeming wing,
   healing and sight,
   health to the sick in mind,
   sight to the inly blind,
   O now to humankind
   let there be light.

3. Spirit of truth and love,
   life-giving, holy Dove,
   speed forth thy flight;
   move on the water's face,
   bearing the lamp of grace,
   and in earth's darkest place
   let there be light.

4. Holy and blessèd Three,
   glorious Trinity,
   Wisdom, Love, Might;
   boundless as ocean's tide
   rolling in fullest pride,
   through the earth far and wide
   let there be light.

685 Gilbert Rorison (1821-1869)

1. Three in One, and One in Three,
   ruler of the earth and sea,
   hear us while we lift to thee
   holy chant and psalm.

2. Light of lights! with morning-shine
   lift on us thy light divine;
   and let charity benign
   breathe on us her balm.

3. Light of lights! when falls the ev'n,
   let it close on sin forgiv'n,
   fold us in the peace of heav'n;
   shed a holy calm.

4. Three in One, and One in Three,
   dimly here we worship thee;
   with the saints hereafter we
   hope to bear the palm.

686 Psalm 34 in 'New Version' (Tate and Brady, 1696)

1. Through all the changing scenes of life,
   in trouble and in joy,
   the praises of my God shall still
   my heart and tongue employ.

Continued overleaf

2. O magnify the Lord with me,
with me exalt his name;
when in distress to him I called,
he to my rescue came.

3. The hosts of God encamp around
the dwellings of the just;
deliv'rance he affords to all
who on his succour trust.

4. O make but trial of his love:
experience will decide
how blest are they, and only they,
who in his truth confide.

5. Fear him, ye saints, and you will then
have nothing else to fear;
make you his service your delight,
your wants shall be his care.

6. To Father, Son and Holy Ghost,
the God whom we adore,
be glory as it was, is now,
and shall be evermore.

688 Charles Wesley (1707-1788)

687 Bernhardt Severin Ingemann (1789-1862)
trans. Sabine Baring-Gould (1834-1924) alt.

1. Through the night of doubt and sorrow
onward goes the pilgrim band,
singing songs of expectation,
marching to the promised land.

2. Clear before us, through the darkness,
gleams and burns the guiding light;
so we march in hope united,
stepping fearless through the night.

3. One the light of God's own presence
o'er his ransomed people shed,
chasing far the gloom and terror,
bright'ning all the path we tread.

4. One the object of our journey,
one the faith which never tires,
one the earnest looking forward,
one the hope our God inspires.

5. One the strain that lips of thousands
lift as from the heart of one:
one the conflict, one the peril,
one the march in God begun.

6. One the gladness of rejoicing
on the far eternal shore,
where the one almighty Father
reigns in love for evermore.

7. Onward, therefore, fellow pilgrims,
onward with the Cross our aid;
bear its shame and fight its battle,
till we rest beneath its shade.

8. Soon shall come the great awaking,
soon the rending of the tomb;
then the scatt'ring of all shadows,
and the end of toil and gloom.

688 Charles Wesley (1707-1788)

1. Thy ceaseless, unexhausted love,
unmerited and free,
delights our evil to remove,
and help our misery.

2. Thou waitest to be gracious still;
thou dost with sinners bear,
that, saved, we may thy goodness feel,
and all thy grace declare.

3. Thy goodness and thy truth to me,
to ev'ry soul, abound,
a vast, unfathomable sea,
where all our thoughts are drowned.

4. Its streams the whole creation reach,
so plenteous is the store,
enough for all, enough for each,
enough for evermore.

5. Faithful, O Lord, thy mercies are,
a rock that cannot move;
a thousand promises declare
thy constancy of love.

6. Throughout the universe it reigns,
   unalterably sure;
   and while the truth of God remains
   the goodness must endure.

689
Edward Hayes Plumptre (1821-1891), alt.

1. Thy hand, O God, has guided
   thy flock, from age to age;
   the wondrous tale is written,
   full clear, on ev'ry page;
   our forebears owned thy goodness,
   and we their deeds record;
   and both of this bear witness:
   one Church, one Faith, one Lord.

2. Thy heralds brought glad tidings
   to greatest, as to least;
   they bade them rise, and hasten
   to share the great King's feast;
   and this was all their teaching,
   in ev'ry deed and word,
   to all alike proclaiming:
   one Church, one Faith, one Lord.

3. Through many a day of darkness,
   through many a scene of strife,
   the faithful few fought bravely
   to guard the nation's life.
   Their gospel of redemption,
   sin pardoned, hope restored,
   was all in this enfolded:
   one Church, one Faith, one Lord.

4. And we, shall we be faithless?
   Shall hearts fail, hands hang down?
   Shall we evade the conflict,
   and cast away our crown?
   Not so: in God's deep counsels
   some better thing is stored:
   we will maintain, unflinching,
   one Church, one Faith, one Lord.

5. Thy mercy will not fail us,
   nor leave thy work undone;
   with thy right hand to help us,
   the vict'ry shall be won;
   and then by all creation,
   thy name shall be adored.
   And this shall be their anthem:
   One Church, one Faith, one Lord.

690
Frederick Lucian Hosmer (1840-1929)

1. Thy kingdom come! on bended knee
   the passing ages pray;
   and faithful souls have yearned to see
   on earth that kingdom's day.

2. But the slow watches of the night
   not less to God belong;
   and for the everlasting right
   the silent stars are strong.

3. And lo, already on the hills
   the flags of dawn appear;
   gird up your loins, ye prophet souls,
   proclaim the day is near.

4. The day in whose clear-shining light
   all wrong shall stand revealed,
   when justice shall be throned in might,
   and ev'ry hurt be healed.

5. When knowledge, hand in hand with
          peace,
   shall walk the earth abroad:
   the day of perfect righteousness,
   the promised day of God.

691
Lewis Hensley (1824-1905) alt.

1. Thy kingdom come, O God,
   thy rule, O Christ, begin;
   break with thine iron rod
   the tyrannies of sin.

Continued overleaf

2. Where is thy reign of peace
and purity and love?
When shall all hatred cease,
as in the realms above?

3. When comes the promised time
that war shall be no more,
and lust, oppression, crime
shall flee thy face before?

4. We pray thee, Lord, arise,
and come in thy great might;
revive our longing eyes,
which languish for thy sight.

5. Some scorn thy sacred name,
and wolves devour thy fold;
by many deeds of shame
we learn that love grows cold.

6. O'er lands both near and far
thick darkness broodeth yet:
arise, O morning star,
arise, and never set.

692 Horatius Bonar (1808-1889)

1. Thy way, not mine, O Lord,
however dark it be;
lead me by thine own hand,
choose out the path for me.

2. Smooth let it be or rough,
it will be still the best;
winding or straight, it leads
right onward to thy rest.

3. I dare not choose my lot;
I would not if I might:
choose thou for me, my God,
so shall I walk aright.

4. The kingdom that I seek
is thine, so let the way
that leads to it be thine,
else I must surely stray.

5. Take thou my cup, and it
with joy or sorrow fill,
as best to thee may seem;
choose thou my good and ill.

6. Choose thou for me my friends,
my sickness or my health;
choose thou my cares for me,
my poverty or wealth.

7. Not mine, not mine, the choice
in things or great or small;
be thou my guide, my strength,
my wisdom, and my all.

693 Shapcott Wensley

1. Thy will be done, the Saviour said,
and bowed to earth his sacred head,
the sands of life had nearly run,
my Father, let thy will be done,
they will, not mine, be done.

2. No watch his spent disciples kept,
amid the shadows deep they slept;
but silent angels waiting there,
beheld his agony of prayer-
thy will, not mine, be done.

3. His soul foresaw the cruel scorns,
the brutal scourge, the crown of thorns,
and, darker than Gethsemane,
the shadows of th' accursed tree,
thy will, not mine, be done.

4. What though he felt in that dread hour,
the storms of human passions low'r;
nor pain, nor death, his soul would shun,
my Father, let thy will be done,
thy will, not mine, be done.

694

Noel Richards
© 1991 Kingsway's Thankyou Music

1. To be in your presence,
   to sit at your feet,
   where your love surrounds me
   and makes me complete.

   This is my desire, O Lord, this is my desire,
   this is my desire, O Lord, this is my desire.

2. To rest in your presence,
   not rushing away,
   to cherish each moment,
   here I would stay.

695

Frances Jane van Alstyne
(Fanny J. Crosby) (1820-1915)

1. To God be the glory!
   great things he hath done;
   so loved he the world
   that he gave us his Son;
   who yielded his life
   an atonement for sin,
   and opened the life-gate
   that all may go in.

   Praise the Lord, praise the Lord!
   let the earth hear his voice;
   praise the Lord, praise the Lord!
   let the people rejoice:
   O come to the Father,
   through Jesus the Son,
   and give him the glory;
   great things he hath done.

2. O perfect redemption,
   the purchase of blood!
   to ev'ry believer
   the promise of God;
   the vilest offender
   who truly believes,
   that moment from Jesus
   a pardon receives.

3. Great things he hath taught us,
   great things he hath done,
   and great our rejoicing
   through Jesus the Son;
   but purer, and higher,
   and greater will be
   our wonder, our rapture,
   when Jesus we see.

696

William Chatterton Dix (1837-1898) alt.

1. To thee, O Lord, our hearts we raise
   in hymns of adoration;
   to thee bring sacrifice of praise
   with shouts of exultation:
   bright robes of gold the fields adorn,
   the hills with joy are ringing,
   the valleys stand so thick with corn
   that even they are singing.

2. And now, on this our festal day,
   thy bounteous hand confessing,
   upon thine altar, Lord, we lay
   the first-fruits of thy blessing:
   by thee our souls are truly fed
   with gifts of grace supernal;
   thou who dost give us earthly bread,
   give us the bread eternal.

3. We bear the burden of the day,
   and often toil seems dreary;
   but labour ends with sunset ray,
   and rest comes for the weary:
   may we, the angel-reaping o'er,
   stand at the last accepted,
   Christ's golden sheaves for evermore
   to garners bright elected.

4. O blessèd is that land of God,
   where saints abide for ever;
   where golden fields spread far and broad,
   where flows the crystal river:
   the strains of all its holy throng
   with ours today are blending;
   thrice blessèd is that harvest-song
   which never hath an ending.

697
William Walsham How (1823-1897)

1. To thee our God we fly
   for mercy and for grace;
   O hear our lowly cry,
   and hide not thou thy face.

   O Lord, stretch forth thy mighty hand,
   and guard and bless our native land.

2. Arise, O Lord of hosts!
   Be jealous for thy name,
   and drive from out our coasts
   the sins that put to shame.

3. Thy best gifts from on high
   in rich abundance pour,
   that we may magnify
   and praise thee evermore.

4. The pow'rs ordained by thee
   with heav'nly wisdom bless;
   may they thy servants be,
   and rule in righteousness.

5. Give peace, Lord, in our time,
   O let no foe draw nigh,
   nor lawless deeds of crime
   insult thy majesty.

6. The Church of thy dear Son
   inflame with love's pure fire,
   bind her once more in one;
   with life and truth inspire.

2. Jesus is the name we treasure,
   name beyond what words can tell;
   name of gladness, name of pleasure,
   ear and heart delighting well;
   name of sweetness passing measure,
   saving us from sin and hell.

3. 'Tis the name for adoration,
   name for songs of victory;
   name for holy meditation
   in the vale of misery;
   name for joyful veneration
   by the citizens on high.

4. 'Tis the name that whoso preacheth
   speaks like music to the ear;
   who in prayer this name beseecheth
   sweetest comfort findeth near;
   who its perfect wisdom reacheth
   heav'nly joy posesseth here.

5. Jesus is the name exalted
   over ev'ry other name;
   in this name, whene'er assaulted,
   we can put our foes to shame:
   strength to them who else had halted,
   eyes to blind, and feet to lame.

6. Therefore we in love adoring
   this most blessèd name revere,
   holy Jesus, thee imploring
   so to write it in us here,
   that hereafter, heav'nward soaring,
   we may sing with angels there.

698
'Gloriosi Salvatoris' (15th century)
trans. John Mason Neale (1818-1866) alt.

1. To the name of our salvation
   laud and honour let us pay,
   which for many a generation
   hid in God's foreknowledge lay,
   but with holy exultation
   we may sing aloud today.

699
Brian A. Wren (b. 1936)
© 1986 Stainer & Bell Ltd.

1. Trav'lling, trav'lling over the world,
   people can be out of place,
   dashing for freedom, looking for work,
   needing a friendly face:

Break the bread of belonging,
welcome the stranger in the land.
We have each been a stranger,
we can try to understand.
Break the bread of belonging,
fear of the foreigner still blows strong;
make a space for the strangers:
give them the right to belong.

2. Some have fled from terror by night,
   hiding from bullets by day,
   weary and hungry, in fear of their life,
   seeking a safe place to stay:

3. Some are far from the people they love,
   driven by family need,
   tired and exploited, doing their job,
   thinking of children to feed:

4. Trav'lling, trav'lling over the world,
   no-one should be out of place.
   What would we say, then, if we were
        alone,
   needing a friendly face?

700 'Puer nobis nasoitor'
     15th century trans. Percy Dearmer, alt.
     © *Oxford University Press*

1. Unto us a boy is born!
   King of all creation;
   came he to a world forlorn,
   the Lord of ev'ry nation,
   the Lord of ev'ry nation.

2. Cradled in a stall was he,
   watched by cows and asses;
   but the very beasts could see
   that he the world surpasses,
   that he the world surpasses.

3. Then the fearful Herod cried,
   'Pow'r is mine in Jewry!'
   So the blameless children died
   the victims of his fury,
   the victims of his fury.

4. Now may Mary's Son, who came
   long ago to love us,
   lead us all with hearts aflame
   unto the joys above us,
   unto the joys above us.

5. Omega and Alpha he!
   Let the organ thunder,
   while the choir with peals of glee
   shall rend the air asunder,
   shall rend the air asunder.

701 Reginald Heber (1783-1826)

1. Virgin-born, we bow before thee:
   blessèd was the womb that bore thee;
   Mary, maid and mother mild,
   blessèd was she in her child.

2. Blessèd was the breast that fed thee;
   blessèd was the hand that led thee;
   blessèd was the parent's eye
   that watched thy slumb'ring infancy.

3. Blessèd she by all creation,
   who brought forth the world's salvation,
   blessèd they, for ever blest,
   who love thee most and serve thee best.

4. Virgin-born, we bow before thee:
   blessèd was the womb that bore thee;
   Mary, maid and mother mild,
   blessèd was she in her child.

702 Michael Forster (b. 1946)
     © *1993 Kevin Mayhew Ltd.*

1. Waken, O sleeper, wake and rise,
   salvation's day is near,
   and let the dawn of light and truth
   dispel the night of fear.

2. Let us prepare to face the day
   of judgement and of grace,
   to live as people of the light,
   and perfect truth embrace.

Continued overleaf

3. Watch then and pray, we cannot know
the moment or the hour,
when Christ, unheralded, will come
with life-renewing power.

4. Then shall the nations gather round
to learn his ways of peace,
when spears are turned to pruning-hooks
and all our conflicts cease.

703 Philipp Nicolai (1556-1608)
trans. Francis Crawford Burkitt (1864-1935) alt.
© Oxford University Press

1. Wake, O wake! with tidings thrilling
the watchmen all
the air are filling:
arise, Jerusalem, arise!
Midnight strikes! no more delaying,
'The hour has come!'
we hear them saying.
Where are ye all, ye maidens wise?
The Bridegroom comes in sight,
raise high your torches bright!
Alleluia!
The wedding song
swells loud and strong:
go forth and join the festal throng.

2. Sion hears the watchmen shouting,
her heart leaps up
with joy undoubting,
she stands and waits with eager eyes;
see her Friend from heav'n descending,
adorned with truth
and grace unending!
her light burns clear, her star doth rise.
Now come, thou precious Crown,
Lord Jesu, God's own son!
Hosanna!
Let us prepare
to follow there,
where in thy supper we may share.

3. Ev'ry soul in thee rejoices;
from earthly and
angelic voices
be glory giv'n to thee alone!
Now the gates of pearl receive us,
thy presence never more
shall leave us,
we stand with angels round thy throne.
Earth cannot give below
the bliss thou dost bestow.
Alleluia!
Grant us to raise,
to length of days,
the triumph-chorus of thy praise.

704 Marie Lydia Pereira (b. 1920)
© 1984 Kevin Mayhew Ltd.

Wake up, O people, the Lord is very near!
Wake up, and stand for the Lord. (Repeat)

1. Your saving Lord is near. Wake up!
His glory will appear. Wake up!
Your hour of grace is nearer than it
ever was.

2. The night of sin has passed. Wake up!
The light is near at last. Wake up!
The day star, Christ, the Son of God, will
soon appear.

3. To live in love and peace. Wake up!
To let all quarrels cease. Wake up!
To live that all you do may stand the
light of day.

4. That Christ may be your shield.
Wake up!
That death to life may yield. Wake up!
That heaven's gate be opened wide again
for you.

705

Hilary Greenwood (b. 1929)
© Society of the Sacred Mission. Used by permission

1. Walking in a garden
   at the close of day,
   Adam tried to hide him
   when he heard God say:
   'Why are you so frightened,
   why are you afraid?
   You have brought the winter in,
   made the flowers fade.'

2. Walking in a garden
   where the Lord had gone,
   three of the disciples,
   Peter, James, and John;
   they were very weary,
   could not keep awake,
   while the Lord was kneeling there,
   praying for their sake.

3. Walking in a garden
   at the break of day,
   Mary asked the gard'ner
   where the body lay;
   but he turned towards her,
   smiled at her and said:
   'Mary, spring is here to stay,
   only death is dead.'

706

Nick Fawcett
© 1999 Kevin Mayhew Ltd

1. Warm as the sun, fresh as the breeze,
   fair as a flower, tall as the trees,
   clear as the dew, pure as the dove,
   so unto me, Lord, is your love.

2. Lovely as dawn, welcome as light,
   peaceful as dusk, restful as night,
   high as the clouds, deep as the sea,
   so is your love, Lord, unto me.

3. Swift as a stream, free as a bird,
   firm as a rock, sure as your word,
   bright as the stars, shining above,
   so unto me, Lord, is your love.

4. Finer than silk, richer than money,
   precious as gold, sweeter than honey,
   priceless as jewels, dear as can be,
   so is your love, Lord, unto me.

5. Bursting with joy, leaping with praise,
   glowing with thanks, heart set ablaze;
   bringing my life, all that I do,
   such is my love, Jesus, for you

707

Graham Kendrick (b. 1950)
© 1990 Make Way Music

1. We are his children, the fruit of
      his suff'ring,
   saved and redeemed by his blood;
   called to be holy, a light to the nations:
   clothed with his pow'r, filled with his love.

   Go forth in his name,
   proclaiming, 'Jesus reigns!'
   Now is the time for the church to arise
   and proclaim him
   'Jesus, Saviour, Redeemer and Lord.'

2. Countless the souls that are stumbling
      in darkness,
   why do we sleep in the light?
   Jesus commands us to go make disciples,
   this is our case, this is our fight.

3. Listen, the wind of the Spirit is blowing,
   the end of the age is so near;
   pow'rs in the earth and the heavens
      are shaking,
   Jesus our Lord soon shall appear!

708

Susan Sayers (b. 1946), based on Psalm 100
© 1995 Kevin Mayhew Ltd.

We are his people, the sheep of his flock,
his people, the sheep of his flock.

1. Shout with gladness to God
   all the earth, joyfully obey him.
   Come and gather before him now,
   singing songs of gladness.

Continued overleaf

2. Understand that the Lord is our God;
   he it is who made us.
   We his people belong to him,
   he our loving shepherd.

   We are his people, the sheep of his flock,
   his people, the sheep of his flock.

3. O how faithful and good is the Lord,
   loving us for ever;
   rich in mercy and faithfulness,
   true through all the ages.

Traditional South African
v.1 trans. Anders Nyberg vs. 2 & 3 trans. Andrew Maries
© v.1 1990 Wild Goose Publications
vs 2 & 3 Sovereign Music UK

709

1. We are marching in the light of God. *(x4)*

   We are marching,
   Oo-ooh! We are marching in the light
   of God. *(Repeat)*

2. We are living in the love of God . . .

3. We are moving in the pow'r of God . . .

710

Brian A. Wren (b. 1936)
© 1989 Stainer & Bell Ltd.

1. We are not our own. Earth forms us,
   human leaves on nature's growing vine,
   fruit of many generations,
   seeds of life divine.

2. We are not alone. Earth names us:
   past and present, peoples near and far,
   family and friends and strangers
   show us who we are.

3. Through a human life God finds us;
   dying, living, love is fully known,
   and in bread and wine reminds us:
   we are not our own.

4. Therefore let us make thanksgiving,
   and with justice, willing and aware,
   give to earth, and all things living,
   liturgies of care.

5. And if love's encounters lead us
   on a way uncertain and unknown,
   all the saints with prayer surround us:
   we are not alone.

6. Let us be a house of welcome,
   living stone upholding living stone,
   gladly showing all our neighbours
   we are not our own!

711

Graham Kendrick (b. 1950)
© 1986 Kingsway's Thankyou Music

1. We believe in God the Father,
   maker of the universe,
   and in Christ, his Son our Saviour,
   come to us by virgin birth.
   We believe he died to save us,
   bore our sins, was crucified;
   then from death he rose victorious,
   ascended to the Father's side.

   Jesus, Lord of all, Lord of all; (4)
   name above all names,
   name above all names!

2. We believe he sends his Spirit
   on his Church with gifts of pow'r;
   God, his word of truth affirming,
   sends us to the nations now.
   He will come again in glory,
   judge the living and the dead:
   ev'ry knee shall bow before him,
   then must ev'ry tongue confess.

712

The Iona Community
© 1989 WGRG/Iona Community

1. We cannot measure how you heal
   or answer ev'ry suff'rer's prayer,
   yet we believe your grace responds
   where faith and doubt unite to care.
   Your hands, though bloodied on the cross,
   survive to hold and heal and warn,
   to carry all through death to life
   and cradle children yet unborn.

2. The pain that will not go away,
   the guilt that clings from things long past,
   the fear of what the future holds,
   are present as if meant to last.
   But present too is love which tends
   the hurt we never hoped to find,
   the private agonies inside,
   the memories that haunt the mind.

3. So some have come who need your help
   and some have come to make amends,
   as hands which shaped and saved
      the world
   are present in the touch of friends.
   Lord, let your Spirit meet us here
   to mend the body, mind and soul,
   to disentangle peace from pain
   and make your broken people whole.

713 Isaac Watts (1674-1748)

1. We give immortal praise
   to God the Father's love
   for all our comforts here
   and better hopes above:
   he sent his own
   eternal Son,
   to die for sins
   that we had done.

2. To God the Son belongs
   immortal glory too,
   who bought us with his blood
   from everlasting woe:
   and now he lives,
   and now he reigns,
   and sees the fruit
   of all his pains.

3. To God the Spirit's name
   immortal worship give,
   whose new-creating pow'r
   makes the dead sinner live:
   his work completes
   the great design,
   and fills the soul
   with joy divine.

4. To God the Trinity
   be endless honours done,
   the undivided Three,
   and the mysterious One:
   where reason falls
   with all her pow'rs,
   there faith prevails,
   and love adores.

714 Richard Godfrey Parsons (1882-1948)
© Copyright control

1. We hail thy presence glorious,
   O Christ our great High Priest,
   o'er sin and death victorious,
   at thy thanksgiving feast:
   as thou art interceding
   for us in heav'n above,
   thy Church on earth is pleading
   thy perfect work of love.

2. Through thee in ev'ry nation
   thine own their hearts upraise,
   off'ring one pure oblation,
   one sacrifice of praise:
   with thee in blest communion
   the living and the dead
   are joined in closest union,
   one Body with one Head.

3. O living bread from heaven,
   Jesu, our Saviour good,
   who thine own self hast given
   to be our souls' true food;
   for us thy body broken
   hung on the cross of shame:
   this bread its hallowed token
   we break in thy dear name.

Continued overleaf

4. O stream of love unending,
   poured from the one true vine,
   with our weak nature blending
   the strength of life divine;
   our thankful faith confessing
   in thy life-blood outpoured,
   we drink this cup of blessing
   and praise thy name, O Lord.

5. May we, thy word believing,
   thee through thy gifts receive,
   that, thou within us living,
   we all to God may live;
   draw us from earth to heaven
   till sin and sorrow cease,
   forgiving and forgiven,
   in love and joy and peace.

715 Michael Forster (b. 1946)
based on the speech by Martin Luther King Jr.
© 1997 Kevin Mayhew Ltd.

1. We have a dream:
   this nation will arise,
   and truly live
   according to its creed,
   that all are equal
   in their maker's eyes,
   and none shall suffer
   through another's greed.

2. We have a dream
   that one day we shall see
   a world of justice,
   truth and equity,
   where sons of slaves
   and daughters of the free
   will share the banquet
   of community.

3. We have a dream
   of deserts brought to flow'r,
   once made infertile
   by oppression's heat,
   when love and truth
   shall end oppressive pow'r,
   and streams of righteousness
   and justice meet.

4. We have a dream:
   our children shall be free
   from judgements based on
   colour or on race;
   free to become
   whatever they may be,
   of their own choosing
   in the light of grace.

5. We have a dream
   that truth will overcome
   the fear and anger
   of our present day;
   that black and white
   will share a common home,
   and hand in hand
   will walk the pilgrim way.

6. We have a dream:
   each valley will be raised,
   and ev'ry mountain,
   ev'ry hill brought down;
   then shall creation
   echo perfect praise,
   and share God's glory
   under freedom's crown!

716 Edward Joseph Burns (b. 1938)
© The Revd. Edward J. Burns
Reproduced by kind permission

1. We have a gospel to proclaim,
   good news for all throughout the earth;
   the gospel of a Saviour's name:
   we sing his glory, tell his worth.

2. Tell of his birth at Bethlehem,
   not in a royal house or hall,
   but in a stable dark and dim,
   the Word made flesh, a light for all.

3. Tell of his death at Calvary,
   hated by those he came to save;
   in lonely suff'ring on the cross:
   for all he loved, his life he gave.

4. Tell of that glorious Easter morn,
empty the tomb, for he was free;
he broke the pow'r of death and hell
that we might share his victory.

5. Tell of his reign at God's right hand,
by all creation glorified.
He sends his Spirit on his Church
to live for him, the Lamb who died.

6. Now we rejoice to name him King:
Jesus is Lord of all the earth.
This gospel-message we proclaim:
we sing his glory, tell his worth.

717 Graham Kendrick (b. 1950)
© 1989 Make Way Music

1. We'll walk the land with hearts on fire;
and ev'ry step will be a prayer.
Hope is rising, new day dawning;
sound of singing fills the air.

2. Two thousand years, and still the flame
is burning bright across the land.
Hearts are waiting, longing, aching,
for awak'ning once again.

Let the flame burn brighter
in the heart of the darkness,
turning night to glorious day.
Let the song grow louder,
as our love grows stronger;
let it shine! Let it shine!

3. We'll walk for truth, speak out for love;
in Jesus' name we shall be strong,
to lift the fallen, to save the children,
to fill the nation with your song.

718 William Bullock (1798-1874) and
Henry Williams Baker (1821-1877)

1. We love the place, O God,
wherein thine honour dwells;
the joy of thine abode
all earthly joy excels.

2. It is the house of prayer,
wherein thy servants meet;
and thou, O Lord, art there
thy chosen flock to greet.

3. We love the sacred font;
for there the holy Dove
to pour is ever wont
his blessing from above.

4. We love thine altar, Lord;
O what on earth so dear?
For there, in faith adored,
we find thy presence near.

5. We love the word of life,
the word that tells of peace,
of comfort in the strife,
and joys that never cease.

6. We love to sing below
for mercies freely giv'n;
but O, we long to know
the triumph-song of heav'n.

7. Lord Jesus, give us grace
on earth to love thee more,
in heav'n to see thy face,
and with thy saints adore.

719 Matthias Claudius (1740-1815)
trans. Jane Montgomery Campbell (1817-1878) alt.

1. We plough the fields and scatter
the good seed on the land,
but it is fed and watered
by God's almighty hand:
he sends the snow in winter,
the warmth to swell the grain,
the breezes and the sunshine,
and soft, refreshing rain.

All good gifts around us
are sent from heav'n above;
then thank the Lord, O thank the Lord,
for all his love.

Continued overleaf

2. He only is the maker
   of all things near and far;
   he paints the wayside flower,
   he lights the evening star;
   he fills the earth with beauty,
   by him the birds are fed;
   much more to us, his children,
   he gives our daily bread.

   All good gifts around us
   are sent from heav'n above;
   then thank the Lord, O thank the Lord,
   for all his love.

3. We thank thee then, O Father,
   for all things bright and good:
   the seed-time and the harvest,
   our life, our health, our food.
   Accept the gifts we offer
   for all thy love imparts,
   and, what thou most desirest,
   our humble, thankful hearts.

3. And thou, creator Spirit,
   look on us, we are thine;
   renew in us thy graces,
   upon our darkness shine;
   that, with thy benediction
   upon our souls outpoured,
   we may receive in gladness
   the body of the Lord.

4. O Trinity of Persons,
   O Unity most high,
   on thee alone relying
   thy servants would draw nigh:
   unworthy in our weakness,
   on thee our hope is stayed,
   and blessed by thy forgiveness
   we will not be afraid.

720 Vincent Stuckey Stratton Coles (1845-1929)

1. We pray thee, heav'nly Father,
   to hear us in thy love,
   and pour upon thy children
   the unction from above;
   that so in love abiding,
   from all defilement free,
   we may in pureness offer
   our Eucharist to thee.

2. Be thou our guide and helper,
   O Jesus Christ, we pray;
   so may we well approach thee,
   if thou wilt be the Way:
   thou, very Truth, hast promised
   to help us in our strife,
   food of the weary pilgrim,
   eternal source of life.

721 Spiritual, alt.

1. Were you there
   when they crucified my Lord? *(Repeat)*
   O, sometimes it causes me to
   tremble, tremble, tremble.
   Were you there
   when they crucified my Lord?

2. Were you there
   when they nailed him to a tree? . . .

3. Were you there
   when they pierced him in the side? . . .

4. Were you there
   when they laid him in the tomb? . . .

5. Were you there
   when he rose to glorious life? . . .

722

Pierre-Marie Hoog and Robert B. Kelly (b. 1948)
© Original text copyright Rev Pierre-Marie Hoog, S.J.
English translation © 1999 Kevin Mayhew Ltd.

Advent 1

We shall stay awake
and pray at all times,
ready to welcome Christ,
the Prince of Justice.
We shall set aside
all fears and worries,
ready to welcome Christ,
the Prince of Peace.

Advent 2

We shall set our sights
on what is righteous,
ready to welcome Christ,
the Prince of Justice.
We shall smooth the path,
prepare the Lord's way,
ready to welcome Christ,
the Prince of Peace.

Advent 3

We shall plunge into
the saving water,
ready to welcome Christ,
the Prince of Justice.
We shall be reborn
and rise to new life,
ready to welcome Christ,
the Prince of Peace.

Advent 4

We shall hold with faith
to what God promised,
ready to welcome Christ,
the Prince of Justice.
We shall be
attentive to his Spirit,
ready to welcome Christ,
the Prince of Peace.

723
Thomas Kelly (1769-1855) alt.

1. We sing the praise of him who died,
   of him who died upon the cross;
   the sinner's hope, though all deride,
   will turn to gain this bitter loss.

2. Inscribed upon the cross we see
   in shining letters, 'God is love';
   he bears our sins upon the tree;
   he brings us mercy from above.

3. The cross! it takes our guilt away:
   it holds the fainting spirit up;
   it cheers with hope the gloomy day,
   and sweetens ev'ry bitter cup.

4. It makes the coward spirit brave
   to face the darkness of the night;
   it takes the terror from the grave,
   and gilds the bed of death with light.

5. The balm of life, the cure of woe,
   the measure and the pledge of love,
   the sinner's refuge here below,
   the angels' theme in heav'n above.

724
John Henry Hopkins (1820-1891), alt.

1. We three kings of Orient are;
   bearing gifts we traverse afar;
   field and fountain, moor and mountain,
   following yonder star.

   O star of wonder, star of night,
   star with royal beauty bright,
   westward leading still proceeding,
   guide us to thy perfect light.

2. Born a King on Bethlehem plain,
   gold I bring, to crown him again,
   King for ever, ceasing never,
   over us all to reign.

3. Frankincense to offer have I,
   incense owns a Deity nigh,
   prayer and praising, gladly raising,
   worship him, God most high.

Continued overleaf

4. Myrrh is mine, its bitter perfume
   breathes a life of gathering gloom;
   sorrowing, sighing, bleeding, dying,
   sealed in the stone-cold tomb.

   O star of wonder, star of night,
   star with royal beauty bright,
   westward leading still proceeding,
   guide us to thy perfect light.

5. Glorious now behold him arise,
   King and God and sacrifice;
   alleluia, alleluia,
   earth to heav'n replies.

725 Fred Kaan (b. 1929)
© 1967, 1991, 1997 Stainer & Bell Ltd

1. We turn to you, O God of ev'ry nation,
   giver of good and origin of life;
   your love is at the heart of all creation,
   your hurt is people's pain in war
       and death.

2. We turn to you, that we may be forgiven
   for crucifying Christ on earth again.
   We know that we have never wholly
       striven,
   to share with all the promise of
       your reign.

3. Free ev'ry heart from pride and self-
       reliance,
   our ways of thought inspire with
       simple grace;
   break down among us barriers of
       defiance,
   speak to the soul of all the human race.

4. On all who rise on earth for right
       relations,
   we pray the light of love from hour
       to hour.
   Grant wisdom to the leaders of
       the nations,
   the gift of carefulness to those in pow'r.

5. Teach us, good Lord, to serve the need
       of others,
   help us to give and not to count the cost.
   Unite us all to live as sisters, brothers,
   defeat our Babel with your Pentecost!

726 John L. Bell (b. 1949) and Graham Maule (b. 1958)
© 1989, WGRG, Iona Community

1. We will lay our burden down,
   we will lay our burden down,
   we will lay our burden down
   in the hands of the risen Lord.

2. We will light the flame of love,
   we will light the flame of love,
   we will light the flame of love,
   as the hands of the risen Lord.

3. We will show both hurt and hope,
   we will show both hurt and hope,
   we will show both hurt and hope,
   like the hands of the risen Lord.

4. We will walk the path of peace,
   we will walk the path of peace,
   we will walk the path of peace,
   hand in hand with the risen Lord.

727 Joseph Medlicott Scriven (1819-1886)

1. What a friend we have in Jesus,
   all our sins and griefs to bear!
   What a privilege to carry
   ev'rything to him in prayer!
   O what peace we often forfeit,
   O what needless pain we bear,
   all because we do not carry
   ev'rything to God in prayer!

2. Have we trials and temptations?
   Is there trouble anywhere?
   We should never be discouraged:
   take it to the Lord in prayer!
   Can we find a friend so faithful,
   who will all our sorrows share?
   Jesus knows our ev'ry weakness –
   take it to the Lord in prayer!

3. Are we weak and heavy-laden,
   cumbered with a load of care?
   Jesus only is our refuge,
   take it to the Lord in prayer!
   Do thy friends despise, forsake thee?
   Take it to the Lord in prayer!
   In his arms he'll take and shield thee,
   thou wilt find a solace there.

1. What a wonderful change in my life has
      been wrought
   since Jesus came into my heart!
   I have light in my soul for which long I
      had sought,
   since Jesus came into my heart!

   Since Jesus came into my heart,
   since Jesus came into my heart,
   floods of joy o'er my soul
   like the sea billows roll,
   since Jesus came into my heart!

2. I have ceased from my wand'ring and
      going astray
   since Jesus came into my heart!
   And my sins which were many are all
      washed away
   since Jesus came into my heart!

3. I'm possessed of a hope that is steadfast
      and sure,
   since Jesus came into my heart!
   And no dark clouds of doubt now my
      pathway obscure,
   since Jesus came into my heart!

4. There's a light in the valley of death now
      for me,
   since Jesus came into my heart!
   And the gates of the city beyond
      I can see,
   since Jesus came into my heart!

5. I shall go there to dwell in that city,
      I know,
   since Jesus came into my heart!
   And I'm happy, so happy, as onward I go,
   since Jesus came into my heart!

1. What child is this who, laid to rest,
   on Mary's lap is sleeping?
   Whom angels greet with anthems sweet,
   while shepherds watch are keeping?
   This, this is Christ the King,
   whom shepherds guard and angels sing:
   come, greet the infant Lord,
   the babe, the Son of Mary!

2. Why lies he in such mean estate,
   where ox and ass are feeding?
   Good Christians, fear: for sinners here
   the silent Word is pleading.
   Nails, spear, shall pierce him through,
   the cross be borne for me, for you;
   hail, hail the Word made flesh,
   the babe, the Son of Mary!

3. So bring him incense, gold and myrrh,
   come rich and poor, to own him.
   The King of kings salvation brings,
   let loving hearts enthrone him.
   Raise, raise the song on high,
   the Virgin sings her lullaby:
   joy, joy for Christ is born,
   the babe the Son of Mary!

1. What shall we bring to give honour
      to God:
   worship and sacrifice, praying and song?
   This is all nothing unless we can bring
   justice and mercy to honour our King.

Continued overleaf

Walk with our God, humbly each day.
Help us to do all that we say.
Justice and mercy should crown all
*   we bring –*
this is the worship we offer our King.

2. Save us, O Lord, from the hypocrite's
   prayer:
   bringing you praise while our deeds
   are unfair.
   Help us to honour all people on earth:
   each one is precious, of infinite worth.

3. Save us, O Lord, from excuse
   and neglect,
   show us the world as you see it today.
   Kindle within us a passion for good;
   give us the strength to do all that
   we should.

731
Jan Struther (1901-1953)
© *Oxford University Press. Used by permission from*
'Enlarged Songs of Praise'

1. When a knight won his spurs,
   in the stories of old,
   he was gentle and brave,
   he was gallant and bold;
   with a shield on his arm
   and a lance in his hand,
   for God and for valour
   he rode through the land.

2. No charger have I,
   and no sword by my side,
   yet still to adventure
   and battle I ride,
   though back into storyland
   giants have fled,
   and the knights are no more
   and the dragons are dead.

3. Let faith be my shield
   and let joy be my steed
   'gainst the dragons of anger,
   the ogres of greed;
   and let me set free,
   with the sword of my youth,
   from the castle of darkness,
   the pow'r of the truth.

732
Joseph Addison (1672-1719) alt.

1. When all thy mercies, O my God,
   my rising soul surveys,
   transported with the view, I'm lost
   in wonder, love and praise.

2. Unnumbered comforts to my soul
   thy tender care bestowed,
   before my infant heart conceived
   from whom those comforts flowed.

3. When in such slipp'ry paths I ran
   in childhood's careless days,
   thine arm unseen conveyed me safe,
   to walk in adult ways.

4. When worn with sickness oft hast thou
   with health renewed my face;
   and when in sins and sorrows sunk,
   revived my soul with grace.

5. Ten thousand thousand precious gifts
   my daily thanks employ,
   and not the least a cheerful heart
   which tastes those gifts with joy.

6. Through ev'ry period of my life
   thy goodness I'll pursue,
   and after death in distant worlds
   the glorious theme renew.

7. Through all eternity to thee
   a joyful song I'll raise;
   for O! eternity's too short
   to utter all thy praise.

1. When God Almighty came to earth,
   he took the pain of Jesus' birth,
   he took the flight of refugee,
   and whispered: 'Humbly follow me.'

2. When God Almighty went to work,
   carpenter's sweat he didn't shirk,
   profit and loss he didn't flee,
   and whispered: 'Humbly follow me.'

3. When God Almighty walked the street,
   the critic's curse he had to meet,
   the cynic's smile he had to see,
   and whispered: 'Humbly follow me.'

4. When God Almighty met his folk,
   of peace and truth he boldly spoke
   to set the slave and tyrant free,
   and whispered: 'Humbly follow me.'

5. When God Almighty took his place
   to save the sometimes human race,
   he took it boldly on a tree,
   and whispered: 'Humbly follow me.'

6. When God Almighty comes again,
   he'll meet us incognito as then;
   and though no words may voice
      his plea,
   he'll whisper: 'Are you following me?'

When I feel the touch
of your hand upon my life,
it causes me to sing a song
that I love you, Lord.
So from deep within
my spirit singeth unto thee,
you are my King,
you are my God,
and I love you, Lord.

When I look into your holiness,
when I gaze into your loveliness,
when all things that surround
become shadows in the light of you;
when I've found the joy
of reaching your heart,
when my will becomes
enthrall'd in your love,
when all things that surround
become shadows in the light of you:
I worship you, I worship you,
the reason I live is to worship you.
I worship you, I worship you,
the reason I live is to worship you.

1. When I needed a neighbour,
   were you there, were you there?
   When I needed a neighbour,
   were you there?

   And the creed and the colour
   and the name won't matter,
   were you there?

2. I was hungry and thirsty,
   were you there, were you there?
   I was hungry and thirsty,
   were you there?

3. I was cold, I was naked,
   were you there, were you there?
   I was cold, I was naked,
   were you there?

4. When I needed a shelter,
   were you there, were you there?
   When I needed a shelter,
   were you there?

Continued overleaf

5. When I needed a healer,
   were you there, were you there?
   When I needed a healer,
   were you there?

   *And the creed and the colour
   and the name won't matter,
   were you there?*

6. Wherever you travel,
   I'll be there, I'll be there,
   wherever you travel,
   I'll be there.

737 Fred Pratt Green (b. 1903)
© 1972 Stainer & Bell Ltd.

1. When, in our music,
   God is glorified,
   and adoration leaves
   no room for pride,
   it is as though
   the whole creation cried:
   Alleluia.

2. How often, making music,
   we have found
   a new dimension
   in the world of sound,
   as worship moved us
   to a more profound
   Alleluia!

3. So has the Church,
   in liturgy and song,
   in faith and love,
   through centuries of wrong,
   borne witness to the truth
   in ev'ry tongue:
   Alleluia!

4. And did not Jesus sing
   a psalm that night
   when utmost evil strove
   against the Light?
   Then let us sing,
   for whom he won the fight:
   Alleluia!

5. Let ev'ry instrument
   be tuned for praise!
   Let all rejoice
   who have a voice to raise!
   And may God give us
   faith to sing always:
   Alleluia!

738 Isaac Watts (1674-1748)

1. When I survey the wondrous cross
   on which the Prince of Glory died,
   my richest gain I count but loss,
   and pour contempt on all my pride.

2. Forbid it, Lord, that I should boast,
   save in the death of Christ, my God:
   all the vain things that charm me most,
   I sacrifice them to his blood.

3. See from his head, his hands, his feet,
   sorrow and love flow mingling down:
   did e'er such love and sorrow meet,
   or thorns compose so rich a crown?

4. Were the whole realm of nature mine,
   that were an off'ring far too small;
   love so amazing, so divine,
   demands my soul, my life, my all.

739 German (19th century)
trans. Edward Caswall (1814-1878)

1. When morning gilds the skies,
   my heart awaking cries,
   may Jesus Christ be praised.
   Alike at work and prayer
   to Jesus I repair;
   may Jesus Christ be praised.

2. The night becomes as day,
   when from the heart we say:
   may Jesus Christ be praised.
   The pow'rs of darkness fear,
   when this sweet chant they hear:
   may Jesus Christ be praised.

3. In heav'n's eternal bliss
   the loveliest strain is this:
   may Jesus Christ be praised.
   Let air, and sea, and sky
   from depth to height reply:
   may Jesus Christ be praised.

4. Be this, while life is mine,
   my canticle divine:
   may Jesus Christ be praised.
   Be this th'eternal song
   through all the ages on:
   may Jesus Christ be praised.

740 Michael Forster (b. 1946)
© 1996 Kevin Mayhew Ltd.

1. When our God came to earth,
   not for him noble birth:
   he affirmed human worth
   from a humble manger,
   just another stranger.

   Let the poor rejoice!
   Let the mute give voice!
   Love is shown,
   God is known,
   Christ is born of Mary.

2. Not for kings was the word
   which the poor shepherds heard:
   hope renewed, grace conferred,
   and the hillside ringing
   with the angels' singing.

3. Bethlehem, humble town
   where the babe wears the crown,
   turns the world upside down:
   God so unexpected,
   homeless and rejected.

4. Let us sing Mary's song,
   bringing hope, righting wrong,
   heard with fear by the strong,
   poor and humble raising,
   God of justice praising.

741 John Henry Sammis (1846-1919)

1. When we walk with the Lord
   in the light of his word,
   what a glory he sheds on our way!
   While we do his good will,
   he abides with us still,
   and with all who will trust and obey.

   Trust and obey,
   for there's no other way
   to be happy in Jesus,
   but to trust and obey.

2. Not a burden we bear,
   not a sorrow we share,
   but our toil he doth richly repay;
   not a grief nor a loss,
   not a frown nor a cross,
   but is blest if we trust and obey.

3. But we never can prove
   the delights of his love
   until all on the altar we lay;
   for the favour he shows,
   and the joy he bestows,
   are for them who will trust and obey.

4. Then in fellowship sweet
   we will sit at his feet,
   or we'll walk by his side in the way.
   What he says he will do,
   where he sends we will go,
   never fear, only trust and obey.

742 Michael Forster (b. 1946), based on 'Ubi Caritas'
© 1998 Kevin Mayhew Ltd.

1. Where true love is found with charity,
   God is present there.
   Christ's own love has called us,
   gathered us together.
   Let us come with songs
   of hope and jubilation,
   worship and adore him,
   God of our salvation,
   loving one another,
   loving one another.

Continued overleaf

2. Where true love is found with charity,
   God is present there.
   As his holy people,
   gathering together,
   let us be united,
   strife and discord ending.
   Christ, our God, among us,
   ev'ry fear transcending,
   known in one another,
   known in one another.

3. Where true love is found with charity,
   God is present there.
   With saints and martyrs,
   one in faith together,
   let us see your glory,
   Christ our great salvation,
   sharing in the great
   eternal celebration,
   there with one another,
   there with one another.

743 Hubert J. Richards (b. 1921),
based on 'Ubi Caritas' Matthew 5:23, 1 John 4:16
© 1997 Kevin Mayhew Ltd.

1. Where true love is present,
   God is present there.
   When we meet together
   let all quarrels cease.

   Leave your gift,
   and make peace with each other. (Repeat)

2. God is loving kindness;
   those who love like him
   live in God most truly,
   and he lives in them.

3. Let us put behind us
   bitterness and strife,
   recognising Jesus
   present in our midst.

744 Refrain: Francis M. Kelly, based on Ruth 1:16
vs 1-4 Robert B. Kelly (b. 1948), based on Ephesians
5: 21-31, vs 5-8 Frances M. Kelly
© 1999 Kevin Mayhew Ltd.

Wherever you go I will go, wherever you
live I will live;
your people will be my people, your God
will be my God.

1. Christ and his Church are but one
      single body;
   Christ is the head, we follow where
      he leads.

2. Christ loves his Church and gave himself
      to save her;
   he made her holy, sinless, without fault.

3. Christ loves his Church, this is a
      sacred myst'ry;
   our human love is graced and speaks
      of God.

4. So may our love, like Christ's, be
      selfless giving;
   and in this giving, Christ is present here.

Other verses for weddings

5. We come today, in Christ a new creation,
   and in this giving we become as one.

6. Together now, our love can grow
      and strengthen;
   love is not selfish, we can share our joy.

7. And may our home become a place
      of welcome,
   an open door for all who pass our way.

8. We ask your blessing, Father, Son
      and Spirit,
   on all our friends and fam'ly
      gathered here.

745 Nahum Tate (1625-1715)

1. While shepherds watched their flocks
      by night,
   all seated on the ground,
   the angel of the Lord came down,
   and glory shone around.

2. 'Fear not,' said he, (for mighty dread
   had seized their troubled mind)
   'glad tidings of great joy I bring
   to you and all mankind.

3. To you in David's town this day
   is born of David's line
   a Saviour, who is Christ the Lord;
   and this shall be the sign:

4. The heav'nly babe you there shall find
   to human view displayed,
   all meanly wrapped in swathing bands,
   and in a manger laid.'

5. Thus spake the seraph, and forthwith
   appeared a shining throng
   of angels praising God, who thus
   addressed their joyful song:

6. 'All glory be to God on high,
   and on the earth be peace,
   goodwill henceforth from heav'n to all
   begin and never cease.'

746 Heinrich Theobald Schenck (1656-1727) trans. Frances Elizabeth Cox (1812-1897) based on Revelation 7:13

1. Who are these like stars appearing,
   these, before God's throne who stand?
   Each a golden crown is wearing:
   who are all this glorious band?
   Alleluia, hark, they sing,
   praising loud their heav'nly King.

2. Who are these in dazzling brightness,
   clothed in God's own righteousness,
   these, whose robes of purest whiteness
   shall their lustre still possess,
   still untouched by time's rude hand –
   whence came all this glorious band?

3. These are they who have contended
   for their Saviour's honour long,
   wrestling on till life was ended,
   following not the sinful throng;
   these, who well the fight sustained,
   triumph by the Lamb have gained.

4. These are they whose hearts were riven,
   sore with woe and anguish tried,
   who in prayer full oft have striven
   with the God they glorified;
   now, their painful conflict o'er,
   God has bid them weep no more.

5. These, th' Almighty contemplating,
   did as priests before him stand,
   soul and body always waiting
   day and night at his command:
   now in God's most holy place
   blest they stand before his face.

747 Graham Kendrick (b. 1950) © 1988 Make Way Music

1. Who can sound the depths of sorrow
   in the Father heart of God,
   for the children we've rejected,
   for the lives so deeply scarred?
   And each light that we've extinguished
   has brought darkness to our land:
   upon our nation, upon our nation
   have mercy, Lord.

2. We have scorned the truth you gave us,
   we have bowed to other lords.
   We have sacrificed the children
   on the altar of our gods.
   O let truth again shine on us,
   let your holy fear descend:
   upon our nation, upon our nation
   have mercy, Lord.

Continued overleaf

(Men)

3. Who can stand before your anger?
   Who can face your piercing eyes?
   For you love the weak and helpless,
   and you hear the victims' cries.

(All)

Yes, you are a God of justice,
and your judgement surely comes:
upon our nation, upon our nation
have mercy, Lord.

(Women)

4. Who will stand against the violence?
   Who will comfort those who mourn?
   In an age of cruel rejection,
   who will build for love a home?

(All)

Come and shake us into action,
come and melt our hearts of stone:
upon your people, upon your people
have mercy, Lord.

5. Who can sound the depths of mercy
   in the Father heart of God?
   For there is a Man of sorrows
   who for sinners shed his blood.
   He can heal the wounds of nations,
   he can wash the guilty clean:
   because of Jesus, because of Jesus
   have mercy, Lord.

748 William Walsham How (1823-1897) alt.

1. Who is this so weak and helpless,
   child of lowly Hebrew maid,
   rudely in a stable sheltered,
   coldly in a manger laid?
   'Tis the Lord of all creation,
   who this wondrous path hath trod;
   he is God from everlasting,
   and to everlasting God.

2. Who is this – a Man of Sorrows,
   walking sadly life's hard way;
   homeless, weary, sighing, weeping
   over sin and Satan's sway?
   'Tis our God, our glorious Saviour,
   who beyond our mortal sight
   now for us a place prepareth
   free from grief and full of light.

3. Who is this – behold him raining
   drops of blood upon the ground?
   Who is this – despised, rejected,
   mocked, insulted, beaten, bound?
   'Tis our God, who gifts and graces
   on his Church now poureth down;
   all his faithful ones empow'ring
   to partake in cross and crown.

4. Who is this that hangeth dying,
   with the thieves on either side?
   Nails his hands and feet are tearing,
   and the spear hath pierced his side.
   'Tis the God who ever liveth
   'mid the shining ones on high,
   in the glorious golden city
   reigning everlastingly.

749 Graham Kendrick (b. 1950)
© 1997 Make Way Music

1. Who sees it all, before whose gaze
   is darkest night bright as the day;
   watching as in the secret place
   his likeness forms upon a face?

   God sees, God knows,
   God loves the broken heart;
   and holds, and binds,
   and heals the broken heart.

2. Who sees it all, the debt that's owed
   of lives unlived, of love unknown?
   Who weighs the loss of innocence,
   or feels the pain of our offence?

775

1. As Jacob with travel
   was weary one day,
   at night on a stone
   for a pillow he lay;
   he saw in a vision
   a ladder so high
   that its foot was on earth
   and its top in the sky:

   Alleluia to Jesus who died on the tree,
   and has raised up a ladder of mercy for me,
   and has raised up a ladder of mercy for me.

2. This ladder is long,
   it is strong and well-made,
   has stood hundreds of years
   and is not yet decayed;
   many millions have climbed it
   and reached Zion's hill,
   and thousands by faith
   are climbing it still:

3. Come let us ascend!
   all may climb it who will;
   for the angels of Jacob
   are guarding it still:
   and remember, each step
   that by faith we pass o'er,
   some prophet or martyr
   has trod it before:

4. And when we arrive
   at the haven of rest
   we shall hear the glad words,
   'Come up hither, ye blest,
   here are regions of light,
   here are mansions of bliss.'
   O who would not climb
   such a ladder as this?

776

Original text: William James Kirkpatrick (1838-1921)
Alternative text, vs. 2 & 3: Michael Forster (b. 1946)
© *Alternative verses 2 and 3 1996 Kevin Mayhew Ltd.*

1. Away in a manger,
   no crib for a bed,
   the little Lord Jesus
   laid down his sweet head.
   The stars in the bright sky
   looked down where he lay,
   the little Lord Jesus,
   asleep on the hay.

2. The cattle are lowing,
   the baby awakes,
   but little Lord Jesus
   no crying he makes.
   I love thee, Lord Jesus!
   Look down from the sky,
   and stay by my side
   until morning is nigh.

3. Be near me, Lord Jesus;
   I ask thee to stay
   close by me for ever,
   and love me, I pray.
   Bless all the dear children
   in thy tender care,
   and fit us for heaven,
   to live with thee there.

An alternative version

1. Away in a manger,
   no crib for a bed,
   the little Lord Jesus
   laid down his sweet head.
   The stars in the bright sky
   looked down where he lay,
   the little Lord Jesus,
   asleep on the hay.

2. The cattle are lowing,
   they also adore
   the little Lord Jesus
   who lies in the straw.
   I love you, Lord Jesus,
   I know you are near
   to love and protect me
   till morning is here.

Continued overleaf

3. Be near me, Lord Jesus;
   I ask you to stay
   close by me for ever,
   and love me, I pray.
   Bless all the dear children
   in your tender care,
   prepare us for heaven,
   to live with you there.

777
Paul Field
© 1991 Daybreak Music Ltd

1. A wiggly, waggly worm, a slipp'ry,
      slimy slug,
   a creepy, crawly, buzzy thing, a tickly,
      wickly bug;
   of all the things to be, I'm happy that
      I'm me.
   Thank you, Lord, I'm happy that
      I'm me.
   I'm happy that I'm me, happy that
      I'm me.
   There's no one else in all the world that
      I would rather be.
   A wiggly, waggly worm, a slippery,
      slimy slug,
   a creepy, crawly, buzzy thing, a tickly,
      wickly bug.

2. A prickly porcupine, a clumsy kangaroo,
   a croaky frog, a hairy hog, a monkey
      in a zoo;
   of all the things to be, I'm happy that
      I'm me.
   Thank you, Lord, I'm happy that
      I'm me.
   I'm happy that I'm me, happy that
      I'm me.
   There's no one else in all the world that
      I would rather be.
   A prickly porcupine, a clumsy kangaroo,
   a croaky frog, a hairy hog, a monkey
      in a zoo.

778
Alan J. Price
© 1990 Daybreak Music Ltd.

1. Be the centre of my life, Lord Jesus,
   be the centre of my life, I pray;
   be my Saviour to forgive me,
   be my friend to be with me,
   be the centre of my life today!

2. Let the power of your presence,
      Lord Jesus,
   from the centre of my life shine through;
   oh, let ev'rybody know it,
   I really want to show it,
   that the centre of my life is you!

779
Winifred Elliott
© Copyright control

1. Boisterous, buzzing, barking things,
   with paws and legs and claws and wings;
   all that swims or crawls or sings;
   or flaps or flops or flips or flings:
   our Creator made all these,
   and big and little you's and me's.

2. Bugs and birds and bears and bees;
   and buds that burst on blossoming trees;
   fluffy clouds before the breeze;
   and stars and skies and streams and seas:
   our Creator made all these,
   and big and little you's and me's.

3. Girls and boys and Mum and Dad,
   the kind and good, or even bad –
   all who please and make him glad,
   and even those who make him sad:
   our Creator made all these,
   and big and little you's and me's.

780
Michael Forster (b. 1946)
© 1993 Kevin Mayhew Ltd.

Break the bread and pour the wine,
break the bread and pour the wine,
break the bread and pour the wine,
share a meal with Jesus,
share a meal with Jesus.

1. Come and meet around the table,
   God prepares the holy food;
   we can share with one another
   ev'rything we have that's good.

2. Come and meet around the table,
   God provides the wine to share;
   we enjoy a meal together,
   show each other how we care.

781
Graham Kendrick (b. 1950)
© 1997 Make Way Music

1. Can you see what we have made
   for this very special day?
   An orange for our planet home
   circling around the sun.

   Candle light, burning bright,
   chase the darkness of the night.
   Christ the light, light our way,
   live inside our hearts today.

2. Count the seasons as we sing,
   summer, autumn, winter, spring.
   Sing to God who sends the rain,
   making all things new again.

3. See the food with colours bright,
   tastebuds tingle at the sight.
   Let's be thankful as we share,
   God's good gifts are ev'rywhere.

4. Why then is the world we made,
   wrapped around with ribbon red?
   Red is for the ransom paid,
   when our Lord was crucified.

5. There's a world I'm dreaming of,
   where there's peace and joy and love.
   Light of Jesus ev'rywhere,
   this is my Christingle prayer.

782
Susan Sayers (b. 1946)
© 1986 Kevin Mayhew Ltd.

1. Caterpillar, caterpillar,
   munching, munching,
   ate through a leaf or two,
   for caterpillar, caterpillar,
   munching, munching,
   didn't have a lot to do.
   But the leaves were very tasty,
   and there seemed a lot to spare,
   so caterpillar, caterpillar, went on
   munching, munching ev'rywhere.

2. Caterpillar, caterpillar,
   feeling sleepy,
   fixed up a silken bed.
   Then caterpillar, caterpillar
   climbed inside
   and covered up his sleepy head.
   In the dark he slept and rested
   as the days and nights went by,
   till on a sunny morning when the
   silk bed burst, he was a butterfly!

3. Butterfly, oh butterfly,
   a flitt'ring, flutt'ring;
   oh what a sight to see.
   And as the lovely butterfly
   was flutt'ring by,
   I heard him sing a song to me:
   'Oh I never knew God could do
   such a wondrous thing for me;
   for he took me as a caterpillar
   and he made a butterfly of me.'

783
Estelle White (b. 1925)
© 1977 Kevin Mayhew Ltd.

1. 'Cheep!' said the sparrow
   on the chimney top,
   'All my feathers are known to God.'
   'Caw!' said the rook in a tree so tall,
   'I know that God gladly made us all.'

2. 'Coo!' said the gentle one,
   the grey-blue dove,
   'I can tell you that God is love.'
   High up above sang the lark in flight,
   'I know the Lord is my heart's delight.'

3. 'Chirp!' said the robin
   with his breast so red,
   'I don't want to work at all, yet I'm fed.'
   'Whoo!' called the owl in a leafy wood,
   'Our God is wonderful, wise and good.'

784
Estelle White (b. 1925)
© 1976 Kevin Mayhew Ltd.

Christ is our King,
let the whole world rejoice!
May all the nations sing out with one voice!
Light of the world,
you have helped us to see that
we are one people and
one day we all shall be free!

1. He came to open the eyes of the blind,
letting the sunlight pour into their minds.
Vision is waiting for those who
     have hope.
He is the light of the world.

2. He came to speak tender words to
     the poor,
he is the gateway and he is the door.
Riches are waiting for all those who hope.
He is the light of the world.

3. He came to open the doors of the goal;
he came to help the downtrodden
     and frail.
Freedom is waiting for all those
     who hope.
He is the light of the world.

4. He came to open the lips of the mute,
letting them speak out with courage
     and truth.
His words are uttered by all those
     who hope.
He is the light of the world.

5. He came to heal all the crippled
     and lame,
sickness took flight at the sound of
     his name.
Vigour is waiting for all those who hope.
He is the light of the world.

6. He came to love everyone on this earth
and through his Spirit he
     promised rebirth.
New life is waiting for all those
     who hope.
He is the light of the world.

785
Jimmy Owens. © 1972 Bud John Songs/EMI
Christian Music Publishing

Clap your hands, all you people.
Shout to our God with a voice of triumph.
Clap your hands, all you people.
Shout to our God with a voice of praise!
Hosanna, hosanna.
Shout to our God with a voice of triumph.
Praise him, praise him.
Shout to our God with a voice of praise!

786
Jean Holloway (b. 1939)
© 1997 Kevin Mayhew Ltd.

1. Clap your hands and sing this song,
all together,
tap your feet and sing along,
all together.

2. Raise your hands up in the air,
God can reach you anywhere.

3. Fold your arms across your chest,
in the arms of God you're blessed.

4. Close your eyes and shut them tight,
God will keep you in his sight.

5. Now sing softly, whisper low,
God will hear you even so.

6. Sing out loud and strong and clear,
so that ev'ryone can hear.

7. Sing with harmony and joy,
God loves ev'ry girl and boy.

787
Unknown

1. Come into his presence, singing,
'Alleluia.' *(x3)*

2. Come into his presence, singing,
'Jesus is Lord.' *(x3)*

3. Come into his presence, singing,
'Glory to God.' *(x3)*

788

Graham Kendrick (b. 1950)
© 1986 Kingsway's Thankyou Music

Come on, let's get up and go.
Let ev'ryone know.
We've got a reason to shout and to sing,
'cause Jesus loves us
and that's a wonderful thing.
Go! go! go! go! get up and go.
Don't be sleepy or slow.
You, you, you, you know what to do.
Give your life to him.

Come on, let's get up and go.
Let ev'ryone know.
We've got a reason to shout and to sing,
'cause Jesus loves us
and that's a wonderful thing.

789

Katherine K. Davis, Henry V. Onorati
and Harry Simeone
© 1941 EMI Mills Music Inc./Delaware Music Corp

1. Come, they told me,
   pah-rum-pum-pum-pum!
   our new-born King to see,
   pah-rum-pum-pum-pum!
   Our finest gifts we bring,
   pah-rum-pum-pum-pum!
   to lay before the King,
   pah-rum-pum-pum-pum!
   Rum-pum-pum-pum!
   Rum-pum-pum-pum!
   So, to honour him,
   pah-rum-pum-pum-pum!
   when we come.

2. Baby Jesus,
   pah-rum-pum-pum-pum!
   I am a poor child too,
   pah-rum-pum-pum-pum!
   I have no gift to bring,
   pah-rum-pum-pum-pum!
   that's fit to give a King,
   pah-rum-pum-pum-pum!
   Rum-pum-pum-pum!
   Rum-pum-pum-pum!
   Shall I play for you,
   pah-rum-pum-pum-pum!
   on my drum?

3. Mary nodded,
   pah-rum-pum-pum-pum!
   The ox and lamb kept time,
   pah-rum-pum-pum-pum!
   I played my drum for him,
   pah-rum-pum-pum-pum!
   I played my best for him,
   pah-rum-pum-pum-pum!
   Rum-pum-pum-pum!
   Rum-pum-pum-pum!
   Then he smiled at me,
   pah-rum-pum-pum-pum!
   me and my drum.

790

Karen Lafferty
© 1981 Maranatha! Music/CopyCare

Don't build your house on the sandy land,
don't build it too near the shore.
Well, it might look kind of nice,
but you'll have to build it twice,
oh, you'll have to build your house
once more.

You'd better build your house upon a rock,
make a good foundation on a solid spot.
Oh, the storms may come and go
but the peace of God you will know.

791

Bev Gammon
© 1988 Kingsway's Thankyou Music

Do what you know is right.
Do what you know is right.
Do what you know is good.
Do what is good.
If no one else does it, don't be afraid.
Jesus says, 'I am with you always'.

792
Michael Forster (b. 1946)
© 1997 Kevin Mayhew Ltd.

1. Do you ever wish you could fly like a bird,
   or burrow like a worm? Well, how absurd!
   Think of all the things that you can do
   and just be glad God made you 'you'!

2. Do you ever wish you could swim
        like a duck?
   Unless your feet are webbed you're
        out of luck!
   Think of all the things that you can do
   and just be glad God made you 'you'!

3. Do you ever wish you could run
        like a hare?
   Well, wishing it won't get you anywhere!
   Think of all the things that you can do
   and just be glad God made you 'you'!

4. Do you ever wish you could hang
        like a bat?
   There's really not a lot of fun in that!
   Think of all the things that you can do
   and just be glad God made you 'you'!

5. Do you ever wish – well, that's
        really enough!
   To wish away your life is silly stuff!
   Think of all the things that you can do
   and just be glad God made you 'you'!

793
Michael Forster (b. 1946)
© 1997 Kevin Mayhew Ltd.

Each of us is a living stone,
no one needs to stand alone,
joined to other living stones,
we're building the temple of God.

1. We're building, we're building
   the temple of God on earth,
   but it needs no walls or steeple,
   for we're making a house of greater worth,
   we're building it with people!

2. The stone that, the stone that
   the builders once cast aside
   has been made the firm foundation,
   and the carpenter who was crucified
   now offers us salvation.

794
Peter Watcyn-Jones
© 1978 Kevin Mayhew Ltd.

1. Ev'ry bird, ev'ry tree
   helps me know, helps me see,
   helps me feel
   God is love and love's around.
   From each river painted blue
   to the early morning dew
   this is love, God is love, love's around.

2. Ev'ry prayer, ev'ry song
   makes me feel I belong
   to a world filled
   with love that's all around.
   From each daybreak to each night,
   out of darkness comes the light,
   this is love, God is love, love's around.

3. Ev'ry mountain, ev'ry stream,
   ev'ry flower, ev'ry dream
   comes from God,
   God is love and love's around.
   From the ever-changing sky
   to a new-born baby's cry,
   this is love, God is love, love's around.

795
Stuart Garrard
© 1995 Kingsway's Thankyou Music

Ev'ry minute of ev'ry day
I get my life from you.
In ev'ry possible kind of way
your life comes bursting through.
You're the one I depend upon,
the source of my life,
you're the only one.
I didn't know living could be such fun,
it's eternal life and it's just begun.

796

Susan Sayers (b. 1946), based on John 12:24
© 1984 Kevin Mayhew Ltd

1. Farmer, farmer, why do you plough?
   What will you do to us grains of
      wheat now?
   'The earth prepared, I'll bury you all,
   for unless the grain dies
   it can never grow tall:
   for unless the grain dies
   it can never grow tall.'

2. Miller, miller, turning your stone,
   why must you grind? Can't you leave
      us alone?
   Why must you change us all with
      your pow'r?
   'You can only be bread
   if you first become flour;
   you can only be bread
   if you first become flour.'

3. Baker, baker, kneading the dough,
   why do you pound us and pummel us so?
   'Unless I work my yeast through you all
   I shall find that my bread
   is not risen at all;
   I shall find that my bread
   is not risen at all.'

4. Jesus, Jesus, use us, we pray;
   use us to further your glory each day.
   'You are my body; you are my bread -
   to be broken and shared
   that the world may be fed;
   to be broken and shared
   that the world may be fed.'

797

Robin Mann
© 1986 Kevin Mayhew Ltd.

Father welcomes all his children
to his fam'ly through his Son.
Father giving his salvation,
life for ever has been won.

1. Little children, come to me,
   for my kingdom is of these.
   Love and new life have I to give,
   pardon for your sin.

2. In the water, in the word,
   in his promise, be assured:
   all who believe and are baptised
   shall be born again.

3. Let us daily die to sin;
   let us daily rise with him –
   walk in the love of Christ our Lord,
   live in the peace of God.

798

Susan Sayers (b. 1946)
© 1986 Kevin Mayhew Ltd.

Father, we want to thank you
for your loving kindness;
and to show you we love you
we will play our music for you.

1. Rum, tum, ta-rum, tum, tum,
   we play our drums for you, Lord Jesus.
   Rum, tum, ta-rum, tum, tum,
   we play our drums for you.

2. Ring, ting, ta-ting, ting, ting,
   we play our triangles for Jesus.
   Ring, ting, ta-ting, ting, ting,
   we play them, Lord, for you.

3. La, la, la-la, la, la,
   we sing our praises for you, Jesus.
   La, la, la-la, la, la,
   we sing our praise for you.

799

Susan Sayers (b. 1946)
© 1986 Kevin Mayhew Ltd.

1. Fishes of the ocean
   and the birds of the air,
   they all declare
   the wonderful works of God
   who has created ev'rything ev'rywhere;
   let the whole earth sing of his love!

Continued overleaf

2. Apples in the orchard
and the corn in the field,
the plants all yield
their fruit in due season,
so the generosity of God is revealed;
let the whole earth sing of his love!

3. Energy and colour
from the sun with its light,
the moon by night;
the patterns of the stars
all winking in the darkness on a frosty
   cold night;
let the whole earth sing of his love!

4. Muddy hippopotamus
and dainty gazelle,
the mice as well,
are all of his making,
furry ones and hairy ones and some with
   a shell;
let the whole earth sing of his love!

5. All that we can hear
and ev'rything we can see,
including me,
we all of us spring from God
who cares for ev'rybody unendingly;
let the whole earth sing of his love!

800 Graham Jeffery
© 1983 Palm Tree Press Ltd
assigned 1984 to Kevin Mayhew Ltd.

1. Forward in faith, forward in Christ,
we are travelling onward;
forward in faith, forward in Christ,
we are trav'ling on.

   *Onward, onward, we are trav'ling on,
   onward, onward, we are trav'ling on.*

2. Jesus is Lord, Jesus is Lord,
we are travelling onward;
Jesus is Lord, Jesus is Lord,
we are trav'ling on.

3. He is our King, he is our King,
we are travelling onward;
he is our King, he is our King,
we are trav'ling on.

801 David Morstad
© Copyright control

Friends, all gather here in a circle.
It has no beginning and it has no end.
Face to face, we all have a place
in God's own circle of friends.
Hey there, *(name)*!
How do you do?
Who's that friend sitting close to you?
Thank the Lord, for *(name)* has a place
in the circle, too.
Take a look around.
Find someone near.
Take him/her by the hand,
say, 'Glad you're here.'
We're together and when we've gone,
God's love, like a circle,
rolls on and on and on.

802 Estelle White (b. 1925)
© 1976 Kevin Mayhew Ltd.

1. Give me peace, O Lord, I pray
in my work and in my play;
and inside my heart and mind,
Lord, give me peace.

2. Give peace to the world, I pray
let all quarrels cease today.
May we spread your light and love:
Lord, give us peace.

803 Janet Morgan
© 1989 Sea Dream Music

   *Give thanks to the Lord for he is good.
   Give thanks to the Lord for ever.
   Give thanks to the Lord for he is good.*

1. When you jump out of bed
and you touch your toes,
when you brush your teeth
and put on your clothes:

2. When you eat your dinner
   and you're all full up,
   when your mum says (name),
   and you help wash up:

3. When you stretch up high
   and you touch the ground,
   when you stretch out wide
   and you turn around:

4. When you click your fingers
   and you stamp your feet,
   when you clap your hands
   and you slap your knees:

   After the last refrain add:

   Give thanks to the Lord. Amen.

804

Caroline Somerville
© *Caroline Somerville. Used by permission.*

1. God almighty set a rainbow
   arching in the sky above,
   and his people understand it
   as a signal of his love.

   Thank you, Father, thank you, Father,
   thank you, Father, for your care,
   for your warm and loving kindness
   to your people ev'rywhere.

2. Clouds will gather, storms come streaming
   on the darkened earth below –
   too much sunshine makes a desert,
   without rain no seed can grow.

3. Through the stormcloud shines your
      rainbow,
   through the dark earth springs the wheat.
   In the future waits your harvest
   and the food for all to eat.

4. God almighty, you have promised
   after rain the sun will show;
   bless the seeds and bless the harvest.
   Give us grace to help us grow.

805

Alan J. Price
© *1994 Daybreak Music Ltd*

God is good, God is great,
he's the one who did create
ev'rything that there is by his power.
God is good, God is great,
he's the one who did create
ev'rything that there is by his power.

1. Thank you, Lord, for the things I can see,
   thank you, thank you, Lord.
   Thank you, Lord, for the sounds I can hear,
   thank you, thank you, Lord.

2. Thank you, Lord, for my family,
   thank you, thank you, Lord.
   Thank you, Lord, for all my friends,
   thank you, thank you, Lord.

3. Thank you, Lord, for the birds in the sky,
   thank you, thank you, Lord.
   Thank you, Lord, for the ants
      on the ground,
   thank you, thank you, Lord.

4. Thank you, Lord, for your love to me,
   thank you, thank you, Lord.
   Thank you, Lord, that you're always near,
   thank you, thank you, Lord.

806

Michael Forster (b. 1946)
© *1999 Kevin Mayhew Ltd*

God made a boomerang and
*   called it love,*
God made a boomerang and
*   called it love,*
God made a boomerang and
*   called it love,*
and then he threw it away!

1. Love's like a boomerang,
      that's what we've found,
   it comes right back when you
      throw it around.
   Something we can share out,
   never seems to wear out,
   love's like a boomerang,
      let's throw it around.

Continued overleaf

2. Love's like a boomerang,
    that's what God planned,
but it's no use if it stays in your hand.
Got to send it spinning
for a new beginning,
love's like a boomerang,
    let's throw it around.

God made a boomerang and
    called it love,
God made a boomerang and
    called it love,
God made a boomerang and
    called it love,
and then he threw it away!

3. Love's like a boomerang, goes
    with a swing,
now ev'rybody can have a good fling.
Families and nations
join the celebrations,
love's like a boomerang,
    let's throw it around.

807 Kathleen Middleton
© 1986 Kevin Mayhew Ltd.

1. God our Father gave us life,
    he keeps us in his care;
    help us care for others too:
    Lord, hear our prayer;
    Lord, hear our prayer.

2. When we're frightened, hurt or tired,
    there's always someone there.
    Make us thankful for their love:
    Lord, hear our prayer;
    Lord, hear our prayer.

3. All God's children need his love,
    a love that we can share.
    So, we pray for everyone:
    Lord, hear our prayer;
    Lord, hear our prayer.

808 Michael Forster (b. 1946)
© 1997 Kevin Mayhew Ltd.

1. God sends a rainbow after the rain,
    colours of hope gleaming through pain;
    bright arcs of red and indigo light,
    making creation hopeful and bright.

    Colours of hope dance in the sun,
    while it yet rains the hope has begun;
    colours of hope shine through the rain,
    colours of love, nothing is vain.

2. When we are lonely, when we're afraid,
    though it seems dark, rainbows are made;
    even when life itself has to end,
    God is our rainbow, God is our friend.

3. Where people suffer pain or despair,
    God can be seen in those who care;
    even where war and hatred abound,
    rainbows of hope are still to be found.

4. People themselves like rainbows are made,
    colours of hope in us displayed;
    old ones and young ones, women
        and men,
    all can be part of love's great 'Amen'!

809 Ian D. Craig
© 1993 Daybreak Music Ltd

1. God's love is deeper than the deepest ocean,
    God's love is wider than the widest sea,
    God's love is higher than the
        highest mountain,
    deeper, wider, higher is God's love to me.

2. God's grace is deeper than the deepest ocean,
    God's grace is wider than the widest sea,
    God's grace is higher than the
        highest mountain,
    deeper, wider, higher is God's grace to me.

3. God's joy is deeper than the deepest ocean,
    God's joy is wider than the widest sea,
    God's joy is higher than the
        highest mountain,
    deeper, wider, higher is God's joy to me.

4. God's peace is deeper than the
      deepest ocean,
   God's peace is wider than the widest sea,
   God's peace is higher than the
      highest mountain,
   deeper, wider, higher is God's peace
      to me.
   Deeper, wider, higher,
   deeper, wider, higher,
   deeper, wider, higher is God to me.

810 Unknown, alt.
© 1986 Greg Leavers and P. J. Horrobin.
Used by permission

God's not dead, (no), he is alive.
God's not dead, (no), he is alive.
God's not dead, (no), he is alive.
Serve him with my hands,
follow with my feet,
love him in my heart,
know him in my life;
for he's alive in me.

811 Michael Forster (b. 1946)
© 1997 Kevin Mayhew Ltd.

1. God turned darkness into light,
   separated day from night,
   looked upon it with delight,
   and declared that it was good.

   God was pleased with ev'rything, (x3)
   and declared that it was good.

2. God divided land and sea,
   filled the world with plants and trees,
   all so beautiful to see,
   and declared that it was good.

3. God made animals galore,
   fishes, birds and dinosaurs,
   heard the splashes, songs and roars,
   and declared that it was good.

4. God made people last of all,
   black and white, and short and tall,
   male and female, large and small,
   and declared that it was good.

812 Michael Forster (b. 1946)
© 1993 Kevin Mayhew Ltd.

1. Goliath was big and Goliath was strong,
   his sword was sharp and his spear
      was long;
   he bragged and boasted but he was wrong:
   biggest isn't always best!

   Biggest isn't always best!
   Biggest isn't always best!
   God told David, 'Don't be afraid,
   biggest isn't always best!'

2. A shepherd boy had a stone and sling;
   he won the battle and pleased the King!
   Then all the people began to sing:
   'Biggest isn't always best!'

3. So creatures made in a smaller size,
   like tiny sparrows and butterflies,
   are greater than we may realise:
   biggest isn't always best!

813 Susan Sayers (b. 1946)
© 1986 Kevin Mayhew Ltd.

1. Go wand'ring in the sun,
      let it warm you through.
      That's how warm and comforting
      God's love can be for you.

2. Just watch a feather fall,
      lay it on your cheek.
      Jesus is as gentle
      with the frightened and the weak.

3. Enjoy the drops of rain,
      sparkling as they fall.
      Jesus is as gen'rous
      with his blessings to us all.

4. Well, can you hold the sea,
      make a living flow'r?
      Neither can we understand
      the greatness of his pow'r.

5. Yet run against the wind –
      very soon you'll see –
      just as strong and free
      is Jesus' love for you and me.

814 *Unknown*

Hallulu, hallelu, hallelu, hallelujah;
we'll praise the Lord! *(Repeat)*
We'll praise the Lord, hallelujah! *(x3)*
We'll praise the Lord!

815 Doug Horley
© 1997 Kingsway's Thankyou Music

Have we made our God too small,
too small?
Have we made our God too small?
He made the heavens and earth
and he reigns on high,
yet he's got the time for you and I.
(Repeat)

See the glory of God light up the sky,
as the clouds proclaim he reigns on high.
See the huge expanse of the oceans wide,
and a billion stars that grace the sky.
I'm awed by the power,
awed by the marks of God all around me,
yet humbled ev'ry day, by my
    unbelieving ways.
I really, really want it to change.

816 Mick Gisbey
© 1985 Kingsway's Thankyou Music

1. Have you got an appetite?
   Do you eat what is right?
   Are you feeding on the word of God?
   Are you fat or are you thin?
   Are you really full within?
   Do you find your strength in him
   or are you starving?

   You and me, all should be
   exercising regularly,
   standing strong all day long,
   giving God the glory.
   Feeding on the living Bread,
   not eating crumbs but loaves instead;
   standing stronger, living longer,
   giving God the glory.

2. If it's milk or meat you need,
   why not have a slap-up feed,
   and stop looking like a weed and
      start to grow?
   Take the full-of-fitness food,
   taste and see that God is good,
   come on, feed on what you should
      and be healthy.

817 Christian Strover
© Christian Strover/Jubilate Hymns

1. Have you heard the raindrops
   drumming on the rooftops?
   Have you heard the raindrops
   dripping on the ground?
   Have you heard the raindrops
   splashing in the streams
   and running to the rivers all around?

   There's water, water of life,
   Jesus gives us the water of life;
   there's water, water of life,
   Jesus gives us the water of life.

2. There's a busy worker
   digging in the desert,
   digging with a spade that
   flashes in the sun;
   soon there will be water
   rising in the well-shaft,
   spilling from the bucket as it comes.

3. Nobody can live
   who hasn't any water,
   when the land is dry,
   then nothing much grows;
   Jesus gives us life if we drink
   the living water,
   sing it so that everybody knows.

818 *Unknown*

He is the King of kings,
he is the Lord of lords,
his name is Jesus, Jesus, Jesus, Jesus
O, he is the King.

819

Traditional

1. He's got the whole world in his hand. *(x4)*

2. He's got you and me, brother . . .

3. He's got you and me, sister . . .

4. He's got the little tiny baby . . .

5. He's got ev'rybody here . . .

820

Orien Johnson.
© 1982 Fred Bock Music Company/Kingsway's Thankyou Music

Hey, now, ev'rybody sing,
ev'rybody sing to the Lord our God!
Hey, now, ev'rybody sing,
ev'rybody sing to the Lord our God!
Ev'rybody join in a song of praise,
come and sing along with me!
Glory, alleluia, glory, alleluia,
I'm so glad I'm free!

Hey, now, ev'rybody sing,
ev'rybody sing to the Lord our God!
Hey, now, ev'rybody sing,
ev'rybody sing to the Lord our God!
Ev'rybody sing, ev'rybody sing,
ev'rybody sing to the Lord our God!
Ev'rybody sing, ev'rybody sing,
ev'rybody sing to the Lord our God!
Ev'rybody sing!

821

Unknown

Ho, ho, ho, hosanna,
ha, ha, hallelujah,
he, he, he, he loves me,
and I've got the joy of the Lord.

822

Hugh Mitchell
© 1973 Zondervan Corporation/Brentwood-Benson Music Publishing

How did Moses cross the Red Sea?
How did Moses cross the Red Sea?
How did Moses cross the Red Sea?
How did he get across?
Did he swim? No! No!
Did he row? No! No!
Did he jump? No! No! No! No!
Did he drive? No! No!
Did he fly? No! No!
How did he get across?
God blew with his wind, puff, puff,
   puff, puff,
he blew just enough, 'nough, 'nough,
   'nough, 'nough,
and through the sea he made a path,
that's how he got across.

823

Martin Smith
© 1994 Curious? Music UK/Kingsway's Thankyou Music

*Oh, I could sing unending songs
of how you saved my soul.
Well, I could dance a thousand miles
because of your great love.*

My heart is bursting, Lord,
to tell of all you've done.
Of how you changed my life
and wiped away the past.
I wanna shout it out,
from ev'ry roof-top sing.
For now I know that God
is for me, not against me.
Ev'rybody's singing now,
'cos we're so happy!
Ev'rybody's dancing now,
'cos we're so happy!
If only we could see your face
and see you smiling over us
and unseen angels celebrate,
for joy is in this place.

824

Susan Sayers (b. 1946)
© 1986, 1987 Kevin Mayhew Ltd.

1. I feel spring in the air today,
   lots of flowers are on their way,
   bursting up to the light of day,
   for the earth is springing to life.

2. I feel spring in the air today,
   lambs are ready to frisk and play;
   nests are built as the tall trees sway,
   for the earth is springing to life.

3. I feel spring in the air today,
   Lord and Father, I want to say
   thanks for showing your love this way,
   for the earth is springing to life.

825

Brian Howard
© 1975 Mission Hills Music. Administered by CopyCare

1. If I were a butterfly,
   I'd thank you Lord, for giving me wings,
   and if I were a robin in a tree,
   I'd thank you, Lord, that I could sing,
   and if I were a fish in the sea,
   I'd wiggle my tail and I'd giggle with glee,
   but I just thank you, Father,
     for making me 'me'.

   For you gave me a heart,
   and you gave me a smile,
   you gave me Jesus
   and you made me your child,
   and I just thank you, Father,
   for making me 'me'.

2. If I were an elephant,
   I'd thank you, Lord, by raising my trunk,
   and if I were a kangaroo,
   you know I'd hop right up to you,
   and if I were an octopus,
   I'd thank you, Lord, for my fine looks,
   but I just thank you, Father,
     for making me 'me'.

3. If I were a wiggly worm,
   I'd thank you, Lord, that I could squirm,
   and if I were a billy goat,
   I'd thank you, Lord, for my
     strong throat,
   and if I were a fuzzy wuzzy bear,
   I'd thank you, Lord, for my fuzzy
     wuzzy hair,
   but I just thank you, Father,
     for making me 'me'.

826

Susan Sayers (b. 1946)
© 1986 Kevin Mayhew Ltd.

1. If I were an astronaut out in space,
   I'd watch the world spin by,
   a bright coloured marble lit up by the sun
   and set in an indigo sky.

   Ours to enjoy, ours to look after,
   oh what a wonderful world.

2. If I were a monkey, and treetop high,
   I'd see the fruits that grow,
   delicious and succulent, fragrant
     and sweet,
   on branches above and below.

3. If I were an octopus in the sea,
   the sun would filter through
   to dapple the corals and brighten
     the shells
   down deep in an ocean of blue.

827

Estelle White (b. 1925)
© 1978 Kevin Mayhew Ltd.

1. I give my hands to do your work
   and, Jesus Lord, I give them willingly.
   I give my feet to go your way
   and ev'ry step I shall take cheerfully,

   O, the joy of the Lord is my strength,
   my strength!
   O, the joy of the Lord is my help, my help!
   For the pow'r of his Spirit is in my soul
   and the joy of the Lord is my strength.

2. I give my eyes to see the world
and ev'ryone, in just the way you do.
I give my tongue to speak your words,
to spread your name and freedom-
giving truth.

3. I give my mind in ev'ry way
so that each thought I have will come
from you.
I give my spirit to you, Lord,
and every day my prayer will spring anew.

4. I give my heart that you may love
in me your Father and the human race.
I give myself that you may grow
in me and make my life a song of praise.

828 Traditional

I gotta home in gloryland that outshines
the sun (3)
way beyond the blue.

Do Lord, oh do Lord, oh do remember
me (3)
way beyond the blue.

829 Susan Sayers (b. 1946)
© 1986 Kevin Mayhew Ltd.

1. I have a friend who is deeper than
the ocean,
I have a friend who is wider than the sky,
I have a friend who always
understands me,
whether I'm happy or ready to cry.

2. If I am lost he will search until he
finds me,
if I am scared he will help me to be brave.
All I've to do is turn to him and ask him.
I know he'll honour the promise he gave.

3. 'Don't be afraid,' Jesus said, 'for I am
with you.
Don't be afraid,' Jesus said, 'for I am here.
Now and for ever, anywhere you travel,
I shall be with you, I'll always be near.'

830 Rob Hayward
© 1985 Kingsway's Thankyou Music

I'm accepted, I'm forgiven,
I am fathered by the true and living God.
I'm accepted, no condemnation,
I am loved by the true and living God.
There's no guilt or fear as I draw near
to the Saviour and Creator of the world.
There is joy and peace as I release
my worship to you, O Lord.

831 Ian Smale
© 1998 Glorie Music
Administered by Kingsway's Thankyou Music

I may live in a great big city,
I may live in a village small,
I may live in a tiny house,
I may live in a tower tall,
I may live in the countryside,
I may live by the sea,
but wherever I live, I know
that Jesus also lives with me,
but wherever I live, I know
Jesus lives with me.

832 Michael Forster (b. 1946)
© 1993 Kevin Mayhew Ltd.

1. I'm black, I'm white, I'm short, I'm tall,
I'm all the human race.
I'm young, I'm old, I'm large, I'm small,
and Jesus knows my face.

The love of God is free to ev'ryone,
free to ev'ryone, free to ev'ryone.
The love of God is free, oh yes!
That's what the gospel says.

2. I'm rich, I'm poor, I'm pleased, I'm sad,
I'm ev'ryone you see.
I'm quick, I'm slow, I'm good, I'm bad,
I know that God loves me.

3. So tall and thin, and short and wide,
and any shade of face,
I'm one of those for whom Christ died,
part of the human race.

833 Alan J. Price
© 1991 Daybreak Music Ltd

1. I'm gonna click, click, click,
   I'm gonna clap, clap, clap,
   I'm gonna click, I'm gonna clap and
      praise the Lord!
   Because of all he's done,
   I'm gonna make him 'Number One'.
   I'm gonna click, I'm gonna clap and
      praise the Lord!

2. I'm gonna zoom, zoom, zoom
   around the room, room, room,
   I'm gonna zoom around the room and
      praise the Lord!
   Because of all he's done,
   I'm gonna make him 'Number One'.
   I'm gonna zoom around the room and
      praise the Lord!

3. I'm gonna sing, sing, sing,
   I'm gonna shout, shout, shout,
   I'm gonna sing, I'm gonna shout and
      praise the Lord!
   Because of all he's done,
   I'm gonna make him 'Number One'.
   I'm gonna sing, I'm gonna shout and
      praise the Lord!

4. I'm gonna click, click, click,
   I'm gonna clap, clap, clap,
   I'm gonna click, I'm gonna clap and
      praise the Lord!
   Because of all he's done,
   I'm gonna make him 'Number One'.
   I'm gonna click, I'm gonna clap and
      praise the Lord!

834 Mike Burn
© 1996 Chasah Music/Daybreak Music Ltd

1. I'm singing your praise, Lord,
   I'm singing your praise,
   to show the world that I love you, Jesus,
   I'm singing your praise.

So many ways, Lord,
so much that I can do
to lift your name in all the earth
to show that I love you.

2. I'm clapping my hands . . .

3. I'm shouting your name . . .

4. I'm jumping for joy . . .

835 Gerard Fitzpatrick
© 1986 Kevin Mayhew Ltd.

1. In the upper room, Jesus and his friends
   met to celebrate their final supper.
   Jesus took a bowl, knelt to wash their feet,
   told them:
   'You must do for others as I do for you.'

2. Peter was annoyed: 'This will never do!
   You, as Master, should not play
      the servant!'
   Jesus took a towel, knelt to dry their feet,
   told them:
   'You must do for others as I do for you.'

836 Judy Bailey
© 1993 Daybreak Music Ltd

I reach up high, I touch the ground,
I stomp my feet and turn around.
I've got to (woo woo) praise the Lord.
I jump and dance with all my might,
I might look funny but that's all right.
I've got to (woo woo) praise the Lord.

1. I'll do anything just for my God,
   'cos he's done ev'rything for me.
   It doesn't matter who is looking on,
   Jesus is the person that I want to please.

2. May my whole life be a song of praise,
   to worship God in ev'ry way.
   In this song the actions praise his name,
   I want my actions ev'ry day to do
      the same.

837
Alan J. Price
© 1992 Daybreak Music Ltd.

Isn't it good to be together,
being with friends old and new?
Isn't it good?
The Bible tells us Jesus our Lord is here too!
Isn't it good to be together,
being with friends old and new?
Isn't it good?
The Bible tells us Jesus our Lord is here too!

He's here!
By his Spirit he's with us. He's here!
His promise is true. He's here!
Though we can't see him, he's here
for me and you. *(Repeat)*

838 Spiritual

*It's me, it's me, it's me, O Lord,
standing in the need of prayer.* (Repeat)

1. Not my brother or my sister,
but it's me, O Lord,
standing in the need of prayer. *(Repeat)*

2. Not my mother or my father . . .

3. Not the stranger or my neighbour . . .

839
Basil Bridge (b. 1927)
© 1990 Oxford University Press
from 'New Songs of Praise 5'

1. It's rounded like an orange,
this earth on which we stand;
and we praise the God who holds it
in the hollow of his hand.

*So Father, we would than you
for all that you have done,
and for all that you have given us
through the coming of your Son.*

2. A candle, burning brightly,
can cheer the darkest night,
and these candles tell how Jesus
came to bring a dark world light.

3. The ribbon round the orange
reminds us of the cost;
how the Shepherd, strong and gentle,
gave his life to save the lost.

4. Four seasons with their harvest
supply the food we need,
and the Spirit gives a harvest
that can make us rich indeed.

5. We come with our Christingles
to tell of Jesus' birth,
and we praise the God who blessed us
by his coming to this earth.

840
Ian White
© 1987 Little Misty Music/Kingsway's Thankyou Music

*It takes an almighty hand,
to make your harvest grow;
it takes an almighty hand,
however you may sow.
It takes an almighty hand,
the world around me shows;
it takes the almighty hand of God.*

1. It takes his hand to grow your garden,
all from a secret in a seed;
part of a plan he spoke and started,
and said is 'very good indeed'.

2. It takes his hand to turn the seasons,
to give the sun and snow their hour;
and in this plan we learn his reason,
his nature and eternal power.

3. It took his hands to carry sorrow,
for ev'ry sin that we have done;
and on a cross he bought tomorrow,
a world of good, like he'd begun.

4. And in his hands there is perfection,
that in this land we only taste;
for now, we see a poor reflection,
then, we shall see him face to face.

841 Spiritual

1. I've got peace like a river,
   I've got peace like a river,
   I've got peace like a river in my soul.

2. I've got joy like a fountain . . .

3. I've got love like an ocean . . .

842 Doug Horley
© 1996 Kingsway's Thankyou Music

I want to be a tree that's bearing fruit,
that God has pruned and caused to shoot,
Oh, up in the sky, so very, very high.
I want to be, I want to be a blooming tree.
God has promised his Holy Spirit
will water our roots and help us grow.
Listen and obey, and before you know it
your fruit will start to grow, grow, grow,
   grow, grow.

You'll be a tree that's bearing fruit,
with a very, very, very strong root,
bright colours like daisies, more fruit
   than Sainsb'ry's,
you'll be a blooming tree.

843 Ian Smale
© 1989 Kingsway's Thankyou Music

I will click my fingers, clap my hands,
stamp my feet and shout hallelujah!
Then I'll whistle as loud as I can.
(Whistle)
I'm happy I'm a child of the Lord.

844 Ian Smale
©1985 Kingsway's Thankyou Music

I will wave my hands
in praise and adoration, *(x3)*
praise and adoration to the living God.
For he's given me hands
that just love clapping:
one, two, one, two, three;
and he's given me a voice
that just loves shouting,
'Hallelujah!'

He's given me feet that just love dancing:
one, two, one, two, three;
and he's put me in a being
that has no trouble seeing
that whatever I am feeling
he is worthy to be praised.

845 Susan Warner (1819-1885)

1. Jesus bids us shine
   with a pure, clear light,
   like a little candle
   burning in the night.
   In this world is darkness;
   so we must shine,
   you in your small corner,
   and I in mine.

2. Jesus bids us shine,
   first of all for him;
   well he sees and knows it,
   if our light grows dim.
   He looks down from heaven
   to see us shine,
   you in your small corner,
   and I in mine.

3. Jesus bids us shine,
   then, for all around:
   many kinds of darkness
   in the world abound
   sin, and want and sorrow,
   so we must shine,
   you in your small corner,
   and I in mine.

846 Michael Forster (b. 1946)
© 1993 Kevin Mayhew Ltd.

Jesus had all kinds of friends,
so the gospel stories say.
Jesus had all kinds of friends,
and there's room for us today.

1. Some were happy, some were sad,
   some were good and some were bad,
   some were short and some were tall,
   Jesus said he loved them all.

2. Some were humble, some were proud,
   some were quiet, some were loud,
   some were fit and some were lame,
   Jesus loved them all the same.

3. Some were healthy, some were sick,
   some were slow and some were quick,
   some were clever, some were not,
   Jesus said he loved the lot!

847 *Gill Hutchinson*
    © 1992 Sea Dream Music

Jesus is greater than the greatest heroes.
Jesus is closer than the closest friends.
He came from heaven and he died to
save us,
to show us love that never ends. ·
(Repeat)
Son of God, and the Lord of glory,
he's the light, follow in his way.
He's the truth that we can believe in,
and he's the life, he's living today.
(Repeat)

848 *Sarah Clark*
    © 1994 CN Publishing/Copycare

1. Jesus is special, special to me,
   he gave his life so I could be free.
   He is my friend who never leaves me.
   He is so special, special to me;
   he is so special, special to me.

2. Jesus forgave me for all of my wrong,
   came to the earth so we could belong
   in his kingdom, close to his heart.
   Making me special, he set me apart;
   making me special, he set me apart.

3. Here in my weakness, his strength
       is so clear,
   thank you, Lord Jesus, you're mighty,
       yet here.
   I praise you for taking all of my fear.
   Help me to trust you and know you
       are near;
   help me to trust you and know you
       are near.

849 *Graham Kendrick (b. 1950)*
    © 1996 Make Way Music

Jesus' love has got under our skin,
Jesus' love has got under our skin.
Deeper than colour oh;
richer than culture oh;
stronger than emotion oh;
wider than the ocean oh.
Don't you want to celebrate
and congratulate somebody,
talk about a family!
It's under our skin, under our skin.

Leader	Ev'rybody say love:
All	**love.**
Leader	Ev'rybody say love:
All	**love,**
Leader	love,
All	**love.**

Isn't it good to be
living in harmony.
Jesus in you and me;
he's under our skin,
under our skin,
he's under our skin,
under our skin.

850 *H. W. Rattle*
    © Scripture Union

Jesus' love is very wonderful,
Jesus' love is very wonderful,
Jesus' love is very wonderful,
oh wonderful love!
So high you can't get over it,
so low you can't get under it,
so wide you can't get round it,
oh wonderful love!

851 *Graham Kendrick (b. 1950)*
    © 1986 Kingsway's Thankyou Music

1. Jesus put this song into our hearts, *(x2)*
   it's a song of joy no one can take away.
   Jesus put this song into our hearts.

Continued overleaf

2. Jesus taught us how to live in
   harmony, *(x2)*
   diff'rent faces, diff'rent races, he made
   us one.
   Jesus taught us how to live in harmony.

3. Jesus turned our sorrow into dancing, *(x2)*
   changed our tears of sadness into rivers
   of joy.
   Jesus turned our sorrow into a dance.

852
Michael Forster (b. 1946)
© 1997 Kevin Mayhew Ltd.

1. Jesus went away to the desert, praying,
   listened for his Father's voice.
   Then he heard the voice
   of the tempter saying,
   'Why not make the easy choice?'

   Ain't list'nin' to no temptation,
   ain't fallin' for no persuasion,
   ain't gonna turn away from salvation,
   I'm a waitin' on the word of the Lord.

2. 'There's an easy way if you'd only
   choose it,
   you can turn the stones to bread!
   What's the good of pow'r
   if you don't abuse it?
   Gotta keep youself well fed!'

3. 'What about a stunt to attract attention,
   showing off your special pow'r?
   You'd get more applause
   than I'd care to mention
   jumping from the Temple tow'r!'

4. 'Ev'rything you want will be right there
   for you,
   listen to the words I say!
   Nobody who matters
   will dare ignore you;
   my way is the easy way.'

853
Greg Leavers
© 1990 Greg Leavers

Jesus will never, ever,
no not ever, never, ever change.
He will always, always,
that's for all days,
always be the same;
so as Son of God and King of kings
he will for ever reign.
Yesterday, today, for ever,
Jesus is the same.
Yesterday, today, for ever,
Jesus is the same.

854
David Hind
© 1992 Kingsway's Thankyou Music

Jesus, you love me more than I can know.
Jesus, you love me more than words can say.
I'm special, I'm planned;
I'm born with a future, I'm in your hands.
I'm forgiven, I've been changed;
loved by my Father who knows me by name.
I'm loved by my Father who knows me
by name.

855
Susan Sayers (b. 1946)
© 1986 Kevin Mayhew Ltd.

1. Just imagine having a world
   where people care,
   glad to help
   and loving in word and deed.

   Well, it can be true
   if we really want it to,
   and the love of Jesus living in us
   is all we need.

2. Just imagine having a world
   where people care,
   glad to give
   without any hate or greed.

856 Spiritual

1. Kum ba yah, my Lord, kum ba yah. *(x3)*
   O Lord, kum ba yah.

2. Someone's crying, Lord,
   kum ba yah, *(x3)*
   O Lord, kum ba yah.

3. Someone's singing, Lord,
   kum ba yah, *(x3)*
   O Lord, kum ba yah.

4. Someone's praying, Lord,
   kum ba yah, *(x3)*
   O Lord, kum ba yah.

857 Susan Sayers (b. 1946)
© 1984 Kevin Mayhew Ltd.

1. Let the mountains dance and sing!
   Let the trees all sway and swing!
   All creation praise its King! Alleluia!

2. Let the water sing its song!
   And the pow'rful wind so strong
   whistle as it blows along! Alleluia!

3. Let the blossom all break out
   in a huge unspoken shout,
   just to show that God's about! Alleluia!

858 Michael Forster (b. 1946)
© 1993 Kevin Mayhew Ltd.

1. Life for the poor was hard and tough,
   Jesus said, 'That's not good enough;
   life should be great and here's the sign:
   I'll turn the water into wine.'

   Jesus turned the water into wine, (x3)
   and the people saw that life was good.

2. Life is a thing to be enjoyed,
   not to be wasted or destroyed.
   Laughter is part of God's design;
   let's turn the water into wine!

3. Go to the lonely and the sad,
   give them the news to make them glad,
   helping the light of hope to shine,
   turning the water into wine!

859 Eric Boswell. © 1959 Warner Chappell Music Ltd.

1. Little donkey, little donkey,
   on the dusty road,
   got to keep on plodding onwards
   with your precious load.
   Been a long time, little donkey,
   through the winter's night;
   don't give up now, little donkey,
   Bethlehem's in sight.

   Ring out those bells tonight,
   Bethlehem, Bethlehem,
   follow that star tonight,
   Bethlehem, Bethlehem.
   Little donkey, little donkey,
   had a heavy day,
   little donkey, carry Mary safely on her way.

2. Little donkey, little donkey,
   on the dusty road,
   there are wise men, waiting for a
   sign to bring them here.
   Do not falter, little donkey,
   there's a star ahead;
   it will guide you, little donkey,
   to a cattle shed.

860 Christopher Massey (b. 1956)
© 1999 Kevin Mayhew Ltd.

1. Little Jesus, sleep away, in the hay,
   while we worship, watch and pray.
   We will gather at the manger,
   worship this amazing stranger:
   little Jesus born on earth,
   sign of grace and human worth.

2. Little Jesus, sleep away, while you may;
   pain is for another day.
   While you sleep, we will not wake you,
   when you cry we'll not forsake you.
   Little Jesus, sleep away,
   we will worship you today.

861

Traditional Czech carol
trans. Percy Dearmer (1867-1936)
© Oxford University Press. Used by permission

1. Little Jesus, sweetly sleep, do not stir;
   we will lend a coat of fur;
   we will rock you, rock you, rock you,
   we will rock you, rock you, rock you,
   see the fur to keep you warm,
   snugly round your tiny form.

2. Mary's little baby sleep, sweetly sleep,
   sleep in comfort, slumber deep; .
   we will rock you, rock you, rock you,
   we will rock you, rock you, rock you;
   we will serve you all we can,
   darling, darling little man.

862

Ian D. Craig
© 1993 Daybreak Music Ltd.

1. Lord of the future, Lord of the past,
   Lord of our lives, we adore you.
   Lord of forever, Lord of our hearts,
   we give all praise to you.

2. Lord of tomorrow, Lord of today,
   Lord over all, you are worthy.
   Lord of creation, Lord of all truth,
   we give all praise to you.

863

Ian Smale
© 1989 Kingsway's Thankyou Music

Lord, we've come to worship you,
Lord, we've come to praise;
Lord, we've come to worship you
in oh so many ways.
Some of us shout and some of us sing,
and some of us whisper the praise we bring,
but Lord, we all are gathering
to give to you our praise.

864

Alan J. Price
© 1992 Daybreak Music Ltd

*Lord, you've promised, through your
   Son,
you'll forgive the wrongs we've done;
we confess them, ev'ry one,
please, dear Lord, forgive us.*

1. Things we've done and things we've said,
   we regret the hurt they spread.
   Lord, we're sorry.
   Lord, we're sorry.

2. Sinful and unkind thoughts too,
   all of these are known to you.
   Lord, we're sorry.
   Lord, we're sorry.

3. And the things we've left undone,
   words and deeds we should have done.
   Lord, we're sorry.
   Lord, we're sorry.

Last refrain:
*Lord, you've promised, through your
   Son,
you'll forgive the wrong we've done;
we receive your pardon,
Lord, as you forgive us.*

865

Traditional

*My God is so big, so strong and
   so mighty,
there's nothing that he cannot do.
My God is so big, so strong and
   so mighty,
there's nothing that he cannot do.*

1. The rivers are his, the mountains are his,
   the stars are his handiwork too.

2. He's called you to live for him ev'ry day,
   in all that you say and you do.

866
Ian Smale
© 1989 Glorie Music/Kingsway's Thankyou Music

1. My mouth was made for worship,
my hands were made to raise,
my feet were made for dancing,
my life is one of praise to Jesus.
And all God's people said: Amen,
hallelujah, amen, praise and glory,
amen, amen, amen, amen.
Wo, wo, wo, wo.

2. My heart was made for loving,
my mind to know God's ways,
my body was made a temple,
my life is one of praise to Jesus.
And all God's people said: Amen,
hallelujah, amen, praise and glory,
amen, amen, amen, amen.
Wo, wo, wo, wo, wo.

867
Susan Sayers (b. 1946)
© 1986 Kevin Mayhew Ltd.

1. Never let Jesus into your heart
unless you are prepared for change.
If you once let Jesus into your heart,
you will never be the same again.
He will change your weakness
   into strength
as suffering turns into joy.
He will wash you clean as the
   drifting snow,
give peace that no one can destroy.

2. Never let Jesus into your heart
unless you are prepared for change.
If you once let Jesus into your heart,
you will never be the same again.
He will use your gifts to help this world,
put you where he needs you to be,
at the end of time he will welcome you,
and love you for eternity.

868
John Hardwick
© 1993 Daybreak Music Ltd.

1. Nobody's a nobody,
believe me 'cause it's true.
Nobody's a nobody,
especially not you.
Nobody's a nobody,
and God wants us to see
that ev'rybody's somebody,
and that means even me.

2. I'm no cartoon, I'm human,
I have feelings, treat me right.
I'm not a super hero
with super strength and might.
I'm not a mega pop star
or super athlete,
but did you know I'm special,
in fact I'm quite unique!

3. *Repeat verse 1*

869
Graham Kendrick (b. 1950)
© 1998 Make Way Music

1. O come and join the dance
that all began so long ago,
when Christ the Lord
was born in Bethelehem.
Through all the years of darkness
still the dance goes on and on,
oh, take my hand
and come and join the song.

Rejoice! Rejoice! Rejoice! Rejoice!
O lift your voice and sing,
and open up your heart to welcome him.
Rejoice! Rejoice! Rejoice! Rejoice
and welcome now your King,
for Christ the Lord was born in Bethlehem.

2. Come shed your heavy load
and dance your worries away,
for Christ the Lord was
born in Bethlehem.
He came to break the pow'r of sin
and turn your night to day,
oh, take my hand
and come and join the song.

Continued overleaf

3. Let laughter ring and angels sing
   and joy be all around,
   for Christ the Lord
   was born in Bethlehem.
   and if you seek with all your heart
   he surely can be found,
   oh, take my hand
   and come and join the song.

4. So whether you're rich or you're poor,
   whatever your race or your sect,
   be you black, white or brown,
   Jesus wants you around,
   there's plenty of room in the net!

872 Unknown

Our God is so great,
so strong and so mighty,
there's nothing that he cannot do.
(Repeat)
The rivers are his,
the mountains are his,
the stars are his handiwork too.
Our God is so great,
so strong and so mighty,
there's nothing that he cannot do.

870 Joanne Pond
© 1980 Kingsway's Thankyou Music

O give thanks to the Lord,
all you his people,
O give thanks to the Lord,
for he is good.
Let us praise, let us thank,
let us celebrate and dance,
O give thanks to the Lord,
for he is good.

873 Michael Forster (b. 1946)
© 1993 Kevin Mayhew Ltd.

Out to the great wide world we go! (3)
and we sing of the love of Jesus.

1. Go and tell our neighbours,
   go and tell our friends,
   Jesus gives his people
   love that never ends. So:

871 Michael Forster (b. 1946)
© 1993 Kevin Mayhew Ltd.

One hundred and fifty-three! (x2)
The number of all the fish in the sea:
one hundred and fifty-three!

1. We'd fished all the night for nothing,
   but Jesus said, 'Try once more.'
   So we doubtfully tried on the other side,
   and found there were fish galore!

2. People sad and lonely,
   wond'ring how to cope;
   let's find ways of showing
   Jesus gives us hope. So:

2. We got all the fish to the shore,
   we wondered how many there'd be,
   So we started to count,
   and what an amount:
   one hundred and fifty-three!

874 Ruth Brown
© Oxford University Press

Over the earth is a mat of green,
over the green is dew,
over the dew are the arching trees,
over the trees the blue.
Across the blue are scudding clouds,
over the clouds the sun,
over it all is the love of God,
blessing us ev'ry one.

3. Now here was a wonderful sight
   we'd never expected to see;
   and the net didn't break,
   it was able to take
   the hundred and fifty-three!

875

Martin Smith
© 1994 Curious? Music UK/Kingsway's
Thankyou Music

Over the mountains and the sea
your river runs with love for me,
and I will open up my heart
and let the Healer set me free.
I'm happy to be in the truth,
and I will daily lift my hands,
for I will always sing of
when your love came down.

I could sing of your love for ever,
I could sing of your love for ever,
I could sing of your love for ever,
I could sing of your love for ever.

O, I feel like dancing,
it's foolishness, I know;
but when the world has seen the light,
they will dance with joy
like we're dancing now.

876 Traditional

1. O when the saints go marching in,
   O when the saints go marching in,
   I want to be in that number
   when the saints go marching in.

2. O when they crown him Lord of all . . .

3. O when all knees bow at his name . . .

4. O when they sing the Saviour's praise . . .

5. O when the saints go marching in . . .

877 Unknown, based on Acts 3

Peter and John went to pray,
they met a lame man on the way.
He asked for alms
and held out his palms
and this is what Peter did say:
'Silver and gold have I none,
but such as I have I give thee,
in the name of Jesus Christ of Nazareth,
rise up and walk!'

He went walking and leaping
and praising God,
walking and leaping and praising God.
'In the name of Jesus Christ of Nazareth,
rise up and walk.'

878 Unknown

Praise and thanksgiving let ev'ryone bring
unto our Father for ev'ry good thing!
All together joyfully sing.

879

Michael Forster (b. 1946), based on Psalm 150
© 1997 Kevin Mayhew Ltd.

1. Praise God in his holy place!
   He's the God of time and space.
   Praise him, all the human race!
   Let ev'rything praise our God!

2. Praise him with the ol' wood block!
   Let it swing and let it rock,
   praising God around the clock!
   Let ev'rything praise our God!

3. Praise him with the big bass drum,
   if you've got guitars, then strum!
   Now let's make those rafters hum!
   Let ev'rything praise our God!

4. Praise him with the chime bars' chime,
   tell the bells it's party time,
   help those singers find a rhyme!
   Let ev'rything praise our God!

5. Violin or xylophone,
   trumpets with their awesome tone;
   bowed or beaten, bashed or blown,
   let ev'rything praise our God!

6. Cymbals, triangles and things,
   if it crashes, howls or rings,
   ev'rybody shout and sing!
   Let ev'rything praise our God!

880

Paul Crouch and David Mudie
© 1991 Daybreak Music Ltd

Prayer is like a telephone
for us to talk to Jesus.
Prayer is like a telephone
for us to talk to God.
Prayer is like a telephone
for us to talk to Jesus.
Pick it up and use it ev'ry day.
We can shout out loud,
we can whisper softly,
we can make no noise at all,
but he'll always hear our call.

881

Susan Sayers (b. 1946)
© 1986 Kevin Mayhew Ltd.

Push, little seed,
push, push, little seed,
till your head pops out of the ground.
This is the air,
and now you are there
you can have a good look round.
You'll see God's sky,
you'll see God's sun,
you'll feel his raindrops one by one,
as you grow, grow, grow, grow,
grow to be wheat for bread.
So push, little seed,
push, push, little seed,
that the world may be fed.

882

Estelle White (b. 1925)
© 1983 Kevin Mayhew Ltd.

1. Put your trust in the man
   who tamed the sea,
   put your trust in the man
   who calmed the waves,
   put your trust in the Lord Jesus,
   it is he who rescues and saves.

2. Put your trust in the man
   who cured the blind,
   put your trust in the man
   who helped the lame,
   put your trust in the Lord Jesus,
   there is healing strength in his name.

3. Put your trust in the man
   who died for you,
   put your trust in the man
   who conquered fear,
   put your trust in the Lord Jesus,
   for he rose from death and he's near.

4. Put your trust in the man
   who understands,
   put your trust in the man
   who is your friend,
   put your trust in the Lord Jesus,
   who will give you life without end.

883

Unknown, based on Genesis 6:4

Rise and shine,
and give God his glory, glory, (x3)
children of the Lord.

1. The Lord said to Noah,
   'There's gonna be a floody, floody.'
   Lord said to Noah,
   'There's gonna be a floody, floody,'
   Get those children out of the muddy,
       muddy,
   children of the Lord.'

2. So Noah, he built him,
   he built him an arky, arky,
   Noah, he built him,
   he built him an arky, arky,
   built it out of hickory barky, barky,
   children of the Lord.

3. The animals, they came on,
   they came on, by twosies, twosies,
   animals, they came on, they came on,
   by twosies, twosies,
   elephants and kangaroosies, roosies,
   children of the Lord.

4. It rained and poured
   for forty daysies, daysies,
   rained and poured
   for forty daysies, daysies,
   nearly drove those animals
       crazies, crazies,
   children of the Lord.

5. The sun came out
   and dried up the landy, landy,
   sun came out
   and dried up the landy, landy,
   ev'rything was fine and dandy, dandy,
   children of the Lord.

6. If you get to heaven
   before I do-sies, do-sies,
   you get to heaven
   before I do-sies, do-sies,
   tell those angels I'm coming
       too-sies, too-sies,
   children of the Lord.

884 W. L. Wallace
© 1997 Kevin Mayhew Ltd.

1. Sing praise to God,
   sing praise to God for life,
   for beauty, hope and love,
   for tenderness and grace.
   Sing praise to God,
   sing praise to God for life,
   with all of earth,
   sing and praise all God's life.

2. Lift up your eyes
   to see the works of God,
   in ev'ry blade of grass,
   in ev'ry human face.
   Lift up your eyes
   to see the works of God,
   through all of life,
   in all time and all space.

3. Open your ears
   to hear the cries of pain
   arising from the poor
   and all who are oppressed.
   Open your mind
   and use your wits to find
   who are the cause
   of this world's unjust ways.

4. Reach out your hands
   to share the wealth God gave
   with those who are oppressed,
   and those who feel alone.
   Reach out your hands
   and gently touch with Christ
   each frozen heart
   which has said 'No' to love.

5. Open our hearts
   to love the world with Christ,
   each person in this world,
   each creature of this earth.
   Open our hearts
   to love the ones who hate,
   and in their hearts
   find a part of ourselves.

6. Live life with love,
   for love encircles all;
   it casts out all our fears,
   it fills the heart with joy.
   Live life with love,
   for love transforms our life,
   as we praise God with our eyes,
   hands and hearts.

885
Gill Hutchinson
© 1994 Sea Dream Music

Step by step, on and on,
we will walk with Jesus till the journey's done.
Step by step, day by day,
because Jesus is the living way.

1. He's the one to follow,
   in his footsteps we will tread.
   Don't worry about tomorrow,
   Jesus knows the way ahead. Oh,

2. He will never leave us,
   and his love he'll always show,
   so wherever Jesus leads us,
   that's the way we want to go. Oh,

886
Susan Sayers (b. 1946)
© 1986 Kevin Mayhew Ltd.

1. Thank you for the summer morning,
   misting into heat;
   thank you for the diamonds
   of dew beneath my feet;
   thank you for the silver
   where a snail has wandered by;
   oh, we praise the name
   of him who made
   the earth and sea and sky.

2. Thank you for the yellow fields
   of corn like waving hair;
   thank you for the red surprise
   of poppies here and there;
   thank you for the blue of
   an electric dragonfly;
   oh, we praise the name
   of him who made
   the earth and sea and sky.

3. Thank you for the splintered light
   among the brooding trees;
   thank you for the leaves that rustle
   in a sudden breeze;
   thank you for the branches
   and the fun of climbing high;
   oh, we praise the name
   of him who made
   the earth and sea and sky.

4. Thank you for the ev'ning
   as the light begins to fade;
   clouds so red and purple
   that the setting sun has made;
   thank you for the shadows
   as the owls come gliding by;
   oh, we praise the name
   of him who made
   the earth and sea and sky.

887
Diane Davis Andrew
adapted by Geoffrey Marshall-Taylor
© 1971 Celebration/Kingsway's Thankyou Music

1. Thank you, Lord, for this new day, *(x3)*
   right where we are.

   Alleluia, praise the Lord, (x3)
   right where we are.

2. Thank you, Lord, for food to eat, *(x3)*
   right where we are.

3. Thank you, Lord, for clothes to wear, *(x3)*
   right where we are.

4. Thank you, Lord, for all your gifts, *(x3)*
   right where we are.

888
Susan Sayers (b. 1946)
© 1986 Kevin Mayhew Ltd.

The clock tells the story of time God gave us,
measured in a tick-tock way.
Don't waste a second of the time God
*   gave us;*
all too soon it flies away.

1. Driving lorries, licking lollies,
   pushing heavy trolleys
   round the supermarket store;
   washing faces, tying laces,
   blinking, winking, drinking
   and much more you can be sure.

2. Time is good for thinking in,
   for helping other people in,
   or playing with a friend;
   time is like a funny kind of
   pocket money given
   ev'ry day for us to spend.

889

David Arkin
© Earl Robinson and David Arkin
Templeton Publishing Co.

1. The ink is black, the page is white,
together we learn to read and write,
to read and write;
and now a child can understand
this is the law of all the land,
all the land;
the ink is black, the page is white,
together we learn to read and write,
to read and write.

2. The slate is black, the chalk is white,
the words stand out so clear and bright,
so clear and bright;
and now at last we plainly see
the alphabet of liberty,
liberty;
the slate is black, the chalk is white,
together we learn to read and write,
to read and write.

3. A child is black, a child is white,
the whole world looks upon the sight,
upon the sight;
for very well the whole world knows,
this is the way that freedom grows,
freedom grows;
a child is black, a child is white,
together we learn to read and write,
to read and write.

4. The world is black, the world is white,
it turns by day and then by night,
and then by night;
it turns so each and ev'ry one
can take his station in the sun,
in the sun;
the world is black, the world is white,
together we learn to read and write,
to read and write.

890

John Gowans. © Salvationist Publishing & Supplies.
Administered by CopyCare

1. There are hundreds of sparrows,
thousands, millions,
they're two a penny, far too many there
must be;
there are hundreds and thousands,
millions of sparrows,
but God knows ev'ry one, and God
knows me.

2. There are hundreds of flowers,
thousands, millions,
and flowers fair the meadows wear for all
to see;
there are hundreds and thousands,
millions of flowers,
but God knows ev'ry one, and God
knows me.

3. There are hundreds of planets,
thousands, millions,
way out in space each has a place by
God's decree;
there are hundreds and thousands,
millions of planets,
but God knows ev'ry one, and God
knows me.

4. There are hundreds of children,
thousands, millions,
and yet their names are written on God's
memory;
there are hundreds and thousands,
millions of children,
but God knows ev'ry one, and God
knows me.

891

Alan J. Price
© 1994 Daybreak Music. Used by permission

1. There is so much to discover,
that God wants us to know.
There is so much to find out for ourselves,
and that's the way to go.
When we learn what God has said,
when we act on what we've read,
there is so much to discover,
there's so much more to know.

Continued overleaf

2. There is so much to discover,
that God wants us to know.
There is so much to find out for
ourselves,
and that's the way to go.
Through the Spirit's pow'r within,
we can change the world for him.
There is so much to discover,
there's so much more to know.

3. There is so much to discover,
that God wants us to know.
There's so much to find out for ourselves,
and that's the way to go.
If we're ever feeling bored,
we just need to ask the Lord
to show to us the things he's planned for
us to do,
and that's the way to go.

892 Michael Forster (b. 1946)
© 1997 Kevin Mayhew Ltd.

There's a great big world out there.
Let's go! (x3)
Celebrate the love of God!

1. We've sung about the love of God,
now it's time to let it show.
If we don't act as though it's true,
how on earth will people know?

2. We've brought to God our prayers
and hymns,
now it's time to live his life,
to sow a little love and peace
in the place of selfish strife.

3. We've listened to the word of God,
now it's time to live it out,
to show by ev'rything we do
what the gospel is about.

893 Michael Forster (b. 1946)
© 1993 Kevin Mayhew Ltd.

There's a rainbow in the sky,
and it's okay! (x3)
It's a sign that God is good.

1. Forty days and nights afloat,
all cooped up on Noah's boat!
Now the rain is almost done;
wake up world, here comes the sun!

2. Now we've got another start,
ev'ryone can play a part:
make the world a better place,
put a smile on ev'ry face!

3. Sometimes, still, the world is bad,
people hungry, people sad.
Jesus wants us all to care,
showing people ev'rywhere:

894 Susan Sayers (b. 1946)
© 1986 Kevin Mayhew Ltd.

1. There's a seed in a flow'r
on a plant in a garden
of the world, as it swirls
through the wideness of space . . .

of our star-speckled galaxy,
speck of the universe,
made and sustained
by the love of our God.

2. There's an ant in a nest
on the floor of a forest
of the world, as it swirls
through the wideness of space . . .

3. There's a crab in a shell
in the depth of an ocean
of the world, as it swirls
through the wideness of space . . .

4. There's a child in a school
of a town in a country
of the world, as it swirls
through the wideness of space . . .

895
Christina Wilde
© 1997, 1999 Kevin Mayhew Ltd.

There was one, there were two,
there were three friends of Jesus,
there were four, there were five,
there were six friends of Jesus,
there were sev'n there were eight,
there were nine friends of Jesus,
ten friends of Jesus in the band.

1. Bells are going to ring in praise of Jesus,
   praise of Jesus, praise of Jesus,
   bells are going to ring in praise of Jesus,
   praising Jesus the Lord.

2. Drums are going to boom in praise
      of Jesus,
   praise of Jesus, praise of Jesus,
   drums are going to boom in praise
      of Jesus,
   praising Jesus the Lord.

3. Tambourines will shake in praise of Jesus,
   praise of Jesus, praise of Jesus,
   tambourines will shake in praise of Jesus,
   praising Jesus the Lord.

4. Trumpets will resound in praise of Jesus,
   praise of Jesus, praise of Jesus,
   trumpets will resound in praise of Jesus,
   praising Jesus the Lord.

Verses can be added ad lib, for example:

Clarinets will swing, in praise of Jesus . . .

Play recorders, too . . .

Triangles will ting . . .

Fiddles will be scraped . . .

Let guitars be strummed . . .

Chime bars will be chimed . . .

Glockenspiels will play . . .

Vibraphones will throb . . .

Trombones slide about . . .

896
Michael Forster (b. 1946)
© 1993 Kevin Mayhew Ltd.

1. The voice from the bush said:
   Moses, look snappy,
   have I got a job for you!
   I've looked around
   and I'm not very happy.
   Here is what you have to do:

   Lead my people to freedom! (3)
   Got to go to the Promised Land!

2. The people of God
   were suff'ring and dying,
   sick and tired of slavery.
   All God could hear
   was the sound of their crying;
   Moses had to set them free:

3. We know that the world
   is still full of sorrow,
   people need to be set free:
   We've got to give them
   a better tomorrow,
   so God says to you and me:

897
Unknown

1. The wise man built his house
   upon the rock, *(x3)*
   and the rain came tumbling down.
   And the rain came down
   and the floods came up,
   the rain came down
   and the floods came up, *(x2)*
   and the house on the rock stood firm.

2. The foolish man built his house
   upon the sand, *(x3)*
   and the rain came tumbling down.
   And the rain came down
   and the floods came up,
   the rain came down
   and the floods came up, *(x2)*
   and the house on the sand fell flat.

898

Michael Forster (b. 1946)
© 1997 Kevin Mayhew Ltd.

The world is full of smelly feet,
weary from the dusty street.
The world is full of smelly feet,
we'll wash them for each other.

1. Jesus said to his disciples,
   'Wash those weary toes!
   Do it in a cheerful fashion,
   never hold your nose!'

2. People on a dusty journey
   need a place to rest;
   Jesus says, 'You say you love me,
   this will be the test!'

3. We're his friends, we recognise him
   in the folk we meet;
   smart or scruffy, we'll still love him,
   wash his smelly feet!

899

Susan Sayers (b. 1946)
© 1986 Kevin Mayhew Ltd.

1. Think big: an elephant.
   Think bigger: a submarine.
   Think bigger: the highest mountain
   that anyone has ever seen.
   Yet big, big, bigger is God,
   and he loves us all!

2. Think old: a vintage car.
   Think older: a full grown tree.
   Think older: a million grains
   of the sand beside the surging sea.
   Yet old, old, older is God,
   and he loves us all!

3. Think strong: a tiger's jaw.
   Think stronger: a castle wall.
   Think stronger: a hurricane
   that leaves little standing there at all.
   Yet strong, strong, stronger is God,
   and he loves us all!

900

Doreen Newport
© 1969 Stainer & Bell Ltd.

1. Think of a world without any flowers,
   think of a world without any trees,
   think of a sky without any sunshine,
   think of the air without any breeze.
   We thank you, Lord, for flow'rs and trees
      and sunshine,
   we thank you, Lord, and praise your
      holy name.

2. Think of a world without any animals,
   think of a field without any herd,
   think of a stream without any fishes,
   think of a dawn without any bird.
   We thank you, Lord, for all your living
      creatures,
   we thank you, Lord, and praise your
      holy name.

3. Think of a world without any people,
   think of a street with no one living there,
   think of a town without any houses,
   no one to love and nobody to care.
   We thank you, Lord, for families and
      friendships,
   we thank you, Lord, and praise your
      holy name.

901

Traditional

This little light of mine,
I'm gonna let it shine, (x3)
let it shine, let it shine, let it shine.

1. The light that shines is the light of love,
   lights the darkness from above,
   it shines on me and it shines on you,
   and shows what the power of love can do.
   I'm gonna shine my light both far
      and near,
   I'm gonna shine my light both bright
      and clear.
   Where there's a dark corner in this land,
   I'm gonna let my little light shine.

2. On Monday he gave me the gift of love,
   Tuesday peace came from above.
   On Wednesday he told me to have
      more faith,
   on Thursday he gave me a little
      more grace.
   On Friday he told me to watch and pray,
   on Saturday he told me just what to say,
   on Sunday he gave me the pow'r divine
   to let my little light shine.

902 Alan J. Price
© 1990 Daybreak Music Ltd

Tick tock, tick tock.
Life is rather like a clock;
I am like a little wheel,
however big or small I feel;
God can use me in his plan,
I can serve him as I am.
Isn't it good? Isn't it good?

903 Michael Forster (b. 1946)
© 1993 Kevin Mayhew Ltd.

1. We can plough and dig the land,
   we can plant and sow,
   we can water, we can weed,
   but we can't make things grow.

   That is something only God can do, (3)
   only God can make things grow.

2. We can edge and we can prune,
   we can rake and hoe,
   we can lift and we can feed,
   but we can't make things grow.

3. We can watch the little shoots
   sprouting row by row,
   we can hope and we can pray,
   but we can't make things grow.

904 Susan Mee
© 1997 Kevin Mayhew Ltd.

1. We eat the plants that grow from
      the seed,
   but it's God who gives the harvest.
   Cures can be made from herbs and
      from weeds,
   but it's God who gives the harvest.
   Ev'rything beneath the sun,
   all the things we claim we've done,
   all are part of God's creation:
   we can meet people's needs
   with things we grow from seed,
   but it's God who gives the harvest.

2. We find the iron and turn it to steel,
   but it's God who gives the harvest.
   We pull the levers, we turn the wheels,
   but it's God who gives the harvest.
   Ev'rything we say we've made,
   plastic bags to metal spades,
   all are part of God's creation:
   we can make lots of things
   from microchips to springs,
   but it's God who gives the harvest.

905 Fred Kaan (b. 1929)
© 1968 Stainer & Bell Ltd.

1. We have a King who rides a donkey, (3)
   and his name is Jesus.

   Jesus the King is risen, (3)
   early in the morning.

2. Trees are waving a royal welcome (3)
   for the King called Jesus.

3. We have a King who cares for people (3)
   and his name is Jesus.

4. A loaf and a cup upon the table, (3)
   bread-and-wine is Jesus.

Continued overleaf

5. We have a King with a bowl and
   towel, (3)
   Servant-King is Jesus.

   Jesus the King is risen, (3)
   early in the morning.

6. What shall we do with our life this
   morning? (3)
   Give it up in service!

906
Alan J. Price
© 1991 Daybreak Music Ltd

We're a bright light together,
with the light of Jesus we shine;
we're a grand band together,
with our friend Jesus it's fine.
We're a swell smell together,
it's the fragrance of Jesus we share!
Whenever we are together,
Jesus is specially there.
Even before time began,
we were part of God's great plan;
'cos of Jesus we would be
part of his great family!

907
Christina Wilde
© 1997 Kevin Mayhew Ltd.

1. We thank God for the harvest
   we gather ev'ry day,
   the things God grows from seeds we sow
   in all our work and play.

   Gotta get out and scatter some seed,
   grow some crops and smother the weeds,
   so much love there's no room for greed,
   gotta go and scatter some seeds.

2. God gives love to be scattered,
   and seeds of faith to sow,
   then sprinkles grace in ev'ry place
   to make the harvest grow.

3. We can work all together,
   with people ev'rywhere:
   in ev'ry place, each creed and race,
   God gives us love to share.

908
Ian Smale
© 1984 Kingsway's Thankyou Music

We will praise, we will praise,
we will praise the Lord,
we will praise the Lord because he is good.
We will praise, we will praise,
we will praise the Lord
because his love is everlasting.

Bring on the trumpets and harps,
let's hear the cymbals ring,
then in harmony lift our voices
and sing, sing.

909
Lucy East
© 1995 Kingsway's Thankyou Music

All **What noise shall we make to
say that God is great?
What noise shall we make
unto the Lord?**

Leader 1. Let's make a loud noise to say
that God is great.
Let's make a loud noise unto
the Lord.

All **Here is my loud noise:
here is my loud noise:
here is my loud noise unto the
Lord.**

2. Let's make a quiet noise . . .
   Here is my quiet noise . . .

3. Let's make a fast noise . . .
   Here is my fast noise . . .

4. Let's make a slow noise . . .
   Here is my slow noise . . .

5. Let's make a joyful noise . . .
   Here is my joyful noise . . .

6. Let's make a praising noise . . .
   **Here is my praising noise: God
   is good!**

**We love making noise
to say that God is great.
We love making noise
unto the Lord.**

910

Paul Booth
© 1977 Stainer & Bell Ltd.

1. When God made the garden of creation,
   he filled it full of his love;
   when God made the garden of creation,
   he saw that it was good.
   There's room for you, and room for me,
   and room for ev'ryone:
   for God is a Father who loves
      his children,
   and gives them a place in the sun.
   When God made the garden of creation,
   he filled it full of his love.

2. When God made the hamper of
      creation,
   he filled it full of his love;
   when God made the hamper of creation,
   he saw that it was good.
   There's food for you, and food for me,
   and food for ev'ryone:
   but often we're greedy, and waste
      God's bounty,
   so some don't get any at all.
   When God made the hamper of
      creation,
   he filled it full of his love.

3. When God made the fam'ly of creation,
   he made it out of his love;
   when God made the fam'ly of creation,
   he saw that it was good.
   There's love for you, and love for me,
   and love for ev'ryone:
   but sometimes we're selfish, ignore
      our neighbours,
   and seek our own place in the sun.
   When God made the fam'ly of creation,
   he made it out of his love.

4. When God made us stewards of creation
   he made us his Vision to share;
   when God made us stewards of creation
   our burdens he wanted to bear.
   He cares for you,
   he cares for me,
   he cares for all in need;
   for God is a father who loves his children
   no matter what colour or creed.
   When God made us stewards of creation
   he made us his vision to share.

911
Susan Sayers (b. 1946)
© 1986 Kevin Mayhew Ltd.

1. When Jesus was my age he played with
      his friends,
   played with his friends, played with his
      friends;
   when Jesus was my age he played with
      his friends,
   and he's friends with each one of us now.

2. When Jesus was my age he laughed and
      he sang,
   laughed and he sang, laughed and he
      sang;
   when Jesus was my age he laughed and
      he sang,
   and he loves hearing us singing now.

3. When Jesus was my age he sometimes
      felt sad,
   sometimes felt sad, sometimes felt sad;
   when Jesus was my age he sometimes
      felt sad,
   and he shares in our sadnesses now.

4. When Jesus was my age he went to his
      school,
   went to his school, went to his school;
   when Jesus was my age he went to his
      school,
   and he goes ev'rywhere with us now.

912 Unknown

1. When the Spirit of the Lord
   is within my heart
   I will sing as David sang. *(Repeat)*
   I will sing, I will sing,
   I will sing as David sang. *(Repeat)*

2. When the Spirit of the Lord
   is within my heart
   I will clap as David clapped . . .

3. When the Spirit of the Lord
   is within my heart
   I will dance as David danced . . .

4. When the Spirit of the Lord
   is within my heart
   I will praise as David praised . . .

913 Alan J. Price
© 1994 Daybreak Music Ltd

When the time is right,
whether day or night,
the Lord Jesus Christ will come again
(he'll come again).
As we wait for that day,
in our work and our play,
we'll let our light shine bright
and live for the King who will reign.

914 Anne Conlon
© 1996 Josef Weinberger Ltd.

1. When your Father made the world,
   before that world was old,
   in his eye what he had made
   was lovely to behold.
   Help your people to care for your world.

   The world is a garden you made,
   and you are the one who planted the seed,
   the world is a garden you made,
   a life for our food, life for our joy,
   life we could kill with our selfish greed.

2. All the world that he had made,
   the seas, the rocks, the air,
   all the creatures and the plants
   he gave into our care.
   Help your people to care for your world.

3. When you walked in Galilee,
   you said your Father knows
   when each tiny sparrow dies,
   each fragile lily grows.
   Help your people to care for your world.

4. And the children of the earth,
   like sheep within your fold,
   should have food enough to eat,
   and shelter from the cold.
   Help your people to care for your world.

915 Paul Booth
© Paul Booth/CopyCare

1. Who put the colours in the rainbow?
   Who put the salt into the sea?
   Who put the cold into the snowflake?
   Who made you and me?
   Who put the hump upon the camel?
   Who put the neck on the giraffe?
   Who put the tail upon the monkey?
   Who made hyenas laugh?
   Who made whales and snails and quails?
   Who made hogs and dogs and frogs?
   Who made bats and cats and rats?
   Who made ev'rything?

2. Who put the gold into the sunshine?
   Who put the sparkle in the stars?
   Who put the silver in the moonlight?
   Who made Earth and Mars?
   Who put the scent into the roses?
   Who taught the honey-bee to dance?
   Who put the tree inside the acorn?
   It surely can't be chance!
   Who made seas and leaves and trees?
   Who made snow and winds that blow?
   Who made streams and rivers flow?
   God made all of these!

916
Unknown

Yesterday, today, forever,
Jesus is the same;
all may change, but Jesus never,
glory to his name!
Glory to his name! Glory to his name!
All may change, but Jesus never,
glory to his name!

917
Susan Sayers (b. 1946)
© 1986 Kevin Mayhew Ltd.

1. You can drink it, swim in it,
cook and wash up in it,
fish can breathe in it,
what can it be?

   It's water!
   God has provided us water!
   Water of life.

2. It's as hard as rock,
yet it flows down a mountain,
and clouds drop drips of it –
what can it be?

3. It's as light as snowflakes
and heavy as hailstones,
as small as dewdrops
and big as the sea.

918
Traditional

1. You've got to move
when the Spirit says move,
you've got to move
when the Spirit says move,
'cause when the Spirit says move,
you've got to move when the Spirit,
move when the Spirit says move.

2. You've got to sing
when the Spirit says sing . . .

3. You've got to clap
when the Spirit says clap . . .

4. You've got to shout
when the Spirit says shout . . .

5. You've got to move
when the Spirit says move . . .

919
Unknown

Zacchaeus was a very little man,
and a very little man was he.
He climbed up into a sycamore tree,
for the Saviour he wanted to see.
And when the Saviour passed that way,
he looked into the tree and said,
'Now Zacchaeus, you come down,
for I'm coming to your house for tea.'

920
Sue McClellan, John Paculabo and Keith Ryecroft
© 1972 Kingsway's Thankyou Music

Zip bam boo, zama lama la boo,
there's freedom in Jesus Christ. (Repeat)
Though we hung him on a cross
till he died in pain,
three days later he's alive again.
Zip bam boo, zama lama la boo,
there's freedom in Jesus Christ.

1. This Jesus was a working man
who shouted 'Yes' to life,
but didn't choose to settle down,
or take himself a wife.
To live for God he made his task,
'Who is this man?' the people ask.
Zip bam boo, zama lama la boo,
there's freedom in Jesus Christ.

2. He'd come to share good news from God
and show that he is Lord.
He made folk whole who trusted him
and took him at his word.
He fought oppression, loved the poor,
gave the people hope once more.
Zip bam boo, zama lama la boo,
there's freedom in Jesus Christ.

3. 'He's mad! He claims to be God's Son
and give new life to men!
Let's kill this Christ, once and for all,
no trouble from him then!'
'It's death then, Jesus, the cross for you!'
Said, 'Man, that's what I came to do!'
Zip bam boo, zama lama la boo,
there's freedom in Jesus Christ.

CHANTS

921
Taizé Community
© Ateliers et Presses de Taizé

Adoramus te, Domine

1. With the angels and archangels:
2. With the patriarchs and prophets:
3. With the Virgin Mary, mother of God:
4. With the apostles and evangelists:
5. With all the martyrs of Christ:
6. With all who witness to the Gospel of the Lord:
7. With all your people of the Church throughout the world.

922
Traditional
© 1997 Kevin Mayhew Ltd.

Adoramus te, Domine Deus.

Translation: We adore you, O Lord God.

923
Taizé Community, from Psalm 103
© Ateliers et Presses de Taizé

Bless the Lord, my soul,
and bless God's holy name.
Bless the Lord, my soul,
who leads me into life.

1. It is God who forgives all your guilt,
   who heals ev'ry one of your ills,
   who redeems your life from the grave,
   who crowns you with love and
   compassion.

2. The Lord is compassion and love,
   the Lord is patient and rich in mercy.
   God does not treat us according to our sins
   nor repay us according to our faults.

3. As a father has compassion on
   his children,
   the Lord has mercy on those who
   revere him;
   for God knows of what we are made,
   and remembers that we are dust.

924
David Adam. © SPCK, Holy Trinity Church

Calm me, Lord, as you calmed the storm;
still me, Lord, keep me from harm.
Let all the tumult within me cease;
enfold me, Lord, in your peace.

Last time:
Lord enfold me in your peace.

925
Psalm 118
© 1981 Ateliers et Presses de Taizé

Confitemini Domino quoniam bonus.
Confitemini Domino. Alleluia!

Translation: Give thanks to the Lord for he
is good

926
Taizé Community, based on Scripture
© Ateliers et Presses de Taizé

Eat this bread, drink this cup,
come to him and never be hungry.
Eat this bread, drink this cup,
trust in him and you will not thirst.

1. Christ is the Bread of Life,
   the true bread sent from the Father.

2. Your ancestors ate manna in the desert,
   but this is the bread come down
   from heaven.

3. Eat his flesh, and drink his blood,
   and Christ will raise you up on the last day.

4. Anyone who eats this bread
   will live for ever.

5. If we believe and eat this bread
   we will have eternal life.

927

Traditional
© 1998 Kevin Mayhew Ltd.

Exaudi nos, Domine;
donna nobis pacem tuam.

*Translation: Hear us, O Lord, give us
your peace.*

928

Kevin Mayhew (b. 1942)
based on the Aaronic Blessing, Numbers 6: 24-26
© 1996 Kevin Mayhew Ltd.

Holy God,
we place ourselves into your hands.
Bless us and care for us,
be gracious and loving to us;
look kindly upon us, and give us peace.

929

Taizé Community
© Ateliers et Presses de Taizé

In the Lord I'll be ever thankful,
in the Lord, I will rejoice!
Look to God, do not be afraid;
lift up your voices: the Lord is near,
lift up your voices: the Lord is near.

930

Margaret Rizza (b. 1929)
© 1998 Kevin Mayhew Ltd.

In the Lord is my joy and salvation,
he gives light to all his creation.
In the Lord is my joy and salvation,
he gives peace and true consolation.
In the Lord is my salvation.
In the Lord is my salvation.

931

Taizé Community, based on Scripture
© Ateliers et Presses de Taizé

Jesus, remember me
when you come into your kingdom.

932

John L. Bell (b. 1949) and Graham Maule (b. 1958)
© WGRG, Iona Community

Kindle a flame to lighten the dark
and take all fear away.

933

Taizé Community, based on Scripture
© Ateliers et Presses de Taizé

*Laudate Dominum,
laudate Dominum,
omnes gentes, alleluia.* (Repeat)

or

*Sing praise and bless the Lord,
sing praise and bless the Lord,
peoples, nations, alleluia.* (Repeat)

1. Praise the Lord, all you nations,
   praise God all you peoples.
   Alleluia.
   Strong is God's love and mercy,
   always faithful for ever. Alleluia

2. Alleluia, alleluia.
   Let ev'rything living give praise to
      the Lord.
   Alleluia, alleluia.
   Let ev'rything living give praise to
      the Lord.

934

Colin Mawby (b. 1936)
© 1991 Kevin Mayhew Ltd.

Lord of creation,
may your will be done.
*Lord of creation,
may your will be done.*

935

Based on Luke 1:46
© 1997 Kevin Mayhew Ltd.

Magnificat, magnificat
anima mea Dominum. *(Repeat)*

*Translation: My soul praises and magnifies
the Lord*

936

Gaelic Blessing, adapted by Margaret Rizza (b. 1929)
© 1998 Kevin Mayhew Ltd.

May the Lord bless you,
may the Lord protect you and guide you,
may his strength uphold you,
his light shine upon you,
his peace surround you,
his love enfold you.

Continued overleaf

Last time:
May the Lord bless you,
the Lord bless you,
the Lord bless you.

937 St. Teresa of Avila
© *Ateliers et Presses de Taizé*

Nada te turbe,
nada te espante.
Quien a Dios tiene nada le falta.
Nada te turbe,
nada te espante.
Solo Dios basta.

or

Nothing can trouble,
nothing can frighten.
Those who seek God shall never go wanting.
Nothing can trouble,
nothing can frighten.
God alone fills us.

938 Taizé Community
© *Ateliers et Presses de Taizé*

O Lord, hear my prayer.
O Lord, hear my prayer:
when I call answer me.
O Lord, hear my prayer.
O Lord, hear my prayer.
Come and listen to me.

939 From Psalm 131
© *The Grail (England) from 'The Psalms. The Grail Translations'*

O Lord, my heart is not proud,
nor haughty my eyes.
I have not gone after things too great,
nor marvels beyond me.
Truly I have set my soul in silence and peace;
at rest, as a child in its mother's arms,
so is my soul.

940 Traditional
© *1998 Kevin Mayhew Ltd.*

Sanctum nomen Domini
magnificat anima mea. *(Repeat)*

Last time:
Sanctum, sanctum nomen Domini.

Translation: My soul magnifies the holy name of the Lord

941 v 1 Pamela Hayes; v 2 Margaret Rizza (b. 1929)
© *1998 Kevin Mayhew Ltd.*

Silent, surrendered, calm and still,
open to the word of God.
Heart humbled to his will,
offered is the servant of God.

*Come, Holy Spirit, bring us light,
teach us, heal us, give us life.
Come, Lord, O let our hearts
flow with love and all that is true.

* *for use at Pentecost*

942 Based on Matthew 26:36–42
© *Ateliers et Presses de Taizé*

*Stay with me, remain here with me,
watch and pray, watch and pray.*

1. Stay here and keep watch with me.
   Watch and pray, watch and pray!

2. Watch and pray not to give way to
   temptation.

3. The Spirit is eager, but the flesh is weak.

4. My heart is nearly broken with sorrow.
   Remain here with me, stay awake
   and pray.

5. Father, if it is possible let this cup pass
   me by.

6. Father, if this cannot pass me by without
   my drinking it, your will be done.

943

From Daniel 3
© Ateliers et Presses de Taizé

Surrexit Christus, alleluia!
Cantate Domino, alleluia!

Translation: Christ is risen. Sing to the Lord.

1. All you heavens, bless the Lord.
   Stars of the heavens, bless the Lord.

2. Sun and moon, bless the Lord.
   And you, night and day, bless the Lord.

3. Frost and cold, bless the Lord.
   Ice and snow, bless the Lord.

4. Fire and heat, bless the Lord.
   And you, light and darkness,
       bless the Lord.

5. Spirits and souls of the just,
       bless the Lord.
   Saints and the humble hearted,
       bless the Lord.

944

Based on Psalm 27
© Ateliers et Presses de Taizé

The Lord is my light,
my light and salvation:
in God I trust,
in God I trust.

945

From Psalm 27
© 1998 Kevin Mayhew Ltd.

The Lord is my light, in him I trust. *(x2)*
The Lord is my light, in him I trust,
in him I trust.

946

Taizé Community
© Ateliers et Presses de Taizé

Ubi caritas et amor.
Ubi caritas Deus ibi est.

Translation: Where there is charity and
love, there is God.

1. Your love, O Jesus Christ,
   has gathered us together.

2. May your love, O Jesus Christ,
   be foremost in our lives.

3. Let us love one another
   as God has loved us.

4. Let us be one in love together
   in the one bread of Christ.

5. The love of God in Jesus Christ
   bears eternal joy.

6. The love of God in Jesus Christ
   will never have an end.

947

Stephen Langton (1160-1228)
© 1998 Kevin Mayhew Ltd.

Veni, lumen cordium.
Veni, Sancte Spiritus.

Translation: Come, light of our hearts.
Come, holy Spirit, come

948

Veni, veni,
veni, Sancte Spiritus.

Translation: Come, Holy Spirit

949

Taizé Community, based on Scripture
© Ateliers et Presses de Taizé

Wait for the Lord, whose day is near.
Wait for the Lord: keep watch take heart!

1. Prepare the way for the Lord.
   Make a straight path for God.
   Prepare the way for the Lord.

2. Rejoice in the Lord always: God is at hand.
   Joy and gladness for all who seek the Lord.

3. The glory of the Lord shall be revealed.
   All the earth will see the Lord.

4. I waited for the Lord. God heard my cry.

5. Our eyes are fixed on the Lord our God.

Continued overleaf

Wait for the Lord, whose day is near.
Wait for the Lord: keep watch take heart!

6. Seek first the kingdom of God.
   Seek and you shall find.

7. O Lord show us your way.
   Guide us in your truth.

950 Taizé Community
© *Ateliers et Presses de Taizé*

Within our darkest night,
you kindle the fire that never dies away,
that never dies away. *(Repeat)*

951 Margaret Rizza (b. 1926)
© *1998 Kevin Mayhew Ltd.*

You are the centre, you are my life,
you are the centre, O Lord, of my life.
Come, Lord, and heal me, Lord of my life,
come, Lord, and teach me, Lord of my life.
You are the centre, Lord, of my life.
Give me your Spirit and teach me your ways,
give me your peace, Lord, and set me free. *
You are the centre, Lord, of my life.

* *Second time:*
You are the centre, you are my life,
you are the centre, O Lord, of my life.

MUSIC FOR THE EUCHARIST

952 A New People's Mass
© McCrimmon Publishing Co. Ltd.

Gregory Murray (1905-1992)

Kyrie

Lord, have mer - cy. Lord, have mer - cy. Christ, have mer - cy.

Christ, have mer - cy. Lord, have mer - cy. Lord, have mer - cy.

Gloria

Glo - ry to God in the high - est, and peace to his peo-ple on earth. Lord God,

hea - ven-ly King, al - migh - ty God and Fa - ther, we wor - ship you, we

give you thanks, we praise you for your glo - ry. Lord Je - sus Christ, on - ly

Son of the Fa - ther, Lord God, Lamb of God, you take a - way the sins of the

world, have mer - cy on us; you are seat-ed at the right hand of the Fa -

ther, re - ceive our prayer. For you a - lone are the Ho - ly One,

you a - lone are the Lord, you a - lone are the Most High, Je - sus Christ,

with the Ho - ly Spi - rit, in the glo - ry of God the Fa - ther. A - men.

Sanctus

Ho - ly, ho - ly, ho - ly Lord. God of pow - er and might, hea-ven and earth are full of your

glo - ry. Ho - san - na in the high - est. Bles - sed is he who comes in the

name of the Lord. Ho - san - na in the high - est.

Memorial Acclamation

Christ has died, Christ is ri-sen, Christ will come a-gain.

Great Amen

A - men.

Agnus Dei

Lamb of God, you take a-way the sins of the world:

1st & 2nd times

have mer-cy on us.

3rd time

grant us peace.

953 A Simple Mass
© 1999 Kevin Mayhew Ltd.

Kyrie

Andrew Moore (b. 1954)

Lord, have mer-cy. Lord, have mer-cy. Christ, have mer-cy.

Christ, have mer-cy. Lord, have mer-cy. Lord, have mer-cy.

Gloria

Glo-ry to God in the high-est, and peace to his peo-ple on earth.

Lord God, heav'n-ly King, al-migh-ty God and Fa-ther, we wor-ship you, we give you

thanks, we praise you for your glo-ry, we praise you for your glo-ry.

Lord Je-sus Christ, on-ly Son of the Fa-ther, Lord God, Lamb of God, you take a-way the

sins of the world: have mer-cy on us; you are seat-ed at the right hand of the

Fa-ther: re-ceive our prayer. For you a-lone are the Ho-ly One, you a-lone are the

Lord, you a - lone are the Most High, Je - sus Christ, with the Ho - ly
Spi - rit, in the glo - ry of God the Fa - ther. A - men. A - men.

Sanctus

Ho - ly, ho - ly, ho - ly Lord, God of pow - er and God of might,
hea - ven and earth are full of your glo - ry. Ho - san - na in the
high - est. Ho - san - na in the high - est. Bless - ed is he who
comes in the name of the Lord. Bless - ed is he who comes in the name of the
Lord. Ho - san - na in the high - est, ho - san - na in the high - est.

Memorial acclamation

Dy - ing, you de - stroyed our death, ris - ing, you re -
stored our life. Lord Je - sus, come in glo - ry.

Agnus Dei

Lamb of God, you take a - way the sins of the world: have
mer - cy on us. Lamb of God, you take a - way the
sins of the world: have mer - cy on us. Lamb of God, you
take a - way the sins of the world: grant us peace.

954 Mass of the Spirit

Kyrie

Kevin Mayhew (b. 1942)

Lord, have mer - cy. Lord, have mer - cy. Lord, have mer - cy.

Christ, have mer - cy. Christ, have mer - cy. Christ, have mer - cy.

Lord, have mer - cy. Lord, have mer - cy. Lord, have mer - cy.

Gloria

Glo - ry to God in the high - est, and peace to his peo - ple on earth.

Lord God, hea - ven - ly King, al - migh - ty God and Fa - ther, we wor - ship you, we

give you thanks, we praise you for your glo - ry. Lord Je - sus Christ, on - ly Son of the

Fa - ther, Lord God, Lamb of God, you take a - way the sin of the world: have

mer - cy on us; you are seat - ed at the right hand of the Fa - ther: re - ceive our

prayer. For you a - lone are the Ho - ly One, you a - lone are the

Lord, you a - lone are the Most High, Je - sus Christ, with the Ho - ly Spi - rit,

in the glo - ry of God the Fa - ther. A - men, a - men.

Sanctus

Ho - ly, ho - ly, ho - ly Lord, God of pow - er and might,

heav - en and earth are full of your glo - ry. Ho - san - na in the high - est.

Bless - ed is he who comes in the name of the Lord. Ho - san - na in the high - est.

Agnus Dei

Lamb of God, you take a - way the sins of the world: have mer - cy on us.

Lamb of God, you take a - way the sins of the world: have mer - cy on us.

Lamb of God, you take a - way the sins of the world: grant us peace.

955 Mass of the Bread of Life

Kyrie

Margaret Rizza (b.1929)

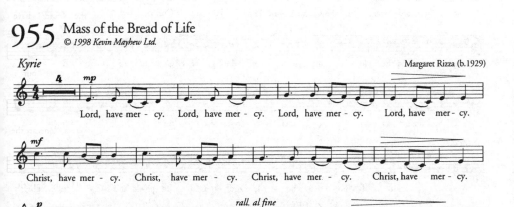

Lord, have mer - cy. Lord, have mer - cy. Lord, have mer - cy. Lord, have mer - cy.

Christ, have mer - cy. Christ, have mer - cy. Christ, have mer - cy. Christ, have mer - cy.

Lord, have mer - cy. Lord, have mer - cy. Lord, have mer - cy. Lord, have mer - cy.

Gloria

Glo - ry, glo - ry to God, glo - ry to God in the high - est; peace to his peo - ple on earth, peace to his peo - ple on earth. Lord God, hea - ven - ly King, al - migh - ty God and Fa - ther, we wor - ship you, we give you thanks, we praise you for your glo - ry. Glo - ry, glo - ry to God, glo - ry to God in the high - est; peace to his peo - ple on earth, peace to his peo - ple on earth. Lord Je - sus Christ, on - ly Son of the Fa - ther, Lord God, Lamb of God, you take a - way the sin of the world: have mer - cy on us; you are seat - ed at the right hand of the Fa - ther: re - ceive our prayer, re - ceive our prayer, re - ceive our prayer. You a - lone are the Ho - ly One, you a - lone are the Lord, you a - lone are the Lord, you a - lone are the Most High, Je - sus Christ, with the Ho - ly Spi - rit, in the glo - ry, the glo - ry, the glo - ry of God the Fa - ther. A - men, a - men, a - men, a - men, a - men, a - men.

Sanctus

Ho - ly, ho - ly, ho - ly Lord, God of pow'r and God of might, hea - ven and earth are full of your glo - ry. Ho - san - na in the high - est; ho - san - na, ho -

san - na, ho - san - na in the high - est; ho - san - na, ho - san - na, ho -

san - na in the high - est. Bless - ed is he, bless - ed is he,

bless - ed is he who comes in the name, he who comes in the name of the Lord. Ho -

san - na in the high - est, ho - san - na, ho - san - na, ho - san - na in the

high - est, ho - san - na, ho - san - na, ho - san - na in the high - est.

Memorial Acclamation

Let us pro- claim the mys- t'ry of faith: Christ has died, Christ is ris - en,

Christ will come a - gain. Christ has died, Christ is ris - en,

Christ will come a - gain. Ho - san - na, ho - san - na, ho - san - na in the

high - est, ho - san - na, ho - san - na, ho - san - na in the high - est.

Great Amen

Through him, with him, in him, in the u - ni- ty of the Ho - ly Spi- rit, all

glo- ry and hon- our is yours, al- migh - ty Fa - ther for e - ver and e - ver. A - men,

a - men, a - men, a - men, a - men, a - men

Agnus Dei

Je - sus, Lamb of God, Je - sus, Lamb of God, you take a - way the sins of the world: have

mer - cy on us. Je - sus, Lamb of God, Je - sus, Lamb of God, you take a - way the

sins of the world: have mer - cy on us. Je - sus, Lamb of God, Je - sus, Lamb of God, you

take a - way the sins of the world: grant us your peace, grant us your peace.

956 The Holy Trinity Service

Christopher Tambling (b.1964)

Kyrie

Lord, have mer - cy. Lord, have mer - cy. Christ, have mer - cy.

Christ, have mer - cy. Lord, have mer - cy. Lord, have mer - cy.

Gloria

Glo - ry to God in the high - est, and peace to his peo-ple on earth.

Lord God, heav n-ly King, al - migh - ty God and Fa - ther, we wor-ship you, we give you thanks, we

praise you for your glo - ry. Lord Je - sus Christ, on-ly Son of the Fa - ther, Lord God, Lamb of

God, you take a-way the sin of the world; have mer - cy on us: you are

seat - ed at the right hand of God the Fa - ther: re - ceive our prayer.

For you a - lone are the Ho - ly One, you a - lone are the Lord;

cresc. *f*

you a - lone are the Most High, Je - sus Christ, with the Ho - ly Spi - rit, in the glo - ry of God the

allarg. *ff* *rit.*

Fa - ther. A - men, a - men. A - men, a - men.

Sanctus

accel. a tempo *cresc.*

Steadily

Ho - ly, ho - ly, ho - ly Lord. God of pow r and might, heav n and earth are

molto allarg. *f* *a tempo* *mf*

full of your glo - ry. Ho-san-na in the high est. Bles-sed is he who comes in the name of the

f

Lord. Ho - san - na in the high - est, ho - san - na in the high - est!

Acclamation

mf cresc. *f* *rit.*

Christ has died. Christ is ris - en. Christ will come a - gain.

Agnus Dei (I)

Flowing but slowly (♩ = 60) *cresc.*

Je - sus, Lamb of God: have mer - cy on us. Je - sus, bear - er of our

mf *mp* *rit.* *p*

sins: have mer - cy on us. Je - sus, Re deem - er of the world: give us your peace.

Flowing but slowly (♩ = 60)

mp

Lamb of God, you take a-way the sins of the world: have mer-cy on us. Lamb of God, you

mf

take a-way the sins of the world: have mer-cy on us.

mp   *rit.*   *p*

Lamb of God, you take a-way the sins of the world: grant us peace.

957 Missa Simplex
© *2000 Kevin Mayhew Ltd.*

Malcolm Archer (b.1952)

Kyrie

With a lilting movement (♩ = 72)

Lord, have mer - cy. Lord, have mer - cy.

Christ, have mer - cy. Christ, have mer - cy.

Lord, have mer - cy. Lord, have mer - cy.

Gloria

Glo - ry to God in the high - est, and peace to his peo - ple on earth.

Lord God, heav'n-ly King, al - migh - ty God and Fa - ther, we wor - ship you, we

give you thanks, we praise you for your glo - ry. Lord Je - sus Christ, on - ly Son of the Fa - ther,

Lord God, Lamb of God, you take a-way the sins of the world: have mer-cy on us; you are seat-ed at the right hand of the Fa-ther; re-ceive our prayer. For you a-lone are the Ho-ly One, you a-lone are the Lord, you a-lone are the Most High, Je-sus Christ, with the Ho-ly Spi-rit, in the glo-ry of God the Fa-ther. A - men.

rall.

Sanctus

Con moto (♩ = 88)

mf

Ho - ly, ho - ly, ho - ly Lord, God of pow'r and might,

cresc. *f*

hea - ven and earth are full of your glo-ry. Ho - san - na in the high - est.

mf *cresc.*

Bles-sed is he who comes in the name of the Lord. Ho -

f

san - na in the high - est, ho - san - na in the high - est.

Memorial Acclamation

With vigour (♩ = 116)

f *ff*

Christ has died. Christ is ri - sen. Christ will come a - gain.

Agnus Dei

(♩ = 66)

Lamb of God, you take a-way the sins of the world: have mer - cy, have mer - cy on us.

Lamb of God, you take a-way the sins of the world: grant us, grant us peace.

958 Kyrie 1.
© *Ateliers et Presses de Taizé*

Jacques Berthier (1923-1994)

Ky - ri - e, Ky - ri - e, e - le - i - son. *(hum under the invocations)*

959 Kyrie
© *1991 Kevin Mayhew Ltd.*

Colin Mawby (b. 1936)

Ky - ri - e, Chri - ste,

Ky - ri - e, e - le - i - son.

Or

Lord, have mer - cy. Christ, have mer - cy.

Lord have mer - cy, have mer - cy.

960 Gloria 3
© *Ateliers et Presses de Taizé*

This setting may be sung as a canon with entries as indicated.

Jacques Berthier (1923-1994)

1 2

Glo - ri - a, glo - ri - a in ex - cel - sis De - o!

3 4

Glo - ri - a, glo - ri - a, al - le - lu - ia, al - le - lu - ia!

961 Halle, halle, halle (Traditional)

Hal- le, hal- le, hal - le - lu - - le - lu - jah! Hal- le -

jah! Hal- le, hal- le, hal - le - - lu-jah, hal - le - lu - jah!

lu - jah! Hal- le, hal - le, hal-

962 Lord, have mercy

Friedrich Filitz (1804-1876)

1. Lord, have mer - cy on us, hear our hum-ble plea; Lord, have mer - cy on us, set our spi-rits free.

2. Christ, have mercy on us,
   hear us as we pray;
   Christ, have mercy on us,
   take our sin away.

3. Lord, have mercy on us,
   hear our humble plea;
   Lord, have mercy on us,
   set our spirits free.

Text: Michael Forster (b. 1946)

963 Coventry Gloria

Peter Jones

Glory to God, glory in the highest, peace to his people, peace on earth.

Glo - ry to God, glo - ry in the high - est, peace to his peo - ple, peace on earth.

Lord God, heavenly King, almighty God and Father.

Glo - ry to God, glo - ry in the high - est, peace to his peo - ple, peace on earth.

We worship you, 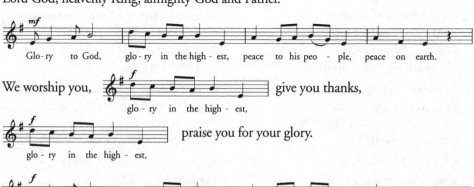 give you thanks,

glo - ry in the high - est,

praise you for your glory.

glo - ry in the high - est,

Glo - ry to God, glo - ry in the high - est, peace to his peo - ple, peace on earth.

Lord Jesus Christ, only Son of the Father, Lord God, Lamb of God, you take away the sin

of the world: have mercy on us,  you are seated at the

have mer - cy on us;

right hand of the Father: receive our prayer,

re - ceive our prayer.

Glory to God, glory in the highest, peace to his people, peace on earth.

Glo - ry   to God,   glo - ry in the high - est,   peace   to his peo - ple,   peace on earth.

For you alone are the Holy One, you alone are the Lord, you alone are the Most High,
Jesus Christ, with the Holy Spirit, in the glory of God, the glory of God the Father.

Glo - ry   to God,   glo - ry in the high - est,   peace   to his peo - ple,   peace on earth.

964
Mike Anderson (b. 1956)
© 1999 Kevin Mayhew Ltd.

Gloria, gloria, in excelsis Deo.
Gloria, gloria, in excelsis Deo.

1. Lord God, heavenly King,
   peace you bring to us;
   we worship you, we give you thanks,
   we sing our song of praise.

2. Jesus, Saviour of all,
   Lord God, Lamb of God,
   you take away our sins,
   O Lord, have mercy on us all.

3. At the Father's right hand,
   Lord receive our prayer,
   for you alone are the Holy One,
   and you alone are Lord.

4. Glory, Father and Son,
   glory, Holy Spirit,
   to you we raise our hands up high,
   we glorify your name.

965
Francesca Leftley (b. 1955)
© 1978 Kevin Mayhew Ltd.

1. Sing to God a song of glory,
   peace he brings to all on earth.
   Worship we the King of heaven;
   praise and bless his holy name.

Glory, glory, sing his glory.
Glory to our God on high.

2. Sing to Christ, the Father's loved one,
   Jesus, Lord and Lamb of God:
   hear our prayer, O Lord, have mercy,
   you who bear the sins of all.

3. Sing to Christ, the Lord and Saviour,
   seated there at God's right hand:
   hear our prayer, O Lord, have mercy,
   you alone the Holy One.

4. Glory sing to God the Father,
   glory to his only Son,
   glory to the Holy Spirit,
   glory to the Three in One.

966
Traditional Peruvian

1. Glory to God, glory to God,
   glory to the Father.
   Glory to God, glory to God,
   glory to the Father.
   To him be glory for ever.
   To him be glory for ever.
   Alleluia, amen,
   alleluia, amen,
   alleluia, amen,
   alleluia, amen.

2. Glory to God, glory to God,
   Son of the Father.
   Glory to God, glory to God,
   glory to the Father.
   To him be glory for ever.
   To him be glory for ever.
   Alleluia, amen.
   Alleluia, amen,
   alleluia, amen,
   alleluia, amen.

3. Glory to God, glory to God,
   glory to the Spirit.
   Glory to God, glory to god,
   glory to the Spirit.
   To him be glory for ever.
   To him be glory for ever.
   Alleluia, amen.
   Alleluia, amen,
   alleluia, amen,
   alleluia, amen.

967
Michael Forster (b. 1946)

1. Glory to God, to God in the height,
   bringing peace to ev'ry nation.
   Lord God almighty, Father and King,
   and the author of salvation.
   'Glory!' let the people sing,
   let the whole creation ring,
   telling out redemption's story,
   as we worship your name
   with thankful songs of praise
   for the love that is your glory.

2. Jesus, the Father's one holy Son,
   all creation bows before you.
   You are the God, the God we acclaim,
   and we worship and adore you.
   Lamb of God, to you we pray,
   you who take our sin away,
   mercy, grace and truth revealing.
   At the right hand of God,
   receive our humble prayer
   for forgiveness, hope and healing.

3. You, Jesus Christ, alone are the Lord,
   by your own eternal merit;
   sharing by right the glory of God
   in the presence of the Spirit.
   You alone are Lord Most High,
   you alone we glorify,
   reigning over all creation.
   To the Father, the Son
   and Spirit, Three in One,
   be eternal acclamation!

968
Michael Forster (b. 1946)

1. Sing glory to God
   in the height of the heavens,
   salvation and peace
   to his people on earth;
   our King and our Saviour,
   our God and our Father,
   we worship and praise you
   and sing of your worth.

   Creation unites in the power of the Spirit,
   in praise of the Father,
   through Jesus, the Son.
   So complex, so simple,
   so clear, so mysterious,
   our God ever Three yet eternally One.

Continued overleaf

2. Our Lord Jesus Christ,
   only Son of the Father,
   Lord God, Lamb of God,
   by the nations adored,
   your blood takes away
   all the sin of creation:
   have mercy upon us,
   for whom it was poured.
   For you are our Saviour,
   our only Redeemer,
   who came all our gladness
   and sorrows to share:
   you sit at the side,
   the right hand of the Father,
   have mercy upon us,
   and answer our prayer.

   Creation unites in the power of the Spirit,
   in praise of the Father,
   through Jesus, the Son.

So complex, so simple,
so clear, so mysterious,
our God ever Three yet eternally One.

3. For you, only you,
   we acknowledge as holy,
   we name you alone as our Saviour
   and Lord;
   you only, O Christ,
   with the Spirit exalted,
   are one with the Father,
   for ever adored.
   Creation unites in the power
   of the Spirit,
   in praise of the Father,
   through Jesus the son.
   So complex, so simple,
   so clear, so mysterious,
   our God ever Three
   yet eternally One.

969 Holy, holy, holy (Deutsche Messe)
© 1984 GIA Publications Inc.

Franz Schubert (1797-1828)
adapted by Richard Proulx

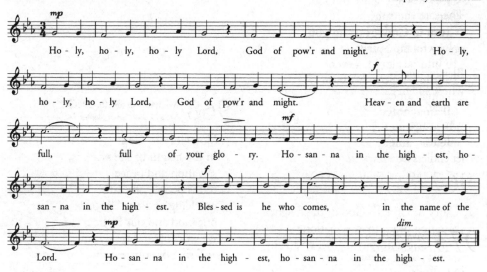

Ho - ly, ho - ly, ho - ly Lord, God of pow'r and might. Ho - ly,
ho - ly, ho - ly Lord, God of pow'r and might. Heav - en and earth are
full, full of your glo - ry. Ho - san - na in the high - est, ho -
san - na in the high - est. Bles - sed is he who comes, in the name of the
Lord. Ho - san - na in the high - est, ho - san - na in the high - est.

970 Sanctus (Taizé)
© Ateliers et Presses de Taizé

Jacques Berthier (1923-1994)

San - ctus, san - ctus, san - ctus Do - mi - nus De - us Sa - ba - oth, De - us Sa - ba - oth.

971 John Ballantine (b. 1945)

1. Holy, holy, holy is the Lord,
   holy is the Lord God almighty!
   Holy, holy, holy is the Lord,
   holy is the Lord God almighty!
   Who was and is, and is to come;
   holy, holy, holy is the Lord.

2. Blessèd, blessèd, blest is he who comes,
   blest is he who comes in the Lord's name.
   Blessèd, blessèd, blest is he who comes,
   blest is he who comes in the Lord's name.
   Hosanna in the heights of heav'n.
   Blessèd, blessèd, blessèd is the Lord.

Hosanna, hosanna
and praise in the height!
How blessèd is he
who is sent to redeem us,
who puts ev'ry fear
and injustice to flight;
who comes in the name
of the Lord as our Saviour.
Hosanna, hosanna
and praise in the height!

972 Michael Forster (b. 1946)

1. Holy, most holy, all holy the Lord,
   in power and wisdom for ever adored.
   The earth and the heavens are full of
        your love;
   our joyful hosannas re-echo above.

2. Blessèd, most blessèd, all blessèd is he
   whose life makes us whole, and whose
        death sets us free:
   who comes in the name of the Father of
        light,
   let endless hosannas resound in the height.

973 Michael Forster (b. 1946)

O holy, most holy,
the God of creation,
for ever exalted
in pow'r and great might.
The earth and the heavens
are full of your glory.

974 Christ has died

Philip Duffy

Christ has died, Christ is ri-sen,

Christ will come a - gain.

975 Christ has died

David Hill

Christ has died, Christ is ri - sen,

Christ will come a - gain.

Christ has died, Christ is ri - sen,

Christ will come a - gain.

976 Lamb of God
© 1986 Kevin Mayhew Ltd.

Gerry Fitzpatrick (b. 1940)

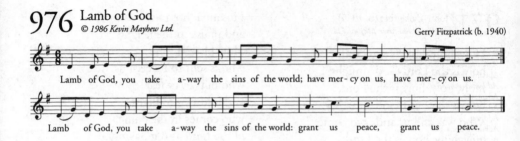

Lamb of God, you take a-way the sins of the world; have mer-cy on us, have mer-cy on us.

Lamb of God, you take a-way the sins of the world: grant us peace, grant us peace.

977 Lamb of God
© 1992 Kevin Mayhew Ltd.

Alan Rees (b. 1941)

Lamb of God, you take a-way the sins of the world: have mer - cy on us.

Lamb of God, you take a-way the sins of the world: grant us peace.

978 Michael Forster (b. 1946)
based on the 'Agnus Dei'
© 1999 Kevin Mayhew Ltd.

1. O Lamb of God, come cleanse our hearts
   and take our sin away.
   O Lamb of God, your grace impart,
   and let our guilty fear depart,
   have mercy, Lord, we pray,
   have mercy, Lord, we pray.

2. O Lamb of God, our lives restore,
   our guilty souls release.
   Into our lives your Spirit pour
   and let us live for evermore
   in perfect heav'nly peace,
   in perfect heav'nly peace.

Index of Authors and Sources of Text

Scriptural Index

JEREMIAH

LAMENTATIONS

EZEKIEL

DANIEL

HOSEA

JOEL

ROMANS

1 CORINTHIANS

2 CORINTHIANS

Index of Uses

Joy, Praise and Thanksgiving
Children's Hymns and Songs

Joy, Praise and Thanksgiving
Chants

TIMES AND SEASONS

Hymns generally applicable to the main seasons are included here. For suggestions more specifically related to the Lectionary, see the Common Worship Lectionary Index.

Morning

Morning
Children's Hymns and Songs

Evening

Evening
Children's Hymns and Songs

Evening
Chants

Advent

THE ORDER FOR HOLY COMMUNION

(See also the Music for the Eucharist section nos 952 - 978)

Opening Hymn

Index of Hymns for the Common Worship Lectionary

Index of First Lines

This index is in four parts

1. General Hymns and Songs
2. Children's Hymns and Songs
3. Chants
4. Music for the Eucharist

This index gives the first line of each hymn. If a hymn is known also by a title (e.g. Jerusalem) this is given as well, but indented and in italics.

GENERAL HYMNS AND SONGS

A

Abba, Father, let me be	1
Abide with me	2
A brighter dawn is breaking	3
Advent acclamations	722
A great and mighty wonder	4
A healing song	403
Ah, holy Jesu, how hast thou offended	5
All creatures of our God and King	6
Alleluia (x8)	7
Alleluia, alleluia, give thanks to the risen Lord	8
Alleluia, alleluia, hearts to heaven and voices raise	9
Alleluia: All the earth	10
Alleluia: Praise God	11
Alleluia, sing to Jesus	12
All for Jesus!	13
All glory, laud and honour	14
All hail and welcome, holy child	15
All hail the power of Jesus' name	16
All heaven declares	17
All I once held dear	18
All my hope on God is founded	19
All over the world	20
All people that on earth do dwell	21
All praise to thee, for thou, O King divine	22
All that I am	23
All the ends of the earth	24
All things bright and beautiful	25
All you who seek a comfort sure	26
Almighty God, we come to make confession	27
A man there lived in Galilee	28
Amazing grace	29
Amazing love	462
Among us and before us	30
An army of ordinary people	31
And can it be	32
And did those feet in ancient time	33
And now, O Father, mindful of the love	34
A new commandment	35
Angels from the realms of glory	36
Angel-voices ever singing	37
An upper room did our Lord prepare	38
A purple robe	39
Arise to greet the Lord of light	40
Around the throne of God	41

Ascribe greatness	42
As gentle as silence	539
As now the sun's declining rays	43
As pants the hart for cooling streams	44
As the deer pants for the water	45
A still small voice	46
As we are gathered	47
As we break the bread	48
As with gladness men of old	49
At even, ere the sun was set	50
A touching place	101
At the cross her station keeping	51
At the dawning of creation	52
At the Lamb's high feast we sing	53
At the name of Jesus	54
At this time of giving	55
Author of life divine	56
Awake, awake: fling off the night	57
Awake, my soul, and with the sun	58
Awake, our souls	59
Away in a manger	776

B

Beautiful world	681
Beauty for brokenness	60
Before the ending of the day	61
Behold, the great Creator	62
Behold, the Saviour of the nations	63
Be humble of heart	129
Beloved, let us love	64
Beneath the cross of Jesus	65
Be still and know that I am God	66
Be still, for the presence of the Lord	67
Be still, my soul	68
Be thou my guardian and my guide	69
Be thou my vision	70
Beyond all mortal praise	71
Bind us together, Lord	72
Bless and keep us, God	73
Blessed assurance	74
Blessed be God	75
Bless the Lord, my soul	76
Blest are the pure in heart	77
Blest are you, Lord of creation	78
Blest Creator of the light	79
Born in the night, Mary's child	80
Bread is blessed	81
Bread of heaven, on thee we feed	82
Bread of the world in mercy broken	83
Break the bread	699
Breathe on me, Breath of God	84
Bridegroom and Bride	213
Brightest and best	85
Bright the vision that delighted	86
Broken for me, broken for you	87
Brother, sister, let me serve you	88
By his grace	89
By your side	90

C

Captains of the saintly band	91
Celebrate	125
Change my heart, O God	92

Child in the manger	93
Christians, awake!	94
Christians, lift up your hearts	95
Christ is alive!	96
Christ is made the sure foundation	97
Christ is our cornerstone	98
Christ is the world's light	99
Christ is the world's true light	100
Christ's is the world	101
Christ, the fair glory of the holy angels	102
Christ the Lord is risen again	103
Christ triumphant	104
Christ, whose glory fills the skies	105
City of God, how broad and far	106
Close to you	334
Cloth for the cradle	107
Colours of day	108
Come and see	109
Come and see the shining hope	110
Come, build the Church	111
Come, come, come to the manger	112
Come, dearest Lord	113
Come down, O Love divine	114
Come, faithful pilgrims all	115
Come, gracious Spirit	116
Come, Holy Ghost, our hearts inspire	117
Come, Holy Ghost, our souls inspire	118
Come, Holy Spirit, come	119
Come, let us join our cheerful songs	120
Come, let us sing	121
Come, Lord, to our souls	122
Come, my Way, my Truth, my Life	123
Come, O Lord, inspire us	124
Come on and celebrate	125
Come, risen Lord	126
Come, thou Holy Spirit, come	127
Come, thou long-expected Jesus	128
Come to me, come, my people	129
Come, wounded healer	130
Come, ye faithful, raise the anthem	131
Come, ye faithful, raise the strain	132
Come, ye thankful people, come	133
Creating God, we bring our song of praise	134
Creator of the starry height	135
Cross of Jesus	136
Crown him with many crowns	137
Cry 'Freedom!'	138

D

Dance and sing	139
Dance in your Spirit	140
Day of wrath and day of wonder	141
Dear Christ, uplifted from the earth	142
Dearest Jesu, we are here	143
Dear Lord and Father of mankind	144
Dear Lord, to you again	145
Deck thyself, my soul, with gladness	146
Deep within my heart	147
Ding dong, merrily on high	148
Disposer supreme	149
Do not be afraid	150
Doxology	560
Drop, drop, slow tears	151

ACKNOWLEDGEMENTS

The publishers wish to express their gratitude to the following for permission to include copyright material in this publication. Details of copyright owners are given above each individual hymn.

Ascent Music, PO Box 263, Croydon, CR9 5AP, UK. International copyright secured. All rights reserved.

The Executors of L.T.J. Arlott, 11 Victoria Street, Alderney, Channel Islands, GY9 3AN.

Ateliers et Presses de Taizé, F-71250, Taizé-Communauté, France.

The Rev'd Glen Baker.

Mr Cliff Barrows.

Canon John E. Bowers.

The Rev'd E. Burns.

The Canterbury Press, St Mary's Works, St Mary's Plain, Norwich, Norfolk, NR3 3BH.

Geoffrey Chapman a division of Cassell Plc, Wellington House, 125 Strand, London, WC2R 0BB.

Church House Publishing, Church House, Great Smith Street, London, SW1P 3NZ.

The Church Pension Fund, 445 Fifth Avenue, New York 10016-0109, USA.

CopyCare Ltd, PO Box 77, Hailsham, East Sussex, BN27 3EF, on behalf of Birdwing Music/EMI Christian Music; Body Songs; Paul Booth; CN Publishing; Deep Fryed Music/Word Music Inc/Maranatha! Music; Hope Publishing; Lillenas Publishing Co.; Maranatha! Music; Mercy/Vineyard Publishing; Mission Hills Music; People of Destiny Int.; The Rodeheaver Co/Word Music; Salvationist Publishing and Supplies; Straightway/Mountain Spring; Abingdon Press; Word of God Music; Word's Spirit of Praise; Zondervan Corporation/Brentwood-Benson Music Publishing, and HarperCollins Religious.

Mrs M. Cross.

J. Curwen & Sons, 8/9 Frith Street, London, W1V 5TZ.

Daybreak Music Ltd., Silverdale Road, Eastbourne, E. Sussex, BN20 7AB. All rights reserved. International copyright secured.

Dr E.F. Downs.